Illustrated
WordPerfect 5.0

Jordan Gold

Wordware Publishing, Inc.

Library of Congress Cataloging-in-Publication Data

Gold, Jordan.
   Illustrated WordPerfect 5.0 / Jordan Gold.

   Includes index.
   1. WordPerfect (Computer program)   2. Word processing.   I. Title.
   II. Title: Illustrated WordPerfect five-point-zero.
   Z52.5.W65G63   1989   652'.5—dc19   88-24083
   ISBN 1-55622-063-4

© 1989 Wordware Publishing, Inc.

All Rights Reserved

1506 Capital Ave.
Plano, Texas 75074

Printed in the United States of America

ISBN 1-55622-063-4

10 9 8 7 6 5 4
8810

All inquiries for volume purchases of this book should be addressed to Wordware Publishing, Inc., at the above address. Telephone inquiries may be made by calling:

(214) 423-0090

Preface

ABOUT WORDPERFECT 5.0 WordPerfect 5.0 is the latest version of WordPerfect Corp.'s popular word processing software package. WordPerfect 5.0 is a vastly improved version of WordPerfect, incorporating such features as integrated text and graphics, styles, automatic reference, document compare, enhanced font support, forms selection, leading and kerning, keyboard layout procedures, and much more. Nearly every menu and keystroke has been redesigned and enhanced from WordPerfect 4.2.

WordPerfect 5.0 retains the powerful features of its predecessor, including automatic table of contents, index, table of authorities, and list generation; sorting; math; password protection; advanced macro generation; timed backup; built-in spelling checker and thesaurus; columns; the ability to add document comments; word search; and much, much more.

WordPerfect 5.0 takes word processing to the level of desktop publishing software. It is useful for letters, reports, articles, and other text-based documents. Its integrated graphics and text capabilities make it a good choice for newsletter generation, books, magazines, technical documents, and more.

ABOUT ILLUSTRATED BOOKS Like all books in the Illustrated Series, this book combines the features of an alphabetic reference guide with a step-by-step tutorial. By following the Recommended Learning Sequence, you proceed in a logical fashion from the most frequently used menu selections to those occasionally needed. Each menu selection is self-contained in a single module. Every module includes numbered operational steps illustrated with exact screen replicas. After using this book as a tutorial, you can refer to it later as a handy reference guide. Modules are arranged in alphabetical order for easy lookup.

Illustrated WordPerfect 5.0 is packed with practical examples to clarify and illustrate word processing, from basic typing to final printout. Whether you are a writer, student, or business professional, this book can help you ease the writing process.

Like WordPerfect, this book is a complete revision of its predecessor, in our case, *Illustrated WordPerfect 4.2*. Every module has been revised or replaced, hundreds of screens have been reshot, and all information has been carefully updated.

ABOUT THE AUTHOR Jordan Gold is vice president/editor-in-chief for Redgate Communications Corp., Vero Beach, FL. Redgate publishes a variety of magazines, including *The Macintosh Buyer's Guide, The Apple IIGS Buyer's Guide,* and *PAQ Review — The Independent Magazine for Compaq Computer Owners.*

Contents

Recommended Learning Sequence

Module 1
ABOUT THIS BOOK

INTRODUCTION

Illustrated WordPerfect describes WordPerfect Corporation's WordPerfect (Version 5.0) word processing program. It describes how the program is used in the office and home and presents detailed information about the many WordPerfect word processing functions. To help you get started right away, each description is accompanied by illustrated, recipe-like examples to help you learn, as well as to provide instant reference information.

The book is designed to meet the needs of a broad range of users. It is for users who are considering buying a word processing system for the first time and want to investigate several before making the purchase. It is also for beginning users who already have access to WordPerfect and want to learn it from scratch. Intermediate and advanced users will find *Illustrated WordPerfect* a valuable quick reference that contains examples of WordPerfect applications and commands. And finally, it is for the classroom instructor as an instructionally designed word processing textbook.

WordPerfect is sophisticated in nature, yet it is easy to learn. You will find WordPerfect's power becomes apparent within an hour or two of practice. You will also find word processing with WordPerfect to be lots of fun. It's easy to create a new document and then format, type, file, and print it.

To prove to yourself how easy WordPerfect is to use, you might want to jump over to Module 3 and read through the sample session. If you already have the program, run through the sample session with your computer. You will create and file a document within a matter of minutes.

Module 3 is for you if you are an adventurous person who likes to "dive in." Once you have experienced a straightforward word processing session, you will have the foundation necessary to tackle the heavy stuff with relative ease.

ORGANIZATION

This book is organized into small, easy-to-read modules. These modules provide descriptions, applications, and illustrations that show you how to use WordPerfect to solve practical word processing problems. Literally hundreds of examples are presented in the Description, Applications, and Typical Operation sections of the modules within this book.

These examples can be used as models for everyday word processing tasks of your own. The working examples, which all use the work of FLG Office Supply, a fictional business in Carbondale, IL, let you experiment with WordPerfect commands. This takes the mystery out of what might otherwise be a technical obscurity. In addition to conducting "hands-on" experiments, you will probably find yourself having a lot of fun.

With the exception of Modules 1 through 3, the modules in this book contain information that pertains to specific WordPerfect commands or families of commands. For experienced users, the book's alphabetical sequence provides a fast reference to WordPerfect's many capabilities. For new users, however, we also provide a Recommended Learning Sequence so you can learn WordPerfect progressively, beginning with basic concepts and working toward the more powerful commands later.

The recommended sequence for learning (or teaching) WordPerfect is at front of this book. As you work your way through the book, you can check off the modules you have completed. The sequence is arranged in a logical progression, where foundation information is provided first and then built upon. The learning sequence can be modified to fit classroom curriculum. If you are a teacher, you may wish to use the learning sequence as a curriculum design aid.

This module provides information about the book and gives an overview of what kind of equipment is required to operate WordPerfect.

Module 2 introduces you to WordPerfect. It provides an overview of WordPerfect functions, editing commands, and control keys. This module makes an excellent quick reference resource when you want to determine the purpose of specific commands.

Module 3 walks you through a sample WordPerfect session. You not only discover how commands are used, but you can follow the sample session using your computer.

In addition to actually using some of the basic WordPerfect system commands, you prepare and save a sample document. By the time you have completed Module 3, WordPerfect's power and ease of use will be apparent, because you will have demonstrated how WordPerfect is used to solve common word processing problems.

Modules 4 through 72 describe and illustrate WordPerfect commands and are arranged in alphabetical order for easy reference. You may want to use the recommended learning sequence and corresponding checklist at the front of the book as a training aid.

Appendix A contains a table of terms and definitions. Most of the entries are intended to help you better understand WordPerfect, but some of the terms include common computer "jargon" that creeps into any computer reference book. Do not be alarmed if the terms and definitions are not immediately clear. They become more understandable as you use the WordPerfect program with Modules 4 through 72. The important thing is that you know where to find the terms and definitions when you need them.

Appendix B shows you how to set up WordPerfect to better work with you. It shows you how to permanently change margins, tabs, and other commands. It also shows you how to make WordPerfect automatically back up your files.

Appendix C helps you better set up WordPerfect to work with your computer monitor. If you have a color monitor, for example, this appendix helps you change the colors of certain functions to fit your needs.

Appendix D explains WordPerfect's File Conversion utility. It shows you how to convert WordPerfect files to work with a variety of software programs. It also shows you how to convert files created with other software to WordPerfect format.

Appendix E includes information to better help you use your printer with WordPerfect.

Appendix F includes troubleshooting tips to help you get over certain difficulties when using WordPerfect.

Appendix G describes the Speller utility. It shows you how to customize the Speller (described in Module 64) for best use with your requirements.

Appendix H describes WordPerfect's Compose feature, which helps you create special characters.

Appendix I lists the many ways you can start WordPerfect when you begin using it each day.

Appendix J describes WordPerfect's Screen Capture utility.

Appendix K is an alphabetical listing of WordPerfect commands.

Appendix L lists the Codes WordPerfect hides in your files. These codes are explained in Module 59.

Appendix M contains WordPerfect exercises. It is provided for both classroom and self-teaching situations. If you are a classroom instructor, you may wish to include these exercises in student assignments. If you are learning WordPerfect on your own, the exercises are a good way to check yourself to see what you have learned about a system or word processing function. If you can answer the questions, you are ready to move to the next module in the learning sequence.

The index helps you locate key ideas in the book.

HARDWARE AND SOFTWARE REQUIREMENTS

WordPerfect operates on most popular 16- and 32-bit microcomputers, such as the IBM® PC and PC AT and PC-compatible computers from such manufacturers as Compaq, Tandy, and PC's Limited. It also works with the IBM line of PS/2 computers and compatibles and PS/2 compatible computers from vendors like Tandy and PC's Limited. You will need the MS-DOS® or PC-DOS® operating system, version 2.0 or later. The computer should have 384 kilobytes of RAM to operate WordPerfect and two disk drives (either two double-sided diskette drives or one hard disk and at least one diskette drive). The diskette drive can be either 5.25-inch or 3.5-inch. A hard disk drive and 512K of RAM are recommended. This book is written with the assumption a hard disk is being used.

You also need either a monochrome or color monitor. In order to get the most out of WordPerfect's graphics capabilities, an EGA or VGA monitor and graphics adapter are recommended. A monochrome monitor and adapter can be used, but you will not be able to import graphics from other programs. See Module 30 for more information about WordPerfect's graphics capabilities.

A printer is not required for learning most word processing functions, but it is needed to print your documents. WordPerfect supports more than 120 printers. See Module 55 for information about printer setup.

Before getting started, you should have 12 WordPerfect system diskettes if you are using 5.25-inch diskettes, or six WordPerfect system diskettes if you are using 3.5-inch drives.

Diskettes include the program and related files, help and tutorial files, font and graphics information, printer files, a thesaurus, a hyphenation dictionary, and a spell checking dictionary. You also need several blank double-sided diskettes to backup each of the WordPerfect diskettes. This lets you store the original WordPerfect (master) diskettes in a safe place.

You also need to format one or two blank diskettes for data. If you are using two double-sided drives, format one of these for your data diskette to store your documents; the other is a backup of your data diskette. The data diskette is used in disk drive B (usually designated as the bottom or right-hand drive) while the working disk containing the WordPerfect programs (called the program disk) is used in disk drive A (the top or left-hand drive). If you are using a hard disk and at least one double-sided disk drive, format one diskette as a backup for the data on the hard disk. Always put program diskettes in drive A and data diskettes in drive B. The procedure for doing this is covered in Module 2.

WHAT YOU SHOULD KNOW

You should know the parts of your computer (see the user's manuals that are available for your computer) and the DOS commands for formatting, copying, renaming, and deleting files (refer to the DOS manual). You should also be familiar with your computer keyboard, since WordPerfect uses every key except the "Scroll Lock" key.

Module 2

WORDPERFECT SYSTEM OVERVIEW

INTRODUCTION

This module offers information about word processors (what they are and what they can do for you) and provides an overview of the WordPerfect 5.0 system, including the word processor, speller, and thesaurus programs. It also describes how to make working copies of WordPerfect and prepare your computer for using WordPerfect.

WORD PROCESSORS A word processor is a software package that turns your personal computer into a machine that changes or "processes" words. A word processor like WordPerfect lets you create and format documents whether they be correspondence, reports, or records and then print the text on paper. WordPerfect also lets you revise a document by simply typing over text; altering the spacing and format of part of a page or entire documents; and moving, inserting, or deleting single characters or large blocks of text. You can also copy an entire document or parts of it from one file to another and then use WordPerfect to check the spelling or count the number of words. If you are stumped for the right word in any situation, you can use the thesaurus included with WordPerfect. You can add graphics through WordPerfect's graphics import facility. And when you are done with a document, you can send and receive WordPerfect files to other computers over phone lines. Best of all, you can create, revise, and print a document at any time.

WordPerfect comes with two templates that list the WordPerfect functions and keys used. If the function keys are on the left-hand side of your keyboard, use the template that fits over the function keys with the function names appearing next to the keys that perform them. If your function keys are on the top of the keyboard, use the template that fits above them. Functions accessible through the Ctrl key are colored red, while those using the Alt key are colored blue, those using the Shift key are colored green, and the function keys alone are colored black on the template. The function keys can perform as many as four functions; these can be accomplished by pressing the key alone, the key and the Shift key, the key and the Ctrl key, or the key and the Alt key.

WORDPERFECT 5.0 SYSTEM DESCRIPTION

WordPerfect 5.0 comes on twelve 5.25-inch diskettes or six 3.5-inch diskettes. The two WordPerfect program diskettes contain the word processing program, which is used to create, file, and print documents. The program diskettes also contain help files to guide you through the execution of the program, auxiliary files containing information that makes the program easier to use, and a number of utility files for macros, document conversion, and other tasks.

The Speller diskette contains WordPerfect's 115,000-word speller/dictionary program and custom dictionaries. These are used to locate and help you correct misspelled words and typographical errors within a WordPerfect document.

The Thesaurus diskette stores the WordPerfect thesaurus that helps you determine the best word to use in any situation.

The Font/Graphics diskette contains clip-art images, characters for the EGA (enhanced graphics adapter) monitor, a screen capture utility, and a number of fonts.

Four of the printer diskettes contain information on each of the more than 100 printers that WordPerfect supports. The PTR program diskette contains the printer definition program.

The Learning diskette contains WordPerfect's automatic installation program, sample learning files, and an on-line tutorial that guides you through much of WordPerfect's functionality.

The Conversion diskette includes programs for converting WordPerfect documents to other formats, a macro conversion utility, a font conversion utility, and a printer test file.

The following paragraphs introduce you to WordPerfect. This introduction helps you become familiar with the various functions of the program, so you better understand the parts of the system you use for different word processing tasks.

MAIN FUNCTIONS   As you load WordPerfect, the WordPerfect copyright logo appears and disappears on the screen. All that is on-screen after that is the Status Line at the bottom. The rest of the screen is blank. While this may be confusing since there is not anything on the screen to tell you what to do next, all you need to do is decide if you want to create a new document or use an old one. If you want to create a new document, just start typing and save the document when you are finished, as described in Module 3. If you want to use an old document, retrieve it by pressing the Retrieve key (Shift-F10) or the List Files key (F5). Module 40 explores this function in more detail.

A document is a generic name for reports, correspondence, papers, and other prepared materials that rely chiefly on words to convey their message. You can file a document, change it, and prepare the final version using WordPerfect, just as you can manually or with a typewriter. The chief difference is that WordPerfect lets you change or ''modify'' the document and its format without having to retype it. And rather than typing, WordPerfect lets you print the document on a printer when you are ready.

When you create a new document, you must give that document a name. The name can be no more than eight characters (with a three character extension). It should be descriptive enough so that you know what the document is without having to look at it. For example, a letter to your partner Sam could be called ''samlet.'' This function is explained in more detail in Module 60.

Either before, during, or after typing, WordPerfect lets you change the margins, tabs, and other formatting characteristics of a document. You can also choose the printer that you want to use, edit more than one document at a time, import pictures, and use WordPerfect's Math functions. All of these functions are described in later modules.

STATUS LINE   The Status Line tells you the filename and directory location of the file you are editing, whether you are editing document 1 or 2 (two documents may be edited simultaneously), what page of the document you are on, which line, and which position in that line. The Status Line is also a message area. It is more fully described in Module 65.

SPELL CHECK A DOCUMENT   Before you give a document to someone else to read, it's nice to use WordPerfect's spell checking feature to make sure no embarrassing errors are in the document. While 115,000 words might seem like a lot, there are times that WordPerfect does not recognize a word that is correctly spelled. In that case, you have the option of adding words to the supplemental dictionary at any time.

The Speller is accessed by pressing Ctrl-F2. WordPerfect compares each word in the specified dictionary with each word in your document. It notifies you of a misspelled word by highlighting that word in the text and giving you the option of replacing that word with one of its suggested correct spellings, typing a corrected spelling yourself, adding that word to the dictionary, or ignoring the word and going on to the next misspelled word. Besides checking your spelling, WordPerfect also counts the number of words in your document, a very useful feature. The WordPerfect Speller is described in Module 64.

THESAURUS   WordPerfect includes a thesaurus to make sure you always have the right word in every sentence. This function is described in Module 71. Thesaurus functions are available by using the WordPerfect and Thesaurus diskettes and by pressing Ctrl-F1. WordPerfect looks at your word and gives you synonyms and antonyms for it. It categorizes the synonyms into groups and lets you choose synonyms. The Thesaurus offers a world of functionality at your fingertips. If you do not like a word, ask the Thesaurus for a better one. If you do not like its initial choices, you can select more. The Thesaurus truly can improve the quality of your writing.

EDITING FUNCTIONS   WordPerfect offers a large number of powerful editing functions. Each is described in detail in Modules 4 through 72. The information provided below gives a brief overview of editing function categories that include:

- Standard Word Processing Functions
- Cursor Positioning Functions
- Advanced Editing and Supporting Functions
- Advanced Functions
- Formatting and Printing Functions

Standard Word Processing Functions   Standard word processing features include such functions as:

- Typeover
- Insert
- Delete
- Move
- Copy
- Search and Replace

Cursor Positioning Functions   WordPerfect offers a wide variety of cursor positioning functions. Among them are:

- Arrow Up, Down, Right, and Left
- End of Screen, Page, and Document
- Top of Screen, Page, and Document
- Go to Specified Page Number
- Scroll Left and Right

Advanced Editing and Positioning Functions   WordPerfect offers a wide variety of editing and supporting functions. These include:

- Automatic Page Break, Page Numbering, and Repagination
- Automatic Alphanumeric and Text Underlining
- Decimal Tab
- Document Merge Functions
- Headers
- Footers
- On-line Help and Status Indicators

Advanced Functions   There are a number of advanced functions, such as:

- Column Calculations (Horizontal and Vertical)
- Column Manipulations (Delete, Insert, and Move)
- Macros
- Graphics
- Split-screen Editing
- Line Drawing
- Automatic generation of indexes, lists, tables of authorities and tables of contents
- Automatic paragraph numbering
- Outline processing

Formatting and Printing Functions   WordPerfect offers a number of formatting and printing options. Some of these are:

- Word and Letter Spacing
- Leading and Kerning
- Merge Print
- Printer Control Codes
- Variable Print Types
- Variable Print Pitch
- Support for a Wide Variety of Forms
- View Document

MODES OF OPERATION   WordPerfect uses modes of operation to let you know what kind of activity or function is in progress. These are indicated by the number next to "Pos" on the Status Line. When you are in boldface type mode, the number is boldface, when you are in caps lock mode, the "Pos" is all caps. "Pos" may change colors as you change modes if you have a color monitor.When you are in underline mode, the number is underlined. During some operations, the left-hand side of the status line notifies you what is occurring. Some modes include:

- Typeover (Ins key)
- Block On (Alt-F4)
- Search and Replace (F2)
- Move (Ctrl-F4)
- Copy (Ctrl-F4)

WORDPERFECT LEARNING DISKETTE   The WordPerfect Learning diskette includes sample exercises to help you get better acquainted with WordPerfect. An on-line tutorial guides you through WordPerfect's features. Type "tutor" at the DOS prompt while in the WordPerfect directory to use the tutorial. If you are using a diskette-based system, put the learning diskette in drive A and type "tutor" to use the tutorial.

WORDPERFECT INSTALLATION

You should prepare extra copies (called "working copies") of all WordPerfect diskettes. The WordPerfect diskettes can be found in the plastic pocket located in the WordPerfect user's manual. You also need to format one or two blank diskettes (called data diskettes) for document storage. (If you are using a system with two floppy drives, format two diskettes. If you are using a hard disk, format one). Read "Using a Dual Floppy System" or "Using a Hard Disk System" to learn how to format your diskettes.

If you are using a computer with a hard, or "fixed," disk and a floppy, WordPerfect designates the floppy disk as drive A and the hard disk as drive C. You may also have a floppy disk in drive B. Store DOS, programs, and data in drive C. Use drive A (and B) to back up your hard drive, store documents, and for other functions.

USING A DUAL FLOPPY DISK SYSTEM   You learn in Appendix B how to set up WordPerfect for your needs, but do not worry about that for now. Format fourteen diskettes as follows:

NOTE

This process varies slightly when using 3.5-inch diskettes. There are only six diskettes with the program and the names of the diskettes are different. Follow the instructions below, substituting the diskette names as required. You only have to format eight 3.5-inch diskettes, six in step 6 and two in step 7.

1.   Open drive A. Remove the original DOS (either MS-DOS or PC-DOS) diskette from your DOS user's manual. Insert the DOS diskette into drive A taking care not to bend or damage the diskette. Close the latch to drive A. Then open drive B, insert a blank diskette, and close the latch to the drive.

2. Turn on the monitor and printer if they have their own On/Off power switches. Then turn on your computer.

Observe disk drive A whirl and notice the red light go on. The DOS system is loading or "booting" into the computer. This may take about a minute, during which time the monitor screen may remain blank.

3. If necessary, respond to the date prompt by typing today's date as MM-DD-YY (Month-Day-Year). Press **Enter** and respond to the current time prompt by typing the time as HH:MM (Hour:Minute). Press **Enter**.

"A>" appears at the upper left-hand corner of the screen when the computer is ready to use. This symbol is the *DOS prompt*, which is always followed by a short blinking symbol called a *cursor*. The cursor signals where you can type on the screen. You always type your DOS commands (instructions that tell your Disk Operating System what to do) immediately after the DOS prompt. After DOS successfully carries out (or "executes") your instructions, the DOS prompt automatically reappears on the next line on the screen.

4. After A>, type **FORMAT B:/S** and press **Enter**. Press any key to start the formatting process.

5. When the first diskette is formatted, a message similar to this appears: "Format another (Y/N)?" Type **Y**. Remove the diskette from drive B and label it "WordPerfect Program #1."

6. Insert the second diskette. Follow the screen instructions to begin formatting. When the second diskette has finished formatting, remove it and label it "WordPerfect Program #2." Insert a third diskette and format it. Then label it "WordPerfect Speller." Follow instructions to format nine other diskettes. Label them Thesaurus, Font/Graphics, Printer 1, Printer 2, Printer 3, Printer 4, Conversion, Learning, and PTR Program. When you have finished, type **N** to the prompt, "Format another (Y/N)?"

7. Insert the second to last (thirteenth 5.25-inch, seventh 3.5-inch) diskette in drive B. After A>, type **FORMAT B:** and press **Enter**. When it is finished, label it "WordPerfect Data." Then follow screen instructions to format one other diskette. When finished, type **N** to return to the DOS prompt. Remove the last diskette you formatted and label it "WordPerfect Data Backup."

Remove your DOS diskette from drive A and copy the WordPerfect programs onto the formatted disks as follows:

1. Insert the original WordPerfect #1 diskette in drive A and the formatted diskette labelled "WordPerfect #1" in drive B. Type **COPY A:*.* B:** and press **Enter**. When the DOS prompt redisplays, remove the two diskettes.

2. Repeat step 1 for each of the other eleven (five 3.5-inch) diskettes, inserting the original WordPerfect labeled diskettes in drive A and the blank formatted diskettes with corresponding names in drive B.

Once the diskettes are prepared, return the original diskettes in their jackets to a safe place away from extremes of temperature and dust. Use the working copies of the program diskettes whenever you use WordPerfect.

Putting the Proper Commands on the WordPerfect #1 Diskette   In order to use WordPerfect, you need to tell DOS how many files can be open at once. The config.sys file on the WordPerfect #1 diskette must be changed. To do this:

1.   Insert the disk you labeled as WordPerfect #1 in drive A. At the A> prompt, type **COPY A:CONFIG.SYS + CON A:CONFIG.SYS**. Press **Enter**.

2.   Type **FILES = 20**. Press **Ctrl-Z**, then **Enter**.

USING A HARD DISK SYSTEM   Make sure your hard disk is formatted before you copy your WordPerfect programs onto the hard disk or format your backup data diskette. See your computer dealer and DOS manual to learn how to do this. Then, make sure the config.sys file in the root directory has a command that says FILES = 20 (or greater). This tells DOS how many files can be open at once. To do this:

1.   Type **CD ** and press **Enter**. Then type **COPYCONFIG.SYS + CON: CONFIG.SYS**.

NOTE
If you are using WordPerfect Library in addition
to WordPerfect, type FILES = 40.

2.   Type **FILES = 20**. Then press **Ctrl-Z** and press **Enter**.

3.   Press **Ctrl-Alt-Del** to restart your system.

Installing WordPerfect On Your Hard Disk   When you are set up, you have two options for installing WordPerfect on your hard disk. You can either manually install the diskettes, or you can use WordPerfect's automatic installation program. Manually install WordPerfect as follows:

1.   After the DOS prompt C> appears, type **CD ** and press **Enter** to return to the root directory. Then type **MD \ WP50** and press **Enter** to make a directory for WordPerfect. Then type **CD \ WP50** and press **Enter** to change the current directory to the WordPerfect directory.

2.   Place the WordPerfect #1 diskette in drive A. Type **COPY A:*.***. Press **Enter** to copy the programs from drive A into the WP directory in drive C. Each program lists on the screen as it copies. When finished, C> reappears. Repeat this step for each of the other WordPerfect diskettes except the Learn diskette.

3.   Type **MD \ WP50 \ LEARN** and press **Enter**. Then type **CD \ WP50 \ LEARN** and press **Enter**.

4.   Put the Learning diskette in drive A. Type **COPY A:*.*** and press **Enter**. The files on the Learning diskette are for use with the WordPerfect Workbook which comes with WordPerfect. When you have finished using the files on the Learning diskette, you can delete them.

5. Store the original program diskettes in a safe place.

To automatically install WordPerfect on the hard disk:

1. Place the Learning diskette in drive A, type **INSTALL**, and press **Enter**.

2. Follow the instructions on the screen.

3. Store the original program diskettes in a safe place.

Setting Up A Data Directory   It's convenient to put all of your data in a different directory than your Wordperfect program files. To do this, type MD \ WP50 \ DOCS and press Enter. This creates a subdirectory for your data. Put all of your WordPerfect data documents in this directory. You can create many subdirectories in this manner. See your DOS manual for more information about subdirectories.

Format a backup data diskette as follows:

1. Insert a blank diskette into drive A. After C>, type **FORMAT A:** and press **Enter**. Follow the screen instructions to begin formatting a diskette.

2. When finished, a screen message similar to this appears, "Format another (Y/N)?" Type **N** and press **Enter** to return to the DOS prompt, C>. Remove the diskette you formatted and label it "WordPerfect Data Backup." Use this to back up your documents.

SELECTING THE PROPER PRINTER   Before WordPerfect can print your documents, you must select a printer. WordPerfect lets you select as many printers as you need. These procedures are outlined in Module 55, Printer Control.

Module 3
A SAMPLE SESSION WITH WORDPERFECT 5.0

INTRODUCTION

This module offers information about word processors (what they are and what they can do for you) and explains how your keyboard works with WordPerfect. It then takes you through a sample session in which you create, save, and edit a document.

GETTING READY

Now that you have made working copies of your WordPerfect program diskettes, you are ready to start a sample session. Before actually loading WordPerfect into your computer, take a quick look at some of the keys you use.

Before you start, apply the template that is located in the WordPerfect user's manual to your keyboard. This lets you read the key labels at a glance, so you do not have to remember the WordPerfect commands. Place the template over or above the function keys (either F1-F10 on the left-hand side of the keyboard or F1-F12 along the top of the keyboard, depending on the type of keyboard you have). At the bottom of the template, commands that use the Ctrl or Shift keys with cursor control keys are listed.

STANDARD TYPING KEYS   The standard typing keys are like those on a conventional typewriter. These include letter, number, Tab, and Shift keys. Your *Shift* key is used to type uppercase letters and the symbols above the upper row of number keys, just as on a typewriter. *Special character keys* are also available on the computer keyboard, such as the vertical bar, back slash, tilde, and brace symbols. These symbols appear in the following list.

Special key	Symbol	Special key	Symbol
Vertical Bar	|	Less Than	<
Back Slash	\\	Open Bracket	[
Tilde	~	Close Bracket	]
Grave		Open Brace	{
Greater Than	>	Close Brace	}

THE ENTER KEY   The *Enter* key works much like the return key on a typewriter. Use it to move the cursor to the beginning of the next line.

The Enter key is also used to complete selected commands. It is usually when a question concerning the command is displayed at the bottom of the screen. The question is also known as a prompt.

FUNCTION KEYS   *Function keys* are special keys that perform very specific tasks. They are used alone and with the Shift, Ctrl, and Alt keys. Combined key sequences appear hyphenated in this book, indicating the keys to press simultaneously.

If you see Shift-F9 in print, for example, press the Shift and F9 keys simultaneously and release them. The same applies to Ctrl-F9, Alt-F9, and so on. On the template, notice Ctrl keys are coded red, Shift keys green, and Alt keys blue. Commands activated by pressing the function keys alone are colored black.

Later modules in this book offer more detailed descriptions of each command, complete with a sample application.

THE CANCEL KEY   The *Cancel* key (F1) works as the "oops" key. It lets you undo any command (like deleting or copying text) or activity (like renaming a document) *before* you touch the keys that complete the action.

MENU SELECTIONS   Menu selections can be activated by typing the number corresponding to that selection or the boldfaced letter in that selection. For example, pressing Shift-F8 brings up the Format Menu. Four choices are available from the Format Menu. Typing 1 or L brings up the Line Format Menu, typing 2 or P brings up the Page Format Menu, 3 or D, the Document Fromat Menu, and 4 or O the Other Format Menu.

SAMPLE SESSION

You are now ready to create, edit, and file a WordPerfect document as well as to learn several WordPerfect editing functions. Observe during the sample session how WordPerfect automatically takes care of formatting and word wrapping for you; other functions are very easy to use.

STARTING WORDPERFECT   Starting WordPerfect is as easy as 1, 2, 3:

1.   If you are using a hard-disk system, proceed to step 2. If you are using a dual-floppy system, insert your working copy of the program gently into drive A and close the latch. Insert your WordPerfect data diskette into drive B and close the latch.

2.   Next to A> or C> (making sure you are in directory \ wp50), type **WP** and press **Enter**. Observe WordPerfect load itself automatically.

3.   Notice the WordPerfect copyright screen on the monitor. Then notice the WordPerfect Status Line at the bottom of the screen.

TYPING A DOCUMENT   When you type a WordPerfect document, there is no need to press Enter at the end of the line, because WordPerfect automatically "word wraps" for you.

Use the following key sequences to correct typographical errors.

- Cursor Movement   Press Backspace and the cursor keys.

- Correct Typos   Press Ins to go into Typeover mode to type over typos. Press Ins again to leave Typeover mode. Use Del to delete characters and spaces.
- Enter blank line   Press Enter at the end of paragraphs and at the beginning of a blank line.
- Adjust gaps in text   Position cursor at beginning of gap and press the Del key.
- Add spaces in text   Press the Spacebar.

As the proprietor of FLG Office Supply, you have to write a letter to Sue, your assistant. Sue is in charge of ordering supplies for you.

NOTE
Combined key sequences are hyphenated, for example, Shift-F6. This indicates the first key is pressed and held while the second key is typed. Both keys are released simultaneously.

1. Press **Enter** three times and type **Dear Sue:** (press **Enter** twice) **We are in need of the following: pencils, pens, dividers, notebooks, pads, and diskettes. Please order them immediately.** (press **Enter** twice, then **Shift-F6**) **Thank You,** (press **Enter** twice, then **Shift-F6** to center text) **FLG**.

2. Press **Enter** to end the paragraph. Notice the following display.

```
Dear Sue:

We are in need of the following: pencils, pens, dividers,
notebooks, pads, and diskettes. Please order them immediately.

                          Thank You,

                             FLG




                                        Doc 1 Pg 1 Ln 2.83" Pos 1"
```

3. Press **F7** and notice the prompt. Then press **Enter**.

```
    Dear Sue:

    We are in need of the following: pencils, pens, dividers,
    notebooks, pads, and diskettes. Please order them immediately.

                        Thank You,

                        FLG










    Document to be saved:
```

4. Type **C:\WP50\DOCS\PRACTICE.WPF**. Press **Enter** to save the document. Notice
    WordPerfect tells you it is saving the document. Notice also the following display.

```
    Dear Sue:

    We are in need of the following: pencils, pens, dividers,
    notebooks, pads, and diskettes. Please order them immediately.

                        Thank You,

                        FLG












    Exit WP? (Y/N) No                              (Cancel to return to document)
```

5. You are now being asked if you want to leave WordPerfect. Since you do not, type **N**.

Notice you now have a blank page except for the Status Line at the bottom of the screen. The document you were writing has now been saved and you are ready to begin something else.

EDITING A WORDPERFECT DOCUMENT   Imagine that you have checked the inventory and realized that you did not need pencils, but you did need marking pens. You are now going to edit your letter to Sue to inform her of this occurrence.

1.   Press **Shift-F10** to retrieve the document. Notice the following display at the bottom of the screen.

```
    Document to be retrieved:
```

2.   Type **C:\WP50\DOCS\PRACTICE.WPF** and press **Enter**. Notice the document is now on the screen as you left it. Notice also that the name of the document is displayed at the lower left-hand corner of the screen.

3.   Using the cursor control keys, move the cursor to the "p" in pencils. Press **Ctrl-Backspace**. Notice the word "pencils" and the comma following it have been deleted.

4.   Type **marking pens,**

Looking at the document, you notice that it looks awkward to list marking pens and pens following each other, so you decide to change the wording a little. The cursor should be in the same position where you left it.

5.   Press the **Spacebar** once, type **ball-point** and press the **Spacebar** again. Notice the following display:

```
Dear Sue:

We are in need of the following: marking pens, ball-point pens, dividers,
notebooks, pads, and diskettes. Please order them immediately.

                Thank You,

                FLG
```

```
C:\WP50\DOCS\PRACTICE.WPF                    Doc 1 Pg 1 Ln 1.83" Pos 6.8"
```

6. Press **F7** to save the document. Press **Enter** twice. Notice the following display at the bottom of the page:

```
    Dear Sue:

    We are in need of the following: marking pens, ball-point pens,
    dividers, notebooks, pads, and diskettes. Please order them
    immediately.

                              Thank You,

                              FLG




          Replace C:\WP50\DOCS\PRACTICE.WPF? (Y/N) No
```

7. Type **Y** to replace the old version of PRACTICE.WPF with the new version. Then type **Y** to exit WordPerfect.

You have just created, edited, and saved a WordPerfect document. Your document is stored on the data disk so you can return to it for further editing or printing later.

8. Turn to Module 60 to continue the learning sequence.

Module 4
ALIGNING TEXT

DESCRIPTION

The Tab Align key (Ctrl-F6) makes it easy to line up columns of numbers or text along a certain *alignment character*. The default alignment character is a decimal point (.).

This feature is most useful for lining up columns of numbers. In fact, the alignment character is used automatically with WordPerfect's Math command (Module 45). Without the Tab Align key, you would have to count the number of spaces in each number to make sure the numbers aligned before typing them. When you press Ctrl-F6, the cursor automatically moves to the next Tab stop. All following text you type moves to the left until you type the alignment character or press Tab or Enter. Then, text or numbers you type once again move to the right.

CAUTION

Numbers are aligned without regard for the left
margin. If you are typing a number that begins
at the first tab stop, make sure it is no more than
15 characters. Otherwise, WordPerfect will not
be able to align it.

For example, create a worksheet with columns of numbers, aligning the characters on a decimal point.

1. Press **Ctrl-F6** twice to move to the second Tab stop.

```
    Align char = .                                    Doc 1 Pg 1 Ln 1" Pos 1.5"
```

2. Type **$125.57** and press **Enter**.
3. Press **Ctrl-F6** twice and type **$3,459.95**. Press **Enter**.

```
      $125.57
    $3,459.95
```

Notice how the characters are aligned on the decimal point. Here are more numbers in that same column:

```
      $125.57
    $3,459.95
  $124,567.90
$1,245,597.63
    $1,345.45
```

Here are the same numbers not aligned:

```
$125.57
$3,459.95
$124,567.90
$1,245,597.63
$1,345.45
```

Notice that the numbers in the aligned illustration look much more organized. They are also much easier to read.

NOTE

You cannot use the Tab Align key to align text
or numbers that are already typed. You must
use it while you are typing and on each line that
you type.

ALIGNMENT CHARACTER   You can change the alignment character with the Format key (Shift-F8). WordPerfect then aligns text based on the new character.

For example, to align a column in a table on a colon (:) do this:

1. Press **Shift-F8** and type **4** or **O**.
2. Type **3** or **D**, then **:** (a colon) to create a new alignment ("decimal") character. Type **,** (a comma) to leave the thousands character separator (Module 48) as a comma. Press **F7** to exit the menu.
3. Press **Ctrl-F6** twice, type **Wilson:** and press **Enter**.
4. Press **Ctrl-F6** twice, type **Jones:** and press **Enter**.
5. Press **Ctrl-F6** twice, type **Robinson:** and press **Enter**.

```
   Wilson:
    Jones:
 Robinson:
```

APPLICATIONS

The Tab Align key is useful in columns of text and numbers. It makes tables look more organized and easier to read. Outlines also look better when the Roman numerals in the outline are aligned (the periods line up even though the numerals often take up from one to three spaces — I, III, VII, etc.). Changing the alignment character lets you align text or numbers around any character you choose.

TYPICAL OPERATION

In this example, you use the Tab Align key to align a table, and you change the alignment character to align text and numbers around different characters in the table.

1. Create a document similar to the following:

```
                        FLG OFFICE SUPPLY
                         HOURS WORKED
                         MARCH, 1987

        EMPLOYEE                        HOURS WORKED
```

2. Press **Shift-F8**, type **4** or **O**, then **3** or **D**.
3. Type **:**, then **,** and press **F7**.
4. Press **Ctrl-F6** three times, type **Mathews:** and press **Enter**.
5. Press **Ctrl-F6** three times, type **Belew:** and press **Enter**.
6. Repeat step five, substituting names until the table looks like this:

```
                        FLG OFFICE SUPPLY
                         HOURS WORKED
                         MARCH, 1987

        EMPLOYEE                        HOURS WORKED
           Mathews:
             Belew:
             Levin:
          Anderson:
               FLG:
     Masters-Jones:
             David:
```

7. Move the cursor to the space after the colon in "Mathews:"
8. Press **Shift-F8**, type **4** or **O**, then **3** or **D**.
9. Type **.**, then **,** and press **F7**. This changes the alignment character back to a period.
10. Press **Tab** five times, then press **Ctrl-F6** and type **175.25**.

11. Press **Down Arrow**, **Tab** five times, then press **Ctrl-F6**. Type **94.50**.

12. Repeat step 11, substituting the number value until the table looks like this:

```
                    FLG OFFICE SUPPLY
                      HOURS WORKED
                      MARCH, 1987

         EMPLOYEE                        HOURS WORKED
         Mathews:                          175.25
           Belew:                           94.50
           Levin:                          225.40
        Anderson:                            9.00
             FLG:                          245.00
   Masters-Jones:                           37.25
           David:                          206.35
```

13. Save the document as TIMESHET.WPF.

14. Turn to Module 8 to continue the learning sequence.

Module 5
APPEARANCE

DESCRIPTION

WordPerfect gives you several different ways to highlight text on-screen. You can boldface and underline text through simple function key commands, or you can use the Appearance key to create italicized, shadow, outline, and other special text. Most of the methods used to highlight text only show up at the printer. But with nearly all monitors, you can create boldfaced and underlined text on-screen. And with many monitors, especially EGA (Enhanced Graphics Adapter) and VGA (Video Graphics Array), you can create italicized text. All text highlighting is intended to be used for emphasis. Each stands out from a document:

Boldfaced text looks like this. <u>Underlined text looks like this.</u> **<u>You can also put text in both underline and boldface.</u>** *Italicized text looks like this.*

USING THE BOLDFACE COMMAND   To use the boldface command, press F6. Everything you type after you press F6 is boldface. To turn off the boldface command, press F6 again. You can tell if the boldface command is on by looking at the Status Line (Module 65).

When WordPerfect is in boldface mode, the number next to "Pos" is boldfaced. Boldface will appear brighter than normal on a single-color monitor. On a color monitor, boldface will generally be blue. (To change colors, see Appendix C).

BOLDFACING A BLOCK OF TEXT   WordPerfect also lets you change a block of text from normal to boldface. (Blocks are discussed in further detail in Module 8.) After you define a block, pressing F6 boldfaces the block.

USING THE UNDERLINE COMMAND   The Underline key (F8) works like the Boldface key. When you press F8, the number next to Pos on the Status Line is reverse video on a single-color monitor, and generally green on a color monitor.

```
                                                   Doc 1 Pg 1 Ln 2.33" Pos 1"
```

In the underline mode, everything you type until you press F8 again is underlined.

UNDERLINING A BLOCK OF TEXT   You can underline a block of text in much the same way as you boldface it. First, define a block using Alt-F4, then press F8 to underline everything in the block.

NOTE

If your printer supports it, underlined text can be printed as either a single underline or a double underline. (Double underlined text appears as a single underline on-screen.) Use Ctrl-F8 to select double underlines.

UNDERLINING SPACES AND TABS   WordPerfect is initially set to underline spaces, but not tabs in text. This means that spaces between words are underlined, but tabs between words, such as in tabular headings, are not. To change this:

1.   Press **Shift-F8** and type **4** or **O**. Notice the following illustration.

```
Format: Other

        1 - Advance

        2 - Conditional End of Page

        3 - Decimal/Align Character         .
            Thousands' Separator            ,

        4 - Language                        EN

        5 - Overstrike

        6 - Printer Functions

        7 - Underline - Spaces              Yes
                        Tabs                No
```

2.   Type **7** or **U**. If you don't want spaces to be underlined, type **N**. If you want tabs to be underlined, type **Y**.

NOTE

You can change these settings throughout a document. If you want to underline tabular headings, for example, you can turn tab underline on at the beginning of the line you want to underline, and turn it off when you are finished. Alternatively, you can change the default settings through the Setup menu (Appendix B).

3. Press **F7** to save the settings. Then type text normally. Alternatively, you can use this command with the block key to change the underline style for a block of text.

COMBINING BOLDFACE AND UNDERLINE   To boldface and underline text, press F6 and F8. All following typed text is boldface and underlined. When both modes are on, the number next to Pos on the Status Line is green on a color monitor, but looks identical to underline mode on a single-color monitor. If you are using a single-color monitor and are not sure whether both boldface and underline are on, you can check this by using the Reveal Codes key, Alt-F3. (Reveal Codes are explained in Module 59.)

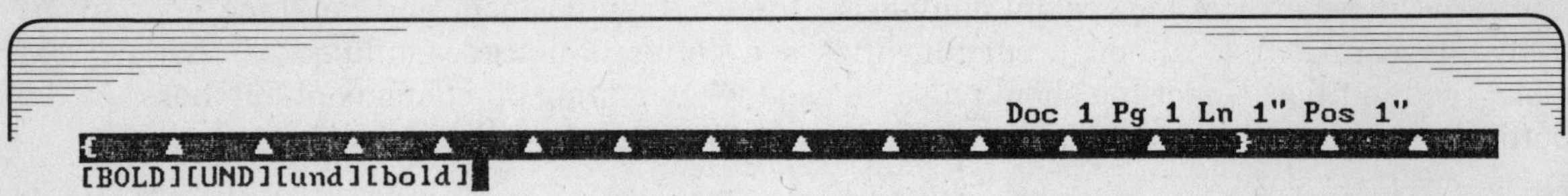

If both the boldface and underline symbols are listed, then anything you type is both boldface and underlined until you press F6 and F8 again.

NOTE

When you are in boldface and underline mode, you can switch to either the boldface or underline mode by pressing F6 or F8 again. For example, pressing F6 turns off boldface but leaves underline still on.

APPEARANCE   While WordPerfect shows normal, boldface, and underlined text on-screen, it also gives you the ability to create outline, italicized, shadow, and small caps text in print. On some monitors (EGA and VGA, for example) you can also create italicized text on-screen. To create special text:

NOTE

Not all of these effects necessarily work with your printer. Some printers are unable to create these effects. Experiment with your printer to see if they work.

1. Press **Ctrl-F8** and type **2**.

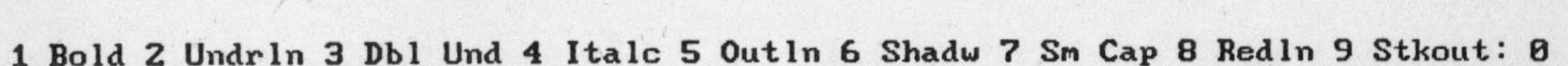

    1 Bold 2 Undrln 3 Dbl Und 4 Italc 5 Outln 6 Shadw 7 Sm Cap 8 Redln 9 Stkout: 0

2. Pick the highlighting you want. For example, type **4** or **I** to italicize text. Notice "Pos" on the Status Line change accordingly.

3. Type text normally. With most of these options, text is highlighted on-screen, but prints in the style chosen. Press **Ctrl-F8** and type **3** or **N** to return text to normal. Alternatively, you can highlight text using the Block key and use the appearance key to change the style of a block of text.

APPLICATIONS

Use all of these effects for special emphasis. Italicized, underlined, and boldface text can be used interchangeably, although certain titles are better italicized. Outlined or shadow text looks good in titles. Underline should also be used when adding up columns of numbers. At the bottom of an accounting column, you might want to switch to a double underline.

Do not get carried away with these effects, however. Using too many of them in a single document tends to make your document look busy and cluttered. The content of the document loses out to the effects in the document.

TYPICAL OPERATION

What happens if you underline a block of text and change your mind? In this example, you switch text from underlined to normal in two ways: first, by using the Reveal Codes key, then by using the Del key.

This operation can be used interchangeably for all special effects discussed in this module.

1. Start WordPerfect and create a document similar to the following:

```
MEMO

FROM: FLG
TO:   JYM
SUBJECT: TARDINESS

John:

Never under any circumstances, are you to let an employee be tardy
without telling me. I was told that last week, Roger came in late
three times. In the future, if this should happen, tell me. I'll
straighten the employee out. Trying to protect Roger or any other
employee might help them in the very short run, but it could cost
them their job in the long run.


FLG




                                          Doc 1 Pg 1 Ln 1" Pos 1"
```

2. Move the cursor to the "N" in "Never." Press **Alt-F3**.

```
MEMO

FROM: FLG
TO:   JYM
SUBJECT: TARDINESS

John:

Never under any circumstances, are you to let an employee be tardy
without telling me. I was told that last week, Roger came in late
three times. In the future, if this should happen, tell me. I'll
                                        Doc 1 Pg 1 Ln 2.33" Pos 1"
John:[HRt]
[HRt]
[UND]Never under any circumstances, are you to let an employee be tardy[SRt]
without telling me.[und] I was told that last week, Roger came in late[SRt]
three times. In the future, if this should happen, tell me. I'll[SRt]
straighten the employee out. Trying to protect Roger or any other[SRt]
employee might help them in the very short run, but it could cost[SRt]
them their job in the long run.[HRt]
[HRt]
FLG

Press Reveal Codes to restore screen
```

3. Press **Backspace** to delete the [UND] symbol.

```
MEMO

FROM: FLG
TO:   JYM
SUBJECT: TARDINESS

John:

Never under any circumstances, are you to let an employee be tardy
without telling me. I was told that last week, Roger came in late
three times. In the future, if this should happen, tell me. I'll
                                        Doc 1 Pg 1 Ln 2.33" Pos 1"
John:[HRt]
[HRt]
Never under any circumstances, are you to let an employee be tardy[SRt]
without telling me. I was told that last week, Roger came in late[SRt]
three times. In the future, if this should happen, tell me. I'll[SRt]
straighten the employee out. Trying to protect Roger or any other[SRt]
employee might help them in the very short run, but it could cost[SRt]
them their job in the long run.[HRt]
[HRt]
FLG

Press Reveal Codes to restore screen
```

4. Press **Alt-F3** to return to the document.

```
MEMO

FROM: FLG
TO:   JYM
SUBJECT: TARDINESS

John:

Never under any circumstances, are you to let an employee be tardy
without telling me. I was told that last week, Roger came in late
three times. In the future, if this should happen, tell me. I'll
straighten the employee out. Trying to protect Roger or any other
employee might help them in the very short run, but it could cost
them their job in the long run.

FLG
```

Doc 1 Pg 1 Ln 2.33" Pos 1"

5. Move the cursor to the "b" in "but." Press **Left Arrow** once if the indicator on the Status Line shows you are in the underline mode. The underline mode should go off. If the indicator shows you're in normal mode, proceed to step 6.

6. Press **Del** and type **Y** at the delete underline prompt.

7. Save the document as TARDY.WPF.

8. Turn to Module 11 to continue the learning sequence.

Module 6
AUTO REWRITE

DESCRIPTION

When you add text to a document that forces other text down to the next line, WordPerfect automatically rewrites the screen. This is because WordPerfect includes an Auto Rewrite feature. Turn off Auto Rewrite to see the effects of changes line-by-line instead of all at once.

When the Auto Rewrite command is turned off, use the Rewrite command to rewrite the screen. Auto Rewrite is selected through the Setup menu (Shift-F1). The Rewrite key is accessed using the Screen key (Ctrl-F3). To turn off Auto Rewrite:

1. Press **Shift-F1** and type **3** or **D**. Notice the Setup menu (Appendix B).
2. Type **1** or **A** and type **N**. This turns Auto Rewrite off. Then press **F7**.

To turn Auto Rewrite back on:

1. Press **Shift-F1**, type **3** or **D**, and type **1** or **A**.
2. Type **Y**. Then press **F7**.

USING THE REWRITE KEY   Use the Rewrite key when Auto Rewrite is off to rewrite the screen to accommodate inserted text.

1. To use the Rewrite key, move the cursor to text you want to rewrite and press **Ctrl-F3**.

```
     0 Rewrite; 1 Window; 2 Line Draw: 0
```

2. Type **0** or **R**. This rewrites the screen.

APPLICATIONS

Auto Rewrite is a useful feature for most WordPerfect applications. If you frequently use columnar text (described in Module 13), or are used to older versions of WordPerfect where Auto Rewrite was not available, you might like to turn Auto Rewrite off. If you want to rewrite the screen at any time with Auto Rewrite off, use the Rewrite key. We recommend that you always leave Auto Rewrite on.

TYPICAL OPERATION

In this example, turn Auto Rewrite off to see the effects the Rewrite function has on a typical business letter. Then turn it back on to contrast the effects.

1. Start WordPerfect and create a document similar to the following:

```
                                        FLG Office Supply
                                        1210 S. Main
                                        Carbondale, IL 62901
                                        (618) 549-1952
                                        June 21, 1987

Mr. Henry Simpson
215 N. Olive
Carterville, IL 62916

Dear Sir:

Thank you for your letter and resume of May 31 in application for
the position of Senior Support Specialist at FLG. We were very
impressed with your qualifications and background and considered
your application very carefully.

Unfortunately, after a long and rigorous interview process, we have
decided to hire someone else for the position. You can be sure that
we will keep your resume on file for future reference.

Thank you for your interest in FLG Office Supply.

                                        Sincerely,

                                        Michael David
                                        Senior Vice President


                                Doc 1 Pg 1 Ln 5.5" Pos 1"
```

2. Press **Shift-F1** and type **3** or **D**.

3. Type **1** or **A**, type **N**, and press **F7**. This turns off Auto Rewrite.

4. Move the cursor to the space after the period at the end of the first sentence. Then type
    It is always gratifying to see someone with your background consider working at FLG.

```
                                        FLG Office Supply
                                        1210 S. Main
                                        Carbondale, IL 62901
                                        (618) 549-1952
                                        June 21, 1987

Mr. Henry Simpson
215 N. Olive
Carterville, IL 62916

Dear Sir:

Thank you for your letter and resume of May 31 in application for
the position of Senior Support Specialist at FLG. It is always
gratifying to see someone with your background consider working at
FLG. We were very
```

5. Press **Ctrl-F3** and type **0** or **R** to rewrite the screen.

```
                                        FLG Office Supply
                                        1210 S. Main
                                        Carbondale, IL 62901
                                        (618) 549-1952
                                        June 21, 1987


Mr. Henry Simpson
215 N. Olive
Carterville, IL 62916

Dear Sir:

Thank you for your letter and resume of May 31 in application for
the position of Senior Support Specialist at FLG. It is always
gratifying to see someone with your background consider working at
FLG. We were very impressed with your qualifications and background
and considered your application very carefully.

Unfortunately, after a long and rigorous interview process, we have
decided to hire someone else for the position. You can be sure that
we will keep your resume on file for future reference.

Thank you for your interest in FLG Office Supply.

                                        Doc 1 Pg 1 Ln 3.5" Pos 1.4"
```

NOTE

Pressing Down Arrow also rewrites the screen.
The advantage of using the Rewrite key is that
the cursor does not move.

6. Move the cursor back to the space after the period at the end of the first sentence.

7. Press **Alt-F4** and type **.** to mark the sentence as a block. Press **Del** and type **Y** to delete the sentence.

8. Move the cursor to the "T" in "Thank" at the beginning of the letter. Press **Shift-F1** and type **3** or **D**.

9. Type **1** or **A**, type **Y**, and press **F7** to turn Auto Rewrite back on.

10. Move the cursor to the space after the period at the end of the first sentence. Then type **It is always gratifying to see someone with your background consider working at FLG.** Notice the difference between the first example and this one. The screen is completely rewritten here.

```
                                    FLG Office Supply
                                    1210 S. Main
                                    Carbondale, IL 62901
                                    (618) 549-1952
                                    June 21, 1987

Mr. Henry Simpson
215 N. Olive
Carterville, IL 62916

Dear Sir:

Thank you for your letter and resume of May 31 in application for
the position of Senior Support Specialist at FLG. It is always
gratifying to see someone with your background consider working at
FLG. We were very impressed with your qualifications and background and
considered your application very carefully.

Unfortunately, after a long and rigorous interview process, we have
decided to hire someone else for the position. You can be sure that
we will keep your resume on file for future reference.

Thank you for your interest in FLG Office Supply.

                                    Doc 1 Pg 1 Ln 3.5" Pos 1.5"
```

11. Save the document as SIMPSON.WPF.

12. Turn to Module 5 to continue the learning sequence.

Module 7

AUTOMATIC REFERENCE

DESCRIPTION

Did you ever read a magazine article that referred to another article in the same issue? It probably said something like, "refer to article on XYZ, page 23." When you read it, you probably did not realize that the page number for the article on XYZ was not determined until well after the article was written. Copy editors had to diligently find the reference to the article, locate the target that the reference cited, and mark the page number for that article on the reference.

WordPerfect's Automatic Reference feature takes care of all that for you. It lets you refer to figures, tables, sections, or other parts of a document without worrying about page numbers changing. It automatically enters the correct page number when the document is complete. This is very useful in large documents. Automatic Reference keeps track of the target — the item you are referring to — at the reference point.

You can use as many automatic references as you want in a document. References can be anywhere — text, endnotes, footnotes, headers, footers, graphics box text areas, or graphics box captions. Targets can be in text, endnotes, footnotes, and graphics box captions.

You can also specify more than one target per reference. This lets you refer to more than one item at a time. For example, you could write "see berries, pages 1, 14, and 27."

Automatic references are especially useful when used in conjunction with WordPerfect's Master Documents feature, described in Module 44. This lets you have the reference and target in two separate, but related, files. To generate an automatic reference:

1. Move to the location of the reference, type an introductory phrase and press the **Spacebar** to create one space between the phrase and the reference. Then press **Alt-F5** and type **1** or **R**.

```
Mark Text: Automatic Reference

     1 - Mark Reference

     2 - Mark Target

     3 - Mark Both Reference and Target


Selection: 0
```

2. If you want to mark only the reference now and the target later, type **1** or **R**. To mark the target only, type **2** or **T**. To mark both the reference and the target, type **3** or **B**. If you type **3** or **B**, the following screen appears:

```
Tie Reference to:

    1 - Page Number

    2 - Paragraph/Outline Number

    3 - Footnote Number

    4 - Endnote Number

    5 - Graphics Box Number

After selecting a reference type, go to the location of the item you want to
reference in your document and press Enter to mark it as the "target".


Selection: 0
```

3. Type **1** or **P** to refer to a page number, **2** or **O** a paragraph or outline number, **3** or **F** a footnote number, **4** or **E** an endnote number, or **5** or **G** a graphics box number. If you select a graphics box, you are asked what type of graphics box you want to refer to (graphics is discussed in Module 30).

4. Move the cursor to the space after the target and press **Enter** to mark it. Then type a name for the target and press **Enter**. This ties the target to the reference. The reference number appears at the reference. If you marked a reference without a target, a question mark appears instead.

NOTE
If you are using a graphics box caption, you have
to mark the target and reference separately.

If you want to define multiple targets for one reference, and/or multiple references for one target, continue this procedure, marking targets and references separately. Use the same target name you created before. When references are generated, targets and references with the same target name are matched.

You can also define multiple types for the same reference (for example, "see paragraph 4, page 36"). To do this, create a second reference type with the same target name.

GENERATING REFERENCES   When locations of targets change after a document is updated, you must generate the references. To do this press Alt-F5 and type 6 or G. Then type y to confirm you want to update the references. Make sure this is one of the last steps you perform before printing a document, since changes made since the last update do not appear when a document is printed.

APPLICATIONS

Automatic references do the legwork of updating references when you have made editing changes. They save you from having to locate every reference in a document and update it. This is especially useful for long documents.

Automatic references are useful in articles, magazines, books, reports, theses, annual reports, legal documents, and a variety of other documents. They refer to page numbers, paragraph numbers, footnotes, endnotes, graphics, and outline numbers.

In books or other multiple document items, you can use the Master Documents feature to place references and targets in separate files. You can refer to more than one item (target) in one reference. And you can refer to one target multiple times.

TYPICAL OPERATION

In this operation, you refer to a variety of items in an annual report.

1. Retrieve the file FINANCES.WPF, which was created in Module 15. Delete the first page, which is the letter that accompanied the financial statements. Also delete the page break between the letter and the income statement. Portions of the remaining two pages are shown here. Refer to Module 15 to see the entire document.

```
                        INCOME STATEMENT
                        FLG OFFICE SUPPLIES
                   FOR YEAR ENDED DECEMBER 31, 1986


   Sales:                 $625,000
   Less: Cost of Goods:    375,000
   Gross Margin:                              $250,000



============================================================================
                        BALANCE SHEET
                        FLG OFFICE SUPPLIES
                   FOR YEAR ENDED DECEMBER 31, 1986


   Assets:

   Cash:                 $ 97,232
   Accounts Receivable:    16,345
   Equipment (depreciated): 150,235
   Total Assets:                              $263,812




   C:\WP50\DOCS\FINANCES.WPF              Doc 1 Pg 2 Ln 2.83" Pos 1"
```

2. Move the cursor to the top of the document and press **Ctrl-Enter** to create a new page. Move the cursor up above the page break and type **The year that passed was a good year for FLG Office Supplies. As you can tell from the income statement on page.**

3. Press the **Spacebar**. Then press **Alt-F5**, type **1** or **R**, then **3** or **B**.

4. Type **1** or **P** to tie the reference to a page number. Move the cursor anywhere on the page where the income statement is located and press **Enter**. Type **income statement** as the target name and press **Enter**.

```
The year that passed was a good year for FLG Office Supplies. As
you can tell from the income statement on page 2
============================================================================
                          INCOME STATEMENT
                          FLG OFFICE SUPPLIES
                     FOR YEAR ENDED DECEMBER 31, 1986

Sales:                  $625,000
Less: Cost of Goods:     375,000
Gross Margin:                               $250,000


============================================================================
                           BALANCE SHEET
                          FLG OFFICE SUPPLIES
                     FOR YEAR ENDED DECEMBER 31, 1986

Assets:

Cash:                   $ 97,232
Accounts Receivable:      16,345
Equipment (depreciated): 150,235
Total Assets:                               $263,812

C:\WP50\DOCS\FINANCES.WPF                       Doc 1 Pg 1 Ln 1.16" Pos 5.8"
```

5. Type **, and the balance sheet on page**.

6. Press the **Spacebar**. Then press **Alt-F5**, type **1** or **R**, then **3** or **B**.

7. Type **1** or **P** to tie the reference to a page number. Move the cursor anywhere on the page where the balance sheet is located and press **Enter**. Type **balance sheet** as the target name and press **Enter**.

```
The year that passed was a good year for FLG Office Supplies. As
you can tell from the income statement on page 2, and the balance
sheet on page 3
===============================================================================
                            INCOME STATEMENT
                            FLG OFFICE SUPPLIES
                    FOR YEAR ENDED DECEMBER 31, 1986


Sales:                      $625,000
Less: Cost of Goods:         375,000
Gross Margin:                                   $250,000



===============================================================================
                            BALANCE SHEET
                            FLG OFFICE SUPPLIES
                    FOR YEAR ENDED DECEMBER 31, 1986


Assets:

Cash:                       $ 97,232
Accounts Receivable:          16,345
Equipment (depreciated):     150,235
Total Assets:                                   $263,812
C:\WP50\DOCS\FINANCES.WPF                        Doc 1 Pg 1 Ln 1.33" Pos 2.5"
```

8. Type , **FLG is doing very well. Our cash flow is healthy, our gross margin is over 30 percent, and business in general is good.**

9. Move the cursor to the top of the document and press **Ctrl-Enter** to create a new page. Then press **Shift-F6** and type **FLG OFFICE SUPPLIES** and press **Enter**. Press **Shift-F6** and type **ANNUAL REPORT**.

10. Press **Shift-F8** and type **2** or **P**. Then type **1** or **C**, then type **Y** and press **F7** to center the text on the page.

11. Press **Alt-F5** and type **6** or **G**. Then type **5** or **G** and **Y**. Notice the new page reference numbers.

12. Move the cursor to the end of the paragraph on page 2 and press **Ctrl-Enter** five times to signify extra pages in the annual report. Then press **Alt-F5**, type **6** or **G**, then **5** or **G**, then **Y**.

```
                          FLG OFFICE SUPPLIES
                          ANNUAL REPORT
===============================================================================
The year that past was a good year for FLG Office Supplies. As you
can tell from the income statement on page 8, and the balance sheet
on page 9, FLG is doing very well. Our cash flow is healthy, our
gross margin is over 30 percent, and business in general is good.
===============================================================================

===============================================================================

===============================================================================

===============================================================================

===============================================================================

===============================================================================
                          INCOME STATEMENT
                          FLG OFFICE SUPPLIES
                    FOR YEAR ENDED DECEMBER 31, 1986

Sales:                    $625,000
Less: Cost of Goods:       375,000
C:\WP50\DOCS\FINANCES.WPF                        Doc 1 Pg 1 Ln 1" POS 1"
```

13. Save the document as ANNUAL.WPF.

14. Turn to Module 36 to continue the learning sequence.

Module 8
BLOCK

DESCRIPTION

The Block key (Alt-F4) lets you break text into blocks for use with other editing features. The block can be as long or as short as you want. You define how large the block is by moving the cursor.

The Block key is very useful for performing one operation to a whole group of text. For example, the Block key lets you move, copy, delete, or underline a group of text.

To use the Block key, press Alt-F4.

```
Block on                                          Doc 1 Pg 1 Ln 1" Pos ▉
```

As you move the cursor through the text, the text becomes highlighted. You can move the cursor either backward or forward to define any text you choose as a block. The highlighted text below is part of a block, while the unhighlighted text isn't.

```
While the main function of the average office is work, many office
personnel rely on their place of work as a hub of social activity.
Therefore, it might be pertinent if we start to sell merchandise
that is not related to the office, like magazines.

I want to investigate this matter. I'm going to put you in charge
of this program, Roger. Go down to the library and do some market
research. Also do some studies. Find out what types of items people
hope to find in office supply stores. Find out what we're missing.


Block on                                     Doc 1 Pg 1 Ln 1.66" Pos ▉
```

After pressing Alt-F4, you can move quickly through text by typing a letter or character. The cursor goes to the next occurrence of that letter or character. This is especially useful for defining sentences (type . to define the sentence as a block) or paragraphs (press Enter to define the paragraph as a block.)

NOTE

You can perform more than one editing operation on the same block of text through the use
of the Go To key. The procedure is described in
Module 29.

After you have defined a block of text, you can perform any of the following editing operations on that block. If the Block On message is still flashing after you have completed the editing operation, press F1 to turn off the block.

NOTE
Before you type any of the following keystrokes,
press Alt-F4 and define the block of text.

Keystrokes	Results
Ctrl-F4, 3, filename	Appends (Module 47) block to another file.
F6 or Ctrl-F8, 2, 1	Makes block boldface (Module 5).
Shift-F6, Y	Centers (Module 12) block.
Ctrl-F4, 1 or B, 2 or C	Copies (Module 14) block.
Ctrl-F4, 2 or C, 2 or C	Copies column (Module 14).
Ctrl-F4, 3 or R, 2 or C	Copies rectangle (Module 14).
Ctrl-F4, 1 or B, 1 or M	Cuts block (Module 47) from text.
Ctrl-F4, 2 or C, 1 or M	Cuts column (Module 47) from text.
Ctrl-F4, 3 or R, 1 or M	Cuts rectangle from text (Module 47).
Del, Y	Deletes (Module 17) block.
Alt-F6, Y	Moves block flush to right margin (Module 26).
Ctrl-F8, 1 or S, 3 or F	Changes font (Module 27) to fine for all text in block.
Ctrl-F8, 1 or S, 4 or S	Changes font (Module 27) to small for all text in block.
Ctrl-F8, 1 or S, 5 or L	Changes font (Module 27) to large for all text in block.
Ctrl-F8, 1 or S, 6 or V	Changes font (Module 27) to very large for all text in block.
Ctrl-F8, 1 or S, 7 or E	Changes font (Module 27) to extra large for all text in block.
Ctrl-F8, 2 or A, 4 or I	Italicizes block (Module 5).
Alt-F5, 2 or L, List Number	Marks block for list (Module 41).
Alt-F5, 3 or I, Index, sub-heading, Enter	Marks block for indexing (Module 36).
Shift-F3, 2 or L	Makes all text in block lowercase (Module 11).
Ctrl-F8, 2 or A, 5 or O	Creates outline text at printer (Module 5).
Shift-F7, Y	Prints (Module 57) block.
Shift-F8, Y	Protects (Module 9) text in block from being separated by a page break.
Ctrl-F8, 2 or A, 8 or R	Redlines (Module 58) text in block for insertion.
Ctrl-Home, Ctrl-Home	Restores a block of text (Module 29).
F10, block name, Enter	Saves (Module 60) block as a file.
Ctrl-F5, Y	Converts block of text into document comments (Module 19).
F2, text to search for, F2	Performs a search operation (Module 61) on the block.
Alt-F2, Y or N, text to search for, F2, text to replace it with, F2	Performs a search and replace (Module 61) operation on the block.
Ctrl-F8, 2 or A, 6 or A	Creates shadow text at printer (Module 5).
Ctrl-F8, 2 or A, 7 or C	Creates small caps text at printer (Module 5).
Ctrl-F9, 1-7, F7	Sorts (Module 62) block.
Ctrl-F2	Checks the spelling on the text in the block (Module 64).
Ctrl-F8, 2 or A, 9 or S	Strikes out (Module 58) text for deletion.
Ctrl-F8, 1 or S, 2 or b	Subscripts (Module 67) all text in block.

Keystrokes	Results
Ctrl-F8, 1 or S, 1 or p	Superscripts (Module 67) all text in block.
Alt-F5, 4 or A, ToA Level, Enter	Marks block for table of authorities (Module 68).
Alt-F5, 1 or C, level number, Enter	Marks block for table of contents (Module 69).
F8 or Ctrl-F8, 2, 2	Underlines (Module 5) block.
Ctrl-F8, 2 or A, 3 or D	Creates double underline of block (Module 5).
Shift-F3, 1 or U	Makes all text in block uppercase (Module 11).

DEFINING A RECTANGULAR OR COLUMNAR BLOCK OF TEXT   You can also use the block key to define a rectangular or columnar block of text, for moving and copying purposes. To define a rectangular block, move the cursor from the upper left corner of the text to the lower right corner. You define the width.

A columnar block of text is text that is in a column, but *not* in column mode (Module 13). WordPerfect defines a column as text that is from one tab, indent, hard return, or alignment character (Module 4). It is similar to a rectangular block of text but is confined only to columns of text or numbers. To define a columnar block of text, move the cursor from anywhere on the first line of the column to anywhere on the last line.

Each feature is especially useful in charts and tables when you might want to copy text in a certain column. Copying columnar blocks of text is often easier than copying rectangular blocks. For example, assume you are trying to copy the names of the employees from the following chart.

```
FLG OFFICE SUPPLIES

WEEKLY HOURS SHEET

PERIOD ENDING JUNE 6, 1987

Employee   Hours Worked
Wilson        47
Mathews       38
Jones         32
Smith         15
Levin         41
Belew         38
```

                                    Doc 1 Pg 1 Ln 2.16" Pos 1"

If you are defining a rectangular block of text, make sure the cursor is on the "W" in "Wilson." If you are defining a columnar block, make sure the cursor is anywhere within the name "Wilson."

1. Press **Alt-F4**. To define a rectangular block, move the cursor to the "w" in "Belew." To define a columnar block, move the cursor to anywhere in the name "Belew."

```
FLG OFFICE SUPPLIES

WEEKLY HOURS SHEET

PERIOD ENDING JUNE 6, 1987

Employee    Hours Worked
Wilson           47
Mathews          38
Jones            32
Smith            15
Levin            41
Belew            38


Block on                                    Doc 1 Pg 1 Ln 3" Pos 1.5"
```

2. Move the cursor to the right until it is under the "s" in "Mathews" and press **Ctrl-F4**. Type **2** or **C** for a columnar block of text, **3** or **R** for a rectangular block.

```
Employee    Hours Worked
Wilson           47
Mathews          38
Jones            32
Smith            15
Levin            41
Belew            38


1 Move; 2 Copy; 3 Delete; 4 Append: 0
```

With either method, you get the same block of text. Notice the difference between it and a normal block of text. All you can do with a rectangular or columnar block of text is move, copy, delete, or append it. No other editing features work with it. To copy the block, type 2 or C.

APPLICATIONS

As the table in this module shows, the Block key helps you perform many editing operations. Its best use is in moving and copying text. This allows you to "cut and paste," possibly the most useful feature of word processing because you can literally rearrange documents — move paragraphs, sentences, or even pages to other locations in a document.

The Block key is also useful for performing operations on only a portion of the text, such as search and replace, indexing, spell checking, printing, and a variety of other tasks. This is useful because it lets you perform a task on any part of the document that you want. It saves you the trouble of having to perform that task on the entire document.

TYPICAL OPERATION

In this example, you define a block of text and redefine it until it is exactly what you want. Once defined, you make the block boldface.

1. Create a document similar to the following:

```
RULES AND REGULATIONS FOR EMPLOYEES OF FLG OFFICE SUPPLY

1. Employees are always to be on time.

2. Each employee must take care to dress appropriately. Jeans and
t-shirts are not permitted on the sales floor.

3. Employees are to conduct themselves in an orderly manner. Loud
arguing or fighting will not be tolerated.


                                         Doc 1 Pg 1 Ln 1.66" Pos 1"
```

2. With the cursor on the number "2," press **Alt-F4**. Then press **Up Arrow** until rule number 1 is highlighted.

```
RULES AND REGULATIONS FOR EMPLOYEES OF FLG OFFICE SUPPLY

1. Employees are always to be on time.

2. Each employee must take care to dress appropriately. Jeans and
t-shirts are not permitted on the sales floor.

3. Employees are to conduct themselves in an orderly manner. Loud
arguing or fighting will not be tolerated.

Block on                                 Doc 1 Pg 1 Ln 1.33" Pos 1"
```

3. Press **Down Arrow** until rule number 2 is highlighted. Since the block began at rule number 2, rule number 1 is no longer highlighted. Press **F6** to boldface all text in the block.

RULES AND REGULATIONS FOR EMPLOYEES OF FLG OFFICE SUPPLY

1. Employees are always to be on time.

2. Each employee must take care to dress appropriately. Jeans and t-shirts are not permitted on the sales floor.

3. Employees are to conduct themselves in an orderly manner. Loud arguing or fighting will not be tolerated.

Doc 1 Pg 1 Ln 2" Pos 1"

4. Save the document as RULES.WPF.

5. Turn to Module 14 to continue the learning sequence.

Module 9
BLOCK PROTECT

DESCRIPTION

The Protect feature lets you keep a block (Module 8) of text on the same page. Text protected in this way cannot be separated by a soft page break (Module 50). You can, however, separate the text with a hard page break (Ctrl-Enter).

This feature is especially useful for tables or figures illustrated in text. You would not want two lines of a four-line table on one page and the other two lines on the next, for example.

To protect a block of text:

1. Press **Alt-F4**. Define the block to protect and press **Shift-F8**.

```
Protect block? (Y/N) No
```

2. Type **Y** to protect the block of text.

WordPerfect will not separate protected text by a page break. If all the text cannot fit on one page, it all moves to the next.

To remove protection from a block of text, use Reveal Codes (Module 59). WordPerfect puts a "Block Pro:On" code at the beginning of the block, and a "Block Pro:Off" code at the end. To remove block protection, move the cursor to the "Block Pro:On" code and press Del to delete it.

CONDITIONAL END OF PAGE   Another way to keep text on the same page is through the Conditional End of Page command. Instead of protecting a block of text, this feature protects a specified number of lines.

Once lines of text are protected, they remain on the same page, even if WordPerfect has to insert a page break before the text.

To use Conditional End of Page:

1. Move the cursor to the line above the text you want to protect and press **Shift-F8**. Then type **4** or **O**.

2. Type **2** or **C**.

    `Number of Lines to Keep Together:`

3. Type the number of lines to keep together and press **Enter**.

To remove the Conditional End of Page command, use Reveal Codes. WordPerfect puts a "CndlEOP:(number of lines)" code at the beginning of the text to protect. Move the cursor to the code and press Del to delete it.

APPLICATIONS

Block Protect and Conditional End of Page are especially useful for keeping together tables and charts that are integrated with text in a document. But either can be used to keep any text together — long paragraphs, names, chapter titles, etc.

TYPICAL OPERATION

In this example, you protect a table to keep it on one page.

1. Create a document similar to the following. Leave enough blank space at the top of the page to simulate the beginning of the memo and to create a page break as indicated by the dotted line:

```
As I mentioned, we hope sales can continue to improve. But
indications are times will be tough. Here are sales for this year
compared to last:

Month 1986  Sales        1987 Sales            Percent Change (+/-)
January    $ 43,345      $ 41,425                 -   4.43
February     42,235        41,895                 -   0.81
March        43,439        44,425                 +   2.32
-------------------------------------------------------------------
April        51,137        45,925                 -  10.19
May          53,120        51,190                 -   3.63
Totals:    $233,276      $224,860                 -   3.61

Notice the difference between March sales this year than last.
March is the only month that is up over last year. And it wasn't
a breathtaking increase.

                                   Doc 1 Pg 2 Ln 2.33" Pos 1"
```

2. Move the cursor to the "M" in "Month" on the first page and press **Alt-F4**. Notice the flashing "Block on" prompt. Then move the cursor to the end of the line under the "T" in "Totals."

```
As I mentioned, we hope sales can continue to improve. But
indications are times will be tough. Here are sales for this year
compared to last:

Month 1986  Sales         1987 Sales            Percent Change (+/-)
January    $ 43,345      $ 41,425                -    4.43
February     42,235        41,895                -    0.81
March        43,439        44,425                +    2.32
---------------------------------------------------------------------
April        51,137        45,925                -   10.19
May          53,120        51,190                -    3.63
Totals:   $233,276      $224,860                -    3.61

Notice the difference between March sales this year than last.
March is the only month that is up over last year. And it wasn't
a breathtaking increase.


Block on                                    Doc 1 Pg 2 Ln 1.5" Pos 1"
```

3. Press **Shift-F8** and type **Y** to protect the block. Notice the entire block is now on page 2.

```
As I mentioned, we hope sales can continue to improve. But
indications are times will be tough. Here are sales for this year
compared to last:
---------------------------------------------------------------------

Month 1986  Sales         1987 Sales            Percent Change (+/-)
January    $ 43,345      $ 41,425                -    4.43
February     42,235        41,895                -    0.81
March        43,439        44,425                +    2.32
April        51,137        45,925                -   10.19
May          53,120        51,190                -    3.63
Totals:   $233,276      $224,860                -    3.61

Notice the difference between March sales this year than last.
March is the only month that is up over last year. And it wasn't
a breathtaking increase.

                                            Doc 1 Pg 2 Ln 2.33" Pos 1"
```

4. Save the document as MONTH.WPF.
5. Turn to Module 61 to continue the learning sequence.

Module 10
CANCEL

DESCRIPTION

The Cancel command (F1) lets you cancel any activity that you decide not to complete. This can help you prevent errors while editing. You can use the Cancel command to:

- Cancel any command that displays a message on the Status Line or creates a menu
- Leave a WordPerfect menu
- Cancel Hyphenation
- Recover, or "undelete," text that has been deleted.

CANCELLING A COMMAND   Suppose you are using the Block On command to define a block of text. (Block commands are explained in Module 8.) You are thinking about moving part of the last sentence to the beginning of the memo and have defined that part of the sentence as a block of text. Your screen might resemble the following display:

```
  MEMO

  CONFIDENTIAL

  While the main function of the average office is for work, many
  office personnel rely on their place of work as a hub of social
  activity. Therefore, it might be pertinent if we start to sell
  merchandise that is not related to the office, like magazines.



  Block on                              Doc 1 Pg 1 Ln 2.16" Pos 7.2"
```

Before you continue with the block move, you decide that you like the memo as is and you'd like to leave it that way. The Cancel command lets you do this. If you press F1, the Block On indicator stops flashing and the command is cancelled.

The Cancel command is used in this way with any command that displays a prompt on the Status Line or creates a menu. It cannot be used with Reveal Codes (Module 59) or Macros (Module 42). To leave Reveal Codes, press the Reveal Codes key again (Alt-F3). To halt macro definition, press the Macro Define key (Ctrl-F10).

USING THE CANCEL KEY TO LEAVE A MENU   Assume you press the wrong key and accidentally access the Format menu (discussed in further detail in Modules 21, 39, 48, and 51). The menu is displayed below.

```
Format

    1 - Line
            Hyphenation                    Line Spacing
            Justification                  Margins Left/Right
            Line Height                    Tab Set
            Line Numbering                 Widow/Orphan Protection

    2 - Page
            Center Page (top to bottom)    New Page Number
            Force Odd/Even Page            Page Numbering
            Headers and Footers            Paper Size/Type
            Margins Top/Bottom             Suppress

    3 - Document
            Display Pitch                  Redline Method
            Initial Codes/Font             Summary

    4 - Other
            Advance                        Overstrike
            Conditional End of Page        Printer Functions
            Decimal Characters             Underline Spaces/Tabs
            Language

    Selection: 0
```

You can press F1 to return to document editing.

TIP: You can cancel commands with other keys when presented with menus in WordPerfect. Consider the preceding Format menu. You can press any key other than the choices on the menu (1 through 4, D, L, P, or O) to cancel the command.

CANCELLING HYPHENATION When Hyphenation (described in Module 34) is on, WordPerfect gives you the option of cancelling the hyphenation of any word. This is illustrated in the following example:

```
MEMO

From: FLG
To:   MDS

Dear Michael:

Some of our new employees have been pursuing their jobs too vigorously


Position hyphen: Press ESC vigoro-usly
```

NOTE

In order for this example to work, hyphenation
must be set to on.

Assume you do not want to hyphenate "vigorously." The prompt at the bottom of the screen is not asking if you want to hyphenate the word or not; it is asking where you want the hyphen. The Cancel key gives you the option to cancel hyphenation.

By pressing F1, "vigorously" is not hyphenated. Instead, it moves to the next line.

UNDELETING TEXT   The Cancel key is also used to "undelete" or restore text that has been deleted. WordPerfect keeps the last three deletions in memory. So, if you change your mind about text after you have deleted it, you can restore it. Notice the following example:

```
MEMO

From: FLG
To:   MDS

Dear Michael:

Some of our employees have been pursuing their jobs too vigorously.
I am afraid that one of them is going to become ill. I would like
to recommend mandatory vacations for Jonathan, Mike, and Laura.
Jonathan should take the first week of March off, Mike the second
and Laura the third.

Let me know what you think.


                                        Doc 1 Pg 1 Ln 3.33" Pos 1"
```

Let's assume you previously deleted the word "week" with a following comma, using the Delete Word command (explained in Module 17). You realize that the memo would read better if that word were left in.

1. Leave the cursor where it is and press **F1** rather than retyping the word.

```
    MEMO

    From: FLG
    To:   MDS

    Dear Michael:

    Some of our employees have been pursuing their jobs too vigorously.
    I am afraid that one of them is going to become ill. I would like
    to recommend mandatory vacations for Jonathan, Mike, and Laura.
    Jonathan should take the first week of March off, Mike the second
    week, and Laura the third.

    Let me know what you think.




    Undelete: 1 Restore; 2 Previous Deletion: 0
```

WordPerfect gives you the option of returning "week," to its original place in the document, or restoring a previous deletion.

2. Type **1** or **R** to restore the word to the document.

APPLICATIONS

Use the Cancel command whenever you are editing a document and have pressed the wrong key. Use the Undelete command to restore deleted text, cancel a command, or leave a menu.

TYPICAL OPERATION

This example shows how to restore deleted text.

1. Create a document similar to the following:

```
CONFIDENTIAL

From: FLG
To:   RAW

While the main function of the average office is for work, many
office personnel rely on their place of work as a hub of social
activity. Therefore, it might be pertinent if we start to sell
merchandise that is not related to the office, like magazines.

I want to investigate this matter. I'm going to put you in charge
of this program, Roger. Go down to the library and do some market
research. Also do some studies. Find out what types of items people
hope to find in office supply stores. Find out what we're missing.

I'd like a full report by the end of the month. I want your report
to list all of the items we aren't carrying that we should be
carrying. I'd also like an estimated sales volume for those items.

Also Roger, please don't discuss this with anyone else, not even
anyone on the staff.

FLG

                              Doc 1 Pg 1 Ln 5.16" Pos 1"
```

2. Move the cursor to the "A" in "Also" at the bottom of the document and press **Alt-F4** to turn on Block Mode.

3. Type . (a period) to move the cursor to the end of the sentence and press **Del**. Notice the prompt asking if you want to delete the block. Type **Y** to delete the sentence.

4. Move the cursor to the "f" in "for" in the first sentence. Press **Ctrl-Backspace** to delete the word.

5. Move the cursor to the next-to-the-last line in the document (before "FLG") and press **F1**. Then type **2** to show the previous deletion.

```
  CONFIDENTIAL

  From: FLG
  To:   RAW

  While the main function of the average office is work, many office
  personnel rely on their place of work as a hub of social activity.
  Therefore, it might be pertinent if we start to sell merchandise
  that is not related to the office, like magazines.

  I want to investigate this matter. I'm going to put you in charge
  of this program, Roger. Go down to the library and do some market
  research. Also do some studies. Find out what types of items people
  hope to find in office supply stores. Find out what we're missing.

  I'd like a full report by the end of the month. I want your report
  to list all of the items we aren't carrying that we should be
  carrying. I'd also like an estimated sales volume for those items.

  Also Roger, please don't discuss this with anyone else, not even
  anyone on the staff.

  FLG
  Undelete: 1 Restore; 2 Previous Deletion: 0
```

6. Type **1** to restore this text.

7. To save the document, press **F7**, then **Enter**. At the prompt "Document to be saved:" type **IDEAS.WPF** and press **Enter**.

8. Turn to Module 40 to continue the learning sequence.

Module 11

CASE CONVERSION

DESCRIPTION

WordPerfect's Case Conversion feature (Shift-F3) is a handy tool that lets you convert an entire block of text from uppercase to lowercase and vice-versa. When converting a block to lowercase, WordPerfect leaves the first word in a sentence capitalized, as well as words like "I" and "I'm."

This feature only works with the Block key (Alt-F4) activated. To convert a block of text to upper or lowercase, press Alt-F4 (notice the flashing "Block on" prompt) and define the block of text you wish to convert. When you press Shift-F3 you see:

```
1 Uppercase; 2 Lowercase: 0
```

Type 1 or U to convert the block to uppercase or 2 or L to convert the block to lowercase. Press F1 to turn the Block mode off.

NOTE
In order to leave the first word in the first sentence capitalized when converting a block to lowercase, begin the block with the period at the end of the previous sentence.

APPLICATIONS

Anytime you have a block of text that you want to convert to uppercase or lowercase, use the Case Conversion command. This command is convenient with both large and small blocks of text. You might want to change book titles, section titles, and other items to uppercase. Uppercase text is useful for emphasis. On the other hand, you might want to change a block of text that is uppercase to lowercase. The Case Conversion command serves that purpose as well.

TYPICAL OPERATION

In this example, you convert various blocks of text in a memo from lowercase to uppercase and then you convert a block of text from uppercase to lowercase.

1. Create a document similar to the following:

```
Notice to all employees:

Friday, March 3 is a special day for us at FLG Office Supply. It's
FLG's birthday! We're not sure how old she is, but we need to get
her a birthday present. I propose that everyone chip in $1 for the
present. And I'll buy the cake!

MD


                                        Doc 1 Pg 1 Ln 1" Pos 1"
```

2. Move the cursor to the "N" in "Notice." Press **Alt-F4**, then press **End** to define the first line as a block.

```
Notice to all employees:

Friday, March 3 is a special day for us at FLG Office Supply. It's
FLG's birthday! We're not sure how old she is, but we need to get
her a birthday present. I propose that everyone chip in $1 for the
present. And I'll buy the cake!

MD

Block on                                Doc 1 Pg 1 Ln 1" Pos 3.4"
```

3. Press **Shift-F3** and type **1** to make the block uppercase.

```
NOTICE TO ALL EMPLOYEES:

Friday, March 3 is a special day for us at FLG Office Supply. It's
FLG's birthday! We're not sure how old she is, but we need to get
her a birthday present. I propose that everyone chip in $1 for the
present. And I'll buy the cake!

MD


                                        Doc 1 Pg 1 Ln 1" Pos 3.4"
```

4. Move the cursor to the "A" in "And" in the last sentence and press **Alt-F4**. Press **End** to highlight the block.

5. Press **Shift-F3** and type **1** to convert the block to uppercase. Notice the sentence is now all uppercase.

6. To change the sentence back to lowercase, move the cursor to the period after "present" and press **Alt-F4**. Press **End** to define the sentence as a block.

7. Press **Shift-F3** and type **2** to convert the block to lowercase. Notice the "A" in "And" is still uppercase.

8. Save the document as BIRTHDAY.WPF.

9. Turn to Module 59 to continue the learning sequence.

Module 12
CENTER

DESCRIPTION

If you were creating your documents with a typewriter instead of a computer, horizontally centering text would be a tedious process. You have to move the carriage to the center of a page, count the number of characters (including spaces) in the text you want centered, move the carriage one space to the left for each two characters in the text, and finally, type.

Luckily, you are not using a typewriter. To center text horizontally in WordPerfect, simply move the cursor to the beginning of the line and press Shift-F6, the Center key. Then type the text you want centered, and press either Enter or Tab. If you have already typed the text, move the cursor to the beginning of the line and press Shift-F6, then Down Arrow. The center key centers all text after the cursor on a chosen line.

NOTE

Press Enter or Tab at the end of any line you want centered. If you do not, WordPerfect attempts to center all text between the Center command and the next time you press Enter or Tab.

If you insert (Module 37) or delete (Module 17) text, WordPerfect automatically accommodates the changes and keeps the line centered.

The reference points for the center key are the left and right margins, unless you are centering text while in column mode (Module 13). In other words, if your margins are 10 and 74, the center of the page is 42. If you are using inches on the Status Line and your margins are 1" on left and right, the center of the page is 4.2" for 10 pitch and 4.25" for 12 pitch.

If you have a block (Module 8) of text that you want centered, WordPerfect does that as well. Define the block of text, press Shift-F6, and confirm you want the block centered.

APPLICATIONS

Use the Center key to center any line or block of text in a document. One of the most common uses for the Center command is centering titles and title pages. You can also use the Center tab (Module 70) to center column headings in tables.

TYPICAL OPERATION

In this example, you center the lines of a memo.

1. Create a document similar to the following:

```
ATTENTION ALL EMPLOYEES!

FLG OFFICE SUPPLY IS HAVING A PARTY!

YOU'RE INVITED!

MARCH 25,1987

8:00 PM

EMPEROR'S PALACE

BE THERE!
```

Doc 1 Pg 1 Ln 1" POS 1"

2. Make sure the cursor is at the top of the page and press **Alt-F4**. Then press **Home**, **Home**, **Down Arrow** to move the cursor to the bottom of the page and define the entire page as a block of text. Then press **Shift-F6**.

```
[Cntr]? (Y/N) No
```

3. Type **Y**.

```
                    ATTENTION ALL EMPLOYEES!

               FLG OFFICE SUPPLY IS HAVING A PARTY!

                        YOU'RE INVITED!

                        MARCH 25,1987

                           8:00 PM

                       EMPEROR'S PALACE

                          BE THERE!
```

Doc 1 Pg 1 Ln 3.16" POS 1"

4. Save the document as PARTY.WPF.
5. Turn to Module 26 to continue the learning sequence.

COLUMN DEFINITION

DESCRIPTION

If you are doing desktop publishing or want to produce documents that are columnar in format, use WordPerfect's Column Definition command (Alt-F7). The Column Definition command lets you put as many as 24 columns on a page. Newspaper style columns are the most common type:

```
        AB Office Supply              staff personnel to assist those
                                      sales people.
    AB Office Supply in Murphysboro            O&G Office Supply
    is probably our toughest
    competitor. Those folks are       Their general tactics border on
    tenacious. They have three        the immoral. Those folks only
    outside salespeople and several   want to close the sale.


                                         Col 2 Doc 1 Pg 1 Ln 2" Pos 6.8"
```

But WordPerfect also lets you create parallel columns. Parallel columns keep common groups of information together on a page. The length of the information in each column is irrelevant. Parallel columns are commonly used for applications like scripts, screenplays, and tables.

There are two types of parallel columns: parallel, and parallel with block protect. Since parallel columns typically consist of independent groups, block protect prevents these groups from being separated. If there is not enough room for both of the columns below on a page, for example, block protect moves both to the next page.

```
        AB Office Supply                  O&G Office Supply

    AB Office Supply in Murphysboro   Their general tactics border on
    is probably our toughest          the immoral. Those folks only
    competitor. Those folks are       want to close the sale.
    tenacious. They have three
    outside salespeople and several
    staff personnel to assist those
    sales people.


                                      Col 2 Doc 1 Pg 1 Ln 1.66" Pos 6.8"
```

There are four steps to creating a column in WordPerfect:

1. Define the columns
2. Turn Column mode on
3. Type the text in the columns
4. Turn column mode off

DEFINE COLUMNS   Before you can go into Column Mode, you must first tell WordPerfect how many columns you want on a page, how you want those columns spaced, where you want the margins to be, and whether you want newspaper or parallel format. All column formats are saved with the document. To define columns:

1. Press **Alt-F7**.

```
1 Math On; 2 Math Def; 3 Column On/Off; 4 Column Def: 0
```

2. Type **4** or **D**.

```
Text Column Definition

    1 - Type                          Newspaper

    2 - Number of Columns             2

    3 - Distance Between Columns

    4 - Margins

    Column    Left      Right    Column    Left      Right
    1:        1"        4"       13:
    2:        4.5"      7.5"     14:
    3:                           15:
    4:                           16:
    5:                           17:
    6:                           18:
    7:                           19:
    8:                           20:
    9:                           21:
    10:                          22:
    11:                          23:
    12:                          24:

Selection: 0
```

3. This is the Text Column Definition menu. Type **1** or **T**.

```
Column Type: 1 Newspaper; 2 Parallel; 3 Parallel with Block Protect: 0
```

4. Select the type of columns you want. Type **1** or **N** for newspaper (the default setting), **2** or **P** for parallel, and **3** or **B** for parallel with block protect.

5. Type the number of text columns you want (4, for example) and press **Enter**. WordPerfect makes all the calculations for you in creating evenly spaced columns on the page.

```
    Column     Left      Right      Column     Left      Right
      1:       1"        2.25"        13:
      2:       2.75"     4"           14:
      3:       4.5"      5.75"        15:
      4:       6.25"     7.5"         16:
```

6. Type **3** or **D**.

```
    3 - Distance Between Columns              0.5"
```

7. Note that WordPerfect automatically sets the distance between columns at ½-inch. You can change this to whatever you want. For example, type **1** and press **Enter**.

```
    3 - Distance Between Columns              1"

    4 - Margins

    Column     Left      Right      Column     Left      Right
      1:       1"        1.87"        13:
      2:       2.87"     3.75"        14:
      3:       4.75"     5.62"        15:
      4:       6.62"     7.5"         16:
```

8. Notice that WordPerfect automatically resets the column settings based on your "distance between columns" choice. Type **4** or **M**. Notice the cursor move to the first column setting. This lets you edit the settings to create columns of unequal width. Unequal columns are appropriate for many parallel columns, including tables and scripts.

9. Make any changes to the columns as necessary and press **F7** to return to the document.

CREATE COLUMNS   To create columns, turn Column mode on and type the text. When you are finished typing one column and want to move to the next, press Ctrl-Enter, the Hard Page Break command (Module 50). To turn Column mode on, press Alt-F7 and type 3 or C. Notice the "Col" indicator appear on the Status Line.

The "Col" indicator on the Status Line tells you that you are in Column mode. Type text normally. When you get to the end of the page (9.83"), WordPerfect moves up to the next column. If you want to move to the next column before you get to the end of the page, press Ctrl-Enter.

NOTE
Most of WordPerfect's commands work normally
inside columns, but margins, footnotes, and sort
do not work.

CURSOR CONTROL INSIDE COLUMNS   Cursor control inside columns is similar to that in any other text document. But if you want to move the cursor between columns, there are a few special procedures as outlined in this table:

Keystrokes	Result
Ctrl-Home, Right Arrow	Moves cursor to next column.
Ctrl-Home, Left Arrow	Moves cursor to the previous column.
Ctrl-Home, Home, Right Arrow	Moves cursor to the last column on the page.
Ctrl-Home, Home, Left Arrow	Moves cursor to the first column on the page.

APPLICATIONS

Use Newspaper style columns when doing desktop publishing or other types of word processing where columns fit. Use parallel columns when presenting groups of ideas that fit in columnar format, such as scripts, tables, and lists.

TYPICAL OPERATION

In this example, create a product listing using parallel columns.

1. Start WordPerfect and press **Shift-F6**, the Center key. Type **FLG OFFICE SUPPLY -- APPROVED VENDOR LIST** and press **Enter** twice.
2. Press **Alt-F7** and type **4** or **D** to begin defining columns.
3. Type **1** or **T** then **3** or **B** to create parallel columns with block protect.
4. Leave the settings as they are for number of columns, column margins, and distance between columns. Press **F7**, then **3** or **C** to turn Column mode on.

```
FLG OFFICE SUPPLY -- APPROVED VENDOR LIST


                              Col 1 Doc 1 Pg 1 Ln 1.33" POS 1"
```

5. Type **Word Process Steno Books** and press **Ctrl-Enter** to move to the next column.

6. Type **Acme Office Products** (press **Enter**), **123 Lawrence Avenue** (press **Enter**), **Chicago, IL 60620** (press **Enter**). Then press **Ctrl-Enter** to move back to the first column.

7. Type **Eye Nice Steno Books** and press **Ctrl-Enter** to move to the next column again.

8. Type **Warren-Johnson Products** (press **Enter**), **158 Samuel Lane** (press **Enter**), **Bedford, TX 76022** (press **Enter**). Then press **Ctrl-Enter** to move back to the first column.

```
        FLG OFFICE SUPPLY -- APPROVED VENDOR LIST

Word Process Steno Books           Acme Office Products
                                   123 Lawrence Avenue
                                   Chicago, IL 60620


Eye Nice Steno Books               Warren-Johnson Products
                                   158 Samuel Lane
                                   Bedford, TX 76022


                              Col 1 Doc 1 Pg 1 Ln 3" Pos 1"
```

9. Save the document as COLUMN.WPF.

10. Turn to Module 20 to continue the learning sequence.

Module 14
COPY

DESCRIPTION

The Copy command (Ctrl-F4) lets you copy text for use in other parts of a document or in other documents. You can copy a block of text, a rectangular block of text, columnar information, a sentence, a paragraph, or a page. Copy is similar to the Move command described in Module 47, except rather than cutting the text from its original location, the Copy command leaves the original text unchanged.

The Copy command also works like the Move command in that the material you want to copy must first be specified and stored either as a block of text or as a sentence, paragraph, or page in the computer's memory. Then you move the cursor to the place where you want to insert a copy of the text and retrieve it. WordPerfect inserts the text and automatically adjusts the document. You can retrieve text as many times as you want, since the text stays in memory until you either define another block, make another copy, or leave WordPerfect.

NOTE

Text defined in blocks and text defined as a
sentence, paragraph, or page are stored in the
same location in WordPerfect. So, for example,
if you define a block of text, it will only stay in
memory until you either define another block or
copy (or move) a sentence, paragraph, or page.

TIP: The Copy command is very useful for copying text and putting that text in other documents. The text you choose to copy stays in memory until you leave WordPerfect. One way to copy between documents is by using WordPerfect's Switch feature (Module 22), which lets you edit two documents at once. Another way is by using the Append command, which lets you copy blocks of text from one document to another.

NOTE

You can also copy the contents of entire documents
from file to file by using the Retrieve Text key
(Shift-F10). This is described in Module 25.

COPYING SENTENCES, PARAGRAPHS, OR PAGES This feature lets you copy text from one location to another without having to define a block of text. It is useful only if you are copying a sentence, paragraph, or page. To use this feature, you have only to make sure that the cursor is anywhere in the sentence, paragraph, or page you want to copy. If the text you want to copy is more complicated, (i.e, two sentences, two paragraphs, two pages), then you have to define and copy a block, as described in the next section. To copy a sentence, paragraph, or page:

1. Make sure the cursor is anywhere in the sentence, paragraph, or page you want to copy and press **Ctrl-F4**.

```
Move: 1 Sentence; 2 Paragraph; 3 Page; 4 Retrieve: 0
```

2. Type **1** or **S** if you want to copy a sentence, **2** or **P** to copy a paragraph, or **3** or **A** to copy a page.

```
1 Move; 2 Copy; 3 Delete; 4 Append: 0
```

Here is your chance to tell WordPerfect if you want to move, copy, delete, or append the sentence, paragraph, or page.

3. Type **2** or **C** for copy.

```
Move cursor; press Enter to retrieve.          Doc 1 Pg 1 Ln 1.33" Pos 1"
```

4. Move the cursor where you want to copy the text and press **Enter**. The selected text is copied.

COPYING BLOCKS OR RECTANGULAR BLOCKS OF TEXT   The Copy command also works with blocks of text. These blocks can be either normal or rectangular. Module 8 tells you how to define blocks of text.

To copy a block of text:

1. Press **Alt-F4** to turn block on. Move the cursor to define a block of text and press **Ctrl-F4**.

```
Move: 1 Block; 2 Tabular Column; 3 Rectangle: 0
```

2. Type **1** or **B** for a normal block of text, **3** or **R** for a rectangular block. Then type **2** or **C** to copy the block.

3. Move the cursor where you want the copied text to appear and press **Enter**.

COPYING TABULAR COLUMN INFORMATION   If you want to copy columnar information, generally a column in a table, use this command. This command identifies text that has been defined by tabs, indents, alignment characters (Module 4) and hard returns. This command is not for copying columns of text (Module 13). To copy columnar information:

CAUTION
Do not use this command for copying text in
Column mode. Use the regular copy command
for doing that.

1. Press **Alt-F4** to turn Block on and define a block of text. This highlights all the text, not just the column. Then press **Ctrl-F4**.

2. Type **2** or **C** to highlight the column of text. Then type **2** or **C** to copy the text.

3. Move the cursor where you want the copied text to appear and press **Enter**.

RETRIEVING BLOCKS MORE THAN ONCE   Text remains in memory until you replace it with another block. WordPerfect lets you retrieve it through the use of the Retrieve key (Ctrl-F4). To retrieve a previously marked block of text:

1. Press **Ctrl-F4**, then type **4** or **R**.

```
Retrieve: 1 Block; 2 Tabular Column; 3 Rectangle: 0
```

2. Type **1** or **B** to retrieve a block of text, **2** or **C** to retrieve a tabular column of text, or **3** or **R** to retrieve a rectangular block of text. The text is retrieved at the current cursor location.

APPENDING TEXT FROM ONE DOCUMENT TO ANOTHER   WordPerfect makes it very easy to copy blocks of text from one document to another. The Append command copies a selected block of text in one document and puts it at the end of another document. If you want to move a block of text to a specific location in another document, use the Switch command to help you.

To append text:

1. Press **Alt-F4** to turn block on. Move the cursor to define a block of text and press **Ctrl-F4**.

2. Type **1** or **B** to select a block of text, **2** or **C** to select a columnar block of text, or **3** or **R** to select a rectangular block. Then type **4** or **A** to append it.

```
Append to:
```

3. Type the name of the file you want to append the block of text to and press **Enter**. WordPerfect copies the block to the end of the specified file.

APPLICATIONS

The Copy command is useful for copying text within a document or from one document to another. It saves time and reduces typing errors. The Retrieve command is handy when you are retrieving the same block of text many times. And the Append command makes it easy to copy text between documents. Use the Copy command whenever you are editing a document.

TYPICAL OPERATION

This example shows you how to copy a sentence from one location in a speech to another.

1. Create a document similar to the following:

```
Most of the concerns that we share as office automation
professionals are vastly different from those we shared just a few
years ago. As computers proliferate into businesses, we find our
customers need things they didn't need before, like continuous-feed
paper, and stop buying items we couldn't order fast enough before,
like typing correction fluid. And does anyone remember pencils and
pens? Do people buy those anymore?

As I've said before,


                                        Doc 1 Pg 1 Ln 1" Pos 1"
```

2. Place the cursor anywhere in the first sentence and press **Ctrl-F4**. Type **1** or **S** to indicate you want to move or copy the sentence.

```
Most of the concerns that we share as office automation
professionals are vastly different from those we shared just a few
years ago. As computers proliferate into businesses, we find our
customers need things they didn't need before, like continuous-feed
paper, and stop buying items we couldn't order fast enough before,
like typing correction fluid. And does anyone remember pencils and
pens? Do people buy those anymore?

As I've said before,

1 Move; 2 Copy; 3 Delete; 4 Append: 0
```

3. Type **2** or **C** to copy the sentence. Then move the cursor to the space after the comma in the last line.

```
As I've said before, _
```

4. Press **Enter** to retrieve the sentence. There should not be a capital "M" in "Most," so press **Ins** to change into Typeover mode and type **m**.

```
As I've said before, most of the concerns that we share as office
automation professionals are vastly different from those we shared
just a few years ago.
```

5. Save the document as CONCERN.WPF.

6. Turn to Module 47 to continue the learning sequence.

Module 15
CURSOR CONTROL

DESCRIPTION

The cursor is the little blinking line that appears on the monitor screen. It is a visual guide that identifies your position in the document. The cursor is your guide in all phases of word processing, from the first typed words to the final stages of editing and printing. Understanding the most efficient ways to move the cursor around a document saves you time while editing, therefore helping you increase the speed at which you process documents. Moving the cursor where you want it on the screen in the fewest keystrokes is called "cursor control."

While you are creating a document, the cursor moves as you type or when you press the Spacebar. You can also move the cursor through the use of arrow keys, the Home key, the End key, the PgUp key, the PgDn key, the Screen Up key, and the Screen Down key. You can also use the Ctrl and Esc keys in conjunction with the preceding keys.

The arrow keys are located on the numeric keypad. The 2, 4, 6, and 8 keys each have an arrow pointing down, left, right, and up, respectively. These are the arrow keys. The direction they point indicates the direction the cursor moves when they are pressed. On some of the newer keyboards there is an additional cursor or arrow keypad. These keys can be used in addition to the arrow keys on the numeric keypad.

Use the arrow keys to move the cursor by one character (letter, number, symbol, or blank space) on the screen. If you move the cursor too far to the right so that it moves beyond the last character in a line, the cursor appears on the first character of the next line. This is called "wrapping around." Also, if you move the cursor too far to the left, it wraps around and appears as the last character of the previous line. The cursor always stays within the screen boundary.

While the arrow keys alone let you move the cursor by one character or line per keystroke, other keystrokes help you move the cursor farther. You can, for example, "jump" the cursor to the beginning or end of a line. Or, you can move the cursor from one word to the next or to the beginning of a page or document.

WordPerfect uses the following keystrokes for cursor control. (Cursor control with the Esc key is described in Module 24 and with the Go To command in Module 29.)

NOTE

For information about cursor control while in
Column mode, see Module 13.

Keystroke	Function
Up Arrow	Moves cursor up one line. Can scroll to previous page if cursor is on line 1 of a page.
Down Arrow	Moves cursor down one line. Can scroll to next page if cursor is on the last line of a page.
Left Arrow	Moves cursor one character to the left, or to the last character on the previous line if the cursor is in position 1.
Right Arrow	Moves cursor one character to the right, or to the first character on the next line if the cursor is in the last position on the previous line.
Ctrl-Left Arrow	Jumps cursor to the first character of the previous word.
Ctrl-Right Arrow	Jumps cursor to the first character of the next word.
Ctrl-Home, Up Arrow	Moves cursor to the top of the current page.
Ctrl-Home, Down Arrow	Moves cursor to the bottom of the current page.
Ctrl-Home, Any Character	Moves cursor to the next occurrence of the character, assuming it occurs in the next 2000 characters.
Ctrl-Home, Ctrl-Home	Moves the cursor to its last location prior to a cursor command.
Ctrl-Home, Alt-F4 (Block on)	Moves cursor to the beginning of the defined block. If Block is not on (Module 8), it moves the cursor to the last location of a block definition.
Esc-Left Arrow	Moves cursor n characters to the left (Module 24). ("n" being the repeat value).
Esc-Right Arrow	Moves cursor "n" characters to the right.
Esc-Up Arrow	Moves cursor "n" lines up.
Esc-Down Arrow	Moves cursor "n" lines down.
Home-Left Arrow	Jumps cursor to the left edge of the screen.
Home, Home, Left Arrow	Jumps cursor to the beginning of the current line, after any codes (Module 59).
Home, Home, Home, Left Arrow	Jumps cursor to the beginning of the current line, before any codes.
Home-Right Arrow	Jumps cursor to the right edge of the screen.
Home, Home-Right Arrow, End	Jumps cursor to the end of the current line.
Home-Up Arrow, Screen Up (– on numeric keypad)	Jumps cursor to the first line of the current screen of text. If cursor is at top line of screen, it moves up to the top of the next screen.
Home-Down Arrow, Screen Down (+ on numeric keypad)	Jumps cursor to the last line of the current screen of text. If cursor is at last line of screen, it moves to the last line of the next screen.
PgUp	Jumps cursor to the previous page.
PgDn	Jumps cursor to the next page.
Home, Home, Up Arrow	Jumps cursor to the beginning of the current document.
Home, Home, Down Arrow	Jumps cursor to the end of the current document.

USING ARROW KEYS   The Up Arrow and Down Arrow keys move the cursor up or down one line at a time. Right Arrow and Left Arrow move the cursor to the right or left one character at a time.

You can move faster through documents by using the arrow keys in conjunction with others. For example, use the Ctrl key and the Left Arrow or Right Arrow keys to move the cursor one word at a time instead of one space at a time. Or, use the Home key with Left Arrow or Right Arrow to move the cursor to the beginning or end of the line the cursor is on.

Another way to move the cursor to the end of a line is by pressing the End key.

Use the Tab key in conjunction with the Ins key to move the cursor quickly through a document. When in Typeover mode, achieved by pressing Ins once (Module 37), pressing Tab moves the cursor to the next tab stop. Pressing Tab continuously moves you from tab stop to tab stop. Similarly, pressing Shift-Tab while in Typeover mode moves you backward throughout a document via tab stops.

The arrow keys help move you from one screen of text (approximately one-half page) to another. Pressing Home-Up Arrow or Home-Down Arrow moves the cursor to the beginning or end of a screen of text.

Another way to move up or down a screenful of text at a time is to use the + and − keys on the numeric keypad. The − key moves the cursor up a screen, while + moves the cursor down a screen.

To move faster, use the PgUp and PgDn keys to move the cursor through the document one page at a time. Or, use the Home key in conjunction with the Up Arrow and Down Arrow keys to move the cursor to the beginning or end of a document. If you press the Home key twice in succession and then press Up Arrow or Down Arrow, the cursor moves to the beginning or end of a document.

APPLICATIONS

Efficient cursor control is essential to word processing. You control the cursor every time you edit or create a document with WordPerfect. Learning new ways to control the cursor helps you work faster and more efficiently.

TYPICAL OPERATION

The following example shows how you use cursor control to help you edit a document more efficiently.

1. Create a document similar to the following. You use this document in other modules. Each financial statement should be on a separate page. Press **Ctrl-Enter** between pages.

NOTE

Refer to Module 12 to center text and Module 5
for instructions on underlining text.

Jack Belew
FLG Office Supplies
124 N. Main
Carbondale, IL 62901
February 24, 1987

William Levin
345 N. Olive
Carterville, IL 62966

Dear Bill:

It was a pleasure speaking with you last week about your new
position with the Bank of Carterville. I hope you can help us with
our financial needs in the future.

Per your request, I am enclosing some recent financial statements.
I think you'll agree that FLG Office Supplies is in fine financial
shape. And with your help, we hope to be even better.

Sincerely,

Jack Belew
Controller

Doc 1 Pg 1 Ln 1" Pos 1"

==

INCOME STATEMENT
FLG OFFICE SUPPLIES
FOR YEAR ENDED DECEMBER 31, 1986

Sales:	$625,000	
Less: Cost of Goods:	375,000	
Gross Margin:		$250,000
Operating Expenses:		
Rent:	$ 36,000	
Utilities:	8,000	
Salaries:	95,000	
Misc. Expenses:	46,525	
Total Operating Expenses:		185,525
Gross Profit:		$64,475
Taxes:		$19,343
Net Profit:		$45,132

Doc 1 Pg 2 Ln 1" Pos 1"

```
================================================================================
                              BALANCE SHEET
                           FLG OFFICE SUPPLIES
                     FOR YEAR ENDED DECEMBER 31, 1986

Assets:

Cash:                        $ 97,232
Accounts Receivable:           16,345
Equipment (depreciated):      150,235
Total Assets:                                    $263,812

Liabilities:

Accounts Payable:            $ 46,525
Taxes Payable:                 13,323
Total Liabilities:                               $ 59,848

Equity:

Owner's Equity:                                  $203,964

Total Liabilities and Equity:                    $263,812



                                          Doc 1 Pg 3 Ln 1" Pos 1"
```

2. Move the cursor to the top of the document by pressing **Home**, **Home**, **Up Arrow**. Then press **Down Arrow** 13 times to move the cursor to the "p" in "position." Then press **Left Arrow** to move it to the end of the previous line.

```
                              Jack Belew
                              FLG Office Supplies
                              124 N. Main
                              Carbondale, IL 62901
                              February 24, 1987

William Levin
345 N. Olive
Carterville, IL 62966

Dear Bill:

It was a pleasure speaking with you last week about your new
position with the Bank of Carterville. I hope you can help us with
our financial needs in the future.

Per your request, I am enclosing some recent financial statements.
I think you'll agree that FLG Office Supplies is in fine financial
shape. And with your help, we hope to be even better.

                              Sincerely,

                              Jack Belew
                              Controller
C:\WP50\DOCS\FINANCES.WPF              Doc 1 Pg 1 Ln 3" Pos 7"
```

3. Press **Right Arrow** to move the cursor back to the beginning of the next line. Then, press **Up Arrow** to move the cursor up one line.

```
It was a pleasure speaking with you last week about your new
position with the Bank of Carterville. I hope you can help us with
our financial needs in the future.

                                        Doc 1 Pg 1 Ln 3" Pos 1"
```

4. You should be at the "I" in "It" at the beginning of line. Press **Ctrl-Right Arrow** to move to the next word.

```
It was a pleasure speaking with you last week about your new
position with the Bank of Carterville. I hope you can help us with
our financial needs in the future.

                                        Doc 1 Pg 1 Ln 3" Pos 1.3"
```

5. Press **Ctrl-Left Arrow** to move back. Then press **Home-Right Arrow** to move the cursor to the end of the line.

```
It was a pleasure speaking with you last week about your new _
position with the Bank of Carterville. I hope you can help us with
our financial needs in the future.

                                        Doc 1 Pg 1 Ln 3" Pos 7"
```

6. Press **Home-Left Arrow** to move to the beginning of the line. Then press **Home-Down Arrow** to move to the beginning of the last line on the screen.

```
                              Sincerely,

                              Jack Belew
                              Controller
                                        Doc 1 Pg 1 Ln 4.83" Pos 1"
```

7. Press **Home-Up Arrow** to move to the beginning of the screen. Then press **PgDn** to move to the beginning of the next page.

```
                          INCOME STATEMENT
                         FLG OFFICE SUPPLIES
                   FOR YEAR ENDED DECEMBER 31, 1986

Sales:                  $625,000
Less: Cost of Goods:     375,000
Gross Margin:                              $250,000


                                     Doc 1 Pg 2 Ln 1" Pos 1"
```

8. Press **Home**, **Home**, **Down Arrow** to move the cursor to the end of the document.

```
Equity:

Owner's Equity:                   $203,964

Total Liabilities and Equity:     $263,812


                              Doc 1 Pg 3 Ln 4.83" Pos 1"
```

9. Save the document and name it FINANCES.WPF.
10. Turn to Module 29 to continue the learning sequence.

Module 16

DATE

DESCRIPTION

The Date command (Shift-F5) inserts the current date and/or the current time at the current cursor location. The date and time is either the current time (as determined by your system) or some later time determined when the document is retrieved or printed.

> **NOTE**
> If you don't have a clock/calendar in your computer that keeps the date and time for you, you must enter the date and time into your computer every time you start it. Otherwise, the date will always be January 1, 1980 at 00:00.

The default date format is month, day, year (February 27, 1989). You can change this format and add the time as well. The Date command is useful for letters, legal papers, or other documents where date and time stamping are important.

USING THE DATE COMMAND   Press Shift-F5 to access the Date menu:

```
    1 Date Text; 2 Date Code; 3 Date Format; 4 Outline; 5 Para Num; 6 Define: 0
```

To insert the date, type 1 or D. The current date appears on-screen.

```
    June 19, 1989
```

SELECTING THE CORRECT FORMAT   There are several variations of the format for date and time. To select a format, type 3 or F from the Date menu.

```
  Date Format

      Character    Meaning
          1        Day of the Month
          2        Month (number)
          3        Month (word)
          4        Year (all four digits)
          5        Year (last two digits)
          6        Day of the Week (word)
          7        Hour (24-hour clock)
          8        Hour (12-hour clock)
          9        Minute
          0        am / pm
          %        Used before a number, will:
                     Pad numbers less than 10 with a leading zero
                     Output only 3 letters for the month or day of the week


  Examples:   3 1, 4         = December 25, 1984
              %6 %3 1, 4     = Tue Dec 25, 1984
              %2/%1/5 (6)    = 01/01/85 (Tuesday)
              8:90           = 10:55am


  Date format: 3 1, 4
```

You can use up to 29 characters to define the date and time format you like. Anything you add to the format, like spelling out date or time, becomes part of the format. You can change the format as many times as you want. Some sample date and time formats are:

Format	Display
3 1, 4	June 19, 1989
3 1, 4 -- 7:9	June 19, 1989 -- 14:26
2/1/5	6/19/89
%2/%1/%5	06/19/89
DATE: 6, 3 1, 4 TIME: 8:9 0	DATE: Friday, February 27, 1987 TIME: 2:26 pm

To change the current format, type the format you like. For example, type 3 1, 4 -- 8:9 0 and press Enter twice. To check the format, press Shift-F5 and type 1 or T.

```
  June 19, 1989 -- 2:26 pm
```

INSERTING A DATE/TIME FUNCTION CODE   The date/time function code inserts the current date and/or time into your text. After the document is retrieved, the date and time are updated to the current time. When a document is printed, the code displays the date and time the document was sent to the printer. To insert a date/time function code, position the cursor where you want the code, press Shift-F5, and type 2 or C.

TIP: If you want to make the date change while you are editing a document, use the Switch command (Shift-F3), which is described in Module 22. When you return to the document after editing a second, the date changes.

USING THE DATE COMMAND IN MERGED TEXT   The Date command inserts the current date and time into a series of merge letters. (The Merge command is described in Module 46.) To use the command, press Shift-F9 and type D in the appropriate place in the document. A "^D" appears on-screen. When the document is merged, the current date is inserted where the "^D" appears.

APPLICATIONS

The Date command is useful for letters, legal briefs, and other documents where the date and time the document was completed is critical.

The date code feature is useful for documents that need the date updated every time they are retrieved. The date code function is not intended for use in documents where the original date is saved for future reference. This is because the date code changes to the current date every time the document is retrieved.

TYPICAL OPERATION

In this example, you insert a date/time code into a time-sensitive memo. The code reflects when the memo is sent out, not when it was written.

1. Create a document similar to the following:

```
MEMO

FROM: FLG
TO: ALL EMPLOYEES
SUBJECT: NEW PAYROLL PROCEDURES
DATE:

Effective immediately, all employees will be paid bi-weekly instead
of weekly. This procedure is necessary because we are growing
faster than our accounting department can handle. I apologize for
any inconvenience this may cause you. If there are any financial
hardships brought about by this situation, please see me.

FLG


                                             Doc 1 Pg 1 Ln 1" Pos 1"
```

2. Move the cursor to the space after "Date:" and press the **Spacebar**, then **Shift-F5**. Type **3** or **F** to check the format.

3.   Type **6, 3 1 -- 8:9 0** and press **Enter**. Type **2** or **C** to insert the code.

```
    MEMO

    FROM: FLG
    TO: ALL EMPLOYEES
    SUBJECT: NEW PAYROLL PROCEDURES
    DATE: Thursday, June 9 -- 9:47 am

    Effective immediately, all employees will be paid bi-weekly instead


                                        Doc 1 Pg 1 Ln 1.83" Pos 4.3"
```

4.   Save the document, calling it MEMO.WPF, but don't exit WordPerfect. Wait ten minutes.
5.   Then press **Shift-F10**, type **MEMO.WPF** and press **Enter**. Notice the difference in the time.
6.   Save the document as MEMO.WPF.
7.   Turn to Module 51 to continue the learning sequence.

Module 17

DELETE

DESCRIPTION

WordPerfect deletes text in many ways; by character, word, line, page, or block of text. WordPerfect offers you several types of delete commands — Delete Right, Delete Left, Delete Word, Delete to End of Word, Delete to Beginning of Word, Delete Block, Delete Sentence, Delete Paragraph, Delete Page, Delete to End of Line, and Delete to End of Page. There is also a function called Undelete, which cancels previous deletions. That is discussed in Module 10.

The delete functions are some of the most commonly used editing commands. They can help you remove small or large amounts of text with only a few keystrokes. In addition, WordPerfect prompts you to delete formatting functions like boldface, underline, and centering.

You can delete as many or as few characters or pages of text as you want. If you want to delete entire files, use the Delete File command, referred to in Module 25. The WordPerfect delete functions are:

Command	Key	Function
Delete Right	Del	Deletes text to right of cursor.
Delete Left	Backspace	Deletes text to left of cursor.
Delete Word	Ctrl-Backspace	Deletes word cursor is within.
Delete to End of Word	Home, Del	Deletes from cursor to end of word.
Delete to Beginning of Word	Home, Backspace	Deletes from cursor to beginning of word.
Delete Block	Alt-F4, Del, Y	Deletes defined block of text.
Delete to End of Line	Ctrl-End	Erases text from cursor position to end of line.
Delete to End of Page	Ctrl-PgDn, Y	Deletes text from cursor position to end of page.
Delete Page	Ctrl-F4, 3 or a, 3 or D	Deletes page cursor is within.
Delete Paragraph	Ctrl-F4, 2 or P, 3 or D	Deletes paragraph cursor is within.
Delete Sentence	Ctrl-F4, 1 or S, 3 or D	Deletes sentence cursor is within.

DELETE RIGHT   Delete Right deletes text to the right of the cursor. It is accomplished using the Del key and is most effective when deleting only a few characters. To use Delete Right move the cursor to the character or characters you want to delete. Then, press Del for each character you want to delete. WordPerfect deletes characters to the right of the cursor.

DELETE LEFT   Delete Left works similarly to Delete Right. It uses the Backspace key (◄—) to delete text to the left of the cursor. To use Delete Left move the cursor to the character or characters you want to delete. Then, press Backspace for each character you want to delete. WordPerfect deletes characters to the left of the cursor.

DELETE WORD   Delete Left and Delete Right are fine for eliminating one or two characters, but it is cumbersome to use those commands to delete entire words as we did above. The Delete Word command deletes an entire word and the space after that word. It is accomplished using the Ctrl-Backspace key combination. To delete words, move the cursor anywhere within the word you want to delete. Then press Ctrl-Backspace for each word you want to delete. WordPerfect deletes words to the right of the cursor.

DELETE TO END OR BEGINNING OF WORD   If you only want to delete part of a word, you can use the Delete to End or Delete to Beginning of Word command. Rather than Ctrl-Backspace, which deletes an entire word no matter where the cursor is, this command deletes from the cursor to either the end of the word (Home, Del) or the beginning of the word (Home, Backspace). This command is useful when you need to delete sections of words. To delete parts of words, move the cursor to the location at which you want to delete either the rest of the word or the beginning of the word. Press Home, Del to delete from the cursor to the end of the word or Home, Backspace to delete from the cursor to the beginning of the word. In either case, the letter the cursor is on is also deleted.

DELETE BLOCK   Sometimes you need to delete large amounts of text. The Delete Block command is convenient for this. It deletes any block of text you define. (For further information on Block commands, see Module 8.) As described in Module 8, you can quickly define a block by pressing any character (letter, number, or symbol). WordPerfect searches for the first appearance of that character and defines a block from the current cursor position to that character. To delete a block of text, move the cursor to the beginning of the block you want to delete and press Alt-F4. Then move the cursor to the end of the block of text and press Del. Type Y in response to the "Delete Block?" prompt.

DELETE TO END OF LINE   The Delete to End of Line feature erases everything to the right of the cursor on the current line. It is accomplished by pressing Ctrl-End. To use the Delete to End of Line feature, move the cursor to the beginning of the text you want to delete. Then press Ctrl-End to delete the rest of the text on that line. To delete an entire line of text, move the cursor to the beginning of the line and press Ctrl-End.

DELETE TO END OF PAGE   The Delete to End of Page command deletes everything to the right of the cursor on the current page. It is accomplished by pressing Ctrl-PgDn. To use the Delete to End of Page feature, move the cursor to the beginning of the text you want to delete. Then press Ctrl-PgDn. To delete an entire page, move the cursor to the beginning of the page and press Ctrl-PgDn. Type Y in response to the "Delete Remainder of Page?" prompt.

DELETE SENTENCE, PARAGRAPH, OR PAGE   The Move key (Module 47) lets you delete sentences, paragraphs, or pages of text at a single keystroke. Your cursor only has to be within the sentence, paragraph, or page to delete the entire item. To delete a sentence, paragraph, or page:

1. Press **Ctrl-F4**.

```
Move: 1 Sentence; 2 Paragraph; 3 Page; 4 Retrieve: 0
```

2. Type **1** or **S** for a sentence, **2** or **P** for a paragraph, or **3** or **a** for a page.

```
1 Move; 2 Copy; 3 Delete; 4 Append: 0
```

3. Type **3** or **D** to delete the text.

APPLICATIONS

You almost always need to delete text while editing documents. WordPerfect helps you do this quickly and efficiently. If you need to delete a little bit of text, use the Del or the Backspace key. If you need to delete more text, you can delete words, sentences, paragraphs and pages at a keystroke. You can also delete text by highlighting it as a block and deleting it. You can also delete text from the current cursor position through the end of a line, paragraph, or page.

TYPICAL OPERATION

In the following example, you delete a large portion of a document by using many of the delete commands described in this module.

1. Create a document similar to the following:

```
                    STATEMENT OF PURPOSE

                    FLG OFFICE SUPPLY

The average office spends thousands of dollars on office supplies
each year. Pens, pencils, paper, ribbons, and other office supplies
are always wearing out. And it doesn't matter what the economy is
like, the need for office supplies never ends. If things are good,
or things are bad, everyone always needs office supplies.


                                        Doc 1 Pg 1 Ln 2" Pos 3.4"
```

2. Position the cursor on the "A" in "And" at the beginning of the third sentence. Press **Del** four times to delete the word and the space that follows. Then position the cursor on the space to the right of the "e" in the word "office" in the second sentence.

3. Press **Backspace** seven times to delete the word and the space preceding it. Then move the cursor to any character in the second occurrence of the word (or in the space after the word) "office" in the first sentence.

```
The average office spends thousands of dollars on office_supplies
each year. Pens, pencils, paper, ribbons, and other office supplies


                                        Doc 1 Pg 1 Ln 1.66" Pos 6.6"
```

4. Press **Ctrl-Backspace** to delete the word. Then position the cursor on the "I" in "If" at the beginning of the last sentence.

5. Press **Alt-F4**. Then type **.** (a period) to define the entire sentence as a block of text.

```
the need for supplies never ends. If things are good, or things are
bad, everyone always needs office supplies.

Block on                                Doc 1 Pg 1 Ln 2.33" Pos 5.3"
```

6. Press **Del**, then type **Y** to delete the block. Then position the cursor on the "i" in "it."

7. Press **Ctrl-End** to delete the rest of the text on that line.

8. Press **Ctrl-PgDn**, then type **Y** to delete the rest of the page.

```
                     STATEMENT OF PURPOSE

                     FLG OFFICE SUPPLY

The average office spends thousands of dollars on supplies each
year. Pens, pencils, paper, ribbons, and other office supplies are
always wearing out.  the need for supplies never ends.


                                        Doc 1 Pg 1 Ln 2" Pos 3"
```

9. Save the document as PURPOSE.WPF.

10. Turn to Module 43 to continue the learning sequence.

Module 18
DIRECTORIES

DESCRIPTION

In the course of using WordPerfect, you will create a great many documents. It is helpful to organize those documents into directories. A computer is like a filing cabinet, and each file in the computer is like a file in the cabinet. A directory, on the other hand, is like a drawer in that cabinet. Just as it may not be appropriate to keep personal data in the same drawer as business data, it may not be appropriate to keep letters about personal business in the same directory as business-related documents. Directories can be either subdirectories of the WordPerfect directory, or top-level directories. (For more information on directories and their structure, refer to your DOS manual.) WordPerfect lets you create and delete directories, much as you create and delete documents. It also lets you set a default directory.

NOTE

Directories are more useful in hard-disk-based systems, largely because there is so much more room in which to store data. Because of this, the examples in this module refer to a hard-disk-based system. If you have a floppy-based system, you should follow along, since you might want to organize your floppies into directories as well.

DEFAULT DIRECTORY   When you first start WordPerfect, your default directory, or the directory that you retrieve and save files in, is the same one in which the WP.EXE file is located. However, this is generally not a good directory in which to save data. It is better to save data in a directory that is organized along a certain subject, such as letters, articles, and books. Each time you start WordPerfect, you can change the default directory to the one you are working in that day. There are three ways to change the default directory. One way is upon start-up at the beginning of a WordPerfect session, as described in Appendix I. The other two are through the use of the List Files key (F5). To change default directories:

1.   Press **F5** from anywhere in the document.

```
   Dir C:\WP50\*.*                            (Type = to change default Dir)
```

2.   Type **=**.

```
   New directory = C:\WP50
```

3.   Type the directory that you want as the new default directory at this time and press **Enter**.

The procedure for changing the default directory from the List Files menu is similar:

1.   Press **F5** from anywhere in the document, then **Enter**.

```
06/07/88   15:21              Directory C:\WP50\*.*
Document size:        0   Free:  8546304   Used:  3041721        Files:  183

. <CURRENT>      <DIR>                      .. <PARENT>      <DIR>
DOCS      .      <DIR>    06/06/88 07:53     ALTRNAT .WPK        919  04/27/88 11:00
APPA      .      12928    06/03/88 08:00     APPB    .         5376  06/03/88 08:01
APPC      .       3584    06/03/88 08:02     APPD    .         8192  06/03/88 08:02
APPE      .       2048    06/03/88 08:03     APPF    .         9728  06/03/88 08:06
APPG      .       2048    06/03/88 08:07     APPH    .         2048  06/03/88 08:07
APPI      .       3840    06/03/88 08:08     APPJ    .        20096  06/03/88 08:08
APPK      .      12928    06/03/88 08:09     CHARACTR.DOC     52655  04/27/88 11:00
CHARMAP   .TST   15239    04/27/88 11:00     CONVERT .EXE     80511  04/27/88 11:00
CURSOR    .COM    1452    04/27/88 11:00     ENHANCED.WPK      3375  04/27/88 11:00
EPFX80    .PRS    6666    06/02/88 08:45     GRAPHCNV.EXE     70656  04/27/88 11:00
INSTALL   .EXE   26944    05/13/88 09:26     KEYS    .MRS      4800  05/05/88 12:47
LIBRARY   .STY     670    04/27/88 11:00     MACROCNV.EXE     23077  04/27/88 11:00
MACROS    .WPK   14214    04/27/88 11:00     MOD03   .        12928  06/03/88 08:45
MOD04     .       7168    06/02/88 16:29     MOD05   .        13184  06/02/88 16:33
MOD06     .      10368    06/02/88 16:30     MOD07   .         6784  06/02/88 16:31
MOD08     .      11136    06/02/88 16:33     MOD09   .         6400  06/02/88 16:34
MOD1-3    .      27648    06/03/88 08:45     MOD10   .         8960  06/02/88 16:34
MOD10-1   .SCR    8128    06/06/88 14:45 ▼   MOD10-2 .SCR      8128  06/06/88 14:49

1 Retrieve; 2 Delete; 3 Move/Rename; 4 Print; 5 Text In;
6 Look; 7 Other Directory; 8 Copy; 9 Word Search; N Name Search: 6
```

2.   Type **7** or **O**. Then type the name of the directory you want as the default and press **Enter** twice.

CREATE A DIRECTORY   The procedures for creating new directories is similar to changing the default directory. WordPerfect lets you create directories in one of two ways, each through the use of the List Files key (F5). To create a directory:

1.   Press **F5** from anywhere in the document, then type **=**.

2.   To create a subdirectory called "LETTERS," type **C:\WP50\LETTERS** and press **Enter**.

```
Create  C:\WP50\LETTERS? (Y/N) No
```

3.   Type **Y** to create the new directory.

The procedure for creating a new directory from the List Files menu is similar.

1.   From the List Files menu, type **7** or **O**. Then, type the name of the directory you want to create and press **Enter**.

2. Type **Y** to create the directory. Notice the new directory is listed in the menu, along with the date and time it was created.

To look at files in the new directory:

1. Move the cursor to the directory, type **6**, and press **Enter**.

2. Since no files have been created for the directory, no files are listed in the menu. To return to the C:\WP50 directory, type **7** or **O**. Then type **C:\WP50**, and press **Enter**.

DELETE A DIRECTORY If you no longer use a directory, WordPerfect lets you delete it just as you delete a file from the List Files menu. Before you delete any directory make sure you have completed the following procedures:

1. Make sure there are no more files in it. Use DOS commands to copy the files to another directory and delete the files in the old directory.

2. Make sure your current directory is one other than the directory you want to delete.

In the following example, assume you want to delete the letters directory created earlier. Since you just created the directory, there are no files to delete. And, your current directory, as you can see, is C:\WP50.

```
08/04/88  13:54              Directory C:\WP50\*.*
Document size:        0   Free:  7127040   Used:  1885620        Files:  57

.  <CURRENT>    <DIR>                        ..  <PARENT>    <DIR>
BOOK      .     <DIR>    06/08/88  13:05     DOCS       .     <DIR>    06/06/88  07:53
LETTERS   .     <DIR>    08/04/88  13:46     ADDRESS   .WPM      192   06/09/88  07:41
ALTRNAT  .WPK      919   04/27/88  11:00     ANTISPE   .        1199   06/14/88  07:46
APLASPLU .PRS    34991   07/19/88  14:45     B         .       10752   07/15/88  09:38
BS4       .      33792   06/21/88  09:18     BS5       .       54784   06/21/88  09:20
CHARACTR .DIC        0   06/15/88  11:32     CHARACTR .DOC     52655   04/27/88  11:00
CHARMAP  .TST    15239   04/27/88  11:00     CONVERT  .EXE     80511   04/27/88  11:00
CURSOR   .COM     1452   04/27/88  11:00     DOTEXPRI .PRS      1013   07/19/88  14:46
ENHANCED .WPK     3375   04/27/88  11:00     EPFX80   .PRS      6666   06/02/88  08:45
EPMX80GR .PRS     2301   07/19/88  14:47     GRAB     .COM     14687   04/27/88  14:24
GRAPHCNV .EXE    70656   04/27/88  11:00     INSTALL  .EXE     26944   05/13/88  09:26
KEYS     .MRS     4800   05/05/88  12:47     LIBRARY  .STY       670   04/27/88  11:00
MACROCNV .EXE    23077   04/27/88  11:00     MACROS   .WPK     14214   04/27/88  11:00
MOD03     .      12928   06/03/88  08:45     MOD04     .        7168   06/02/88  16:29
MOD05     .      13184   06/02/88  16:33     MOD06     .       10368   06/02/88  16:30
MOD07     .       6784   06/02/88  16:31     MOD08     .       11136   06/02/88  16:33
MOD09     .       6400   06/02/88  16:34     MOD1-3    .       27648   06/03/88  08:45
MOD10     .       8960   06/02/88  16:34  ▼  MOD10-1  .SCR      8128   06/06/88  14:45
```

1. Move the cursor to "LETTERS" and type **2** or **D**.

```
Delete C:\WP50\LETTERS? (Y/N) No
```

2. Type **Y**. WordPerfect deletes the directory.

APPLICATIONS

When you start WordPerfect, you almost always change the default directory to one that you are accessing that day or session. The more often you are in the default directory, the less steps you have to take to retrieve a file. There are many reasons to create new directories and delete old ones. You usually create a new directory because you realize that you have created a lot of documents about a certain subject. It is more convenient to organize those documents into their own directory. You usually delete a directory when you find you are not creating or using any more documents that relate to it. Even if you are no longer using documents about that subject, it is always a good idea to copy those documents to a floppy disk before you delete them. You never know when you might need to refer to them again.

TYPICAL OPERATION

In this example, you create a directory in which to keep all correspondence with a certain vendor, Leonard's Paper Company. Then, you delete it when the vendor goes out of business.

1. Start WordPerfect and press **F5**. Then, type **=**.

2. To create a subdirectory called "LEONARDS," type **C:\WP50\LEONARDS** and press **Enter**. Type **Y** to create the new directory.

3. Assume Leonard's has ceased operations. Also assume all files about Leonard's have been backed up on floppy disks and that all the data files in the directory have been deleted. From the List Files menu, move the cursor to "LEONARDS" and type **2** or **D**.

```
    Delete C:\WP50\LEONARDS? (Y/N) No
```

4. Type **Y**. WordPerfect deletes the directory.

5. Turn to Module 37 to continue the learning sequence.

Module 19
DOCUMENT COMMENTS

DESCRIPTION

There are times that you want to add comments to a document that will not be printed in the final version but can be seen on-screen. WordPerfect's Document Comments feature gives you capabilities not unlike electronic Post-It notes.

The default setting of WordPerfect displays document comments. Appendix B outlines the procedure for not displaying document comments.

WordPerfect adds comments to your document automatically if you are a user of previous versions of WordPerfect. WordPerfect occasionally adds comments to WordPerfect 4.2 documents to remind you of certain changes between the programs.

To create document comments:

1. Press **Ctrl-F5**. Type **5** or **C**.

```
Comment: 1 Create; 2 Edit; 3 Convert to Text: 0
```

2. Type **1** or **C**. The Document Comment screen is displayed:

```
Document Comment




Press Exit when done
```

3. Type text just as you would for any other document. You can enter up to 1,024 characters (about 12½ 80-character lines of text) per comment. You can use both boldface and underline while creating comments. You can have as many comments per document as you want.

4. Press **F7** when you are finished. Comments are displayed on-screen at the cursor location at which they were created (unless you choose not to display them). If you choose to display them, they are enclosed in a box like this:

Doc 1 Pg 1 Ln 1" Pos 1"

EDITING DOCUMENT COMMENTS   Comments can be edited as easily as they are created. To edit document comments:

1. Move the cursor to a position following the comment. Press **Ctrl-F5** and type **5** or **C**, then **2** or **E**. WordPerfect looks backward and selects the first comment it finds.

2. Edit the comments as you would any other document. Press **F7** when you are finished.

CHANGING DOCUMENT COMMENTS TO TEXT   While document comments are always displayed on-screen, they are never printed. If you want to print them, you must change them to text. To do this:

1. Move the cursor to a position after the comment you want to change. Press **Ctrl-F5** and type **5** or **C**.

2. Type **3** or **T**. WordPerfect searches backward for the first comment it sees and converts it to text.

CHANGING TEXT TO DOCUMENT COMMENTS   WordPerfect also lets you turn text into document comments. This is helpful if you make notations in documents and want to save them, but not print them in a finished document. To convert text to comments:

1. Press **Alt-F4** and define the block of text you want to convert. Press **Ctrl-F5**.

2. Type **Y**. The text is converted into a document comment.

APPLICATIONS

Use the Document Comments feature as you would a stick-on note. Make remarks while editing someone else's document. Add comments to aid the writer in improving the document. If you created the document, add comments that you want the editor to see, but that are not for public consumption.

If you find that a comment adds so much to the document that it should be printed, convert it to text. On the other hand, if you are a compulsive note taker who finds it necessary to always add comments to a document, you can convert that text to comments.

Use document comments in any document that will be read by more than one person. This includes articles, theses, reports, and public and private corporate memos.

TYPICAL OPERATION

In this example, you add a document comment to a memo.

1. Create a document similar to the following:

```
To: FLG
From: JYM
Subject: Our Handling of the Turner Fiasco

I think we ought to give up now, FLG. This is not turning out the
way we planned. I'm not happy with how things went last week, and
Turner seems to be getting meaner every day.


                                        Doc 1 Pg 1 Ln 2" Pos 5.4"
```

2. Assume you are FLG and you have just received this memo electronically and you want to add comments to it. Move the cursor after FLG at the top of the document and press **Ctrl-F5**. Type **5** or **C**. Then type **1** or **C**.

3. Type **John:** (press **Enter** twice), **This defeatist attitude on your part is both uncharacteristic and alarming. I disagree completely.** Press **F7** to save the comments. The document now looks like this:

```
To: FLG

    ┌────────────────────────────────────────────────────────────┐
    │ John:                                                        │
    │                                                              │
    │ This defeatist attitude on your part is both uncharacteristic and │
    │ alarming. I disagree completely.                             │
    └────────────────────────────────────────────────────────────┘

From: JYM
Subject: Our Handling of the Turner Fiasco

I think we ought to give up now, FLG. This is not turning out the
way we planned. I'm not happy with how things went last week, and
Turner seems to be getting meaner every day.


                                        Doc 1 Pg 1 Ln 1" Pos 1.7"
```

4. Save the document as TURNER.WPF.

5. Turn to Module 72 to continue the learning sequence.

Module 20
DOCUMENT COMPARE

DESCRIPTION

Have you ever started editing a document and wondered what changes you have made? WordPerfect's Document Compare feature lets you do that. It compares a document on screen with that same document on disk — before any changes were made.

Document Compare analyzes documents phrase-by-phrase. It divides the document into a series of phrases separated by phrase markers — punctuation marks, hard returns, hard page breaks, footnote codes, and endnote codes. It also compares the last page break and the end of the document.

On-screen text that isn't on the file on disk is redlined (Module 58). Text that is on the file on disk but isn't on the on-screen version is displayed on-screen as strikeout text (Module 58). To perform a Document Compare operation:

1.   With a document on-screen, press **Alt-F5**. Type **6** or **G**.

```
Mark Text: Generate

    1 - Remove Redline Markings and Strikeout Text from Document

    2 - Compare Screen and Disk Documents and Add Redline and Strikeout

    3 - Expand Master Document

    4 - Condense Master Document

    5 - Generate Tables, Indexes, Automatic References, etc.


Selection: 0
```

2.   Type **2** or **C**. Press **Enter**.

```
Other Document: C:\WP50\DOCS\FILENAME.WPF
```

3.   This is your chance to compare the document on-screen to either a file on disk of the same name or another file on disk. Press **Enter** to compare to the file of the same name. Or, if you want to compare the file on-screen to another file, type that filename and press **Enter**.

You are then returned to the document with changes marked accordingly.

REMOVING REDLINE AND STRIKEOUT MARKINGS   When you have finished comparing the documents, you can remove the redline and strikeout markings from the text. To do this:

1. Press **Alt-F5** and type **6** or **G**.

2. Type **1** or **R**, then type **Y** in response to the "delete redline markings and strikeout text?" prompt.

APPLICATIONS

Document Compare is a useful utility that helps you trace changes made to a document. It comes in handy when two or more people have edited a file and you want to see the changes they made. It is also a good way to see what changes you have made since the last time a file was saved.

TYPICAL OPERATION

In this operation, compare a memo to the original version.

1. Start WordPerfect and create a document similar to the following:

```
                                  MEMO

        To: FLG
        From: JYM
        Subject: August Sales Figures

        Thanks to the start of another new school year, August sales
        figures were the highest for 1989. Sales of textbooks, school
        supplies and SIU merchandise led the way. There is no greater way
        to increase sales of merchandise than for the Sulukis to do well
        in sports. The success of the 1988-89 Salukis was a big part of
        this.

        The growth of the student body also had a lot to do with this
        situation. There are 1,000 more students on campus this year than
        last. This is due largely to increased recruiting in the Chicago
        area. But part of this is also due to the success of the Saluki
        sports team.

                                        Doc 1 Pg 1 Ln 4" Pos 1"
```

2. Save the document as AUGSALES.WPF.

3. Move the cursor to the "T" in "There" in the third sentence in the first paragraph. Press **Alt-F4** and press **Enter** to highlight the rest of the paragraph as a block of text.

4. Press **Ctrl-F4**, type **1** or **B**, then **1** or **M** to remove the block from the text.

5. Move the cursor to the end of the document and press **Enter** to insert the block.

```
                                MEMO


     To: FLG
     From: JYM
     Subject: August Sales Figures

     Thanks to the start of another new school year, August sales
     figures were the highest for 1989. Sales of textbooks, school
     supplies and SIU merchandise led the way.
     The growth of the student body also had a lot to do with this
     situation. There are 1,000 more students on campus this year than
     last. This is due largely to increased recruiting in the Chicago
     area. But part of this is also due to the success of the Saluki
     sports team. There is no greater way to increase sales of
     merchandise than for the Sulukis to do well in sports. The success
     of the 1988-89 Salukis was a big part of this.

     C:\WP50\DOCS\AUGSALES.WPF                  Doc 1 Pg 1 Ln 3.16" Pos 2.3"
```

6. Move the cursor to the end of the first paragraph and press **Enter**. Then delete "this situation" at the end of the first sentence in the second paragraph and type **our success**.

7. Move the cursor to the middle of the second-to-last sentence and delete "of merchandise." Then move to the last word in the document, delete "this," and type **ours**.

8. Press **Alt-F5**. Type **6** or **G**. Then type **2** or **C** and press **Enter**.

Notice that text that has been added or moved to a new position in the document is redlined. Text that has been deleted or moved from its original location is marked as strikeout.

9. Press **Alt-F5** and type **6** or **G**. Then type **1** or **R** and then **Y**.

```
                                MEMO


     To: FLG
     From: JYM
     Subject: August Sales Figures

     Thanks to the start of another new school year, August sales
     figures were the highest for 1989. Sales of textbooks, school
     supplies and SIU merchandise led the way.

     The growth of the student body also had a lot to do with our
     success. There are 1,000 more students on campus this year than
     last. This is due largely to increased recruiting in the Chicago
     area. But part of this is also due to the success of the Saluki
     sports team. There is no greater way to increase sales than for the
     Sulukis to do well in sports. The success of the 1988-89 Salukis
     was a big part of ours.

     C:\WP50\DOCS\AUGSALES.WPF                  Doc 1 Pg 1 Ln 3.83" Pos 1"
```

10. Save the document.

11. Turn to Module 42 to continue the learning sequence.

Module 21
DOCUMENT FORMAT

DESCRIPTION

The Document Format menu helps format text on the screen. Because changes made from this menu do not result in codes (Module 59) being inserted in the text, they have no effect on a document when it is printed. The Document Format menu lets you change settings for redline method (described in Module 58), display pitch, initial document settings, and initial fonts. The Document Format menu is also the place where you create the document summary. To access the menu, press Shift-F8 and type 3 or D.

```
Format: Document

   1 - Display Pitch - Automatic        Yes
                       Width            0.1"

   2 - Initial Codes

   3 - Initial Font                     10 CPI

   4 - Redline Method                   Printer Dependent

   5 - Summary

Selection: 0
```

DISPLAY PITCH   The display pitch is the width of one character on the screen. The larger the pitch, the smaller the number, and the more characters you can fit on the screen. Modifying the display pitch has no effect on a document when it is printed. It only affects text as it is displayed on the screen. This lets you optimize the display pitch to work best with your monitor.

Normally, the display pitch is 10, or .1" per character. WordPerfect automatically adjusts it to prevent character overlapping. It is best to leave display pitch alone in most instances.

Occasionally, a situation arises where you are fitting so many characters on-screen that they overlap. This can be the case when you try to put several columns across a page with many tabs and indents already being used. To change display pitch, press Shift-F8, type 3 or D, then 1 or D. Type N and change the width to your desired setting. The larger the number, the smaller the pitch, therefore, more characters can fit on the screen. Press F7 to save the settings.

INITIAL CODES   While the setup menu lets you change the default or initial settings for WordPerfect, the initial codes selection lets you change the defaults for the current document only. It then saves those codes at the top of the document. To set the initial codes, press Shift-F8, type 3 or D, then 2 or I.

```
Press Exit when done                                          Ln 1" Pos 1"
```

As when Reveal Codes is pressed, WordPerfect splits the screen into two parts. For example, let's say you want to turn on widow and orphan protection (Module 39). Press Shift-F8, type 1 or L, then 9 or W then y to change the widows/orphans setting. Press F7.

```
                                                     Doc 1 Pg 1 Ln 1" Pos 1"

[W/O On]
```

```
Press Reveal Codes to restore screen
```

Change as many settings as you want, then press F7 to save them. The codes are placed at the top of the document.

DOCUMENT SUMMARY   Document summary lets you identify documents by more than just a filename. It is useful when performing a word search through a document (Module 61). You can list the filename, creation date, subject, author, and typist of a document, plus up to 780 characters of comments about the document.

A document summary is not required when using WordPerfect, but the Setup menu, described in Appendix B, can prompt you to create a document summary when you save or exit a document.

To create document summaries, press Shift-F8 and type 3 or D. Then type 5 or S. This is what the summary for this module looks like:

```
Document Summary

        System Filename            A:\DOCFORM.WPF

        Date of Creation           July 18, 1988

   1 - Descriptive Filename

   2 - Subject/Account

   3 - Author

   4 - Typist

   5 - Comments

     ┌──────────────────────────────────────────────────────────────────┐
     │ This is a description of the document summary feature of WordPerfect. This │
     │ feature is very interesting in that it really includes a lot of    │
     │ information about each document. There is more information than meets the │
     │ eye, as much of it is hidden behind the cloak of secrecy. There is very │
     │ little that is left out of this software program. Very little. In fact, th │
     └──────────────────────────────────────────────────────────────────┘


Selection: 0
```

Notice the filename and creation date are automatically entered, as are the first 400 characters of text as a document comment. Type 1 or D to enter a descriptive filename for the document. Type 2 or S to enter a subject. Type 3 or A to enter an author for the document. Type 4 or T to enter a typist. Each entry can be up to 38 characters long. Press F7 when finished with each.

NOTE

If you enter a descriptive filename before you save the document, WordPerfect saves the document for you and gives it a name that consists of the first seven letters of the subject.

Type 5 or C to add your own comments about the document. Since 400 characters are already in the comments, you can add another 380. Or, you can delete the comments in the comments box using normal cursor control keys, and add more of your own comments, up to 780 characters. Press F7 to return to the document.

INITIAL FONT   The initial font is selected from the font you selected when you first chose your printer. This is explained in Module 55, the next module in the learning sequence. The initial font selection lets you change the initial font for this document only. To change the initial font, press Shift-F8. Type 3 or D, then type 3 or F.

```
  Document: Initial Font

     05 CPI
     06 CPI
     08.5 CPI
   * 10 CPI
     12 CPI
     12pt (PS)
     17 CPI
     Italic 12pt (PS)
     Subscript (05 CPI)
     Subscript (06 CPI)
     Subscript (10 CPI)
     Subscript (12 CPI)

   1 Select; N Name search: 1
```

This is a listing of fonts available from your printer. The selection with the asterisk is the current font. To change fonts, move the cursor to the font you want to change to and press 1 or S. Then press F7 to save your selection.

If your printer is capable of many fonts, use the Name Search feature. Type 1 or N. Then type the first few letters or numbers in the font. As you type the numbers or letters, WordPerfect moves to the first font with those numbers or letters. For example, in the previous illustration, typing I moves quickly to Italic. When you have found your selected font, press F7 to save your settings.

APPLICATIONS

If you are using a document that requires a lot of columns and needs overlapped text to fit on the screen, use the display pitch setting. If you want to change format settings for the current document only, use the initial codes feature. Document summaries provide a useful roundup of information about a document. When used in conjunction with the Word Search feature, document summary provides a powerful way to quickly locate documents. The initial font setting comes in handy when using documents that require a different font than others you might be using.

TYPICAL OPERATION

This operation illustrates the creation of a document summary.

1. Create a document similar to the following:

```
        SPEECH TO BE GIVEN BY FLG TO CARBONDALE CITY COUNCIL

Dear Ladies and Gentlemen of the City Council:

Thank you for letting me speak to you this evening. I speak to you
as a concerned citizen and also as a concerned business person. I
urge you not to approve construction of a mall on Illinois Avenue.
There is no room for such a development. There is no parking, no
land, and not enough business to justify a development like this.


                                        Doc 1 Pg 1 Ln 2.5" Pos 1"
```

2. Press **Shift-F8**, type **3** or **D**, then **5** or **S**.

```
Document Summary

        System Filename                (Not named yet)

        Date of Creation               July 18, 1988

    1 - Descriptive Filename

    2 - Subject/Account

    3 - Author

    4 - Typist

    5 - Comments

  ┌─────────────────────────────────────────────────────────────┐
  │  SPEECH TO BE GIVEN BY FLG TO CARBONDALE CITY COUNCIL ; Dear Ladies and │
  │ Gentlemen of the City Council:  Thank you for letting me speak to you this │
  │ evening. I speak to you as a concerned citizen and also as a concerned │
  │ business person. I urge you not to approve construction of a mall on │
  │ Illinois Avenue. There is no room for such a development. │
  └─────────────────────────────────────────────────────────────┘

Selection: 0
```

3. Notice that System Filename tells you the document hasn't been named. Type **1** or **D** and type **Anti-mall speech**. Press **F7**. Notice WordPerfect saves and names the document "antispe."

4. Type **2** or **S** and type **FLG Speeches - 1989**. Press **F7**.

5. Type **3** or **A** and type **FLG**. Press **F7**.

6. Type **4** or **T** and type **BDM**. Press **F7**.

7. Type **5 or C** and type **Impassioned speech before Carbondale City Council**. Press **F7**.

```
Document Summary

          System Filename          ANTISPE

          Date of Creation         July 18, 1988

    1 - Descriptive Filename        Anti-mall speech

    2 - Subject/Account             FLG Speeches - 1989

    3 - Author                      FLG

    4 - Typist                      BDM

    5 - Comments

   ┌─────────────────────────────────────────────────────────────────┐
   │ Impassioned speech before Carbondale City Council. SPEECH TO BE GIVEN BY │
   │ FLG TO CARBONDALE CITY COUNCIL ; Dear Ladies and Gentlemen of the City   │
   │ Council:  Thank you for letting me speak to you this evening. I speak to  │
   │ you as a concerned citizen and also as a concerned business person. I urge │
   │ you not to approve construction of a mall on Illinois Avenue. There is no  │
   └─────────────────────────────────────────────────────────────────┘

Selection: 0
```

8. Press **F7** twice to save the document summary.

9. Save the document as SPEECH.WPF.

10. Turn to Module 55 to continue the learning sequence.

Module 22
DUAL DOCUMENT EDITING

DESCRIPTION

WordPerfect's dual document editing capability lets you edit two documents at once. This is useful if you are transferring information from one document to another, or using a document as a reference while creating another.

WordPerfect lets you edit two documents at once in two ways — through the Switch key (Shift-F3) and through Windows (Ctrl-F3).

SWITCH   The Switch feature puts one document on-screen at a time. You can retrieve separate documents into each file and edit them nearly simultaneously. You can also move text (Module 47) between documents using the Move key. To switch between documents:

1.   Assume you are in document one. It may contain a blank screen, a document you just created, or a file you just retrieved.

2.   Press **Shift-F3**.

```
                                                        Doc 2 Pg 1 Ln 1" Pos 1"
```

3.   You are now in document 2, as you can tell on the Status Line. You can retrieve an existing file or create a new document. To switch back, press **Shift-F3**.

When you are ready to save one or both documents, you must save them individually. You can exit one document without leaving WordPerfect.

WINDOWS   You do not have to completely leave either document. You can split the screen and view both documents at once. You can view 24 lines on the screen. Those lines can be divided between the documents, with as little as 2 in one document and 22 in the other. To split the screen:

1.   Press **Ctrl-F3**.

```
    0 Rewrite; 1 Window; 2 Line Draw: 0
```

2.   Type **1** or **W**.

```
    Number of lines in this window: 24
```

3. Type the number of lines you want in this window.

TIP: It is recommended that you split the screen evenly, 12 lines on top and 12 lines on bottom. This gives you the best possible view of each document.

4. Press **Enter**. The rest of the lines are automatically given to the other document. Both documents appear on-screen simultaneously. They are separated by WordPerfect's tab ruler.

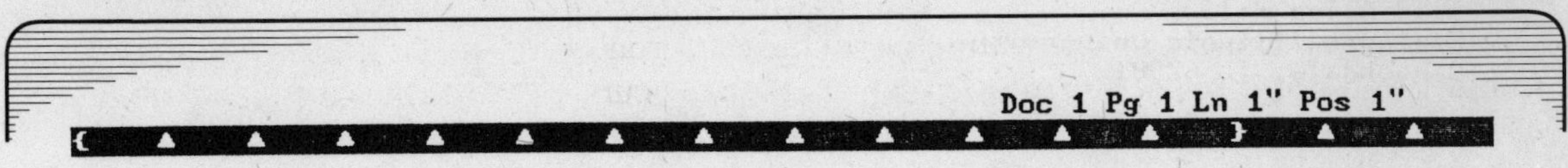

When you are in the top document, the arrows in the tab ruler, which correspond to the tab settings in your document, point up. When you are in the bottom document, the arrows point down. Use the Switch key, (Shift-F3) to switch between documents.

5. To return WordPerfect to normal, press **Ctrl-F3**, type **1**, type **24** to set the current window to 24 lines and press **Enter**.

6. If you want to look at the other document, press **Shift-F3**.

APPLICATIONS

Dual document editing is useful if you are editing one document and using the other as a reference. It is especially useful if you need to move or copy information from one document to another. The Windows feature lets you see both documents on-screen at once.

TYPICAL OPERATION

In this example, use the Switch feature to copy information from one document to another.

1. Create the following document:

```
                                        Jack Belew
                                        FLG Office Supplies
                                        124 N. Main
                                        Carbondale, IL 62901
                                        February 24, 1987

Dr. Arthur Schuff
1118 Allen Hall
Southern Illinois University
Carbondale, IL 62901

Dear Sir:

Thank you for your letter of February 1. I studied it with great
care and discussed it with others at FLG. We decided that since you
are not going to be using the information for financial gain, we
would give you access to our financial records.

It is to be understood that you are using this information for
class purposes only. Since you were kind enough to sign a non-
disclosure agreement earlier, our latest income statement is
enclosed.

                            Jack Belew
                                    Doc 1 Pg 1 Ln 1" Pos 1"
```

2. Press **Ctrl-Enter** to create a new page. Then press **Shift-F3** to switch to the other document.

3. Retrieve the financial statements. You saved them as "FINANCES.WPF" in Module 15, Cursor Control. Press **PgDn** to move to page 2. Then press **Alt-F4** to turn on Block mode and move the cursor to the end of the page to define it as a block.

4. Press **Ctrl-F4**, **1** or **B**, then **2** or **C** to copy the block.

5. Press **Shift-F3** to switch back to the first document. Make sure the cursor is at the beginning of page 2 and press **Enter** to retrieve the block of text. Move the cursor to view the Income Statement.

```
                        INCOME STATEMENT
                        FLG OFFICE SUPPLIES
                  FOR YEAR ENDED DECEMBER 31, 1986

Sales:                      $625,000
Less: Cost of Goods:         375,000
Gross Margin:                               $250,000

Operating Expenses:

Rent:                       $ 36,000
Utilities:                     8,000
Salaries:                     95,000
Misc. Expenses:               46,525
Total Operating Expenses:                    185,525
Gross Profit:                               $64,475
Taxes:                                      $19,343

Net Profit:                                 $45,132
                                    Doc 1 Pg 2 Ln 4" Pos 1"
```

6. Press **F7** and type **Y**. Save the document as SCHUFFLT.WPF. Press **Enter**.

```
Exit doc 1? (Y/N) No
```

7. Type **Y**. WordPerfect switches you to document 2.
8. Save FINANCES.WPF and exit document 2 and WordPerfect.
9. Turn to Module 19 to continue the learning sequence.

Module 23
ENDNOTES

DESCRIPTION

Endnotes provide further information about a subject that is referenced in a document. While footnotes (Module 28) are reference notes that are placed at the end of a page, endnotes are placed at the end of a document. WordPerfect lets you create endnotes and footnotes in the same document. WordPerfect also lets you place endnotes anywhere you want in a document.

There is one blank line separating the end of the text from endnotes, so it is advisable to create a new page and a heading at the end of the document that introduces the endnotes.

WordPerfect automatically numbers endnotes in your document. All you have to do is create them. After you have created an endnote, WordPerfect puts a superscripted number, character, or letter in the text referencing the endnote (superscripts are described in Module 67). You can view endnotes by editing them or by printing out the document. The Reveal Codes key (Alt-F3) lets you see the first 50 characters in an endnote.

CREATE ENDNOTES   The creation of endnotes is similar to that of headers and footers (Module 32). To create an endnote:

1.   Make sure the cursor is where you want the endnote referenced in the text and press **Ctrl-F7**.

```
1 Footnote; 2 Endnote; 3 Endnote Placement: 0
```

2.   Type **2** or **E**, then **1** or **C** to create an endnote.

```
1.



Press Exit when done                                      Ln 1" Pos 1.2"
```

3.   To create an endnote, type the information as you want it to look at the top or bottom of the page. Use any of WordPerfect's formatting commands, like boldface, underline, italics, or center. The "1." at the top of the screen signifies the number of the endnote. Notice the Status Line at the bottom right of the screen.

4.   Press **F7** when you are finished typing the endnote. WordPerfect also puts a superscript 1 at this location in the document.

EDITING AN ENDNOTE   Endnotes can be edited after they are created. To edit an endnote:

1. Place the cursor anywhere in the document and press **Ctrl-F7**. Then type **2** or **E** twice.

```
Endnote number? 2
```

WordPerfect automatically inserts the next endnote number. That is, if you have created four endnotes and your cursor is located between endnote numbers 1 and 2, the prompt will read "Endnote number? 2."

2. Type the number of the endnote you want to edit if it's not the one listed. Press **Enter**.
3. Make your changes to the endnote. Then press **F7** to save those changes.

ENDNOTE OPTIONS   WordPerfect gives you a number of options for formatting endnotes. To see the options and the defaults for those options:

1. Press **Ctrl-F7**. Type **2** or **E**. Then type **4** or **O**. The Endnote Options menu appears:

```
Endnote Options

      1 - Spacing Within Endnotes            1
                Between Endnotes             0.16"

      2 - Amount of Endnote to Keep Together 0.5"

      3 - Style for Numbers in Text          [SUPRSCPT][Note Num][suprscpt]

      4 - Style for Numbers in Note          [Note Num].

      5 - Endnote Numbering Method           Numbers




      Selection: 0
```

2. Press **Enter** to leave the menu, or see the following sections for descriptions of each option.

SPACING WITHIN AND BETWEEN ENDNOTES   The default setting for spacing within endnotes is single spacing, but you may change that to double spacing, triple spacing, one and one-half line spacing, etc. WordPerfect also puts one blank line (0.16 inches) between each endnote. To change the number of spaces within and between endnotes:

1. Type **1** or **S** from the Endnote Options menu. Then type the spacing you want within endnotes and press **Enter**.

2. Type the number of inches you want between each endnote and press **Enter**. Type 0.32"for two lines, 0.48" for three lines, etc. Press **Enter** again to leave the menu and return to the document.

LINES TO KEEP TOGETHER   WordPerfect keeps at least three lines of an endnote on a page. If there is not room for at least three lines, WordPerfect puts the entire endnote on the next page. To change the number of lines to keep together:

1. Type **2** or **A** from the Endnote Options menu. Type the minimum number of lines you want to keep on a page from each endnote and press **Enter**. Use 0.32" for two lines, 0.66" for four lines, etc.

2. Press **Enter** again to leave the menu and return to the document.

STYLE FOR NUMBERS IN TEXT   WordPerfect automatically superscripts (Module 67) the characters, numbers, or letters that identify endnotes in text. You have the option, however, of changing that. You can underline the characters, numbers, or letters, or you can have them appear as normal characters. You can also mix and match, both underlining and superscripting the identifying symbol. To change the way endnotes are identified in text:

1. Type **3** or **T** from the Endnote Options menu. To have endnotes identified by an underline, press **F8**. Press **Enter**. Notice the string by selection 3.

```
    3 - Style for Numbers in Text          [UND][Note Num][und]
```

2. Press **Enter** again to return to the document.

STYLE FOR NUMBERS IN NOTE   In the endnotes section at the end of a document, endnotes are identified by a number, letter, or character followed by a period. WordPerfect lets you change this. You can underline the identifier, remove the period, superscript the identifier, or any combination of the above. To change the way endnotes are identified in the notes:

1. Type **4** or **N** from the Endnote Options menu. To have endnotes identified by an underline, press **F8**.

2. Press **Ctrl-F7**. Then type **2** or **E**. This lets you insert the [Note] code into the string.

```
    1 Note; 2 Number Code; 3 New Number; 4 Options: 0
```

3. Type **1** or **N**.
4. Type **.** and press **Enter**. Notice the string by selection 4.

```
4 - Style for Numbers in Note          [UND].[Note Num][und]
```

5. Press **Enter** again to return to the document.

ENDNOTE NUMBERING METHOD   WordPerfect automatically numbers endnotes, but you get to choose whether they are identified by numbers, letters, or characters. Numbers are the default, but letters and characters are also a good choice. If you choose to use characters to identify endnotes, you can choose up to five different ones (for example, @,#,$,%,*). If there are more than five endnotes in a document, WordPerfect repeats the characters in multiples. For example, if you selected only one character, asterisks, endnote number three would be identified by "***." To change the numbering mode from numbers to letters or characters:

1. Type **5** or **M** from the Endnote Options menu.
2. Select the endnote numbering mode of your choice. Type **1** or **N** for numbers, **2** or **L** for letters, or **3** or **C** for characters. If you choose characters, type the character or characters you want to use for endnotes. Then press **Enter** to leave the menu and return to the document.

NOTE

If you change the endnote numbering method
after you have created endnotes, the previous
numbers do not change. So if you create two
endnotes and decide to switch to letters, the
endnotes will be numbered 1, 2, c, d, etc. You can
change this by editing the old endnotes yourself.

RENUMBERING ENDNOTES   You are not stuck with the numbers you have chosen for endnotes. You can always renumber them. This comes in handy, especially when you change the style of the endnotes in the middle of a document. To renumber endnotes:

1. Press **Ctrl-F7**. Type **2** or **E**, then **3** or **N**.
2. In response to the "endnote number?" prompt, type the new number for the next endnote and press **Enter**.

APPLICATIONS

Endnotes are most often used in formal research documents such as term papers, theses, research papers, and dissertations. They can be used in any document, however. Use them to elaborate on points made in the text when the extra information does not fit in the document.

TYPICAL OPERATION

This example teaches you how to put endnotes into a document.

1. Create a document similar to the following:

```
MEMO

FROM: MD
TO: FLG

Do you remember Tinkers to Evers to Chance? Have you ever heard of
them? I think we should have a double play sale to honor those
gentlemen since they were on the last Chicago Cubs World Series
champions in 1908. The Cubs have just won the World Series, after
all, and I think the folks are a little nostalgic (at least those
that aren't Cardinal fans). Of course, those that aren't nostalgic
are in shock, but let's not worry about that now.
As you might have guessed, the double play sale will have two
parts. Those are outlined below:

                                            Doc 1 Pg 1 Ln 3.16" Pos 4.2"
```

2. With the cursor to the right of the question mark next to "Chance," press **Ctrl-F7**. Type **2** or **E**, then **1** or **C**.

3. Press the **Spacebar** and type the following:

Joe Tinker was the shortstop, Johnny Evers the second baseman, and Frank Chance the first baseman of baseball's first celebrated double play combination. There were other double play combinations that were better, but none are more famous.

4. Press **F7** to save the endnote.

```
Do you remember Tinkers to Evers to Chance?1 Have you ever heard of
them? I think we should have a double play sale to honor those

                                            Doc 1 Pg 1 Ln 1.83" Pos 5.3"
```

5. Press **Ctrl-F7**. Then type **2** or **E** twice and type **1** and press **Enter** to edit the endnote.

```
1. Joe Tinker was the shortstop, Johnny Evers the second baseman,
and Frank Chance the first baseman of baseball's first celebrated
double play combination. There were other double play combinations
that were better, but none are more famous.

Press Exit when done                                    Ln 1" Pos 1"
```

6. Move the cursor to the space after the "n" in "first baseman." Then press the **Spacebar** and type **(and manager)**. Then press **Down Arrow**.

```
1. Joe Tinker was the shortstop, Johnny Evers the second baseman,
and Frank Chance the first baseman (and manager) of baseball's
first celebrated double play combination. There were other double
play combinations that were better, but none are more famous.

Press Exit when done                                Ln 1.5" Pos 5.8"
```

7. Press **F7** to save the changes.
8. Save the document as CUBSWIN.WPF.
9. Turn to Module 64 to continue the learning sequence.

Module 24
ESCAPE

DESCRIPTION

Most software programs use Esc (Escape) to cancel a command. In contrast, WordPerfect uses Esc as a repetition counter for advanced cursor control, text insertion and deletion, and macro execution. The default repeat value is 8, but you can change this to any value you like.

For example, if you want to move the cursor eight pages ahead in a document, you can press Esc and PgDn and quickly move the cursor that distance. The Esc key makes it easier to move around documents, insert and delete text, and execute macros.

CHANGING THE REPEAT VALUE   The repeat value can be easily changed, either temporarily or permanently. When you press Esc, you see:

```
  Repeat Value = 8
```

To change the repeat value, type another number. The repeat value will change to any number you like. When changing the repeat value to another number, you have the option of saving that value or using it for one time only. To save a new repeat value, type the new value and press Enter. To change it for one operation only, type the new value and press the appropriate key to execute the desired operation.

Pressing Esc after you type a new value returns it to its previous value.

USING THE ESC KEY FOR CURSOR CONTROL   Pressing Esc lets you move around a document faster than any other method. Esc used in conjunction with cursor control keys lets you move "n" spaces, words, lines, screens, or pages through a WordPerfect document. The options for cursor control with Esc are listed in the following table:

NOTE

In the keystroke sequences in this module, it is not necessary to hold down the Esc key. Simply press Esc, release it, then complete the keystroke sequence. For example, perform the sequence Esc, Ctrl-End by pressing Esc, then Ctrl-End.

CURSOR CONTROL USING THE ESC KEY REPEAT VALUE (n)

Keystroke	Results
Esc, Up Arrow	Moves the cursor n lines up.
Esc, Down Arrow	Moves the cursor n lines down.
Esc, Left Arrow	Moves the cursor n spaces to the left.
Esc, Right Arrow	Moves the cursor n spaces to the right.
Esc, Ctrl-Left Arrow	Moves the cursor n words to the left.
Esc, Ctrl-Right Arrow	Moves the cursor n words to the right.
Esc, PgUp	Moves the cursor n pages backward.
Esc, PgDn	Moves the cursor n pages forward.

USING ESC TO INSERT TEXT   Pressing Esc lets you insert the same character multiple times into a document with very few keystrokes. (The Insert function is explained in more detail in Module 37.) For example, if you want to create a dotted line at the bottom of a page in a document, move the cursor to the desired location and press Esc. Type 64, then -. You see:

```
Doc 1 Pg 1 Ln 1" Pos 7.4"
```

USING ESC TO DELETE CHARACTERS   While using Esc to insert characters is a relatively limited command, pressing Esc to delete characters is not. WordPerfect lets you delete ''n'' lines, characters, or words. It is very handy for deleting large blocks of text in a minimum of keystrokes. (The Delete function is explained in more detail in Module 17). It actually takes less keystrokes than the Block command (described in Module 8) in many instances.

The keystrokes necessary to delete text using Esc are listed in the following table:

TEXT DELETION USING THE ESC KEY REPEAT VALUE (n)

Keystroke	Results
Esc, Del	Deletes n characters to the right.
Esc, Ctrl-Backspace	Deletes n words to the right.
Esc, Ctrl-End	Deletes n lines starting to the right of the cursor.

USING ESC TO INVOKE A MACRO   Esc can be used to perform a macro multiple times. (Macros are described in Module 42.) This feature quickly gives you numerous on-screen copies of data generated by the macro.

APPLICATIONS

Esc can be used whenever a WordPerfect document is being edited. It allows for quick movement through a document, deletion and insertion of text, and multiple performance of a macro.

TYPICAL OPERATION

In this operation, you use Esc to control the cursor and move through a document very quickly.

1. Retrieve FINANCES.WPF, created in Module 15, Cursor Control. The first page of the document is shown here:

```
                                        Jack Belew
                                        FLG Office Supplies
                                        124 N. Main
                                        Carbondale, IL 62901
                                        February 24, 1987


William Levin
345 N. Olive
Carterville, IL 62966

Dear Bill:

It was a pleasure speaking with you last week about your new
position with the Bank of Carterville. I hope you can help us with
our financial needs in the future.

Per your request, I am enclosing some recent financial statements.
I think you'll agree that FLG Office Supplies is in fine financial
shape. And with your help, we hope to be even better.

                                        Sincerely,

                                        Jack Belew
                                        Controller
C:\WP50\DOCS\FINANCES.WPF                    Doc 1 Pg 1 Ln 1" Pos 1"
```

2. Press **Esc** and **Down Arrow**. Notice the cursor move eight lines down. Press **Esc** and **Down Arrow** again, notice the cursor move another eight lines down.

```
Per your request, I am enclosing some recent financial statements.
C:\WP50\DOCS\FINANCES.WPF                    Doc 1 Pg 1 Ln 3.66" Pos 1"
```

3. Press **Esc** and **Ctrl-Right Arrow**. Notice the cursor move eight words to the right.

```
Per your request, I am enclosing some recent financial statements.
C:\WP50\DOCS\FINANCES.WPF                    Doc 1 Pg 1 Ln 3.66" Pos 5.5"
```

4. Press **Esc** and **PgDn**. Since there aren't eight pages left in the document, notice the cursor move to the end of the document. Press **Esc** and **PgUp** to move the cursor to the beginning of the document.

5. Save the document as FINANCES.WPF.

6. Turn to Module 32 to continue the learning sequence.

Module 25

FILE MANAGEMENT

DESCRIPTION

A computerized file is much the same as a file kept in a filing cabinet. It holds information. As with DOS filenames, WordPerfect lets you put as many as eight letters into your filenames, followed by a period and an optional three-letter extension. The name distinguishes the file from all the others, and the three letter extension divides the files into groups. In a file like SAMPLE.WPF, for example, "sample" is the name of the file, and "wpf" is the group it is in. Similarly, the file that contains most of the WordPerfect program you are now using is WP.EXE. "wp" is the name of the file and "exe" (for "execute") is the group it is in.

Once a file is created, WordPerfect gives you many options for file management. The List Files key (F5), described in Module 40, gives you access to the files in a particular directory, diskette, or category. While other features are available in the List Files menu, the file management features covered in this module let you retrieve, rename, delete, copy, or look at a file. You can also directly retrieve a file without referring to the List Files menu.

You retrieve files for editing purposes. You can change the filename through the rename feature. If you delete a file, you remove it from the directory, or "throw it away." If you copy a file, you make a "clone," or "backup copy" of the file. Backup copies protect you against the danger of accidentally losing a file due to inadvertent erasure or a damaged diskette or hard disk. WordPerfect's Look feature lets you quickly examine the contents of a file without retrieving it. This helps you look at a number of files quickly to find the one you want to edit.

There are two ways to retrieve a file — using the List Files menu and using the Retrieve key (Shift-F10).

RETRIEVE A FILE USING LIST FILES   The List Files menu shows all the files in a particular directory. To retrieve a file from the List Files menu:

1.   Press **F5**. Then type **C:\WP50\DOCS*.*** and press **Enter**.

> **NOTE**
> An alternative way to move through the menu is
> to use the Name Search feature described in
> Module 61.

2.   Press **Down Arrow** to move the cursor to the file you want to retrieve. Type **1** or **R**, then type **Y** to confirm that this is the file you want to retrieve.

RETRIEVE A FILE WITH RETRIEVE KEY   You don't have to use the List Files key to retrieve files. If you know the name of the file you want to retrieve, use the Retrieve key (Shift-F10). To do this, press Shift-F10, type the name of the document you want to retrieve, and press Enter.

RETRIEVE A FILE TO COMBINE WITH ANOTHER FILE   Normally, when you retrieve a file, you do so with a blank screen. But WordPerfect lets you retrieve files while another file in on-screen. This lets you combine the contents of two files.

CAUTION

When retrieving a file with another file on-screen, make sure the cursor is in the position where you the new file should begin. If it isn't, the new file might be retrieved in the middle of a sentence, or even a word, depending on the position of the cursor.

If you have one file on-screen and want to add the contents of another file, move the cursor to the location at which the other file is to be retrieved. Then, press Shift-F10, type the name of the document and press Enter.

NOTE

You can also retrieve files through the List Files menu.

RENAME A FILE   If you don't like the name of a file, or you don't think the name of the file conveys the contents of the file, you can rename the file. To rename a file:

1. Press **F5**, type **C:\WP50\DOCS*.*** and press **Enter**. The display should look similar to the following:

```
06/07/88  14:18              Directory C:\WP50\DOCS\*.*
Document size:        0   Free:  8622080   Used:        4833        Files:   5

. <CURRENT>     <DIR>              | .. <PARENT>      <DIR>
IDEAS    .WPF    1158  06/07/88 14:15   PRACTICE.WPF      720  06/06/88 08:20
REST     .WPF     895  06/06/88 16:15   SAVE     .WPF     657  06/07/88 13:36
SORRY    .WPF    1403  06/07/88 13:58

1 Retrieve; 2 Delete; 3 Move/Rename; 4 Print; 5 Text In;
6 Look; 7 Other Directory; 8 Copy; 9 Word Search; N Name Search: 6
```

2. Move the cursor to the file you want to rename, for example, "IDEAS.WPF" and type **3** or **M**.

```
New name: C:\WP50\DOCS\IDEAS.WPF
```

3. Type the new filename and press **Enter**. WordPerfect renames the file. You will see the new filename in its correct alphabetical position in the List Files menu the next time you access List Files.

COPY A FILE   The copy file feature is useful for making backup copies of files or for copying files for use on other computers. To copy a file:

1.   From the List Files menu, move the cursor to the file you want to copy. Then type **8** or **C**.

```
Copy this file to:
```

2.   Let's say you are copying a file from the hard disk to a data diskette. Put a data diskette in drive A, type **A:** and press **Enter**.

If a file of the same name exists on the destination directory and drive, WordPerfect asks if you want to replace the existing file. If you do, type Y. If not, rename the original file and copy it again. When the copying process starts, the disk drive lights flash on and off while the file is being copied from one drive to another. When the lights go out, the file has been copied.

3.   Remove the data diskette from drive A.

DELETE A FILE   The Delete File command often comes in handy. Sometimes, a file has outlived its usefulness. Or, you may be running out of room on a particular diskette and decide to delete a file. To delete a file:

1.   From the List Files menu, move the cursor to the file you want to delete, for example, "PRACTICE.WPF" and type **2**.

```
Delete C:\WP50\DOCS\PRACTICE.WPF? (Y/N) No
```

2.   Type **Y**. Notice the disk drive light come on as WordPerfect deletes the file.

Notice "Free" disk space in the middle of the screen has increased. That is because a file has been removed from the disk.

COPY OR DELETE SEVERAL FILES AT A TIME   If you want to copy or delete several files at once, you can. The Mark Text key (Alt-F5) marks every file in a directory. You can then either delete or copy all of those files. If you want to mark only certain files for copying or deletion:

1.   From the List Files menu, move the cursor to the first file you want and type *. Then move the cursor to the next file you want and continue marking files in this manner. If you change your mind about marking a file, type * again with the cursor at that file to remove the mark.

2.   Type **8** or **C** or press **F8** if you want to copy the files you marked. If you are deleting the marked files, proceed to step 5.

```
Copy marked files? (Y/N) No
```

3. Type **Y** and press **Enter**.

```
Copy all marked files to:
```

4. Type the location (either directory, or drive and directory) for the files to be copied. If necessary, replace the WordPerfect diskette with a data diskette for this operation. Press **Enter** to begin the copying process. If necessary, when the procedure is complete, remove the data diskette from drive A and replace it with the WordPerfect diskette.

TIP: This feature is very useful for copying a large number of files to data diskettes. If the space required by the files you are copying exceeds that for one data diskette, WordPerfect prompts you to change data diskettes, then continues the copying process.

5. If you are deleting the marked files, type **2** or **D** or press **Del**.

```
Delete marked files? (Y/N) No
```

6. Type **Y** and press **Enter** to delete the files.

LOOK AT A FILE WordPerfect's Look command is unique among word processing software. It is one of the most useful commands in WordPerfect. If you use WordPerfect a great deal, you will find yourself creating a good number of files. Sometimes, you won't be able to remember what data is in a particular file. That is where the Look command comes in. It lets you look at a file without having to go through the trouble of retrieving it and then saving it again. To look at a file:

1. Starting at the List Files menu, move the cursor to the file you want to look at, type **6** or **L**, and press **Enter** to look at the file. The file appears and at the bottom of the file, a message is displayed:

```
Press Exit when done                          (Use Cursor Keys for more text)
```

This gives you a peek at the file, but not much else. You can't edit the file, since you haven't actually retrieved it. And, the file is not in WordPerfect format, so it does not look exactly as it should. The command keeps the filename and file size at the top of the page at all times, thereby reminding you what file you are viewing and how large it is.

You can move through the file using PgUp, PgDn, Screen Up, Screen Down, Up Arrow, Down Arrow, and the Search key (F2). Pressing any other key will have no effect.

2. Press **F7** to leave the file and return to the List Files menu.

APPLICATIONS

There are many reasons for performing the file management tasks mentioned in this module. In order to edit a file, you must first retrieve it. If you are not sure which file you want, use WordPerfect's Look feature to examine a file's contents before retrieving it. Use the Rename feature if you decide the name doesn't tell you enough about the file. Delete files that are either backed up on another diskette or of no further use to you. Copy a file to save a backup as "insurance" or to use the file on another computer. Use the Mark Text key to copy or delete a number of files at once.

TYPICAL OPERATION

This example demonstrates the use of WordPerfect's retrieve file capabilities.

1. Start WordPerfect and create a document similar to the following:

```
MEMO

From: FLG
To:   MDS

Dear Michael:

Some of our employees have been pursuing their jobs too vigorously.
I am afraid that one of them is going to become ill. I would like
to recommend mandatory vacations for Jonathan, Mike, and Laura.
Jonathan should take the first week of March off, Mike the second
and Laura the third.

Let me know what you think.
```

2. Press **F7**, press **Enter**, and then type **REST.WPF** and press **Enter** to save the document. Type **N** to continue with the next step.

3. Press **Shift-F10**. At the "document to be retrieved" prompt, type **IDEAS.WPF** and press **Enter**. If you have been following along, "IDEAS.WPF" was created in the Typical Operation section of Module 10, Cancel.

```
        MEMO

        CONFIDENTIAL

        From: FLG
        To:   RAW

        While the main function of the average office is work, many office
        personnel rely on their place of work as a hub of social activity.
        Therefore, it might be pertinent if we start to sell merchandise
        that is not related to the office, like magazines.

        I want to investigate this matter. I'm going to put you in charge
        of this program, Roger. Go down to the library and do some market
        research. Also do some studies. Find out what types of items people
        hope to find in office supply stores. Find out what we're missing.

        I'd like a full report by the end of the month. I want your report
        to list all of the items we aren't carrying that we should be
        carrying. I'd also like an estimated sales volume for those items.

        Also, Roger, please don't discuss this with anyone else, not even
        anyone on the staff.

                                              Doc 1 Pg 1 Ln 1" Pos 1"
```

4. Press **Home**, **Home**, **Down Arrow** to move the cursor to the bottom of the screen. Press **Enter** to add an extra space. Then, press **Shift-F10**, type **REST.WPF** and press **Enter**.

```
        Also, Roger, please don't discuss this with anyone else, not even
        anyone on the staff.

        FLG

        MEMO

        From: FLG
        To:   MDS

        Dear Michael:

        Some of our employees have been pursuing their jobs too vigorously.
        I am afraid that one of them is going to become ill. I would like
        to recommend mandatory vacations for Jonathan, Mike, and Laura.
        Jonathan should take the first week of March off, Mike the second
        week, and Laura the third.

        Let me know what you think.



        C:\WP50\DOCS\IDEAS.WPF                 Doc 1 Pg 1 Ln 7.66" Pos 1"
```

5. Save this file as a new document called MEMOS.WPF.

6. Turn to Module 15 to continue the learning sequence.

Module 26

FLUSH RIGHT

DESCRIPTION

Normally, typed text is flush against the left margin. There are times, however, when you want text flush against the right margin instead. The Flush Right key (Alt-F6) lets you do this.

The Flush Right key is useful for several applications. For example, the headers and footers on odd-numbered pages in this book are flush right. Another example is dates. This text is normal:

        June 9, 1988

This text is flush right:

                                                                June 9, 1988

The Flush Right key works best with short lines of text (40 columns or less). If you make longer lines flush right, you'll either move some text down to the next line, or not notice that the text is flush right.

To use the Flush Right key, press Alt-F6 and type the text you want flush against the right margin. Text looks like it is moving to the left. Then press Enter.

If you have already typed the text and want to make it flush right, move the cursor to the beginning of the text and press Alt-F6. Text moves to the right margin.

CAUTION

If you are putting flush right text on the same
line with normal text, make sure the flush right
text doesn't "run over" the normal text.
WordPerfect deletes any normal text that gets
in the way of flush right text.

If you have a block (Module 8) of text that you want to make flush right:

1. Move the cursor to the beginning of the block and press **Alt-F4**. Then move the cursor to the end of the block and press **Alt-F6**.

        [Flsh Rt]? (Y/N) No

2. Type **Y**. The block moves to the right margin.

APPLICATIONS

Use the Flush Right key for effect. Dates and headings often look best when they are flush against the right margin. Headers and footers also are often flush right. This is not a key you use often, but it is very useful when needed.

TYPICAL OPERATION

In this example, you move an address flush against the right margin. Notice this is not the way a normal address looks since the lines are not aligned with each other on the left.

1. Start WordPerfect and create a document similar to the following:

```
FLG Office Supply
124 N. Main
Carbondale, IL 62901
March 13, 1989


                                      Doc 1 Pg 1 Ln 1" Pos 1"
```

2. Make sure the cursor is at the top of the page and press **Alt-F4**. Press **Home, Home, Down Arrow** to move the cursor to the bottom of the page. Then press **Alt-F6**.

3. Type **Y** in response to the prompt.

```
                                      FLG Office Supply
                                           124 N. Main
                                 Carbondale, IL 62901
                                       March 13, 1989

                                 Doc 1 Pg 1 Ln 1.66" Pos 1"
```

4. Save the document as ADDRESS.WPF.
5. Turn to Module 35 to continue the learning sequence.

Module 27

FONT

DESCRIPTION

Fonts are typefaces of a specific weight and point size. WordPerfect lets you select the font or fonts in which you want your document printed. You can only select the fonts supported by your printer. In fact, the Font command (Ctrl-F8) is intended only for your printer. The way fonts are displayed on-screen is determined by their setting in the Colors/Fonts/Attributes setting on the Setup menu (Appendix B).

The base font is the way normal text is printed. All other fonts are variations of the base font — boldface, underline, italics, large, small, extra large, etc.

NOTE

The value of the Font command is completely determined by the fonts and attributes your printer supports. To see what attributes your printer supports, print the "PRINTER.TST" file, as described in Appendix E.

CHANGING THE BASE FONT   Changing font appearance is described in Module 5. Another option on the Appearance menu is redlining and strikeout, described in Module 58. To change the base font, press Ctrl-F8 and type 4 or B.

```
  Base Font

      05 CPI
      06 CPI
      08.5 CPI
    * 10 CPI
      12 CPI
      12pt (PS)
      17 CPI
      Italic 12pt (PS)
      Subscript (05 CPI)
      Subscript (06 CPI)
      Subscript (10 CPI)
      Subscript (12 CPI)

   1 Select; N Name search: 1
```

These are the fonts available to a particular printer (Gemini). The font with the asterisk next to it is the current base font. To change the base font, move the cursor to the desired font and type 1 or S.

If you have a lot of fonts available to your printer, type N to select Name Search. Then type the first letter or number of the font you want to select. The cursor moves either to that font or toward that font. Continue typing the font name or number until the cursor reaches that font (Name Search is described in Module 61).

CHANGING FONT SIZE   Once you've selected the base font, you can then change the font size or appearance of text. Font sizes range from fine to extra large. This typically varies from 10 point, or pica, for normal text, to 6 point for fine text and 24 point for extra large. Another option on the Size menu, subscript and superscript, is discussed in Module 67. The size of text does not change on the screen. It only changes at the printer.

To change font size:

1. Press **Ctrl-F8** and type **1** or **S**.

```
1 Suprscpt; 2 Subscpt; 3 Fine; 4 Small; 5 Large; 6 Vry Large; 7 Ext Large: 0
```

2. Type **3** or **F** to change text to fine; **4** or **S** to change it to small; **5** or **L** to change it to large; **6** or **V** to change it to very large; **7** or **E** to change it to extra large.

3. Type the text you want to be in this font. Then press **Ctrl-F8** and type **3** or **N** to change the font back to normal (the base font).

NOTE

If you've already typed the text and you want to
change its font size, define the text you want to
change as a block, then select the font size to
change it to.

APPLICATIONS

The Font feature can help you dramatically change the appearance of printed text. Use large, very large, or extra large fonts in titles, section headings, and other special text. This draws the reader to them, especially when used in conjunction with appearance changes like outline, italics, boldface, or shadow text.

Small or fine fonts often elicit just as much reader attention, because the reader tends to notice text that is not the same size as the rest of the text on the page. Use these fonts for effect as well. Also use them for extraneous, but necessary information. These fonts come in handy in "the fine print" portions of contracts, documents, and other publications.

TYPICAL OPERATION

This typical operation illustrates the use of the Font command in sprucing up a document.

1. Start WordPerfect and create a document similar to the following:

```
FLG OFFICE SUPPLIES IS HAVING AN END OF THE SCHOOL YEAR SALE!

ONE DAY ONLY - MAY 19

EVERYTHING IN THE STORE IS 50% OFF!*


*Does not apply to certain electronic items.

                                    Doc 1 Pg 1 Ln 2.33" Pos 1"
```

2. Move the cursor to the top of the document, press **Alt-F4**, and define the first line as a block of text. Press **Ctrl-F8**, type **2** or **A**, then type **6** or **a** to define the block as shadow text.

NOTE
On a color monitor with EGA graphics, shadow
text is light green.

3. Redefine the same line of text as a block. Press **Ctrl-F8**, type **1** or **S**, and type **6** or **V**. Notice the text turn orange if you have a color monitor. Notice also that the text now is on two lines on-screen.

4. Move the cursor to the next line. Define the next two lines as a block of text. Press **Ctrl-F8** and type **2** or **A**. Then type **1** or **B** to boldface the block of text.

5. Redefine the same block of text. Press **Ctrl-F8**, type **1** or **S**, and type **5** or **L** to make the font large.

6. Move the cursor to the last line. Define the line as a block of text. Press **Ctrl-F8**, type **1** or **S**, and type **3** or **F** to make the font fine. The final document looks like this when printed:

7. Save the document as SALE.WPF.
8. Turn to Module 21 to continue the learning sequence.

Module 28

FOOTNOTES

DESCRIPTION

Footnotes are reference notes placed at the end of each page in a document. They are generally a point of reference guiding the reader to further information.

While endnotes (Module 23) are reference notes generally placed at the end of a document, footnotes are placed at the end of each page. WordPerfect lets you create endnotes and footnotes in the same document.

WordPerfect automatically numbers footnotes in your document. All you have to do is create them. After you have created a footnote, WordPerfect puts a superscripted number, character, or letter in the text referencing the footnote (superscripts are described in Module 67). You can view footnotes by editing them or by printing out the document. The Reveal Codes key (Alt-F3), lets you see the first 50 characters in a footnote.

CREATE FOOTNOTES   The creation of footnotes is similar to that of headers and footers (Module 32). To create a footnote:

1. Make sure the cursor is where you want it in the text. Press **Ctrl-F7**. Then type **1** or **F**.

```
     Footnote: 1 Create; 2 Edit; 3 New Number; 4 Options: 0
```

2. Type **1** or **C**.

```
     Press Exit when done                          Doc 1 Pg 1 Ln 1.5" Pos 1.58"
```

This is the area in which you create a footnote. The "1" at the top of the screen signifies the number of the footnote. WordPerfect also puts a superscript 1 at this location in the text. Notice the Status Line at the bottom right of the screen.

3. To create a footnote, type the information as you want it to look at the top or bottom of the page and press F7. Use any of WordPerfect's formatting commands, like boldface, italics, underline, or center.

EDITING A FOOTNOTE   Footnotes can be edited after they are created. To edit a footnote:

1. Your cursor can be anywhere in the document. Press **Ctrl-F7**, type **1** or **F**, then type **2** or **E**.

```
Footnote number? 2
```

WordPerfect automatically inserts the next footnote number. If you have created four footnotes and your cursor is located between footnote number 1 and 2, the prompt will read "Footnote number? 2."

2. Type the number of the footnote you want to edit. Then press **Enter**.

3. Make your changes to the footnote and press **F7** to save those changes.

RENUMBERING FOOTNOTES   WordPerfect lets you renumber your footnotes. This is useful when you have a document that is broken up into two or more files and you want the footnotes numbered consecutively for both files. If you have a book or report broken up into chapters but contained in one file, you can start the numbering process over at the beginning of each chapter. To renumber footnotes, move the cursor to the left of the footnote to renumber and press Ctrl-F7. Type 1 or F, then 3 or N. Type the number for the next footnote and press Enter. All footnotes will be numbered consecutively starting with the number you've chosen.

FOOTNOTE OPTIONS   WordPerfect gives you a number of options for formatting footnotes. To see the options and the defaults for those options, press Ctrl-F7, type 1 or F, then type 4 or O.

```
  Footnote Options

      1 - Spacing Within Footnotes              1
                  Between Footnotes             0.16"

      2 - Amount of Note to Keep Together       0.5"

      3 - Style for Number in Text              [SUPRSCPT][Note Num][suprscpt]

      4 - Style for Number in Note                  [SUPRSCPT][Note Num][suprscp

      5 - Footnote Numbering Method             Numbers

      6 - Start Footnote Numbers each Page      No

      7 - Line Separating Text and Footnotes    2-inch Line

      8 - Print Continued Message               No

      9 - Footnotes at Bottom of Page           Yes


  Selection: 0
```

Spacing Within And Between Notes   The default setting for spacing within notes is single spacing. But you may change that to double spacing, triple spacing, one and one-half line spacing, etc. WordPerfect also puts one blank line (0.16 inches) between each footnote. To change the number of spaces within and between footnotes, type 1 or S from the Footnote Options menu. Then type the spacing you want and press Enter. Then type the number of inches you want between each footnote and press Enter. Type 0.32" for two lines, 0.48" for three lines, etc. Press Enter again to leave the menu and return to the document.

Lines To Keep Together   WordPerfect keeps at least three lines of a footnote on a page (0.50"). If there isn't room for at least three lines, WordPerfect puts the entire footnote at the bottom of the next page. To change the number of lines to keep together, type 2 or A from the Footnote Options menu. Type the minimum number of lines you want to keep on a page from each footnote and press Enter. Use 0.32" for two lines, 0.66" for four lines, etc. Press Enter again to leave the menu and return to the document.

Style For Numbers In Text   WordPerfect automatically superscripts (Module 67) the characters, numbers, or letters that identify footnotes in text. You have the option, however, of changing that. You can underline the characters, numbers, or letters, or you can have them appear only as characters. You can also mix and match, both underlining and superscripting the identifying symbol. To change the way footnotes are identified in text:

1. Type **3** or **T** from the Footnote Options menu. To have footnotes identified by an underline, press **F8**.

2. Press **Enter**. Notice the string by selection 3.

```
    3 - Style for Number in Text          [UND][Note Num][und]
```

3. Press **Enter** again to return to the document.

Style For Numbers In Note   In the footnotes section at the bottom of the page, footnotes are identified by a number, letter, or character followed by a period. WordPerfect lets you change this. You can underline the identifier, remove the period, superscript the identifier, or any combination of the above. To change the way footnotes are identified on a page, type 4 or N from the footnote options menu. To have footnotes identified by an underline, press F8. Press Enter.

```
    [UND][Note Num][und]
```

Press Enter again to return to the document.

Footnote Numbering Method   WordPerfect automatically numbers footnotes, but you get to choose whether they are identified by numbers, letters, or characters. Numbers are the default, but letters and characters are also a good choice. If you choose to use characters to identify footnotes, you can choose up to five different ones (for example, @,#,$,%,*). If there are more than five footnotes in a document, WordPerfect repeats the characters in multiples. For example, if you selected only one character, asterisks, footnote number three would be identified by "***." To change the numbering mode from numbers to letters or characters, type 5 or M from the Footnote Options menu. Select the footnote numbering mode of your choice. Type 1 or N for numbers, 2 or L for letters, or 3 or C for characters. If you choose characters, type the character or characters you want to use for footnotes. Then press Enter to leave the menu and return to the document.

NOTE

If you change the footnote numbering method after you have created footnotes, the previous numbers will not change. So if you create two footnotes and decide to switch to letters, the footnotes will be numbered 1, 2, c, d, etc. You can change this by editing the old footnotes yourself.

Start Footnote Numbering Each Page   WordPerfect lets you begin each page with footnote number one. The default is consecutive numbers throughout the document. To number the footnotes on each page separately, type 6 or P from the Footnote Options menu. Type Y and press Enter to leave the menu and return to the document.

Line Separating Text And Footnotes   WordPerfect puts a two-inch line at the bottom of the page between text and footnotes. You can change this to either no line between text and footnotes or a line across the entire page separating text and footnotes. To change the line between text and footnotes:

1.   Type **7** or **L** from the Footnote Options menu.

```
   1 No Line; 2 2-inch Line; 3 Margin to Margin: 0
```

2.   Type **1** or **N** for no line, **2** for a two-inch line, or **3** or **M** for a line from margin-to-margin across the page. Then press **Enter** to leave the menu and return to the document.

Print Continued Message   When a footnote continues on to the next page, WordPerfect can add a (Continued. . .) message to the last line of the footnote. To add a continued message, type 8 or C from the Footnotes Option menu. Type Y, then press Enter. Press Enter again to return to the document.

Footnotes At Bottom Of Page   If there is space for blank lines left on the page, WordPerfect puts it between text and footnotes. You have the option of putting the blank space at the bottom of the page, after the footnotes. To put the blank lines at the bottom of the page, rather than before the footnotes, type 9 or B from the Footnote Options menu. Type N to move the blank lines after the footnotes. Then press Enter to leave the menu and return to the document.

APPLICATIONS

Footnotes are most often used in formal research documents such as term papers, theses, research papers, and dissertations. They can be used in any document, however. Use them to reference sources when you make key points in a document.

TYPICAL OPERATION

This example teaches you how to put footnotes into a document.

1.   Create a document similar to the following.

```
The Paperless Office is a Myth
by John Mathews, Executive Vice-President

FLG Office Supply,
Carbondale, IL

For decades, people have spoken of the so-called "paperless
office." It was first mentioned in the early 1900s in a book by
James Young.

                                        Doc 1 Pg 1 Ln 2.5" Pos 1"
```

2. Press **Ctrl-F7**. Type **1** or **F**, then type **1** or **C**.
3. Press the **Spacebar** and type **Office of the Future, Snyder and Sons, 1908**. Then press **F7**.
4. Press **Ctrl-F7**. Type **1** or **F**, then type **2** or **E** to edit the footnote.
5. Type **1** and press **Enter** to edit footnote number 1.

```
     1 Office of the Future, Snyder and Sons, 1908.

Press Exit when done                    Doc 1 Pg 1 Ln 3" Pos 1"
```

6. Move the cursor to the "O" in "Office" and type **Young, James,**. Then press the **Spacebar**.

```
     1 Young, James, Office of the Future, Snyder and Sons, 1908.

Press Exit when done                    Doc 1 Pg 1 Ln 3" Pos 3.08"
```

7. Press **F7** to save the changes and return to the document.
8. Save the document as PAPERLES.WPF.
9. Turn to Module 23 to continue the learning sequence.

Module 29
GO TO

DESCRIPTION

The Go To command is a specialized cursor control feature in WordPerfect that quickly moves you from one part of a document to another. Other cursor control features are described in Modules 15 and 24.

There are six major uses for the Go To command:

- Moving to a specific page number.
- Moving to the next occurrence of a certain character.
- Moving to the top or bottom of a specific page.
- Moving around a particular block of text. (Blocks are described in Module 8.)
- Moving back to a particular part of a document after a major motion command.
- Moving through columns of text. (Columns are described in Module 13.)

Another use of the Go To command lets you leave the program to temporarily go to DOS. This uses a different command sequence than the rest of the features in this module. This feature lets you directly move between other programs if you have installed WordPerfect Library or WordPerfect Shell.

To use the Go To command, press Ctrl-Home. The following screen appears:

```
Go to
```

The next step is up to you. Do you want to go to a specific page, or to the top or bottom of the current page? Your options are listed below:

Keystroke	Result
Ctrl-Home, (Page Number), Enter	Jumps cursor to the page of your choice.
Ctrl-Home, Up Arrow	Jumps cursor to the top of the current page.
Ctrl-Home, Down Arrow	Jumps cursor to the bottom of the current page.
Ctrl-Home, Right Arrow	Jumps cursor to the next column. (See Module 13 for a description of the column mode.)
Ctrl-Home, Left Arrow	Jumps cursor to the previous column.
Ctrl-Home, Home, Right Arrow	Jumps cursor to the last column on the page.
Ctrl-Home, Home, Left Arrow	Jumps cursor to the first column on the page.
Ctrl-Home, x	Jumps cursor to the next occurrence of the character "x," as long as that occurrence is within the next 2,000 characters (10 pages).

Keystroke	Result
Ctrl-Home, Ctrl-Home	Cancels the last major positioning command (PgUp, PgDn, Screen Up, Search, Replace, Escape, any arrow key, or Home).
Ctrl-Home, Alt-F4 (Block On)	Jumps cursor to the beginning of a block.
Alt-F4, Ctrl-Home Ctrl-Home	Restores a block of text.
Ctrl-F1, 1 or G	Temporarily leaves WordPerfect and goes to DOS. Pressing F7 moves you back to WordPerfect.

APPLICATIONS

The Go To command lets you move from any page in a document to any other page very quickly. This is especially advantageous in a large document. It also lets you quickly find a specific character. This is helpful when you are moving to a seldom-used letter, like x or z, or a character, like * or #. It also lets you move to the top or bottom of a page and move around in blocks or columns of text. The Go To command is a very efficient method of cursor movement.

The other type of Go To command, for going to DOS, is also very useful. It lets you temporarily run other applications (assuming you have enough memory to do so), or run DOS commands such as looking for a document or formatting a diskette without having to quit WordPerfect. If you have WordPerfect Library or the WordPerfect Shell, this command moves you to those programs. Both the Shell and Library make it easy to run other applications and go to DOS.

Two commands not really associated with going to any cursor location, but accessed by pressing Ctrl-Home, are those for restoring a block of text and for cancelling a motion command like a Page Up or Page Down command.

TYPICAL OPERATION

Many of the uses of the Go To command are illustrated in the following example.

1. Start WordPerfect and retrieve the FINANCES.WPF file created in Module 15.

```
                                      Jack Belew
                                      FLG Office Supplies
                                      124 N. Main
                                      Carbondale, IL 62901
                                      February 24, 1987


William Levin
345 N. Olive
Carterville, IL 62966

Dear Bill:

It was a pleasure speaking with you last week about your new
position with the Bank of Carterville. I hope you can help us with
our financial needs in the future.

C:\WP50\DOCS\FINANCES.WPF                      Doc 1 Pg 1 Ln 1" Pos 1"
```

2. Press **Ctrl-Home**, type **3**, and press **Enter** to move to page 3.

```
                        BALANCE SHEET
                     FLG OFFICE SUPPLIES
               FOR YEAR ENDED DECEMBER 31, 1986


   C:\WP50\DOCS\FINANCES.WPF                    Doc 1 Pg 3 Ln 1" Pos 1"
```

3. Press **Ctrl-Home**, type **1**, and press **Enter** to return to the top of the document. Then press **Ctrl-Home** and type **R** to jump to the next occurrence of the capital letter R.

```
                      INCOME STATEMENT
                     FLG OFFICE SUPPLIES
               FOR_YEAR ENDED DECEMBER 31, 1986


   C:\WP50\DOCS\FINANCES.WPF                    Doc 1 Pg 1 Ln 1" Pos 1"
```

NOTE

After finding the next occurrence of a certain character the cursor moves to the space *after* the occurrence.

4. Press **Ctrl-Home** and press **Up Arrow** to move to the top of the page. Then, press **PgUp** to move to the top of the document.

5. Press **Ctrl-Home Ctrl-Home** to cancel the Page Up command and return to page 2.

6. Press **Alt-F4**. Move the cursor to the line after "gross margin" and press **Alt-F4** again to turn the block off. Then, press **Ctrl-Home** and **Alt-F4** to move to the beginning of the block.

7. Press **Alt-F4** and then press **Ctrl-Home Ctrl-Home**. Notice the block is redefined.

8. Press **F1** to turn off the Block command.

9. Save the FINANCES.WPF document.

10. Turn to Module 18 to continue the learning sequence.

Module 30
GRAPHICS

DESCRIPTION

Just as a newspaper includes pictures, sketches, graphs, etc., WordPerfect's Graphics feature (Alt-F9) lets you merge graphics and text in your document. The Graphics feature gives you limited, but useful, desktop publishing capabilities to help you create newsletters, technical manuals, presentation materials, and other graphics-related documents.

Graphics are not displayed on-screen. Instead, WordPerfect puts a box on-screen to represent the graphic and wraps text around it. You can move or resize the box as needed.

NOTE

WordPerfect lets you create graphics whether or not you have a graphics card in your computer. But for best use of this command, a graphics card is recommended. A VGA card works best.

There are four types of boxes available in WordPerfect — figure, table, text, and user-defined. Figure boxes are good for graphics images, graphs, charts, and other images. Table boxes are good for tabular and statistical information. Text boxes are useful for sidebars, quote outs, and other text information that is separate from the rest of the document. User-defined boxes are for specialized images that do not fall into the above categories.

A type feature determines the box location in the document. A paragraph-type box moves with the text that wraps around it. A page-type box remains at a fixed position on a page. A character-type box is treated as a character. The line after a character box starts below it. This is the only box type that can be used with footnotes and endnotes.

Boxes can be placed in the main portion of a document as well as in headers, footers, footnotes, and endnotes. Graphics boxes cannot be placed in a table of authorities (Module 68), in document comments (Module 19), or inside other boxes. Text or empty graphics boxes can be placed in styles (Module 66).

While graphics cannot be viewed on-screen during regular editing operations, you can see graphics when in View Document mode (Module 57) and in Graphics Editing mode.

In addition to boxes, the graphics feature also lets you put vertical and horizontal lines on-screen as well as shaded rectangles. Vertical and horizontal lines are discussed in Module 38, Line Drawing.

Each type of box is automatically numbered in WordPerfect. You can optionally type a caption, either in addition to the number given to the box, or instead of.

CREATING GRAPHICS BOXES   To create a box, press Alt-F9.

```
    1 Figure; 2 Table; 3 Text Box; 4 User-defined Box; 5 Line: 0
```

Select the type of box you want to create. Type 1 or F to create a figure, 2 or T to create a table, 3 or B to create a text box, or 4 or U to create a user-defined box. (The Line option is described in Module 38.) A screen similar to the following appears:

```
    Figure: 1 Create; 2 Edit; 3 New Number; 4 Options: 0
```

Type 1 or C to create a figure, table, text, or user-defined box. The appropriate Definition menu appears:

```
    Definition: Figure

        1 - Filename

        2 - Caption

        3 - Type                      Paragraph

        4 - Vertical Position         0"

        5 - Horizontal Position       Right

        6 - Size                      3.25" wide x 3.25" (high)

        7 - Wrap Text Around Box      Yes

        8 - Edit

    Selection: 0
```

Filename   To import a graphics image, type 1 or F from the Definition menu and type a filename of a graphics document, which can be any graphics document from a wide variety of graphics programs. WordPerfect comes with 30 sample graphics files from Publisher's PicturePaks For WordPerfect from Marketing Graphics, Inc. For example, type C:\WP50\ANNOUNCE.WPG to retrieve one particular graphics file. If you have a floppy-based system put the Fonts/Graphics diskette in drive A and type A:ANNOUNCE.WPG. Press Enter. WordPerfect pauses momentarily, and a message at the bottom of the screen informs you it is retrieving the file. Then WordPerfect changes the vertical and horizontal position and the box size to fit the graphic image.

Caption   Type 2 or C from the Definition menu to type the caption.

```
┌──────────────────────────────────────────────────────────────────────┐
│                              Figure 1                                   │
│                                                                         │
└──────────────────────────────────────────────────────────────────────┘
   Press Exit when done                                    Ln 1" Pos 5.05"
```

This is the caption editing screen. You can revise the caption as you want. You can delete the figure or box number by pressing the Backspace key and reposition it anywhere in the caption by pressing Alt-F9. You can type as much text as you want, but the text wraps according to the width of the box you are defining. Press F7 when you are done defining the caption. All or part of it, depending on space, is displayed on the caption line.

Type   Type 3 or T from the Definition menu to define the box type.

```
┌──────────────────────────────────────────────────────────────────────┐
│                                                                         │
│                                                                         │
│     Type: 1 Paragraph; 2 Page; 3 Character: 0                           │
└──────────────────────────────────────────────────────────────────────┘
```

Type 1 or P to define a paragraph box, 2 or a to define a page box, and 3 or C to define a character box.

Vertical Position   Type 4 or V from the Definition menu to define the vertical position of the box.

```
┌──────────────────────────────────────────────────────────────────────┐
│                                                                         │
│                                                                         │
│     Offset from top of paragraph: 0"                                    │
└──────────────────────────────────────────────────────────────────────┘
```

Type the distance you want the box vertically separated from the top of the current paragraph and press Enter.

If you define a page box instead of a paragraph box, the following display appears:

```
┌──────────────────────────────────────────────────────────────────────┐
│                                                                         │
│                                                                         │
│     Vertical Position: 1 Full Page; 2 Top; 3 Center; 4 Bottom; 5 Set Position: 0 │
└──────────────────────────────────────────────────────────────────────┘
```

If you want the box to take up an entire page, type 1 or F. To position the box at the top of the page, type 2 or T. To center it vertically on the page, type 3 or C. To put it on the bottom of the page, type 4 or B. To set its position manually on the page, type 5 or S.

If you are using character-type boxes, the following screen appears:

```
┌──────────────────────────────────────────────────────────────────────┐
│                                                                         │
│                                                                         │
│     Align Text with: 1 Top of Box; 2 Center of Box; 3 Bottom of Box: 0  │
└──────────────────────────────────────────────────────────────────────┘
```

Typing 1 or T aligns the rest of the text on the line with the top of the box. Typing 2 or C aligns the rest of the text on the line with the center of the box. Typing 3 or B aligns the rest of the text on the line with the bottom of the box.

Horizontal Position   Type 5 or H from the Definition menu to define the horizontal position of the box.

```
Horizontal Position: 1 Left; 2 Right; 3 Center; 4 Both Left & Right: 0
```

Typing 1 or L puts the box flush with the left edge of the text; 2 or R puts it flush with the right edge; 3 or C centers the box between the text; and 4 or B makes the box fill the entire area from between the left and right edge of the text.

If you define a page box instead of a paragraph box, the following display appears:

```
Horizontal Position: 1 Margins; 2 Columns; 3 Set Position: 0
```

Typing 1 or M lets you put the box either flush against the left or right margin, centered between the margins, or filling the entire space between the left and right margins. Typing 2 or C gives you the same options, except instead of positioning the box between margins, you are positioning it between columns. Typing 3 or S lets you enter a specific distance from the left edge of the page to fix the position of the box on the page.

Character boxes do not require horizontal positioning; they are always positioned directly after the character to the left.

Size   Type 6 or S from the Definition menu to set the box size.

```
1 Width (auto height); 2 Height (auto width); 3 Both Width and Height: 0
```

Typing 1 or W allows you to set the width of the box, letting WordPerfect set the height automatically to preserve the shape of the image. Typing 2 or H lets you set the height, letting WordPerfect set the width automatically to preserve the image's shape. Typing 3 or B lets you set both the height and the width. Option 2 is not available on text boxes.

Wrap Text Around   Type 7 or W from the Definition menu. Then type y to wrap text around the box, or n to not wrap text around the box. If you select not to wrap text around the box, the box is not shown on screen. The only way to see a box in this instance is to select View Document, accessible from the Print command (Shift-F7), described in Module 57.

Edit   Type 8 or E from the Definition menu.

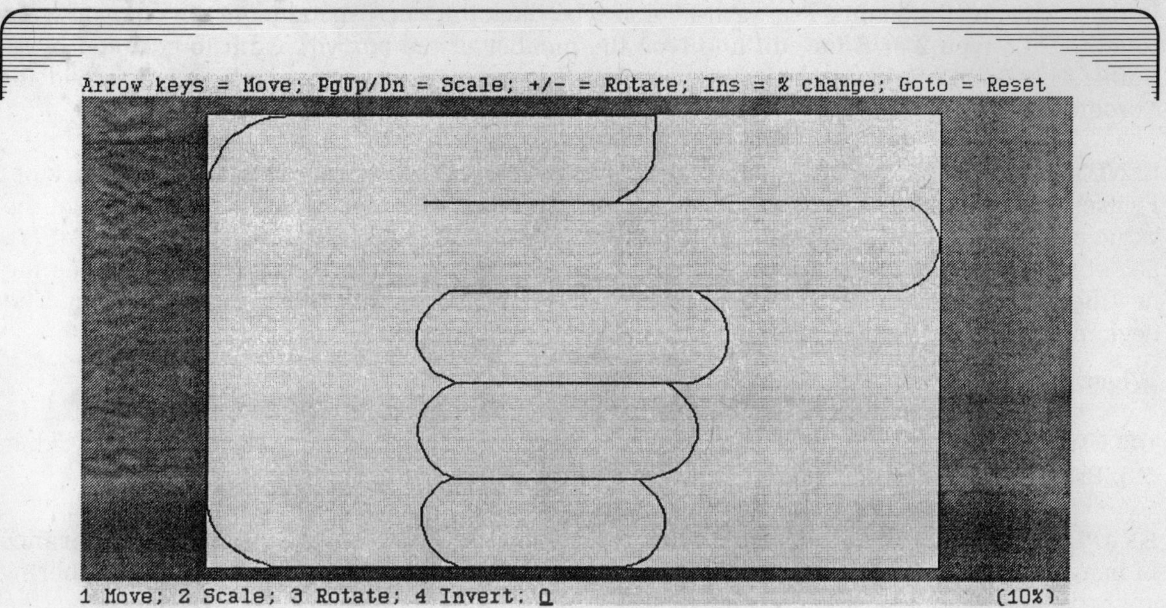

This is the graphics editing screen. It lets you see the image on-screen and gives you the option of moving, scaling, rotating, inverting, or changing the image. Graphics editing is controlled in two ways — typing 1 or M lets you move the image by typing the vertical and horizontal distance you want to move it. Or, you can use the cursor control arrow keys (Module 15) to move the image around the box. The distance the image moves with each keystroke is specified in the lower right-hand portion of the screen. As you would expect, pressing Up Arrow moves the image up, Down Arrow moves it down, Left Arrow moves it left, and Right Arrow moves it right. Typing 2 or S lets you scale the image (expand or contract it) horizontally or vertically by a specific percentage. Pressing PgUp expands the image both horizontally and vertically by a percentage indicated in the lower right-hand corner. Pressing PgDn contracts the image by the same percentage.

Typing 3 or R lets you rotate the image in a circle by a specific number of degrees. Pressing Screen Up (– on the numeric keypad) rotates the image clockwise by the percentage in the lower right-hand portion of the screen (100% equals 360 degrees, 50% equals 180 degrees, etc.). Pressing Screen Down (+ on the numeric keypad) rotates the image in a counter-clockwise direction. When you select any of these options, you are also given the option of mirroring the image, that is, reversing it. Typing 4 or I inverts the image, that is, white dots become black and black dots become white. Typing 4 or I again inverts the image back. Pressing Ins changes the percentage value in the lower right-hand corner to 1, 5, 10, or 25 percent.

Press Ctrl-Home at any time during the editing process to return the image to its pre-edited state.

Press F7 to save the graphics image and return to the document.

EDITING GRAPHICS BOXES   After you have created it, you can edit a graphics box at any point in the document. To do this, Press Alt-F9 and type the letter corresponding to the box you want to edit. Then type 2 or E for edit and type the number of the box you want to edit and press Enter. The Box Definition menu appears. Edit the box using the same options described for "creating graphics boxes."

RENUMBERING GRAPHICS BOXES   Graphics boxes are numbered according to box type. Figures are numbered separately, as are tables and text boxes (if applicable). To change the value of a box, move the cursor to the point you want renumbering to begin and press Alt-F9. Select the type of box you want to renumber. Then type 3 or N for New Number and type the new figure number for the box. From that point forward, all boxes of that type are numbered beginning with that number.

When you have finished adjusting the options, press F7 to return to the document.

DELETING GRAPHICS BOXES   If you decide to delete a graphics box, use Reveal Codes (Module 59). Press Alt-F3, look for the figure code, and delete the figure.

GRAPHICS OPTIONS   WordPerfect offers a great deal of variety in altering the appearance of images. Among other things, you can change shading, adjust the borders, change numbering methods, and caption positioning and style. To set graphics options, press Alt-F9 and select the type of box you want to set options for. Then type 4 or O. The appropriate Options menu appears:

```
    Options:     Figure

        1 - Border Style
                Left                            Single
                Right                           Single
                Top                             Single
                Bottom                          Single
        2 - Outside Border Space
                Left                            0.16"
                Right                           0.16"
                Top                             0.16"
                Bottom                          0.16"
        3 - Inside Border Space
                Left                            0"
                Right                           0"
                Top                             0"
                Bottom                          0"
        4 - First Level Numbering Method        Numbers
        5 - Second Level Numbering Method       Off
        6 - Caption Number Style                [BOLD]Figure 1[bold]
        7 - Position of Caption                 Below box, Outside borders
        8 - Minimum Offset from Paragraph       0"
        9 - Gray Shading (% of black)           0%

    Selection: 0
```

Border Style   Type 1 or B from the Options menu.

```
 1 None; 2 Single; 3 Double; 4 Dashed; 5 Dotted; 6 Thick; 7 Extra Thick: 0
```

These are the options available to you when creating borders. Typing 1 or N gives you no border; 2 or S gives you a single-line border (the default); 3 or D gives you a double-line border; 4 or a gives you a dashed line; 5 or o a dotted line; 6 or T a thick line; and 7 or E an extra thick line. WordPerfect lets you set borders individually for left, right, top, and bottom of the boxes. Enter a setting for the border style or press Enter to leave the setting as it is and go on to the next one.

Outside Border Space   Type 2 or O from the Options menu. This option lets you set the outside border space, or the space between the outside of the border and any text. It is automatically set at 0.16 inches. You can manually change it to any setting you like. Like the border style setting, you can set border space individually for the left, right, top, and bottom. Enter a setting for the border space or press Enter to leave the setting as it is and go on to the next one.

Inside Border Space   Type 3 or I from the Options menu. This is the inside border space, or the space between the border and the image inside the border. It is typically set at 0" all around. You have the option of resetting it to any setting you like. Like the outside border settings, you can set inside border space individually for the left, right, top, and bottom. Enter a setting for the border space or press Enter to leave the setting as it is and go on to the next one.

First Level Numbering Method   Type 4 or F from the Options menu.

```
 1 Off; 2 Numbers; 3 Letters; 4 Roman Numerals: 0
```

This is the numbering style for the type of box you have chosen. The default numbering style for figures is numbers (Figure 1, Figure 2, etc.). Typing 1 or O turns the numbering off; 2 or N is the aforementioned number style; 3 or L is letters; 4 or R is Roman numerals.

Second Level Numbering Method   Type 5 or S from the Options menu. This is the second level numbering method. Second level numbering comes in handy when you are using figures in a variety of chapters. Figure 1,1, for example, is Figure 1 in Chapter 1. Figure 1-2 is figure 2 in Chapter 1. Type 1 or O to turn numbering off (the default); 2 or N is the aforementioned number style; 3 or L is letters; 4 or R is Roman numerals.

Caption Number Style   Type 6 or C from the Options menu. This is the caption number style option. It lets you change the caption number style to whatever you want. You can underline the caption, italicize it, etc. If you have selected second level paragraph numbering, you can change the style from Figure 1 to Figure 1-1 or Illustration 1-1 or even just plain 1-1.

Position of Caption   Type 7 or P from the Options menu.

```
Caption Position: 1 Below Box; 2 Above Box: 1
```

This is the caption positioning option. It lets you position the caption above or below and inside or outside the box. Type 1 or B if you want the caption above the box, 2 or A if you want the caption above the box. Then type 1 or O if you want the caption outside the border, 2 or I if you want it inside the border.

Minimum Offset From Paragraph   Type 8 or M from the Options menu and type the minimum amount of space you want the box separated from the text. The default setting is zero inches. If WordPerfect can set the box off from the text the amount you select, it will. But if it cannot keep the box as far from the text as you selected and still keep the box on the page, it adjusts the amount slightly. When you have selected the correct measurement, press Enter.

Gray Shading   Type 9 or G from the Options menu. Then type the amount of shading you want in the box. The default setting is 0%, or none. The higher the percentage, the darker the box. Press Enter when you have typed the desired shading.

APPLICATIONS

The Graphics feature of WordPerfect is useful for any type of document that needs graphics, text-based sidebars, tables, or other illustrations. This makes it worthwhile for graphics presentations, newsletters, technical documentation, reports, and other documents. The Graphics feature lets you create some rather sophisticated illustrations, adding such features as shading, rotation, mirror images, and others.

TYPICAL OPERATION

This typical operation illustrates the use of graphics in an employee newsletter.

1. Create a document similar to the following:

```
                       FLG OFFICE SUPPLY
                       The Summer Report
```

```
Summer was a pretty nice time for FLG Office Supply. We had sales
that indicated many students were down here at SIU for summer
school. Whether that means they're down here because they're
working extra hard or making up for lost time, remains to be seen.
But we thank them for being here just the same.
```

2. Move the cursor to the blank line above "Summer was" and press **Alt-F9**. Type **1** or **F**, then **1** or **C** to move to the Figure Definition menu.

3. Type **1** or **F**. Then type **C:\WP50\NEWSPAPR.WPG** and press **Enter** to retrieve the graphic image. If you have a floppy-based system, put the Fonts/Graphics diskette in drive A, type **NEWSPAPR.WPG** and press **Enter**. Type **2** or **C** and press **Backspace** to delete the caption. Press **F7**.

4. Type **6** or **S** to set box size. Then type **2** or **H** to select auto height adjustment. Type **1** and press **Enter** to resize the graphic to one inch high. Type **5** or **H**, then **1** or **L** to reposition the graphic at the left margin. Then press **F7** to return to the document.

5. Move the cursor to the end of the document and press **Enter** twice. Then press **Alt-F9** and type **1** or **F**, then **1** or **C**.

6. Type **1** or **F**, then **C:\WP50\RPTCARD.WPG** and press **Enter**. If you have a floppy-based system, put the Fonts/Graphics diskette in drive A and type **A:RPTCARD.WPG** and press **Enter**.

7. Type **2** or **C** and press **Backspace** to delete the caption. Press **F7**.

8. Type **6** or **S** to set box size and type **2** or **H** to select auto height adjustment. Type **1.2** and press **Enter** to resize the graphic to 1.2 inches high. Press **F7** to return to the document. When it is printed, the document looks like this:

9. Save the document as REPORT.WPF.

10. Turn to Module 27 to continue the learning sequence.

Module 31
HARD SPACE

DESCRIPTION

The Hard Space command inserts a mandatory space between text. Words or symbols separated by a hard space will not split apart when word wrapping occurs. This is useful for dates, numbers, and names.

To introduce a hard space, press Home, Spacebar. Here is a passage of text without hard spaces:

```
    Please remember that our company's holiday will occur on December
    26 of this year.
```

If you delete the space between "December" and "26," and then insert a hard space, the text looks as follows:

```
    Please remember that our company's holiday will occur on
    December 26 of this year.
```

To reveal hard spaces in the text, use the Reveal Codes key (described in Module 59). The symbol for a hard space is [ ].

You can use hard spaces between several words in a row to create a string of one long combined word. WordPerfect treats words separated by hard spaces as one. You will occasionally be prompted to hyphenate these combined words.

APPLICATIONS

Insert a hard space to keep strings of numbers, proper names, and dates together so they do not separate during word wrapping.

TYPICAL OPERATION

In this example, you insert hard spaces between a series of words, numbers, and symbols.

1. Start WordPerfect and create a document similar to the following:

```
MEMO

FROM: JYM
TO: FLG
SUBJECT: MEN'S BASKETBALL LEAGUE

It's that time of year again! We have received a request from
Schneider Hall to sponsor the eleventh floor basketball team.
Remember them last year? That group played the most fundamentally-
sound basketball I've ever seen from a group of amateurs in my
life! I think we should sponsor them. Practice commences September
15. The costs wouldn't be too high. I estimate one hundred dollars
or less. And think of all that free advertising!

                                          Doc 1 Pg 1 Ln 1" Pos 1"
```

2. Move the cursor to the space between "September" and "15." Press **Del** and press **Home**, **Spacebar**. Press **Down Arrow** to auto-wrap the rest of the paragraph.

```
    life! I think we should sponsor them. Practice commences
    September 15. The costs wouldn't be too high. I estimate one
    hundred dollars or less. And think of all that free advertising!

                                       Doc 1 Pg 1 Ln 3.16" Pos 1"
```

3. Move the cursor to the space between the "one" and "hundred." Press **Del** and press **Home**, **Spacebar**. Press **Down Arrow** to auto-wrap the rest of the paragraph.

```
MEMO

FROM: JYM
TO: FLG
SUBJECT: MEN'S BASKETBALL LEAGUE

It's that time of year again! We have received a request from
Schneider Hall to sponsor the eleventh floor basketball team.
Remember them last year? That group played the most fundamentally-
sound basketball I've ever seen from a group of amateurs in my
life! I think we should sponsor them. Practice commences
September 15. The costs wouldn't be too high. I estimate
one hundred dollars or less. And think of all that free
advertising!

                                       Doc 1 Pg 1 Ln 3.33" Pos 1"
```

4. Save the document as BASKET.WPF.

5. Turn to Module 24 to continue the learning sequence.

Module 32
HEADERS AND FOOTERS

DESCRIPTION

The Header and Footer command lets you print information at the top or bottom of every page or on odd or even pages throughout a document. Headers are located at the top of the page, footers at the bottom. Header and footer information can be located in any horizontal part of a page. For example, information can be centered, flush against the left margin, or flush against the right margin. Header and footer information can contain text, numbers, and symbols. It can be boldfaced, underlined, italicized, or otherwise highlighted. Common headers and footers include chapter titles, page numbers, and names. For example:

```
   Simpson/Chapter 2                                              Page 1
```

This is a typical header. It includes information that is repeated on the left side of every page, and a page number that changes on the right. This information can be moved anywhere on a page. Page numbers, for example, could be on the next line or in the footer.

WordPerfect lets you create up to two headers and two footers at any point in a document. In reality, this lets you create an unlimited number of headers and footers. For example, if you have a 100-page document with ten chapters, WordPerfect lets you create two headers and footers for chapter one, discontinue them, create two headers and footers for chapter two, and so on.

Headers start on the first text line on the page, footers on the last. WordPerfect allows for one blank line between the header and the start of the text. For example, if you type a header that is two lines long, WordPerfect subtracts those lines plus one more from the text lines available on a page (54). For footers, WordPerfect allows for one blank line between the document text and the footer. If your footer is more than one line long, the rest of it is printed in the bottom margin (6 lines).

So, if you have one header that is three lines long and one footer that is two lines, there are 48 lines of text available per page in the document. Four lines are used in the header and two lines in the footer. Further, there is one less blank line in the bottom margin. Because headers and footers take up a lot of space on the page, it is suggested that no more than five lines at the top and five lines at the bottom be used for headers and footers.

NOTE

If you are using two headers (or two footers) on the same page, make sure that one is either flush right or located on a different line. If you do not, one may print over another.

Headers and footers are not visible on-screen after they are created. They are visible only when a document is printed. Use the Reveal Codes key to see a header or footer on screen (Reveal Codes is described in Module 59). The header created in the previous example looks like this in Reveal Codes:

Translated, this code tells you that this is a header that occurs on every page (see the following menu), and prints Simpson/Chapter 2 on the left side, and the current page number flush against the right margin.

CREATING A HEADER OR FOOTER   You create headers and footers using the Page Format command (press Shift-F8 and type 2 or P). The other page formatting commands are described in Module 51. The Page Format menu looks like this:

```
Format: Page

    1 - Center Page (top to bottom)     No

    2 - Force Odd/Even Page

    3 - Headers

    4 - Footers

    5 - Margins - Top                   1"
                  Bottom                1"

    6 - New Page Number                 1
          (example: 3 or iii)

    7 - Page Numbering                  No page numbering

    8 - Paper Size                      8.5" x 11"
          Type                          Standard

    9 - Suppress (this page only)

Selection: 0
```

1.   Type **3** or **H** for Headers, **4** or **F** for Footers. Then type **1** or **A** for either header A or footer A.

```
    1 Discontinue; 2 Every Page; 3 Odd Pages; 4 Even Pages; 5 Edit: 0
```

2. To create a header or footer that appears on every page, type **2** or **P**. To create one for odd pages, type **3** or **O**, to create one for even pages, type **4** or **v**.

```
Press Exit when done                                      Ln 1" Pos 1"
```

This is the area in which you create a header or footer. Notice the Status Line at the bottom right of the screen.

3. To create a header or footer, type the information as you want it to look at the top or bottom of the page, and press **F7**. Use any of WordPerfect's formatting commands, such as boldface, underline, or center. To create other headers or footers, repeat the above steps.

4. Press **F7** twice to exit the Page Format menu.

EDITING A HEADER OR FOOTER   You can edit headers or footers after they are created. To edit a header or footer, make sure the cursor is after the location where the header or footer was created. In other words, if you created the header or footer on page 2, do not try to edit it on page 1. There are two steps to editing a header or footer:

1. From the Page Format menu, type **3** or **H** for headers or **4** or **F** for footers.

2. Type the appropriate header or footer letter (**1** or **A** or **2** or **B**) and type **5** or **E** to edit that header or footer. After you have made your changes to the document, press **F7** to save those changes.

DISCONTINUING A HEADER OR FOOTER   To cancel a header or footer at any point in the document:

1. Move to the point where you want to cancel the header or footer, press **Shift-F8**, and type **2** or **P** to access the Page Format menu.

2. Type **3** or **H** for headers or **4** or **F** for footers.

3. Type the appropriate header or footer letter (**1** or **A** or **2** or **B**) and type **1** or **D** to discontinue that header or footer.

PAGE NUMBERS IN HEADERS OR FOOTERS   You can select page numbering from the Page Format menu (see Module 51). You can also select page numbering from Headers and Footers. The command for a page number in a header or footer is Ctrl-B, which looks like ^B. However, if you are starting from a point other than page 1 and would like page numbering to start with the current page number, use Ctrl-N instead.

APPLICATIONS

There are many uses for headers and footers. The most common are a company name, an author name, a date, a subject, a chapter number, and a page number. These items can appear in either the header or the footer. Headers and footers are used in reports, memos, articles, books, magazines, technical manuals, and a variety of other publications.

TYPICAL OPERATION

This example illustrates the use of headers and footers in a trip report. It uses all available headers and footers and alternates them on odd and even pages.

1. Create a document similar to the following:

```
To: FLG
From: JYM
Subject: Hawaii Convention

The Hawaii convention was very informative. Besides learning gobs
about the office supply business, we also had a wonderful time. I
never tried poy before. What a beautiful state!

Anyway, the office supply industry is booming. Everyone is adding
computer supplies like diskettes, printers, ribbons, and other
accessories. They're also adding books, telephones, and other items
that never used to be in our stores before.
....
================================================================================
On Wednesday, chairman Peterson discussed the evolution of the
office and its impact on modern society. Ergonomic furniture,
software, anti-radiation screens, paper, ribbons, and other
computer-related merchandise are also revolutionizing the office
supply store. We're so much less reliant on typewriters than we
used to be.

Peterson cautioned against giving up on typewriter-related items.
He mentioned that fully 70 percent of office workers still aren't
using computers.
                                             Doc 1 Pg 2 Ln 2.5" Pos 2.6"
```

2. Move the cursor to the top of the document. Press **Shift-F8**. Type **2** or **P**.

3. Type **3** or **H** and **1** or **A** to access the first header.

4. Type **3** or **O** to make it appear only on odd pages. The header screen appears.

5. Press **Alt-F6** to put all text flush against the right margin and type **Mathews/Trip Report**. Press **F7** to save the header and press **F7** again to return to your document.

6. Press **Alt-F3** to view the header in Reveal Codes.

7. Press **Alt-F3** to return to the document.

8. Press **Shift-F8** and type **2** or **P** to access the Page Format menu again.

9. Type **3** or **H**, then **2** or **B** to select the second header. Type **4** or **v** to select it only for even pages.

10. Type **Mathews/Hawaii** and press **F7** to save the header.

11. Type **4** or **F**, then **1** or **A** to select footer number 1. Type **3** or **O** to select it for odd pages only.

12. Press **Alt-F6** to put the footer flush against the right margin. Then, type **Page**, press the **Spacebar**, and press **Ctrl-B**. Press **F7** to save the footer.

13. Type **4** or **F**, then **2** or **B** to select the second footer. Type **4** or **v** to select it for even pages only.

14. Type **Page** and press the **Spacebar**. Then, press **Ctrl-B** to put the page number at the left margin for even-numbered pages. Press **F7** to save the footer and **F7** again to return to the document.

15. Press **Alt-F3** to view reveal codes for the headers and footers.

The headers on the printed document look like this:

Odd-numbered pages:

```
                                                        Mathews/Trip Report



                                                             Page 1
```

Even-numbered pages:

```
   Mathews/Hawaii



   Page 2
```

16. Press **Alt-F3** to exit Reveal Codes.

17. Save the document as HAWAII.WPF.

18. Turn to Module 16 to continue the learning sequence.

Module 33
HELP

DESCRIPTION

We all run into difficulties with WordPerfect commands from time to time. WordPerfect offers you a convenient solution to your problems with its Help function. Help is available at any time for any WordPerfect function, command, or keystroke. Simply press the Help key (F3) and then the keystroke you want help with. WordPerfect furnishes you a complete description of the command. This is called *on-line* help because it is available on the screen at any time.

On-line help is available while you are performing any editing function with WordPerfect. It is not available while a menu is on-screen, however. To use help:

1. If you are using a floppy-based system, put the Learning diskette, where the help files are located, in drive B. If you are using a hard disk system, you should have installed the help files in Module 2. Press **F3**. If you have a floppy-based system, you are asked where the help files are located. Type **B**.

```
Help                                                    WP 5.0   05/05/88


        Press any letter to get an alphabetical list of features.

            The list will include the features that start with that letter,
            along with the name of the key where the feature is found.  You
            can then press that key to get a description of how the feature
            works.


        Press any function key to get information about the use of the key.

            Some keys may let you choose from a menu to get more information
            about various options.  Press HELP again to display the template.

        Press Enter or Space bar to exit Help.
```

2. When you are finished, if necessary, replace the Learning diskette with the data diskette.

GETTING HELP WITH A SPECIFIC COMMAND Suppose you want information about a command, but don't know the keystroke for that command. WordPerfect lets you get help by pressing the first letter of that command. For example, if you want to change the margins of your text:

1. Look at the keyboard template. Notice margins are not listed.
2. Put the Learning diskette in drive B (if necessary), press **F3**, and type **B** to access help.

3. Type **M**, since that is the first letter in margins. You see this display:

```
Key              Feature                          Key Name

Ctrl-PgUp        Macro Commands                   Macro Commands
Ctrl-F10         Macro Commands, Help on          Macro Definition
Ctrl-F10         Macro, Define                    Macro Define
Ctrl-F10         Macro Editor                     Ctrl-F10, Edit
Alt-F10          Macro, Execute                   Macro
Shft-F1          Main Dictionary(s) Location      Setup,7
Shft-F8          Manual Hyphenation               Format,1
Shft-Tab         Margin Release                   Shft-Tab
Shft-F8          Margins - Left and Right         Format,1
Shft-F8          Margins - Top and Bottom         Format,2
Alt-F5           Mark Text                        Mark Text
Alt-F5           Master Document                  Mark Text,2
Alt-F7           Math                             Math/Columns
Alt-F7           Math Define                      Math/Columns
Shft-F1          Menu Letter Display              Setup,3
Ctrl-F9          Merge                            Merge/Sort
Shft-F9          Merge Codes                      Merge Codes
F9               Merge R                          Merge R
Alt-F9           Minimum Offset from Paragraph    Graphics,1,4
Ctrl-F4          Move                             Move
F5               Move a File                      List Files
Ctrl-F4          Move text                        Move
```

These are all the commands in WordPerfect that start with the letter "m." Now you know that
the keystroke for margins is Shift-F8.

GETTING INFORMATION ON A SPECIFIC KEYSTROKE   Suppose you want information on how
the margins work. Help is still activated.

1. Press **Shift-F8**.

```
Format

    Contains features which change the current document's format.  Options on
    the Line, Page and Other menus change the setting from the cursor
    position forward.  Document Format options change a setting for the
    entire document.  To change the default settings permanently, use the
    Setup key.

    1 - Line

    2 - Page

    3 - Document

    4 - Other


              Type a menu option for more help: 0
```

2. Type **1** or **L**, then **7** or **M** to receive help about margins.

```
Margins

        Sets the left and right margins from the cursor forward.  If your cursor
        is not at the left margin when you set margins, [HRt] is inserted before
        the setting.
```

3. If necessary, replace the Learning diskette with the data diskette.
4. Press the **Spacebar** or **Enter** to resume editing.

APPLICATIONS

Use Help whenever you need more information about a command or you aren't sure what the keystroke is for a certain command.

TYPICAL OPERATION

In this illustration, assume you are editing a letter. You have used the same word ("order") too many times and want a substitute for it, but you don't know how to use WordPerfect's Thesaurus (described in Module 71).

1. Start WordPerfect and create a document similar to the following:

```
                                        FLG Office Supply
                                        124 N. Main
                                        Carbondale, IL 62901
                                        January 21, 1990

Mr. Garry J. Levin
2746 Fremont
Murphysboro, IL 62957

Dear Sir:

Thank you for your order of December 27. We want you to know that
we really appreciate your business. However, Mr. Levin, we want to
notify you that there has been a problem with your order. The 5000
manila file folders that you ordered (part number - FM2467) are
temporarily out of stock. We want you to know that we are making
every effort to fill your order as soon as possible and apologize
for any delay.

                                        Sincerely,

                                        Michael David
                                        Office Manager

                                        Doc 1 Pg 1 Ln 4.66" Pos 6.9"
```

2. If necessary, place the Learning diskette in drive B, press **F3**, and type **B**. If you have a hard-disk system, just press **F3**.

3. Press **Alt-F1** to get help on using the thesaurus.

Thesaurus

Provides a list of synonyms (words with the same or very similar meaning) and antonyms (words with the opposite meaning). Words in the list that are marked with a bullet may be used to look up additional lists.

Any word in the list may be used to replace the original word in the document. Move the reference menu (the column of bolded letters next to the words) to the correct column and type the letter next to the word.

4. Press **Enter** or the **Spacebar** to return to your original position in the document. If necessary, replace the Learning diskette with the data diskette.

5. Press **F7**, press **Enter**, then type **C:\WP50\DOCS\SORRY.WPF**. Press **Enter** to save the document.

6. Type **Y** to exit WordPerfect.

7. Turn to Module 10 to continue the learning sequence.

Module 34

HYPHENATION

DESCRIPTION

Normally, WordPerfect does not hyphenate words. That's because WordPerfect automatically justifies text when a document is printed (Module 39). However, if you want your documents to have more evenly spaced lines as well as a uniform right margin, you can use WordPerfect's Hyphenation feature. Two types of hyphenation are available — manual and automatic. To set hyphenation:

1.   Move the cursor where you want hyphenation to begin and press **Shift-F8**. Type **1** or **L**.

```
   Format: Line

         1 - Hyphenation                     Off

         2 - Hyphenation Zone - Left         10%
                              Right          4%

         3 - Justification                   Yes

         4 - Line Height                     Auto

         5 - Line Numbering                  No

         6 - Line Spacing                    1

         7 - Margins - Left                  1"
                       Right                 1"

         8 - Tab Set                         0", every 0.5"

         9 - Widow/Orphan Protection         No

   Selection: 0
```

2.   Type **1** or **y**.

```
   1 Off; 2 Manual; 3 Auto: 0
```

3.   To turn manual hyphenation on, type **2** or **M**. To turn automatic hyphenation on, type **3** or **A**. Either option will turn on WordPerfect's hyphenation mode from the cursor position through the rest of the document or until you turn hyphenation off.

4.   Press **F7** to return to the document.

MANUAL HYPHENATION   Manual hyphenation lets you make the decisions as to where a word should be hyphenated. With manual hyphenation on, WordPerfect prompts you to position hyphens in text.

```
    Position hyphen; Press ESC per-severance
```

The hyphen in the prompt is located at WordPerfect's best guess as to where the hyphen should be. To select a different location, use the Left Arrow or Right Arrow key to move the hyphen to a break between syllables, for example, between the ''r'' and ''a.'' Press Esc.

```
    There were many periods I considered giving it away. But persever-
ance
```

NOTE
Whenever WordPerfect prompts you to hyphenate a word, you always have the option of not hyphenating that word. Press the Cancel key, F1 (Module 10), and the word in question is shifted down to the next line.

AUTOMATIC HYPHENATION   In automatic hyphenation, WordPerfect uses a set of rules to hyphenate text. With automatic hyphenation, WordPerfect inserts soft hyphens for you into the text as needed. If it cannot determine where a hyphen should be, it prompts you to choose for that word only.

HYPHENATION ZONE   Hyphenation is governed by a hyphenation zone. This zone determines how much or how little text will be hyphenated. The initial setting is 10% or .7" (seven characters) to the left of the right margin and 4% or .25" (2.5 characters) to the right. With a right margin of 74, for example, a zone is established between 67 and 76. If a word begins before or at 67 and continues past 76, WordPerfect designates the word for hyphenation. However, if a word starts after the beginning of the zone, say at 70, and continues to 80, WordPerfect wraps the word to the next line.

The wider the hyphenation zone, the less hyphenating is required. A smaller hyphenation zone has the advantage of more uniform-looking text.

To change the hyphenation zone:

1.   Press **Shift-F8**. Type **1** or **L**. Then type **2** or **Z**.

```
    2 - Hyphenation Zone - Left      10%
                           Right      4%
```

2. Type the amount of space you want on the left side of the hyphenation zone, realizing that in 10-pitch text, there are about 10 characters to the inch. Then type the amount of space to allow on the right side of the zone.

3. Press **F7** to return to the document.

SOFT HYPHEN   When you tell WordPerfect where to hyphenate a word, it puts a soft hyphen into the word you are hyphenating. A soft hyphen goes away when you edit. For example:

```
There were many times I considered giving it away. But persever-
ance
```

If you insert the word "when" between "times" and "I" and press Down Arrow, you see:

```
There were many times when I considered giving it away. But
perseverance
```

Notice the hyphen is no longer there. A soft hyphen disappears when it is no longer needed. You can add soft hyphens to any word in a document. Press Ctrl- - to put a soft hyphen into the middle of any word. This tells WordPerfect where you want to split the word if it needs to be hyphenated.

HARD HYPHEN   You can also add hard hyphens to text. A hard hyphen is a required hyphen that is not removed when a word wraps to the next line. Hard hyphens are useful for words or phrases like jack-of-all-trades or sister-in-law. Type - to add a hard hyphen to text.

HYPHEN CHARACTER   Hyphen characters look just like hard hyphens, but WordPerfect treats text with hyphen characters as one word, while it treats text with hard hyphens as separate words. To create a hyphen character, press Home- -.

DASHES   To create a dash, or double hyphen, type a hyphen character then a hard hyphen.

APPLICATIONS

Hyphenation gives the right margin a more even appearance. Use hyphenation in documents where you consider that to be important. Use hard hyphens in all words that have required hyphens in them. Use soft hyphens to tell WordPerfect where you want a word to be hyphenated if it becomes necessary.

TYPICAL OPERATION

This example illustrates the use of hyphenation.

1. Create a document similar to the following:

```
MEMO

FROM: JOG
TO: FLG
SUBJECT: TALLAHASSEE BRANCH

        I am honored that you asked me to open the store in
Tallahassee. I want you to know that I consider it an honor to be
a part of your operation. There aren't too many companies like
yours in existence anymore. I only hope that yours and others like
it can continue to prosper. My answer to your question has to
automatically be yes!

                                        Doc 1 Pg 1 Ln 3" Pos 1"
```

2. Move the cursor to the beginning of the document and press **Shift-F8**. Type **1** or **L**, **1** or **y**, then **2** or **M** to turn on manual hyphenation.

3. Type **2** or **Z**. Type **5**, then press **Down Arrow** twice to set the hyphenation zone at 5% for the left and 4% for the right. Then press **Enter**. Press **F7** to return to the document.

```
Position hyphen; Press ESC Tallahas-see.
```

4. Since the hyphen is located at a good break, press **Esc**.

```
Position hyphen; Press ESC automatical-ly
```

5. Press **Left Arrow** to move the cursor between the "c" and "a." Press **Esc**.

```
MEMO

FROM: JOG
TO: FLG
SUBJECT: TALLAHASSEE BRANCH

        I am honored that you asked me to open the store in Tallahas-
see. I want you to know that I consider it an honor to be a part
of your operation. There aren't too many companies like yours in
existence anymore. I only hope that yours and others like it can
continue to prosper. My answer to your question has to automatic-
ally be yes!

                                        Doc 1 Pg 1 Ln 3" Pos 1"
```

6. Save the document as JOG.WPF.

7. Turn to Module 67 to continue the learning sequence.

Module 35

INDENT

DESCRIPTION

The Indent key (F4) indents each line of a paragraph. In contrast, the Tab key (Module 70) indents only the first line. The Indent key and the Tab key share the same tab stops. The paragraph indents one tab stop each time you press F4. Once you press F4, WordPerfect indents all text from that point until you press Enter. The Indent key is useful for indenting paragraphs in reports, outlines, and other documents.

To indent text you have already typed, move the cursor to the beginning of the paragraph you want to indent and press F4. Then move the cursor to the bottom of the paragraph to rewrite the screen. Or, use the Block key (Module 8) to indent a block of text.

TIP: You don't have to indent text at the beginning of a line. You can use the Indent key to indent text in the middle of a line, such as in lists where numbers would not be indented.

The Left/Right Indent (Shift-F4) is similar to Indent. Each time you press Shift-F4, it indents text one tab stop from the left and an equal amount from the right. This feature is useful for centering paragraphs, for long quotes, or in other instances where you want text to stand out from the rest of the document. All notes, cautions, and warnings in this book are examples of left/right indented text.

Here is an example of two normal paragraphs. Notice the first line in each paragraph is indented to the first tab stop.

```
     Officers of the Office Automation Society, thank you for
attending my speech. My name is Michael David and I am Vice
President of FLG Office Supply, an office automation and supply
store based in Carbondale, Illinois, the home of the SIU Salukis.
I am indeed pleased to be addressing you tonight.
     Most of the concerns that we share as office automation
professionals are vastly different from those we shared just a few
years ago. As computers proliferate into businesses, we find our
customers need things they didn't need before, like continuous-feed
paper, and stop buying items we couldn't order fast enough before,
like typing correction fluid.
```

In the following example, the second paragraph is indented to the first tab stop.

```
        Officers of the Office Automation Society, thank you for
attending my speech. My name is Michael David and I am Vice
President of FLG Office Supply, an office automation and supply
store based in Carbondale, Illinois, the home of the SIU Salukis.
I am indeed pleased to be addressing you tonight.
        Most of the concerns that we share as office automation
        professionals are vastly different from those we shared just
        a few years ago. As computers proliferate into businesses, we
        find our customers need things they didn't need before, like
        continuous-feed paper, and stop buying items we couldn't order
        fast enough before, like typing correction fluid.
```

Now, the second paragraph is left/right indented.

```
        Officers of the Office Automation Society, thank you for
attending my speech. My name is Michael David and I am Vice
President of FLG Office Supply, an office automation and supply
store based in Carbondale, Illinois, the home of the SIU Salukis.
I am indeed pleased to be addressing you tonight.
        Most of the concerns that we share as office automation
        professionals are vastly different from those we shared
        just a few years ago. As computers proliferate into
        businesses, we find our customers need things they didn't
        need before, like continuous-feed paper, and stop buying
        items we couldn't order fast enough before, like typing
        correction fluid.
```

APPLICATIONS

Use the Indent key to give paragraphs a uniform left margin in outlines, reports, tables, charts, and other documents. Use Left/Right Indent to make paragraphs stand out from the rest of the document.

TYPICAL OPERATION

In this example, you use Indent, Left/Right Indent, and Tab keys to format a report. This example also demonstrates the use of tabs on the same line as indents.

1. Create a document similar to the following:

```
FROM: FLG
TO: MSD
SUBJECT: PERFORMANCE OF STAFF

Michael:

I am not pleased with the latest numbers. They indicate a lack of
effort by the staff in certain areas. Here is what I propose:

1. There must be a special effort to sell Acme Lumber Company on
Michaels. Those people come in here all the time and walk away. It
seems they are disappointed with our prices. Why can't we make a
volume deal with them? Assign Garry Levin to that task please.

NOTE: Large companies like Acme are the foundation on which we can
grow. This should be our number one priority!

2. I would appreciate it if our new hire, Brian Samuelson, showed
some enthusiasm. That man has been on staff for nearly four weeks
and I've barely noticed him smiling. Why don't you give him a pep
talk and encourage him to show customers that he's really
interested in our products? If he doesn't I'm afraid we'll have to
fire him.
                                        Doc 1 Pg 1 Ln 2.5" Pos 1"
```

2. Move the cursor to the number "1" in the second paragraph and press **Tab**.

3. Move the cursor to the "T" in "There" and press **F4**. Move the cursor to the next paragraph.

```
I am not pleased with the latest numbers. They indicate a lack of
effort by the staff in certain areas. Here is what I propose:

    1.      There must be a special effort to sell Acme Lumber
            Company on Michaels. Those people come in here all the
            time and walk away. It seems they are disappointed with
            our prices. Why can't we make a volume deal with them?
            Assign Garry Levin to that task please.

NOTE: Large companies like Acme are the foundation on which we can
grow. This should be our number one priority!
                                        Doc 1 Pg 1 Ln 3.5" Pos 1"
```

4. With the cursor on the "N" in "NOTE," press **Shift-F4** three times. This creates a left/right indent that is three tab stops in on both the left and the right. Move the cursor to the next paragraph.

```
            NOTE: Large companies like Acme are
            the foundation on which we can grow.
            This should be our number one
            priority!

2. I would appreciate it if our new hire, Brian Samuelson, showed
some enthusiasm. That man has been on staff for nearly four weeks
and I've barely noticed him smiling. Why don't you give him a pep
talk and encourage him to show customers that he's really
                                    Doc 1 Pg 1 Ln 4.33" Pos 1"
```

5. With the cursor on the number "2," press **Tab**. Move the cursor to the word "I" and press **F4**.
6. Move the cursor to the end of the document.

```
Michael:

I am not pleased with the latest numbers. They indicate a lack of
effort by the staff in certain areas. Here is what I propose:

    1.    There must be a special effort to sell Acme Lumber
          Company on Michaels. Those people come in here all the
          time and walk away. It seems they are disappointed with
          our prices. Why can't we make a volume deal with them?
          Assign Garry Levin to that task please.

              NOTE: Large companies like Acme are
              the foundation on which we can grow.
              This should be our number one
              priority!

    2.    I would appreciate it if our new hire, Brian Samuelson,
          showed some enthusiasm. That man has been on staff for
          nearly four weeks and I've barely noticed him smiling.
          Why don't you give him a pep talk and encourage him to
          show customers that he's really interested in our
          products? If he doesn't I'm afraid we'll have to fire
          him.
    _
                                    Doc 1 Pg 1 Ln 5.5" Pos 1"
```

7. Save the document as SAMUEL.WPF.
8. Turn to Module 4 to continue the learning sequence.

Module 36
INDEX

DESCRIPTION

WordPerfect helps you generate an index automatically. If you have ever created one by hand, you know what a useful feature this is. You can create an index for a document as large as this book or as small as a one-page report. It is, of course, most useful for large documents. Use the Mark Text key (Alt-F5) to define the index.

Text for the index comes from both the document and written information. This is because indexes are created on two levels: master heading and subheading. Therefore, if you have written a book about nature, for example, you can have headings for flowers, trees, and animals, and subheadings for roses, maples, and dogs, among others. While the subheadings will be in the text, the master headings may not.

If you use WordPerfect's Master Document feature, an index can be generated for a series of linked documents. Master Documents are explained in Module 44.

There are three steps to creating an index:

1. Mark the text to be included in the index and/or create a concordance file
2. Define the style of the index
3. Generate the index

MARKING TEXT FOR AN INDEX   The best way to mark text for an index is as you create the document. Whenever you type a word or phrase that you feel should be indexed, mark it. The text you mark for your index is given a code that cannot be seen without using Alt-F3, the Reveal Codes key (Module 59). If you make a mistake while marking text, use the Reveal Codes key to delete the code and then re-mark the text. To mark text for an index:

1. Move the cursor to the beginning of the text to mark and press **Alt-F4**, the Block key (Module 8). Then move the cursor to define the block of text to mark and press **Alt-F5**.

```
   Mark for: 1 ToC; 2 List; 3 Index; 4 ToA: 0
```

2. Type **3** or **I**.

```
   Index heading: Test
```

3. Text after the Index Heading prompt will be the text you have marked in the block. If that is how you want the heading in the index to read, press **Enter**. If you want the heading to read as something else, type what you want and press **Enter**.

```
    Subheading:
```

4. If you did not select the block of text for an index heading, it is listed again after the subheading prompt. If you want this text to be a subheading in the index, press **Enter**.

5. If you did select the block of text for the index heading, the subheading is blank. Type a new subheading, if desired, and press **Enter**. If you do not want a subheading, leave the line blank and press **Enter**.

MARKING TEXT WITHOUT THE BLOCK KEY   You can mark text for an index without using the Block key.

1. Move the cursor to a word you want in the index and press **Alt-F5**.

```
    1 Auto Ref; 2 Subdoc; 3 Index; 4 ToA Short Form; 5 Define; 6 Generate: 0
```

2. Type **3** or **I**. Notice the "Index Heading:" prompt. The word the cursor is on is listed after "Index Heading." If you want that word as the index heading, press **Enter**. Or, enter a different heading and press **Enter**. Notice the "Subheading Prompt."

3. If you did not select the word in your text for an index heading, it is listed again. If you want this text to be a subheading in the index, press **Enter**.

4. If you did select the word in your text for the index heading, the subheading is blank. You may type a new subheading and press **Enter**. Or, if you do not want a subheading, press **Enter**.

CONCORDANCE   By definition, a concordance is an alphabetical index. WordPerfect lets you create a concordance file, telling WordPerfect what words or phrases you want in an index. WordPerfect then searches through your document for the words or phrases and adds them to the index. This saves you the trouble of searching through the document and marking the words for indexing.

Create a concordance file in the same manner as any other file:

1. Start with a blank screen. Use the index headings you want. Then type the words you want listed in the index, separating each word or phrase with a hard return (by pressing **Enter** after it).

2. Save the file.

When WordPerfect generates the index, it searches for words in the concordance file. If those words are in the document, it indexes them. If the word has not been marked for indexing, WordPerfect indexes the word the way it is marked in the concordance file with no subheading. If the word is marked, WordPerfect uses the heading and subheading information included in the document.

DEFINE THE STYLE OF THE INDEX   Before you can generate the index, you must define a style for it. Would you like page numbers? Where would you like them? How would you like them to look? WordPerfect gives you several choices to help you answer these questions. To define the style:

NOTE
The index must be generated with the cursor in
a location that is after all marked text in the
document.

1. Move the cursor to the place you want the index to begin, usually at the very end of a document. Type a heading for the index and press **Alt-F5**. Then type **5** or **D**.

```
Mark Text: Define

        1 - Define Table of Contents

        2 - Define List

        3 - Define Index

        4 - Define Table of Authorities

        5 - Edit Table of Authorities Full Form

    Selection: 0
```

2. Type **3** or **I**.

```
Concordance Filename (Enter=none):
```

3. Type the name of the concordance file, if any, and press **Enter**. You see the Index Definition menu.

```
Index Definition

        1 - No Page Numbers

        2 - Page Numbers Follow Entries

        3 - (Page Numbers) Follow Entries

        4 - Flush Right Page Numbers

        5 - Flush Right Page Numbers with Leaders


Selection: 0
```

4. Type **1** or **N** if you want index headings with no page numbers, **2** or **P** if you want page numbers following index entries, **3** or **(** if you want page numbers in parentheses following index entries, **4** or **F** if you want flush right page numbers, and **5** or **L** if you want flush right page numbers with leaders (a dotted line usually used only in Tables of Contents).

GENERATE AN INDEX   Once you have marked the text and defined the page numbering style for your index, you are ready to generate it. To generate an index:

1. Leave the cursor where you defined the style and press **Alt-F5**. Then type **6** or **G**.

```
Mark Text: Generate

        1 - Remove Redline Markings and Strikeout Text from Document

        2 - Compare Screen and Disk Documents and Add Redline and Strikeout

        3 - Expand Master Document

        4 - Condense Master Document

        5 - Generate Tables, Indexes, Automatic References, etc.
```

2. Type **5** or **G**.

```
Existing tables, lists, and indexes will be replaced.  Continue? (Y/N) Yes
```

3. WordPerfect automatically deletes the old index when you generate a new one. If you have previously created an index in this document, either delete it before continuing or WordPerfect deletes it for you. Use the Block delete command to delete it (Module 17). If you have deleted the index, type **Y**.

4. WordPerfect now generates the index. While the index is being generated, a "counter" at the bottom left of the screen counts from one to ten to inform you of its progress. When it is completed, the index appears on-screen.

NOTE

If you are generating a particularly large index,
you might need to create a separate document.
WordPerfect prompts you in this case to switch
documents by pressing Shift-F3 (Module 22) and
will generate the index there.

APPLICATIONS

The Index feature is useful for reports, chapters, books, or a variety of large and small documents. Indexes can be useful in documents as short as two pages. The Master Document feature makes it possible to link several documents together and generate one index for all the documents. The Concordance feature makes it easy to generate an index without having to first mark the text.

TYPICAL OPERATION

In this example, you use the mark text feature to index the annual report created in Module 6. This example includes only two pages of the report. Imagine the rest of the index is included.

1. Start WordPerfect and retrieve the file ANNUAL.WPF, which was created in Module 6. Portions of the report are shown here. Refer to Module 6 to see the entire document.

```
                        INCOME STATEMENT
                        FLG OFFICE SUPPLIES
                 FOR YEAR ENDED DECEMBER 31, 1986

Sales:                    $625,000
Less: Cost of Goods:       375,000
Gross Margin:                              $250,000
=================================================================================
                        BALANCE SHEET
                        FLG OFFICE SUPPLIES
                 FOR YEAR ENDED DECEMBER 31, 1986

C:\WP50\DOCS\ANNUAL.WPF                      Doc 1 Pg 9 Ln 1.5" Pos 1"
```

2. Move the cursor to the "I" in INCOME STATEMENT and press **Alt-F4**. Then move the cursor to the right until "INCOME STATEMENT" is highlighted and press **Alt-F5**. Type **3** or **I**.

```
Index heading: INCOME STATEMENT
```

3. Type **Income Statement** so the heading is not all uppercase and press **Enter**. Then at the prompt for (reference to) subheading, press **Enter**.

4. Move the cursor to the "S" in "Sales" and press **Alt-F5**. Type **3** or **I**. At the index heading prompt, type **Income Statement** and press **Enter**. Sales should appear at the subheading prompt. Press **Enter**.

5. Move the cursor to the "O" in "Operating Expenses," press **Alt-F4**, and define "Operating Expenses" as a block of text. Then press **Alt-F5** and type **3** or **I**. Type **Income Statement** and press **Enter** at the index heading prompt. Then press **Enter** to index "Operating Expenses" as a subheading.

6. Move the cursor to the "N" in "Net Profit" and press **Alt-F4**. Define "Net Profit" as a block of text. Then Press **Alt-F5** and type **3** or **I**. Type **Income Statement** and press **Enter** at the index heading prompt. Then press **Enter** again to index "Net Profit" as a subheading.

7. Move the cursor to the "B" in "BALANCE SHEET" and press **Alt-F4**. Define "BALANCE SHEET" as a block of text. Then press **Alt-F5** and type **3** or **I**. Type **Balance Sheet** and press **Enter** to create Balance Sheet as another major heading. Then press **Enter** so you do not create a subheading for this entry.

8. Repeat these procedures to define "Assets," "Liabilities," and "Equity" as subheadings under Balance Sheet.

9. Move the cursor to the end of the document and press **Ctrl-Enter** to create a new page (Module 41). Then press **F6**, type **INDEX**, and press **F6** again. Press **Enter** twice.

10. Press **Alt-F5** and type **5** or **D**. Then type **3** or **I**. Press **Enter** to signify no concordance file. Then type **2** or **P** to define an index where page numbers follow entries.

11. Leave the cursor in the same location where you defined the style and press **Alt-F5**. Then type **6** or **G**.

12. Type **5** or **G** and then **Y**. The completed index looks like this:

```
INDEX

Balance Sheet  9
     Assets  9
     Equity  9
     Liabilities  9
Income Statement  8
     Net Profit  8
     Operating Expenses  8
     Sales  8
```

13. Save the document as INDEX.WPF.

14. Turn to Module 41 to continue the learning sequence.

Module 37
INSERT

DESCRIPTION

When editing a document, you often want to insert some text to add information, make something more grammatically correct, or correct spelling errors.

WordPerfect lets you insert text anytime. It is naturally in the insert mode, meaning you can go to any line of text in a document and add something to it. When you type, text that is to the right of the cursor is pushed forward and new text is inserted in its place. To insert text you move the cursor to where you want the text and type normally.

TYPEOVER   There are other times you want to type over certain text, deleting the old text and replacing it with new words. To use the typeover mode you move the cursor to the text to type over and press Ins. A "Typeover" message appears at the bottom left of the screen. Any text you type now will type over other text in your document.

NOTE
The typeover mode does not work for text that is boldface or underlined. The code for bold or underline must be deleted before you attempt to type over text.

APPLICATIONS

Use the insert mode to add text to a document without deleting anything. Use the typeover mode to add new text and delete old text at the same time.

TYPICAL OPERATION

In this example, you use both the typeover mode and the insert mode to edit a letter.

1. Start WordPerfect and create a document similar to the following:

```
                                        FLG Office Supply
                                        124 N. Main
                                        Carbondale, IL 62901
                                        January 21, 1987

Mr. Garry J. Levin
2746 Fremont
Murphysboro, IL 62957

Dear Sir:

Thank you for your order of December 27. We want you to know that
we really appreciate your business. However, Mr. Levin, we want to
notifi you that there has been a problem with your order. The 5000
manila file folders that you ordered are temporarily out of stock.
We want you to know that we are making every effort to fill your
order as soon as possible and apologize for any delay.

                                        Sincerely,

                                        John Mathews
                                        Office Manager


Typeover                                    Doc 1 Pg 1 Ln 4.66" Pos 1"
```

2. Move the cursor to the "i" in "notifi" in the third sentence and press **Ins**. Then type **y**. Notice the "y" replaces the "i."

```
we really appreciate your business. However, Mr. Levin, we want to
notify_you that there has been a problem with your order. The 5000
manila file folders that you ordered are temporarily out of stock.

Typeover                                    Doc 1 Pg 1 Ln 3.16" Pos 1.6"
```

3. Press **Ins** to turn the typeover mode off. Move the cursor to the space after the "d" in "ordered" and type **(Part Number J4278W)**. Press the **Spacebar** and then **Down Arrow** to reformat the paragraph.

```
notify you that there has been a problem with your order. The 5000
manila file folders that you ordered (Part Number J4278W)_are
temporarily out of stock. We want you to know that we are making

                                        Doc 1 Pg 1 Ln 3.5" Pos 6.8"
```

4. Move the cursor to the "d" in "delay" in the last sentence of the letter, press **Ins** to turn the typeover mode on and type **incon**. Then, press **Ins** to turn the typeover mode off and type **venience this may have caused you.**

```
                                  FLG Office Supply
                                  124 N. Main
                                  Carbondale, IL 62901
                                  January 21, 1987


Mr. Garry J. Levin
2746 Fremont
Murphysboro, IL 62957

Dear Sir:

Thank you for your order of December 27. We want you to know that
we really appreciate your business. However, Mr. Levin, we want to
notify you that there has been a problem with your order. The 5000
manila file folders that you ordered (Part Number J4278W) are
temporarily out of stock. We want you to know that we are making
every effort to fill your order as soon as possible and apologize
for any inconvenience this may have caused you.


                                  Sincerely,

                                  John Mathews
                                  Office Manager


                                  Doc 1 Pg 1 Ln 3.83" Pos 5.6"
```

5. Save the document as SORRY2.WPF.

6. Turn to Module 17 to continue the learning sequence.

Module 38

LINE DRAWING

DESCRIPTION

It is often necessary to draw lines for tables, charts, boxes, and the like. WordPerfect gives you that ability with its Line Drawing feature (Ctrl-F3).

You can draw on a blank screen or around other characters. Use the cursor control keys (Module 15) to create lines, double lines, asterisks, and other graphics characters. Eleven characters are available to you, and WordPerfect gives you the option of adding your own. Corners are inserted automatically. And, you can change characters in the middle of a session.

While everything might look right on-screen, there could be a problem when you send the document to your printer. You can substitute characters your printer can handle like "¦" for vertical lines, the " + " sign for corners, and the " − " sign for horizontal lines.

When you draw lines, it takes twice as many keystrokes to move the cursor to the left or right as it does to move up or down (with single-spaced text).

Line Draw works in typeover mode (Module 37). It deletes any characters in its path.

WordPerfect also lets you draw lines with its Graphics feature. Graphics lines can be shaded, adjusted, positioned on the page, and scaled for length. To use Line Draw:

1. Press **Ctrl-F3** and type **2** or **L**.

This is the Line Draw menu. Use it to select the major character in your line. For normal lines, type 1, for double lines, type 2, for asterisks, type 3, for other characters, type 4. To erase a line, type 5, and to move a line, type 6.

If you type 1, 2, or 3, you immediately go into line drawing mode. Use the cursor control keys to draw the line or shape you want to create.

2. For example, type **1** to select single lines and press **Right Arrow** eight times and **Down Arrow** four times. Then press **Left Arrow** eight times and **Up Arrow** four times.

TIP: The easiest way to draw lines is to use the Esc key (Module 24). If you want to draw a line that is 38 spaces long, for example, change the repeat value to 38 and press Right Arrow.

NOTE

Remember to exit the Line Draw menu before
trying to type your document. If you do not, you
may delete several characters from your text.

3. Press **F7** or type **0** to return to your document.

CHANGING THE THIRD CHARACTER   Single and double lines, the first two characters in the Line Draw menu, are fixed. The asterisk, the third character, however, is not. To change the third character:

1. Press **Ctrl-F3** and type **2** or **L**, then **4**.

```
   1 ▌: 2 ▓: 3 ▐: 4 ▉: 5 ▪: 6 │: 7 ▏: 8 ▀: 9 Other: 0
```

2. Type any number between **1** and **8** to replace the asterisk with that character. If you want to use another character, or if you have replaced the asterisk and would like to make it the third character again, type **9**.

```
   Solid character:
```

3. Type any character, either from your keyboard, or by using an Alt-key sequence with your numeric keypad. The Alt-key sequence lets you select from 256 ASCII characters, of which the characters on your keyboard are many. Alt-56, for example, is the number eight (8). Be aware that your printer may not support many of these characters.

CAUTION

If you use these characters, press the keys on the
numeric keypad. If you press an Alt-key sequence
using the numbers along the top of the keyboard,
chaos may result.

4. To use the selected character in line drawing mode, type **3**.
5. When you are finished, press **F7** or type **0** to leave the line drawing mode.

ERASING CHARACTERS   The Erase command makes the blank space a character in line drawing mode. It erases everything in its path. To erase characters:

1. If you are not already in line drawing mode, move the cursor to the desired location and press **Ctrl-F3**. Type **2** or **L**, then type **5**.

2. Use the cursor control keys as if you are drawing a line. Notice that every time you press a cursor control key, the character in that space is erased. You can even use the **Esc** key as described above to erase a number of spaces at once.

3. Type **1**, **2**, or **3** to continue line drawing, or press **F7** or type **0** to leave the line drawing mode.

MOVING THE CURSOR   The Move option lets you move the cursor from one location to another without creating characters. This is useful if you want to begin another box, or draw a box inside of another box, for example. To use the Move option:

1. Press **Ctrl-F3**, type **2**, then type **6**.

2. Position the cursor where you want to begin drawing the line and type **1**, **2**, or **3**, to select a character.

GRAPHICS LINES   The Graphics Lines feature makes it easy to draw horizontal or vertical lines on a page. You can position the line on the page, adjust it for length and width, and shade it.

Graphics lines do not appear on-screen during normal editing. To see them, select WordPerfect's View Document feature (Module 57). This lets you see what a printed version of a document looks like before it's printed.

To use graphics lines:

1. Press **Alt-F9**.

```
1 Figure; 2 Table; 3 Text Box; 4 User-defined Box; 5 Line: 0
```

2. Type **5** or **L**, then type **1** or **H** to create a horizontal line; **2** or **V** to create a vertical line. This is the display for a vertical line; the horizontal line screen is very similar.

```
Graphics: Vertical Line

     1 - Horizontal Position          Left Margin

     2 - Vertical Position            Full Page

     3 - Length of Line

     4 - Width of Line                0.01"

     5 - Gray Shading (% of black)    100%


Selection: 0
```

3. Type **1** or **H**.

```
 Horizontal Position: 1 Left; 2 Right; 3 Between Columns; 4 Set Position: 0
```

This option lets you position the line horizontally on the page. The default setting is to the left of the left margin selected by typing 1 or L. Typing 2 or R puts it just to the right margin; 3 or B puts it between two specific column numbers that you name; and 4 or S lets you set the position of the line on the page.

4. Type **2** or **V**.

```
 Vertical Position: 1 Full Page; 2 Top; 3 Center; 4 Bottom; 5 Set Position: 0
```

This lets you position the line vertically on the page. The default setting creates a full page vertical line, selected by typing 1 or F. If you want the line to go from one end of the page to the other, type 1 or F. To position the line at the top of the page, type 2 or T. To center it vertically on the page, type 3 or C. To put it on the bottom of the page, type 4 or B. To set its position manually on the page, type 5 or S.

5. Type **3** or **L** to set the length of the line on the page. Type the length you want the line to be, in inches, and press **Enter**.

6. Type **4** or **W** to set the width, or thickness, of the line. Type the width you want the line to be, in inches, and press **Enter**.

7. Type **5** or **G** to set the shading for the line. The higher the percentage, the darker the line.

8. Press **F7** to save your changes.

APPLICATIONS

Line drawing is useful for boxes, graphs, and other pictures. Use it whenever you need to draw boxes or create illustrations. Graphics lines are good for dividing columns on newsletters, putting a horizontal line on a page for effect, and for other desktop publishing applications.

TYPICAL OPERATION

This example shows you how to draw a border around a document title.

1. Start WordPerfect and retrieve FINANCES.WPF, the document you created in Module 15. Press **PgDn** to move to the next page.

```
                        INCOME STATEMENT
                      FLG OFFICE SUPPLIES
                 FOR YEAR ENDED DECEMBER 31, 1986

   Sales:                  $625,000
   Less: Cost of Goods:     375,000
   Gross Margin:                          $250,000

   C:\WP50\DOCS\FINANCES.WPF              Doc 1 Pg 2 Ln 1.16" Pos 1"
```

2. Press **Enter** twice. Then press **Ctrl-F3** and type **2** or **L**.

3. Type **6**, then press **Up Arrow**.

4. Move the cursor to position 2.3 and type **1**. Then press **Esc**. Type **38** to set the repeat value to 38 and press **Enter**.

5. Press **Esc-Right Arrow**.

```
         <------------------------------------------->
                        INCOME STATEMENT
                      FLG OFFICE SUPPLIES
                 FOR YEAR ENDED DECEMBER 31, 1986
```

6. Press **Down Arrow** four times and then press **Esc-Left Arrow**.

7. Press **Up Arrow** four times.

```
              +------------------------------------+
              |          INCOME STATEMENT          |
              |         FLG OFFICE SUPPLIES         |
              |    FOR YEAR ENDED DECEMBER 31, 1986 |
              +------------------------------------+
```

8. Press **F7** or type **0** to leave the line drawing mode.

9. Save the document as STATMENT.WPF.

   This is the last Module of the recommended learning sequence.

Module 39
LINE FORMAT

DESCRIPTION

The Line Format option provides a number of ways to manipulate and arrange text on a line. It helps you set spacing, tabs, line height, margins, and hyphenation. It also lets you number lines, turn justification on and off, and provide for widow/orphan protection.

Many of these options are covered in other modules. Hyphenation is discussed in Module 34, margins in Module 43, spacing and leading (line height) in Module 63, and Tabs in Module 70. The rest of the options are discussed in this module.

JUSTIFICATION   Text is always left-justified, meaning it always lines up at the left margin. You can also make text line up at the right margin. This is called right justification. WordPerfect does this by adjusting the spacing between characters to make text line up at the right margin. While you cannot see this on the screen, the document is right-justified when it is printed. WordPerfect normally turns right justification on. However, you can turn this option off if you like. To set justification:

1.   Move the cursor to the place where you want right justification to be turned on or off. Then, press **Shift-F8** and type **1** or **L**.

```
   Format: Line

        1 - Hyphenation                          Off

        2 - Hyphenation Zone - Left              10%
                               Right             4%

        3 - Justification                        Yes

        4 - Line Height                          Auto

        5 - Line Numbering                       No

        6 - Line Spacing                         1

        7 - Margins - Left                       1"
                      Right                      1"

        8 - Tab Set                              0", every 0.5"

        9 - Widow/Orphan Protection              No

   Selection: 0
```

2.   Type **3** or **J**. Type **Y** to turn justification on or **N** to turn justification off. Press **F7** to return to the document.

LINE NUMBERING   WordPerfect already numbers lines on-screen, just look at the Status Line. The line numbering feature lets you see the line numbers when the document is printed. This is often helpful for reference purposes. To perform Line Numbering:

1. Press **Shift-F8** and type **1** or **L**. Type **5** or **N** and type **Y**. Notice the following display:

```
Format: Line Numbering

        1 - Count Blank Lines                          Yes

        2 - Number Every n Lines, where n is           1

        3 - Position of Number from Left Edge          0.6"

        4 - Starting Number                            1

        5 - Restart Numbering on Each Page             Yes


    Selection: 0
```

2. Line numbering usually counts blank lines. If you don't want it to count blank lines, type **1** or **C**, then **N**.

3. To have line numbering not count every line, set "n" higher than one. For example, to count every other line, type **2** or **N**, then type **2**.

4. Type **3** or **P** to position the line number on the page. Then type the distance, in inches from the left margin, where you want line numbers to appear. Press **Enter**.

5. Type **4** or **S** to change the starting line number from 1 to another number. Type the number you want numbering to begin with and press **Enter**.

6. Type **5** or **R**. Type **Y** if you want line numbering to start over on each page. Type **N** if you want continuous line numbering for an entire document.

7. Press **F7** to return to the document.

WIDOWS AND ORPHANS   A widow is the first line of a paragraph appearing by itself on the last line of a page. An orphan is the last line of a paragraph appearing by itself as the first line of a page. By default, WordPerfect does not offer protection against widows and orphans. However, you can prevent widows and orphans from occurring if you prefer. If Widow and Orphan Protection is on, widows and one line preceding an orphan are moved to the next page.

To protect against widows and orphans:

1. With the cursor at the top of the document, press **Shift-F8** and type **1** or **L**.

2. Type **9** or **W** and type **Y**. Press **F7** to return to the document.

APPLICATIONS

Justification results in more appealing documents since right-justified documents are generally more attractive than non-justified ones. Line numbering is useful for lists, instructions, tables, legal documents, and other applications where line numbers are helpful. Widow and orphan protection generally provides documents that are easier to read.

TYPICAL OPERATION

This operation illustrates the use of line numbering in a list.

1. Start WordPerfect and create a document similar to the following:

```
Textbooks
Pens
Steno Pads
Notebooks
Pencils
Erasers
Illustrator Pads
Printer Paper
Ribbons
Toner
Diskettes
Paperbacks
```

2. This is a "shopping list" of items for FLG to purchase at the office supply distributor. Move the cursor to the "T" in "Textbooks." Press **Alt-F4**. Then move the cursor to the bottom of the page to define the entire page as a block of text.

3. Press **Ctrl-F9** and type **1** or **P** to sort the block (Module 62).

```
Diskettes
Erasers
Illustrator Pads
Notebooks
Paperbacks
Pencils
Pens
Printer Paper
Ribbons
Steno Pads
Textbooks
Toner
```

4. Press **Shift-F8** and type **1** or **L**. Type **5** or **N** and type **Y** to turn Line Numbering on.

5. Type **1** or **C**, then type **N** so blank lines aren't counted.

6. Press **F7** to return to the document. This is what the document looks like when it is printed:

```
        1       Diskettes
        2       Erasers
        3       Illustrator Pads
        4       Notebooks
        5       Paperbacks
        6       Pencils
        7       Pens
        8       Printer Paper
        9       Ribbons
       10       Steno Pads
       11       Textbooks
       12       Toner
```

7. Save the document as SHOP.WPF.

8. Turn to Module 6 to continue the learning sequence.

Module 40

LIST FILES

DESCRIPTION

Normally, if you want to edit a file that has been edited before, the first thing you do after starting WordPerfect is use the List Files key (F5) to look at the files on a particular diskette or directory. A typical file listing is shown here:

```
06/07/88  14:16              Directory C:\WP50\DOCS\*.*
Document size:       0   Free:  8622080   Used:      4833          Files:  5

.  <CURRENT>    <DIR>                  ..  <PARENT>    <DIR>
IDEAS    .WPF      1158  06/07/88 14:15    PRACTICE.WPF      720  06/06/88 08:20
REST     .WPF       895  06/06/88 16:15    SAVE    .WPF      657  06/07/88 13:36
SORRY    .WPF      1403  06/07/88 13:58
1 Retrieve; 2 Delete; 3 Move/Rename; 4 Print; 5 Text In;
6 Look; 7 Other Directory; 8 Copy; 9 Word Search; N Name Search: 6
```

Move the cursor to highlight a file. To move from one file to another, use the cursor control keys. In large directories, you may find it easier to use the PgUp, PgDn, and Screen Up and Screen Down keys. WordPerfect also has a search feature that searches for a file as you type the letters of that file.

WordPerfect lets you choose the files you want to list and lets you change directories to list files in any particular directory. You can also change the default directory (for this session). This makes it easier to retrieve files if you keep your data files in a different directory than the default. (That is highly recommended, by the way.)

The List Files command gives you the filename (the letters before the period) and the extension (the last three letters after the period) of the file, the current document size, the current date and time, the number of files in the current directory, the size of all files, the amount of free space left on the disk, and the date and time each file was last worked on.

A menu at the bottom of the screen gives you the option of *retrieving*, *deleting*, *renaming*, *printing*, or *retrieving* a DOS text file, *looking* at a file, or *copying* a file. You also have the option of *changing* the directory, and performing a *word search* or *name search* of all files to find the file that covers a particular subject. Many of these topics are covered in Module 25, File Management. To leave List Files, press either F7, F1, the Spacebar, or the number 0.

ACCESSING A DIRECTORY WITH LIST FILES   When you press F5 to access the List Files directory, the following message appears on-screen:

```
Dir C:\WP50\*.*                          (Type = to change default Dir)
```

The message indicates that the file directory you are accessing is everything (*.*) in the \ WP50 directory on drive C. If you want to access everything in this directory, press Enter.

NOTE

To access the List Files menu, after you press F5, press any key except F1, the Cancel key. We are using Enter for consistency.

The following display appears:

```
06/07/88  07:48              Directory C:\WP50\*.*
Document size:          0   Free:   8796160   Used:   2806904          Files:   155

MOD65-4 .SCR    8128  06/06/88 09:23  ▲   MOD65-5 .SCR    8128  06/06/88 09:35
MOD65-6 .SCR    8128  06/06/88 09:46      MOD65-7 .SCR    8128  06/06/88 09:46
MOD65-8 .SCR    8128  06/06/88 09:47      MOD65-9 .SCR    8128  06/06/88 09:47
MOD66   .       7296  06/02/88 17:20      MOD67   .       4352  06/02/88 17:20
MOD68   .      11648  06/02/88 17:21      MOD69   .      13696  06/02/88 17:22
MOD70   .       6144  06/02/88 17:24      MOD71   .      25984  06/02/88 17:25
MOD72   .       9216  06/02/88 17:25      PRINTER .TST   17524  04/27/88 11:00
README  .      10516  04/27/88 11:00      README  .WP    12421  04/27/88 11:00
REST    .WPF     895  06/06/88 16:15      RLS     .       4608  06/03/88 13:18
RLS     .BAK    4992  06/02/88 16:26      SPELL   .EXE   37888  04/27/88 14:13
STANDARD.CRS    1932  04/27/88 11:00      STANDARD.PRS    1025  05/05/88 12:47
WP      .EXE  244736  05/05/88 12:47      WP      .FIL  298884  05/05/88 12:47
WP      .MRS    3756  05/05/88 12:47      WPBATCH .        896  06/03/88 08:46
WPBATCH .BAK     896  06/03/88 08:26      WPHELP  .FIL   47587  05/05/88 12:47
WPHELP2 .FIL   52121  05/05/88 12:47      WPSMALL .DRS   13822  05/05/88 12:47
WP{WP}  .SET     863  06/02/88 08:46      WP{WP}EN.LEX  292095  04/27/88 14:13
WP{WP}EN.THS  362269  04/27/88 14:17      WP}WP{  .BV1       0  06/07/88 07:47
WP}WP{  .CHK       0  06/07/88 07:47      WP}WP{  .SPC    4096  06/07/88 07:47
WP}WP{  .TV1       0  06/07/88 07:47

1 Retrieve; 2 Delete; 3 Move/Rename; 4 Print; 5 Text In;
6 Look; 7 Other Directory; 8 Copy; 9 Word Search; N Name Search: 6
```

These are all the files on a hypothetical WordPerfect diskette. Notice all the information on the display. The date and time are in the upper left-hand corner. The directory being accessed is in the middle at the top of the screen. The size of the current document is listed on the second line at left (since you haven't typed anything, the size is 0), space left and used on the diskette is listed to the right, and the number of files in the directory is listed to the far right.

Each filename is listed, plus file size and the date and time of the last time the file was changed. A menu at the bottom of the screen list your options.

LISTING SELECTED FILES WITH LIST FILES If you have a hard disk, all the WordPerfect command files might be in the same directory as the data files. We do not recommend this, as it is better to create sub-directories. In any case, you would not want to have to look through all the files to find the ones you wanted.

If you use a particular three-letter extension, like ".WPF" to distinguish WordPerfect data files from other files, it is a simple matter to look only at those. On a hard disk, the default directory might be "C:\WP50*.*" So the screen looks like this after you press the List Files key:

```
Dir C:\WP50\*.*                                    (Type = to change default Dir)
```

Rather than pressing Enter, type the filename extension of the files you want to retrieve, C:\WP50\DOCS*.WPF. Then press Enter. This retrieves a listing of all the data files on the directory.

```
08/03/88  09:18              Directory  C:\WP50\DOCS\*.WPF
Document size:        0   Free:  6289408   Used:      75896      Files:  52

.  <CURRENT>      <DIR>                 ..  <PARENT>     <DIR>
ANNUAL   .WPF      2611  06/13/88 08:43  ATTACK   .WPF      880  06/10/88 15:50
AUGSALES .WPF       946  06/14/88 13:48  AVERAGE  .WPF     2619  06/08/88 10:28
AVGS     .WPF      1068  08/03/88 08:25  BANQUET  .WPF     1184  06/13/88 13:11
BIRTHDAY .WPF       566  06/08/88 14:29  COLUMN   .WPF      870  06/14/88 13:23
COMMENT  .WPF       658  06/15/88 09:59  CONCERN  .WPF      886  06/09/88 14:41
DRESS    .WPF       582  06/08/88 15:36  FINANCES .WPF     3719  07/18/88 11:53
HISTORY  .WPF      2262  07/19/88 12:59  HOURS    .WPF     1193  06/09/88 13:01
IDEAS    .WPF      1050  06/13/88 08:11  INDEX    .WPF     3338  06/13/88 09:16
JAMES    .WPF      1922  06/09/88 16:37  JOG      .WPF      713  07/18/88 15:00
LEAGUE   .WPF       798  06/08/88 15:57  LEGALDOC .WPF     1102  06/09/88 11:36
LIPSON   .WPF       890  06/09/88 15:07  LIST     .WPF      429  06/13/88 08:04
LISTS    .WPF      2600  07/19/88 07:40  MACROS   .WPF      792  06/14/88 14:46
MASTER   .WPF      3574  07/19/88 08:09  MEMO     .WPF      968  06/09/88 10:08
MEMOS    .WPF      1751  06/07/88 15:54  MEMOTOP  .WPF      462  06/14/88 14:55

1 Retrieve; 2 Delete; 3 Move/Rename; 4 Print; 5 Text In;
6 Look; 7 Other Directory; 8 Copy; 9 Word Search; N Name Search: 6
```

MOVING AROUND THE DIRECTORY In order to use any of the files in the list, you need to move the cursor to those files. Using the arrow keys or the PgUp, PgDn, or Screen Up and Screen Down keys is usually sufficient. But WordPerfect includes another feature that makes accessing files even easier — Name Search. For example, if you typed N (for Name Search) in the preceding directory, then typed m, the cursor would move to "MACROS.WPF," the first file that starts with the letter you typed. Then, if you type e, the cursor would move to "MEMO.WPF."

The Name Search feature of WordPerfect lets you move quickly through large directories to locate files simply by typing a few letters in the filename. To exit the Name Search feature, you press either Enter or any of the arrow keys.

APPLICATIONS

The List Files command is used nearly every time you use WordPerfect, often more than once each session. Use the List Files command anytime you need to look at a list of files on a particular diskette or directory or perform a file management task. Use the Name Search feature to find files quickly.

TYPICAL OPERATION

Assume that you have a directory on your hard disk that includes several files that you want to edit. To make it easier to continuously retrieve those files, you want to change the default directory to C:\WP50\DOCS.

1. Start WordPerfect. Press **F5**, then type = .

2. Type **C:\WP50\DOCS** and press **Enter**.

3. Press **Enter** to access the List Files menu. Then either retrieve or print a document or press the **Spacebar** to return to the document. This changes the default directory to C:\WP50\DOCS until you either change the default directory again, or exit WordPerfect.

4. Turn to Module 25 to continue the learning sequence.

Module 41

LISTS

DESCRIPTION

Some long documents include lists of illustrations, figures, tables, and the like. WordPerfect helps you automatically generate a list. It also helps you generate a table of authorities (Module 68), a table of contents (Module 69) and an index (Module 36). You can create up to nine lists per document. Use the Mark Text key (Alt-F5) to define lists.

Text for the list comes from the document, usually table headings or figure numbers. For example, a list of WordPerfect commands can be generated from the information in this book.

There are three steps to creating a list:

1. Mark the text
2. Define the style of the list
3. Generate the list

If you use WordPerfect's Master Document feature, a list can be generated for a series of linked documents. Master Documents are explained in Module 44.

MARKING TEXT FOR A LIST   The best way to mark text for a list is as you create the document. Whenever you type a word or phrase that you feel should be in a list, mark it and tell WordPerfect which list it should be in. The text you mark for the lists is given a code that cannot be seen without using Alt-F3, the Reveal Codes key (Module 59). If you make a mistake while marking text, use the Reveal Codes key to delete the code and then re-mark the text. To mark text for a list:

1. Move the cursor to the beginning of the text to mark and press **Alt-F4**, the Block key (Module 8). Move the cursor to define the block of text and press **Alt-F5**. Then type **2** or **L**.

```
   List Number:
```

2. Type the number of the list where you want the text included.

DEFINE THE STYLE OF THE LIST   Before you can generate a list, you must define a style for it. Would you like page numbers? Where would you like them? How would you like them to look? WordPerfect gives you several choices to help you answer these questions. To define the style:

NOTE

The list can be generated anywhere in a
document.

1. Position the cursor where you want the list to begin, usually at the very end or very beginning of a document. Then type a heading for the list.

2. Press **Alt-F5**. Type **5** or **D**, then **2** or **L**.

```
List Number (1-9):
```

3. Type the appropriate number between 1 and 9 for the list you are generating. You see the List Definition menu.

```
List 1 Definition

     1 - No Page Numbers

     2 - Page Numbers Follow Entries

     3 - (Page Numbers) Follow Entries

     4 - Flush Right Page Numbers

     5 - Flush Right Page Numbers with Leaders

Selection: 0
```

4. Type **1** or **N** if you want list headings with no page numbers, **2** or **P** if you want page numbers following list entries, **3** or **(** if you want page numbers in parentheses following list entries, **4** or **F** if you want flush right (Module 26) page numbers, or **5** or **L** if you want flush right page numbers with leaders. Leaders are a dotted line between the title and the flush right page number.

GENERATE A LIST   Once you have marked the text and defined the page numbering style for your list, you are ready to generate it. To generate a list:

1. Leave the cursor in the same location where you defined the style and press **Alt-F5**. Type **6** or **G**.

```
Mark Text: Generate

     1 - Remove Redline Markings and Strikeout Text from Document

     2 - Compare Screen and Disk Documents and Add Redline and Strikeout

     3 - Expand Master Document

     4 - Condense Master Document

     5 - Generate Tables, Indexes, Automatic References, etc.

Selection: 0
```

2. Type **5** or **G**.

> Existing tables, lists, and indexes will be replaced. Continue? (Y/N) Yes

3. WordPerfect automatically deletes old lists, tables, and indexes when you generate new ones. If you have previously created a list of the same number in this document, either delete it before continuing or WordPerfect deletes it for you. Use the Block Delete command to delete it (Module 17). If you have deleted the list, type **Y**.

4. WordPerfect now generates the list. While the list is being generated, a note at the bottom left of the screen informs you of its progress. When it is completed, the list appears on-screen.

NOTE

If you are generating a particularly large list, you might need to create a separate document. WordPerfect prompts you in this case to switch documents by pressing Shift-F3 (Module 22) and generates the list there.

APPLICATIONS

Use the List feature to create lists of figures, tables, commands, or any other repetitive item for books, articles, reports, chapters, or any document that would benefit from them.

TYPICAL OPERATION

In this example, you generate two lists, one of tables and one of figures in a fictional document. Use the Page Format key (Module 51) to change the page numbers as indicated in the operation. The dashed line signifies a new page in the document.

1. Create a document that looks similar to the following:

```
                    DETAILS OF FINANCIAL POSITION
                         FLG OFFICE SUPPLY
                         CARBONDALE, IL


    ===========================================================================
    Figure 1. Fixed Assets 1980-1986
    ===========================================================================
    Figure 2. Cash on Hand 1980-1986
    ===========================================================================
    Table 1. Creditors of Record
    ===========================================================================
    Figure 3. Accounts Payable vs. Accounts Receivable
    ===========================================================================
    Figure 4. Equity 1980-86
    ===========================================================================
    Table 2. Equity Holders
    ===========================================================================
```

2. Move the cursor to "Figure 1," which is located on page two and press **Alt-F4**. Then press **End** to highlight the entire figure title and press **Alt-F5**.

3. Type **2** or **L**. Then type **1** to mark this figure for list 1.

4. Move the cursor to Figure 2, which is located on page three, and press **Alt-F4**. Press **End** to highlight the entire figure title and press **Alt-F5**.

5. Type **2** or **L**. Then type **1** to mark this figure for list 1.

6. Move the cursor to Table 1, which is located on page four, and press **Alt-F4**. Then press **End** to highlight the entire table title and press **Alt-F5**.

7. Type **2** or **L**. Then type **2** to mark the table for list 2.

8. Repeat the above procedures, putting figures in list 1, and tables in list 2.

9. Move the cursor to the top of the document and press **Ctrl-Enter** to create a new page.

NOTE
The page locations of the figures and tables
change now that you have created a new page.

10. Move the cursor up to the new page and press **Shift-F6**, the Center key (Module 10) and **F6**, the Boldface key (Module 7). Then type **LIST OF FIGURES** and press **F6**. Press **Enter** twice.

11. Press **Alt-F5**. Type **5** or **D**. Then type **2** or **L**.

12. Type **1** to define list 1. Then type **4** or **F** to define a list with flush right page numbers.

13. Leave the cursor where you defined the style and press **Alt-F5**. Type **6** or **G**. Then type **5** or **G**.

14. Type **Y** in response to the prompt. WordPerfect generates list 1. The completed list looks like this:

```
                        LIST OF FIGURES

   Figure 1. Fixed Assets 1980-1986                       3
   Figure 2. Cash on Hand 1980-1986                       4
   Figure 3. Accounts Payable vs. Accounts Receivable     6
   Figure 4. Equity 1980-86                               7
```

15. Move the cursor just past the list of figures. Press **Enter** twice to separate the lists. Then press **Shift-F6** and **F6** and type **LIST OF TABLES**.

16. Press **F6** and press **Enter** twice.

17. Press **Alt-F5**. Type **5** or **D**. Then type **2** or **L**.

18. Type **2** to define list 2. Then type **5** or **L** to define a list with flush right page numbers and leaders.

19. Leave the cursor where you defined the style and press **Alt-F5**. Type **6** or **G**. Then type **5** or **G**.

20. Type **Y** in response to the prompt. WordPerfect generates list 2. The completed list looks like this:

LIST OF TABLES

```
Table 1. Creditors of Record . . . . . . . . . . . . . . . . . . . 5
Table 2. Equity Holders. . . . . . . . . . . . . . . . . . . . . . 8
```

21. Save the document as LISTS.WPF.
22. Turn to Module 69 to continue the learning sequence.

Module 42
MACROS

DESCRIPTION

A macro is a handy tool that lets you record a series of keystrokes into a file for "playback" at a later time. Macros can save you a lot of time by performing tasks that you do repeatedly, such as typing your name and address at the top of a letter, printing a number of documents, performing search and replace operations, or saving a file.

Macros can perform simple tasks, such as the preceding examples, or a series of tasks, such as searching for words, replacing them with other words, marking them in an index, saving the file, and printing it.

WordPerfect lets you chain macros together — when one macro ends, the next one begins; nest macros — execute one macro inside another; and repeat a macro through the use of the Esc key (Module 24).

Macros in WordPerfect are "visible." In other words, you can see them as they are being executed. You can make them invisible using the Macro Commands key (Ctrl-PgUp). The Macro Commands key also lets you insert a pause into a macro so that you can enter text or perform another command. When you press Enter, the macro resumes execution.

The Macro Commands key also lets you insert variables for advanced macro execution and comments for use in editing macros.

DEFINING A MACRO   Before you use a macro, you must first define, or "record," it. To define a macro:

1. Press **Ctrl-F10**.
2. Type the name of the macro. The name you give it depends on the type of macro you create: permanent or temporary. Permanent macros are those that are saved by WordPerfect for use in later sessions. Names can be one to eight characters or an Alt-key sequence (Alt plus a key on the keyboard). It is more convenient to retrieve a macro that was named with an Alt-key sequence. Temporary macros are those that you do not want to save for another session. To name those, either type one character, or nothing. WordPerfect gives the named macro a .wpm extension. Press **Enter**. Then type a description of the macro that tells you what the macro does and press **Enter** again.
3. Create the macro. Everything you do at this point is included in the macro. You can place a pause in the macro (so users can insert text while invoking the macro) by pressing **Ctrl-PgUp** and typing **2** or **P** and pressing **Enter**. You can even chain another macro to the macro you are defining by pressing **Alt-F10**, typing the name of the old macro, and pressing **Enter** while you are defining another macro.

You cannot start a merge (Module 46) during macro creation. When a merge starts, macro creation automatically stops.

4. To end macro definition, press **Ctrl-F10**.

INVOKING A MACRO   Once you define a macro, you can play it back, or invoke it. If you defined a permanent macro, you can do this anywhere in any document. If you defined a temporary macro, you can only invoke it during that session. If you named a macro with an Alt-key sequence, press the key sequence to invoke the macro. If you used an alternative method to name your macro, press Alt-F10, type the name of the macro, and press Enter. WordPerfect invokes the macro.

NOTE

If you want to repeat the execution of a macro several times, use the Repeat Value (n) in conjunction with the Esc key, as described in Module 24.

EDITING A MACRO   Once you create a macro, you can change how it works through the use of WordPerfect's built-in macro editor. To edit a macro:

1. Press **Ctrl-F10** and type the name of a macro that has already been defined.

```
MARGIN1.WPM is Already Defined.   1 Replace; 2 Edit: 0
```

2. If you wish to replace the macro, type **1** or **R** and define a new macro as described earlier in this module. To edit it, type **2** or **E**.

NOTE

Macro editing is for advanced users only. Those without programming experience should not try to edit macros or use WordPerfect's advanced macro commands.

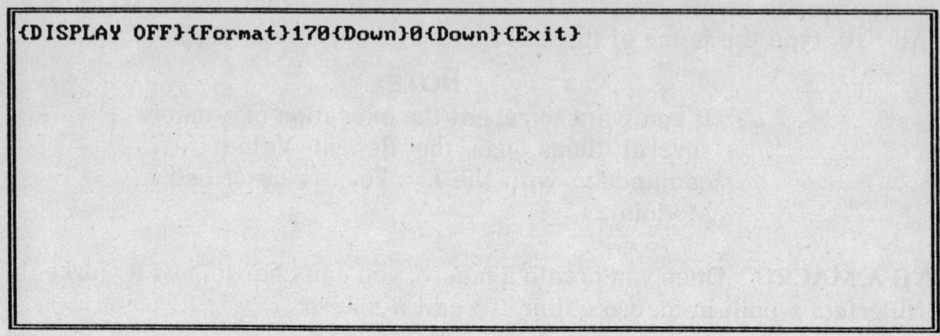

3. Type **1** or **D** to read a description of this macro as created in the macro definition stage. Type **2** or **A** to begin editing. To see a list of commands while editing macros, press **Ctrl-PgUp**, the Macro Commands key.

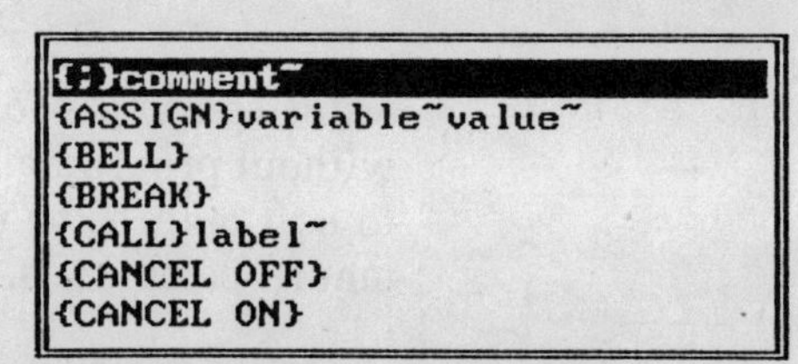

(Name Search; Enter or arrows to Exit)

4. To insert a command inside the macro, move the cursor where you want the command inserted, press **Ctrl-PgUp**, select the command, and press **Enter**. Repeat this procedure as necessary.

5. When you are finished, press **F7** to exit the editor.

CHAINING MACROS   Chaining is a process where two or more macros are chained together. When one macro is completed, the next one automatically starts. There are three types of chains:

- *Simple chain,* where one macro is invoked while another one is being defined. To create a simple chain, define a macro by pressing Ctrl-F10, naming it, and typing all the keystrokes necessary to execute the macro. Press Alt-F10 and type the name of another macro. Then press Ctrl-F10 again to end definition of the first macro. At this point, if the second macro is not defined, you can define it as you would any other macro.

- *Repeating chain,* where one or more macros are repeatedly invoked. A repeating chain only works in conjunction with a Search command (Module 61) because WordPerfect automatically stops invoking a macro when the search command has finished its search through the document. This is especially useful for marking text for indexes, lists, and the table of contents. Use the same procedures to define a repeating chain as you would a simple chain, only make sure a Search command is included in the macro.

- *Conditional chain,* where two or more macros are chained to a macro with a Search command. This makes the macro make a decision. If the Search command finds what it is looking for, WordPerfect invokes one macro, if it does not, WordPerfect invokes another. To create a conditional chain, press Ctrl-F10 and name the macro, for example, "long." Then press Alt-F10 and name the macro to invoke if the search is unsuccessful; call it "short." Then type the keystrokes for the definition of the macro (long), making sure to include at least one Search and Replace operation. When you have completed these procedures, press Alt-F10 and name the macro to invoke if the search is successful; call it "medium." Press Ctrl-F10 to end macro definition.

NESTING MACROS   While a macro chain invokes a second macro only after the first has completed, a nested macro is invoked as part of another macro. Nested macros only work with macros named with Alt-key sequences. To nest a macro, press Ctrl-F10 and name a macro using an Alt-key sequence, type any keystrokes necessary before invoking the nested macro and then press the Alt-key sequence for the nested macro. Then type the rest of the keystrokes for the first macro and press Ctrl-F10 to end macro definition.

MACRO COMMANDS   Pressing Ctrl-PgUp during macro execution invokes the Macro Commands key. This lets you insert a pause in a macro, make macros invisible as they are executed, assign a value to a variable, or insert comments about the macro.

During any macro execution, press Ctrl-PgUp.

```
   1 Pause; 2 Display; 3 Assign; 4 Comment: 0
```

Typing 1 or P lets you pause a macro; 2 or D lets you select whether a macro will be executed visibly or invisibly; 3 or A lets you assign functions and variables to the definition; 4 or D lets you insert comments in the macro that do not appear during macro execution. Options 1 and 2 are suitable for most users; 3 and 4 are intended for advanced users and programmers.

APPLICATIONS

Any time you find yourself repeatedly typing the same keystrokes, a macro can save you time. Macros are useful for a variety of purposes. In all cases, a well-designed macro can save you a lot of time and effort. Use macros to save keystrokes with any procedure that you perform often. For example, if you change margins a lot, you can create a macro that automatically changes the margins for you. Or if you perform the same search and replace task many times, you can create a macro that does this for you at the touch of a keystroke.

Macros can also perform more than one task at a time. For example, you can create a macro that changes boldface to italics while changing margins from 1" left and right to 2" left and right. Macros are also very useful in merge documents (Module 46).

Nested and chained macros are useful for complicated search and replace operations that mark text and move it from one document to another. And advanced macros are useful for any number of purposes. Since WordPerfect includes its own programming language for creating macros, there is very little that cannot be done.

TYPICAL OPERATION

In this example, create a macro that searches for the beginning of each paragraph and inserts a typesetting code.

1. Start WordPerfect and press **Ctrl-F10**. Type **paragraf** and press **Enter**. Then type **inserts paragraph codes** to describe the macro and press **Enter** again.

2. Press **Alt-F2**, the Search and Replace key, and type **N**, indicating you want to perform a search and replace operation without confirming changes. Press **Enter** twice to make WordPerfect search for every instance where return has been pressed twice in a row. Then press **F2**.

```
Replace with:
```

3. Press **Enter** twice and type **+pp**. This leaves the returns in, but adds a typesetting code, +pp, to indicate the beginning of a new paragraph. Press **F2**, then **Ctrl-F10** to save the macro.

4. Create a document similar to the following:

```
The Paperless Office is a Myth
by John Matthews, Executive Vice-President
FLG Office Supply,
Carbondale, IL

For decades, people have spoken of the so-called "paperless
office." It was first mentioned in the early 1900s in a book by
James Young.

Well, paper will never be replaced. There is no way that we can
ever, try as we might, get paper out of our lives. In fact, studies
show that even though we are computerized, we are actually handling
more paper today than ever before.

                                            Doc 1 Pg 1 Ln 1" Pos 1"
```

5. Move the cursor to the top of the document, press **Alt-F10**, type **paragraf**, and press **Enter**.

```
The Paperless Office is a Myth
by John Matthews, Executive Vice-President
FLG Office Supply,
Carbondale, IL

+ppFor decades, people have spoken of the so-called "paperless
office." It was first mentioned in the early 1900s in a book by
James Young.

+ppWell, paper will never be replaced. There is no way that we can
ever, try as we might, get paper out of our lives. In fact, studies
show that even though we are computerized, we are actually handling
more paper today than ever before.

                                         Doc 1 Pg 1 Ln 2.33" Pos 1"
```

The typesetting codes are inserted at the beginning of each paragraph. Imagine the convenience of this in a large document.

6. Save the document as PAPRLESS.WPF.

7. Turn to Module 66 to continue the learning sequence.

Module 43
MARGINS

DESCRIPTION

Margins are the boundaries in which you create your document. The left margin is where text begins on a line, the right margin is the approximate boundary where it ends. When WordPerfect inserts a soft carriage return and wraps a word to the next line, it does so because the right margin has been reached.

WordPerfect lets you change margins as many times as you like in a document. WordPerfect's default margin setting is one inch from the left margin (10 spaces with pica type) and one inch (10 spaces) from the right, or 10 and 74. If you are using 12-pitch, or elite type, your margin settings are effectively 12 and 89.

Only the text after a margin change is affected by the change. If you change margins in the middle of a line of text, WordPerfect inserts a carriage return in your document.

NOTE
If you want to change the way margins are displayed (from inches to spaces or some other measure), use the units of measure setting in the Setup menu, which is accessed by pressing Shift-F1. This is explained in Appendix B.

SETTING MARGINS   Margins are changed using the Line Format key (Shift-F8). To set margins:

1.   Press **Shift-F8** and type **1** or **L**.

```
  Format: Line


      1 - Hyphenation                      Off

      2 - Hyphenation Zone - Left          10%
                             Right         4%

      3 - Justification                    Yes

      4 - Line Height                      Auto

      5 - Line Numbering                   No

      6 - Line Spacing                     1

      7 - Margins - Left                   1"
                    Right                  1"

      8 - Tab Set                          0", every 0.5"

      9 - Widow/Orphan Protection          No
```

2. Type **7** or **M**. Then type the appropriate setting for the left margin and press **Down Arrow**. Type the appropriate setting for the right margin and press **Down Arrow**. Then press **F7** to save the new settings.

USING THE MARGIN RELEASE KEY   Sometimes, you might want to change the left margin for only one line. Instead of changing the margins, use the Left Margin Release key (Shift-Tab). This key moves the cursor back to the first tab before the left margin. Tabs are explained in Module 70. In 10 pitch type, tabs are initially placed five spaces apart in WordPerfect. For example, if you want to move back to position 0, with margins set at 10 and 74, move the cursor to the left margin and press Shift-Tab twice.

APPLICATIONS

There are any number of reasons to change margin settings. One of the most common is to adjust to the type size of the text you wish to print. You also change margins for the type of paper you are using. Envelopes, for example, require a different margin setting than legal- or standard-size paper.

TYPICAL OPERATION

In this example, you change margins from 1 inch on each side of the page to 2 inches.

1. Start WordPerfect, press **Shift-F10**, type **C:\WP50\DOCS\IDEAS.WPF**, and press **Enter** to retrieve the file created in Module 10, Cancel. If you have a floppy-based system, put the proper diskette in drive B and type B:IDEAS.WPF. The document looks similar to the following:

```
MEMO

CONFIDENTIAL

From: FLG
To:   RAW

While the main function of the average office is work, many office
personnel rely on their place of work as a hub of social activity.
Therefore, it might be pertinent if we start to sell merchandise
that is not related to the office, like magazines.

I want to investigate this matter. I'm going to put you in charge
of this program, Roger. Go down to the library and do some market
research. Also do some studies. Find out what types of items people
hope to find in office supply stores. Find out what we're missing.

I'd like a full report by the end of the month. I want your report
to list all of the items we aren't carrying that we should be
carrying. I'd also like an estimated sales volume for those items.

Also, Roger, please don't discuss this with anyone else, not even
anyone on the staff.

C:\WP50\DOCS\IDEAS.WPF                        Doc 1 Pg 1 Ln 1" Pos 1"
```

2. Move the cursor to the "M" in "MEMO" at the top of the page. Press **Shift-F8** and type **1** or **L**, then **7** or **M**.

3. Type **2**, press **Down Arrow**, type **2** again, and press **Down Arrow**. Then press **F7**. Notice the following illustration:

```
MEMO

CONFIDENTIAL

From: FLG
To:   RAW

While the main function of the average office is work, many office
personnel rely on their place of work as a hub of social activity.
Therefore, it might be pertinent if we start to sell merchandise
that is not related to the office, like magazines.

I want to investigate this matter. I'm going to put you in charge
of this program, Roger. Go down to the library and do some market
research. Also do some studies. Find out what types of items people
hope to find in office supply stores. Find out what we're missing.

I'd like a full report by the end of the month. I want your report
to list all of the items we aren't carrying that we should be
carrying. I'd also like an estimated sales volume for those items.

Also, Roger, please don't discuss this with anyone else, not even
anyone on the staff.

C:\WP50\DOCS\IDEAS.WPF                             Doc 1 Pg 1 Ln 1" Pos 2"
```

4. Save the document as IDEAS2.WPF.

5. Turn to Module 63 to continue the learning sequence.

Module 44

MASTER DOCUMENTS

DESCRIPTION

When indexing large books or chapters, WordPerfect's Master Documents feature comes in very nicely. It lets you set up a master document that incorporates an unlimited number of subdocuments. A master document creates indexes (Module 36), lists (Module 41) tables of authorities (Module 68), and/or tables of contents (Module 69) that incorporate all subdocuments with just a few keystrokes.

Create a master document when you begin a book or other document that is made up of a series of separate files. Then add each file as a subdocument as you go. The master document can be expanded or contracted at any time.

Master documents are useful for more than just generating lists and indexes, however. Any formatting changes, codes, or other options created in the master document are included in subdocuments. Any such changes in subdocuments are included in all following subdocuments. To create a master document:

1. Start WordPerfect. Press **Alt-F5**.

```
    1 Auto Ref; 2 Subdoc; 3 Index; 4 ToA Short Form; 5 Define; 6 Generate: 0
```

2. Type **2** or **S**.

```
  Subdoc Filename:
```

3. Type a subdocument name, for example, **TEXTGRAF.WPF** and press **Enter**. WordPerfect displays the subdocument in a box at the top of the screen.

```
  Subdoc: TEXTGRAF.WPF
```

4. Repeat these procedures for as many subdocuments as you want in the master document.

EXPANDING THE MASTER DOCUMENT In order to replace subdocument codes with the entire file for each subdocument, you have to expand the master document. To do this:

1. Press **Alt-F5**, then type **6** or **G**.

```
Mark Text: Generate

        1 - Remove Redline Markings and Strikeout Text from Document

        2 - Compare Screen and Disk Documents and Add Redline and Strikeout

        3 - Expand Master Document

        4 - Condense Master Document

        5 - Generate Tables, Indexes, Automatic References, etc.

Selection: 0
```

2. Type **3** or **E**. WordPerfect expands the master document, importing the entire text of each subdocument. WordPerfect puts a subdocument start message at the beginning of each subdocument and a subdocument end message at the end. While in expanded form, you can edit, print, and otherwise alter the subdocuments.

CONDENSING THE MASTER DOCUMENT   After you have made changes to the subdocuments, you can keep the master document in expanded form, that is, with the entire contents of all subdocuments constantly displayed, or you can condense them. It's really a waste of storage space to keep all of the subdocuments in the master document, so it's usually best to condense a master document after you are finished using it. To condense the master document:

1. Press **Alt-F5**, then type **6** or **G**.

2. Type **4** or **o**.

```
Save Subdocs? (Y/N) Yes
```

3. Type **Y**. If you made changes to the subdocs, the following screen appears:

```
Replace FILENAME.WPF? 1 Yes; 2 No; 3 Replace All Remaining: 0
```

4. Type **1** or **Y** to update this document, **2** or **N** not to update it, or **3** or **R** to update all subdocuments. Selecting either of the first two options means you decide whether to update each of the other subdocuments. (Updating any subdocument incorporates changes made during this session.) Typing **3** or **R** updates them all. WordPerfect then condenses the master document, saving the updated versions of the subdocuments in their original files. If you type **N**, it condenses the master document without saving the edited versions of the subdocuments. When the master document has been condensed, it only includes subdocument codes.

SAVING THE MASTER DOCUMENT   When you are finished with the master document, save it in either expanded or condensed form. When you save it in expanded form, WordPerfect prompts you to update the subdocuments. If you do not, they are not updated with the changes you have made to them.

APPLICATIONS

Master documents are most useful for making formatting changes to a number of documents at once and for generating lists, indexes, tables of contents, and tables of authorities in a large number of related files. They are also useful for retrieving a large number of documents (on-screen) at one time. Master documents help most when preparing books, reports, theses, or other text that includes a large number of related files.

TYPICAL OPERATION

This typical operation illustrates how to create an index from a master document made up of a number of subdocuments.

1. Press **Alt-F5**. Type **2** or **S**. Then type **FINANCES.WPF** and press **Enter**.

2. Press **Alt-F5** again. Type **2** or **S**. Then type **REST.WPF** and press **Enter**.

3. Press **Alt-F5** again. Type **2** or **S**. Then type **IDEAS.WPF** and press **Enter**.

```
Subdoc: FINANCES.WPF
```

```
Subdoc: REST.WPF
```

```
Subdoc: IDEAS.WPF
```

4. Press **Shift-F3** and create a document similar to the following:

```
Michael
Laura
Balance Sheet
Accounts Receivable
FLG
Jack Belew
 Income Statement
Sales
Net Profit
Memo
Confidential
Matt
Mike
```

5. Save the document as NAMES.WPF and type **Y** to exit Doc 2.

6. Press **Alt-F5**, type **6** or **G**, then type **3** or **E** to expand the master document. Press **Home**, **Home**, **Down Arrow** to move the cursor to the end of the document.

7. Press **Alt-F5** and type **5** or **D**. Then type **3** or **I** to define an index (Module 36). Type **NAMES.WPF** as the concordance filename and press **Enter**. (Concordance is explained in Module 36.) Type **4** or **R** to define an index with flush right page numbers.

8. Press **Alt-F5**. Type **6** or **G**, then type **5** or **G** and type **Y**. The completed index looks like this:

```
    Accounts Receivable                                    3
    Balance Sheet                                          3
    FLG                                                  1-4
    Income Statement                                       2
    Jack Belew                                             1
    Laura                                                  3
    Memo                                                   3
    Michael                                                3
    Mike                                                   3
    Net Profit                                             2
    Sales                                              2, 3
```

9. Press **Alt-F5**, type **6** or **G**, then type **4** or **o** to condense the master document. Type **Y** to save all the subdocuments.

10. Save the document as MASTER.WPF.

11. Turn to Module 7 to continue the learning sequence.

Module 45

MATH

DESCRIPTION

The Math command (Alt-F7) lets you use WordPerfect as a calculator in its simplest form, and a spreadsheet at its most complex. WordPerfect performs many detailed math operations to let you prepare different types of financial documents. Math can be used anywhere in a WordPerfect document, or it can be used in its own document.

There are six steps to using WordPerfect's Math command:

1. Set tabs to correspond to your desired math columns.
2. Define the math columns.
3. Turn Math on.
4. Enter numbers and values.
5. Calculate values.
6. Turn Math off.

SETTING TABS   Tabs are described in Module 70. When you use the Math command, you have to set the tabs to correspond to the number of columns in your document. For example, if you are expecting five columns, one at the left margin and four others, you need to set four tab stops in essentially a 6.5-inch space. When you set the tabs, first clear the old tabs, then make sure you leave enough room for the numbers in each column. It is a good idea to leave more room than you think you need.

MATH DEFINITION   After you have reset the tabs, you can define the math columns. Four types of columns are available — calculation, text, numeric, and total. A calculation column is one that includes the result of a formula, like "2*A," or two times the value in column A. This is similar to formulas used in spreadsheets, because you can change the numbers and the formula recalculates.

A text column is one that includes text, not numbers. These are usually column headings or text information that explains about the numbers. A numeric column is one that includes numbers. A total column is one that includes the results of adding the results of all columns to its left. This is a useful tool for accountants.

Assume you have tabs set at 2", 3", 4.5", and 6" (spaces 20, 30, 45, and 60) with margins at 1" on each side (10 and 74). To define math columns, press Alt-F7 and type 2 or e.

```
  Math Definition            Use arrow keys to position cursor

  Columns                    A B C D E F G H I J K L M N O P Q R S T U V W X

  Type                       2 2 2 2 2 2 2 2 2 2 2 2 2 2 2 2 2 2 2 2 2 2 2 2

  Negative Numbers           ( ( ( ( ( ( ( ( ( ( ( ( ( ( ( ( ( ( ( ( ( ( ( (

  Number of Digits to        2 2 2 2 2 2 2 2 2 2 2 2 2 2 2 2 2 2 2 2 2 2 2 2
     the Right (0-4)

  Calculation     1
     Formulas     2
                  3
                  4

  Type of Column:
        0 = Calculation    1 = Text      2 = Numeric    3 = Total

  Negative Numbers
        ( = Parentheses (50.00)          - = Minus Sign  -50.00



  Press Exit when done
```

At first glance, the Math Definition menu looks confusing. But realize that each column corresponds to a tab stop. With four tab stops, we have only five columns to deal with: A, B, C, D, and E. Set the type for each column. Type 0 to define calculation columns, 1 for text columns, 2 for numeric columns, and 3 for total columns.

If you define calculation columns, you must also enter a formula. You can have up to four formulas in any set of columns. The formulas can either rely on a column value or just be the result of a calculation. You can change the calculation whenever you like. Use the following symbols when creating a formula:

+   for addition
–   for subtraction
*   for multiplication
/   for division

The preceding four symbols can be used interchangeably in formulas. The following four symbols cannot be used with any other symbols, values, or even with each other:

+   When used alone, this symbol tells WordPerfect to add the numbers in the numeric columns.
+/   This tells WordPerfect to average the numbers in the numeric columns.
=   This adds the numbers in the total columns.
=/   This averages the numbers in the total columns.

You can also select the way you want negative numbers displayed for each column. Your options are either in parentheses or with the minus sign. The default, which is actually a standard for financial statements, is in parentheses.

You can also select the number of digits (up to four) you want in the decimal column. Since the usual procedure is to add dollars and cents, the default is two digits.

When you are finished defining math columns, press F7 to exit the Math Definition menu. At this point, you can either turn Math on, or return to your document. To turn Math on, type 1 or M. To return to the document, press Enter.

USING MATH   If Math is on, the following message appears on the Status Line:

```
    Math                                          Doc 1 Pg 1 Ln 1" Pos 1"
```

To use math, press Tab.

```
    Align char = . Math                           Doc 1 Pg 1 Ln 1" Pos 1.5"
```

This is the alignment character symbol (Module 4). It means that numbers are aligned on the decimal point in math columns. Type the numbers as usual, pressing Tab to move from column to column.

TIP: The decimal point aligns on the tab space. So if you are using column headings for a table, set the tab halfway through the column heading.

When you get to the end of a column, you use a variety of operators to tell WordPerfect to add up certain numbers:

- A + tells WordPerfect to add all numbers above it and get a subtotal.
- An = tells WordPerfect to add all the subtotals above it and get a total.
- An * tells WordPerfect to add all the totals together for a grand total.
- If a subtotal is only one number, use a small "t" in front of that number to identify it.
- If a total is only one number, use a large "T" in front of that number to identify it.
- Typing N in front of a number forces it to be negative. This is useful when subtracting one column of numbers from another.

After you have entered all the numbers and identified columns as subtotals, totals, and grand totals, you are ready to calculate.

1.   Press **Alt-F7**.

```
    1 Math Off; 2 Calculate; 3 Column On/Off; 4 Column Def: 0
```

2.   Type **2** or **a**.

After a few seconds, WordPerfect calculates the answers. Numbers derived through the calculation of a formula have an exclamation mark (!) after them.

3.   When you are finished calculating, press **Alt-F7**. Then type **1** or **M** to turn Math off.

APPLICATIONS

Use the Math feature to calculate totals in invoices, financial statements, and other documents where numbers are involved.

TYPICAL OPERATION

In this example, you calculate the pay for a group of salespeople. The salespeople are paid a guarantee plus commission.

1.   Start WordPerfect. Then change margins (Module 43) to 0" on both the left and right (0 and 80).

2.   Set Tabs (Module 69) to 1.5", 3.5", 5.2", and 7" (15, 35, 52, and 70).

3.   Create a document similar to the following:

```
                        FLG OFFICE SUPPLY
                        SALES PERFORMANCE
              FOR QUARTER ENDED, MARCH 31, 1989

Employee  Guarantee                 Sales        Commission      Pay
Levin
Snyder
Weil
Total


                                     Doc 1 Pg 1 Ln 1.83" Pos 0.73"
```

4.   Move the cursor to the space following the "n" in "Levin." Press **Alt-F7** and type **2** or **e**.

5.   Move the cursor to the "2" under column C and type **0** to define column C as a calculation column. Then type **.05∗B** as the formula for column C and press **Enter**. The cursor moves to column D.

6.   Type **0** to define column D as a calculation column and type **A + C** as the formula for column D.

7.   Press **F7** twice to save the math definition. Then type **1** or **M** to turn Math on.

8.   Press **Tab** and type **4500.00**.

9.   Press **Tab** and type **65,349.50**.

10.   Press **Tab**. An exclamation mark appears. This indicates a calculated result will appear here.

11.   Press **Tab**. Another exclamation mark appears.

12.   Press **Right Arrow** to move to the next line. Then position the cursor after the "r" in "Snyder."

```
                        FLG OFFICE SUPLY
                        SALES PERFORMANCE
                  FOR QUARTER ENDED, MARCH 31, 1989

   Employee      Guarantee          Sales        Commission      Pay
   Levin         4500.00        65,349.50            !           !
   Snyder
   Weil
   Total
```

13. Press **Tab** and fill in the table as follows, making sure to press **Tab** between each column.

```
                        FLG OFFICE SUPLY
                        SALES PERFORMANCE
                  FOR QUARTER ENDED, MARCH 31, 1989

      Employee      Guarantee          Sales        Commission      Pay
      Levin         4500.00        65,349.50            !           !
      Snyder        4000.00        69,789.25            !           !
      Weil          3850.00        59,397.45            !           !
      Total                                             !           !
```

14. Press **Alt-F7** and type **2** or **a**. After a few seconds, the display looks as follows when WordPerfect completes all its calculations.

```
                        FLG OFFICE SUPPLY
                        SALES PERFORMANCE
                  FOR QUARTER ENDED, MARCH 31, 1989

      Employee  Guarantee          Sales        Commission        Pay
      Levin     4500.00        65,349.50        3,267.48!      7,767.48!
      Snyder    4000.00        69,789.25        3,489.46!      7,489.46!
      Weil      3850.00        59,397.45        2,969.87!      6,819.87!
      Total    12,350.00+     194,536.20+       9,726.81!     22,076.81!
```

15. Press **Alt-F7** and type **1** or **M** to turn Math off.

16. Save the document as SALES389.WPF.

17. Turn to Module 22 to continue the learning sequence.

Module 46
MERGE

DESCRIPTION

Those form letters that you get in the mail that say you may have won a million dollars in a sweepstakes are actually two documents merged into one, creating a third. The body of the letter is sent to everyone on the mailing list. It is kept in one file, called the *primary file*. Since everyone on the mailing list has a different name and address, it is necessary to personalize portions of the letter. The mailing list is kept in another file, called the *secondary file*. The Merge command (F9) is used to combine information in those files to create a third file.

WordPerfect gives you the power to send the same document to a variety of people through the Merge command. Its most common use is in form letters, but it can actually be used for any task where you are sending the same message to a group of people.

SECONDARY FILE   It's easier to understand merge files if you look at secondary files first. The secondary file is a collection of records. And a record is a collection of fields.

For example, if you are creating an address list, each person on the list has a name, address, city, state, zip code, and phone number. The information on each person, which is unique to that person, is a record. Each category of information (name, address, city, etc.), which is common to all people on the list, is a field.

While records may contain as many fields as desired, the field numbers must be consistent throughout the document. If field one in one record is a name, field one of all records must be a name. You can leave information for a field blank, but you must be consistent when creating a secondary file.

This is because when you create a primary file, you tell WordPerfect that you want field one, which may be the person's name, inserted in a particular place in the document. If field one in one record is a name, and in another, an address, some of those form letters are going to look pretty funny.

NOTE

Take care when selecting field numbers. If you have a large number of records in a file, you might want to sort (Module 62) those records by a variety of categories. It's advised that you separate city, state, and zip code into separate fields.

To create a secondary file:

1. Start WordPerfect, type **Bob Williams** and press **F9** for the first field.

The (^R) symbol marks the end of each field in a record and inserts a hard return into the document.

NOTE
Never add an extra hard return to a record.
If you do, WordPerfect will not know which
field number is which when creating the
primary file.

2. Type the information for the next field, **123 Maple Street**, and press **F9**.

3. Type the information for the next field, **Carbondale**, and press **F9**.

4. Type **IL**, press **F9**, type **62901**, and press **F9** again. Continue entering information for individual fields. When you are finished, press **Shift-F9** and type **E**.

```
Bob Williams^R
123 Maple Street^R
Carbondale^R
IL^R
62901^R
^E
================================================================================
```

^E is the "end of record" symbol. It tells WordPerfect you have finished the information for this record and are ready to go on to the next one. If you'd like to leave a field blank, type ^R and press Enter.

Continue entering information in this way, making sure that fields are consistent throughout the file. Then save the file when you are finished.

PRIMARY FILE   The primary file is the form letter. It includes codes that tell WordPerfect where to put the information it gets from the secondary file, as well as a variety of other commands. Most primary files contain only a few merge commands. But WordPerfect gives you a great deal of power for creating a variety of merge documents. The following table lists all the merge commands available to you when creating a primary file.

Merge Command	Meaning
^C	Stops the creation of the merge document. Use this if you want to add additional information while the document is being created.
^D	Inserts today's date at the cursor location.
^E	Marks the end of a record in a secondary file.
^F and number	Inserts the specific field number at the cursor location.
^Gmacroname ^G	Invokes the selected macro at end of the merge.
^N	Tells WordPerfect to look for the next record in the secondary file. If there are no more records, it ends the merge process.

Merge Command	Meaning
^ Omessage ^ O	If you are stopping a merge document, you might want to insert a message on the Status Line that tells you what to do next. This command inserts that message on the Status Line. "Insert the latest price for widgets," is an example of a message.
^ Pfilename ^ P	If you want to change to another primary file in the middle of a merge, use this command.
^ Q	Stops the merge process, even if there are more records in the secondary file to merge.
^ R	Marks the end of a field in a secondary file.
^ Sfilename ^ S	If you want to change to another secondary file in the middle of a merge, use this command.
^ T	Tells WordPerfect to send all text that has been merged to this point to the printer.
^ U	Rewrites the screen.
^ V	Lets you transfer merge codes from one document to another.
?	Eliminates blank lines when a file is printed. Use this to let WordPerfect eliminate printing fields that are not required. For example, if an address field typically takes up two lines, type a ? so WordPerfect won't automatically print two lines on a one-line address.

To create a primary file, create the document as you normally would. If you are typing a business letter, it might start like this:

```
                              FLG Office Supplies
                              124 N. Main
                              Carbondale, IL 62901
                              _
```

1. If you want to insert today's date here when the document is printed, press **Shift-F9**.

```
    ^C; ^D; ^E; ^F; ^G; ^N; ^O; ^P; ^Q; ^S; ^T; ^U; ^V:
```

2. These are the merge commands mentioned in the earlier table. To enter the merge command for date, type **D**.

3. Move the cursor where you want to insert the first field from the secondary file and press **Shift-F9**. Then type **F**.

```
    Field:
```

4. Type **1** to insert field number one at this location (field one in the prior example is name). Press **Enter**.

```
   ^F1^
```

5. Move the cursor where you want the second field inserted and press **Shift-F9**. Type **F**, then **2**, and press **Enter**.

Continue this process for all field numbers that you want in the merge document.

Create the rest of the primary file in much the same way you create any other file, inserting merge commands where appropriate. Then save the file as you normally would.

MERGING A PRIMARY AND SECONDARY FILE After you have created primary and secondary files, you can merge the files to create a number of merge documents. These documents can be saved on disk, or sent directly to the printer. If you want merge documents sent directly to the printer, insert a $^\wedge$T at the end of the primary file, and a $^\wedge$N to tell WordPerfect to proceed to the next record. To create a merge document:

1. Start with a blank screen. Press **Ctrl-F9**.

```
   1 Merge; 2 Sort; 3 Sort Order: 0
```

NOTE
Sort and sorting order are described in Module 62.

2. Type **1** or **M**. Then type the name of the primary file and press **Enter**.

```
   Secondary file:
```

3. Type the name of the secondary file and press **Enter**.

```
   *merging*
```

After a few moments, WordPerfect creates the merge document. Each resulting merge occupies a separate page (or pages) in the same document. Save or print the document as you wish.

APPLICATIONS

The variety of applications for merge documents is almost as unlimited as your imagination. Secondary files, in addition to serving in merge documents, can also be used as address lists, for mailing labels, and for addressing envelopes. Advanced merge documents can include macros, mathematical equations, and a good deal of personalized information.

TYPICAL OPERATION

This example shows you how to create a merge document that is sent directly to the printer.

1. Start WordPerfect and turn on your printer. Then type **Roger Walton** and press **F9**.

2. Type **1720 North Brian Ave** (press **F9**) **Carbondale** (press **F9**) **IL** (press **F9**) **62901** (press **F9**).

3. Type **618-549-6924** (press **F9**) **Roger** (press **F9**). Then press **Shift-F9** and type **E**.

```
Roger Walton^R
1720 North Brian Ave^R
Carbondale^R
IL^R
62901^R
618-549-6924^R
Roger^R
^E
```

4. Add the following records to the list, pressing the indicated keys at the end of each line:

```
Harry Weil(F9)              A.J. Berlau(F9)
4356 W. 53rd St.(F9)        190 S. Orola(F9)
Marion(F9)                  Murphysboro(F9)
IL(F9)                      IL(F9)
62958(F9)                   62904(F9)
618-452-0851(F9)            618-496-5003(F9)
Harry(F9)                   Mr. Berlau(F9)
(Shift-F9, E)               (Shift-F9, E)

Delores Weberman(F9)
9 Summit Circle(F9)
Benton(F9)
IL(F9)
62809(F9)
618-292-0596(F9)
Delores(F9)
(Shift-F9, E)
```

5. Press **F7**, type **y**, **ADDRESS1.SF**, and press **Enter**. Then type **N** to stay in WordPerfect.

6. Create a document similar to the following:

```
                                        FLG Office Supply
                                        124 N. Main
                                        Carbondale, IL 62901

Dear       :

Thanks,    , for your support of FLG Office Supply. We appreciate
your kindness and generosity in making our company a better place
to work and a positive force in the community.

                                        Sincerely,


                                        Michael David
                                        Vice-President

                                        Doc 1 Pg 1 Ln 1" Pos 1"
```

7. Make sure the cursor is on the "D" in "Dear;" then press **Enter** four times.

8. Move the cursor to the line under "Carbondale, IL 62901" at the top of the document. Press **Tab** repeatedly until the cursor gets to position 5". Then press **Shift-F9** and type **D** to put today's date right here. Then press **Enter**.

9. Press **Shift-F9** and type **F**. Type **1** to put field number 1, the name field, here; then press **Enter** twice.

10. Press **Shift-F9**, type **F**, and type **2** to put field number 2, the address field, here. Press **Enter**. twice.

11. Press **Shift-F9**, type **F**, and type **3** to put field number 3, the city field, here. Press **Enter**.

12. Type , and press the **Spacebar**. Then press **Shift-F9**, type **F**, and type **4** to put field number 4, the state field, here. Press **Enter**.

13. Press the **Spacebar**. Then press **Shift-F9**, type **F**, and type **5** to put field number 5, the zip code field, here. Press **Enter** twice.

14. Press **Del** three times to delete some of the blank lines between the address and beginning of the letter. Then move the cursor two spaces after the word "Dear." Press **Shift-F9**, type **F**, and type **7** to put field number 7, the first name field (in the case of A.J. Berlau, it is still a form of personal address), here. Press **Enter**.

15. Move the cursor to the two spaces after the comma following "Thanks." Press **Shift-F9**, type **F**, and type **7** to put field number 7 here also. Press **Enter**.

16. Move the cursor to the bottom of the document. Press **Shift-F9**. Type **T** to send all merged text to the printer.

17. Press the **Spacebar**. Press **Shift-F9** and type **N** to make WordPerfect look for the next record in the secondary file.

18. Use the **Del** key to delete any unneeded spaces.

Your primary file should look like this:

```
                                      FLG Office Supply
                                      124 N. Main
                                      Carbondale, IL 62901
    ^F1^                              ^D
    ^F2^
    ^F3^, ^F4^ ^F5^

    Dear ^F7^:

    Thanks, ^F7^, for your support of FLG Office Supply. We appreciate
    your kindness and generosity in making our company a better place
    to work and a positive force in the community.

                                      Sincerely,


                                      Michael David
                                      Vice-President
    ^T ^N
```

19. Save the document as THANKS.PF, but do not exit WordPerfect.

20. Press **Ctrl-F9**. Then type **1** or **M**.

21. Type **THANKS.PF** and press **Enter** to indicate the primary file. Then type **ADDRESS1.SF** and press **Enter** to indicate the secondary file.

After a few moments, your document starts printing.

Your first merged document should look like this:

```
                                      FLG Office Supply
                                      124 N. Main
                                      Carbondale, IL 62901
                                      August 3, 1988

    Roger Walton
    1720 North Brian Ave
    Carbondale, IL 62901


    Dear Roger:

    Thanks, Roger, for your support of FLG Office Supply. We appreciate
    your kindness and generosity in making our company a better place
    to work and a positive force in the community.

                                      Sincerely,


                                      Michael David
                                      Vice-President
```

22. Turn to Module 62 to continue the learning sequence.

Module 47

MOVE

DESCRIPTION

The Move command (Ctrl-F4) lets you move text for use in other parts of a document or in other documents. You can move a block of text, a column in a table, a rectangular block of text, a sentence, a paragraph, or a page. It is similar to the Copy command described in Module 14, except instead of leaving the text in its original location, the Move command cuts it from the document. You then move the cursor to where you want the text and retrieve it.

The Move command also works like the Copy command in that the material you want to move must first be specified and stored either as a block of text, or as a sentence, paragraph, or page in the computer's memory. Then you can move the cursor to the place where you want to insert the text and retrieve it. WordPerfect inserts the text and automatically adjusts the document. You can retrieve text as many times as you wish, since the text stays in memory until you either define another block, make another move, or leave WordPerfect.

NOTE

Text defined in blocks and text defined as a
sentence, paragraph, or page are stored in the
same location in WordPerfect. So, for example,
if you define a block of text, it only stays in
memory until you either define another block, or
move (or copy) a sentence, paragraph, or page.

TIP: The Move command is very useful for moving text and putting that text in other documents. The text you choose to move stays in memory until you leave WordPerfect. The easiest way to move between documents is by using WordPerfect's Switch feature (Module 22), which lets you edit two documents at once.

MOVING SENTENCES, PARAGRAPHS, OR PAGES   This feature lets you move text from one location to another without having to define a block of text. It is useful if you are moving a sentence, paragraph, or page. In order to use it, you have only to make sure that the cursor is anywhere in the sentence, paragraph, or page you want to move. If the text you want to move is more complicated, (i.e, two sentences, two paragraphs, two pages), then you have to define a block, as described in the next section.

To move a sentence, paragraph, or page:

1. Make sure the cursor is anywhere in the sentence, paragraph, or page you want to move and press **Ctrl-F4**.

```
Move: 1 Sentence; 2 Paragraph; 3 Page; 4 Retrieve: 0
```

2. Type **1** or **S** if you want to move a sentence, **2** or **P** to move a paragraph, or **3** or **a** to move a page.

```
   1 Move; 2 Copy; 3 Delete; 4 Append: 0
```

Here is your chance to tell WordPerfect if you want to move, copy, delete, or append the sentence, paragraph, or page.

3. Type **1** or **M** for Move.

```
   Move cursor; press Enter to retrieve.
```

4. Move the cursor where you want to move the text and press **Enter**. The selected text is moved.

MOVING BLOCKS OR RECTANGULAR BLOCKS OF TEXT   The Move command also works with blocks of text. These blocks can be either normal or rectangular. Module 8 tells you how to define blocks of text.

To move a block of text:

1. Press **Alt-F4** to turn block on. Move the cursor to define a block of text and press **Ctrl-F4**.

```
   Move: 1 Block; 2 Tabular Column; 3 Rectangle: 0
```

2. Type **1** or **B** for a normal block of text, **3** or **R** for a rectangular block. Then type **1** or **M** to move the block from its current location in the text.

3. Position the cursor where you want the text to appear and press **Enter**.

MOVING COLUMNAR INFORMATION   If you want to move columnar information, that is, a column in a table, use this command. This command identifies text that has been defined by tabs, indents, alignment characters (Module 4) and hard returns. This command is not for moving columns of text (Module 13). To move columnar information:

CAUTION

Do not use this command for moving text in
Column mode (Module 13). Use the regular Move
command for doing that.

1. Press **Alt-F4** to turn Block on and define a block of text. This highlights all the text, not just the column. Then press **Ctrl-F4**.

2. Type **2** or **C** to highlight the column of text. Then type **1** or **M** to move the text.

3. Move the cursor where you want the copied text to appear and press **Enter**.

RETRIEVING BLOCKS MORE THAN ONCE   Text remains in memory until you replace it with another block. WordPerfect lets you retrieve it through the use of the Retrieve key (Ctrl-F4). To retrieve a previously marked block of text:

1. Press **Ctrl-F4**, then type **4** or **R**.

```
    Retrieve: 1 Block; 2 Tabular Column; 3 Rectangle: 0
```

2. Type **1** or **B** to retrieve a block of text, **2** or **C** to retrieve a tabular column of text, or **3** or **R** to retrieve a rectangular block of text. The text is retrieved at the current cursor location.

APPLICATIONS

The Move command is useful for moving text within a document or from one document to another. It saves time and reduces typing errors. It is helpful when editing, because you can rearrange paragraphs (cut and paste). This often improves the quality of your writing. The Retrieve command is handy when you are retrieving the same block of text many times.

TYPICAL OPERATION

In this example, use the Move command to move a paragraph from one location to another in a document.

1. Create a document similar to the following:

```
MEMO

TO: FLG
FROM: GWL
SUBJECT: Lipson Motors Account

As you remember, Lipson Motors purchased $10,000 worth of office
supplies from us last year, making them one of our top 15 accounts.

In the first three months of this year, Lipson Motors has only
purchased $200 of supplies from us. It appears Lipson is buying
from Campus Office Supplies on West Elm.

I would like to give Lipson Motors preferred customer status. This
would involve discounts of up to 60% on certain supplies, and
volume discounts that would take last year's sales into account.

What do you think of this?

GWL
                                      Doc 1 Pg 1 Ln 3.16" Pos 1"
```

2. Move the cursor anywhere in the third paragraph and press **Ctrl-F4**. Type **2** or **P**. Then type **1** or **M** to remove the paragraph from the text.

3. Move the cursor to the "A" in "As" at the beginning of the first paragraph and press **Enter** to retrieve the paragraph.

```
MEMO

TO: FLG
FROM: GWL
SUBJECT: Lipson Motors Account

I would like to give Lipson Motors preferred customer status. This
would involve discounts of up to 60% on certain supplies, and
volume discounts that would take last year's sales into account.

As you remember, Lipson Motors purchased $10,000 worth of office
supplies from us last year, making them one of our top 15 accounts.

In the first three months of this year, Lipson Motors has only
purchased $200 of supplies from us. It appears Lipson is buying
from Campus Office Supplies on West Elm.

What do you think of this?

GWL
                                        Doc 1 Pg 1 Ln 2" Pos 1"
```

4. Save the document as LIPSON.WPF.

5. Turn to Module 9 to continue the learning sequence.

Module 48
OTHER FORMAT

DESCRIPTION

WordPerfect offers line formatting (Module 39), page formatting (Module 51), and document formatting (Module 21) options. But that's not enough. Some formatting options just do not fit in any of the above.

The Other Format selection on the Format menu is a potpourri of formatting options. It lets you select the language you are using WordPerfect in; set kerning, word spacing, overstrike, and other printer commands; and decide whether to underline spaces and tabs.

It also lets you decide your alignment character, useful in formulas and tables (discussed in Module 4); set printer advance (Module 54), which lets you print text a specified distance up or down from the current printing position; and provide conditional end of page protection (Module 9), which ensures that certain text stays together on a page. To access the Other Format menu, press Shift-F8 and type 4 or O.

```
Format: Other

      1 - Advance

      2 - Conditional End of Page

      3 - Decimal/Align Character            .
          Thousands' Separator               ,

      4 - Language                           EN

      5 - Overstrike

      6 - Printer Functions

      7 - Underline - Spaces                 Yes
                      Tabs                    No
```

THOUSANDS' SEPARATOR   Both the decimal alignment character and the thousands' separator are used in WordPerfect's Math mode (Module 45). The default thousands' separator is a comma. This option lets you change the character, which automatically separates hundreds from thousands and thousands from millions during Math mode. You can, for example, eliminate the thousands' separator. Or, you can change it to a period or some other character. To do this type 3 or D from the Other Format menu. Either type a new alignment character, press Del to eliminate it, or press Down Arrow to let it remain the same. Press F7 to return to the document.

LANGUAGE   WordPerfect operates in 14 different languages. Changing the language lets WordPerfect select the appropriate speller, thesaurus, and hyphenation dictionary for the language. To change the language, type 4 or L from the Other Format menu. Then type the code for the desired language and press Enter. Press F7 to return to the document. Supported languages and codes are:

NOTE

WordPerfect is shipped with support for only one language. Files to support other languages are available from the company.

Code	Language
CA	Canadian French
DA	Danish
DE	German
EN	American English
ES	Spanish
FR	French
IC	Icelandic
IT	Italian
NE	Dutch
NO	Norwegian
PO	Portuguese
SU	Finnish
SV	Swedish
UK	British English

OVERSTRIKE   Overstrike lets you print two or more characters on the same position on the page. This is helpful when you try to create symbols — chemical symbols, special characters, etc. — that are not supported by your printer. To overstrike characters:

1.   Type **5** or **O** from the Other Format menu.

```
1 Create; 2 Edit: 0
```

2.   Type **1** or **C** to create an overstrike character. Type the characters you want to be overstruck and press **Enter**. Then press **F7** to return to the document. Only the last character you typed will be visible on the screen. You can see all of the characters by pressing **Alt-F3**, the Reveal Codes key (Module 59).

3.   Type **2** or **E** to edit characters that have already been created. They appear at the bottom of the screen with an "Overstrk" code. Edit them normally, press **Enter**, then press **F7** to return to the document.

PRINTER FUNCTIONS   WordPerfect provides a number of printer functions in the Other Format menu. These let you set kerning, or space between letter pairs, send commands to the printer, set word and letter spacing, and set word spacing in justified text. To use these printer functions, type 6 or P from the Other Format menu.

CAUTION
These printer functions are not for casual users.
Unless you are very familiar with desktop
publishing, it is advisable not to use these.

```
Format: Printer Functions

    1 - Kerning                                No

    2 - Printer Command

    3 - Word Spacing                           Optimal
        Letter Spacing                         Optimal

    4 - Word Spacing Justification Limits
        Compressed to (0% - 100%)              60%
        Expanded to (100% - unlimited)         400%

  Selection: 0
```

Kerning   Type 1 or K from the Printer Functions menu. If you want WordPerfect to adjust for space between characters to remove excess white space between letter pairs like "l" and "t," type Y to turn kerning on.

Printer Command   Type 2 or P from the Printer Functions menu.

```
    1 Command; 2 Filename: 0
```

To send commands to the printer, type 1 or C, type a printer command, and press Enter. Printer commands are generally special commands that you can send to your printer to change typesize or style, change modes, initialize the printer, or perform a variety of other functions. If you have a series of printer commands saved as a file that you want to send to the printer, type 2 or F, type the filename, and press Enter.

Word Spacing   Type 3 or W from the Printer Functions menu.

```
  Word Spacing: 1 Normal; 2 Optimal; 3 Percent of Optimal; 4 Set Pitch: 2
```

This is the word or letter spacing option. It defines the way WordPerfect puts space between words and letters. Type 1 or N for normal word and letter spacing. This selects the setting that looks best according to the manufacturer of your printer. Type 2 or O, the default setting, to select the setting that looks best according to WordPerfect. Type 3 or P to select some percent of optimal. Type a percentage and press Enter. The lower the number the less space between words and letters — optimal spacing is 100 percent. Type 4 or S to set the exact character pitch (characters per inch), putting a uniform number of letters in one inch. The resulting measurement is displayed as a percentage of optimal spacing. Ten- or 12-pitch, for example, is 84 percent of optimal, meaning letters and words are a little bit closer together.

Justification Limits   Type 4 or J from the Printer Functions menu. This is the spacing between words for justified text (Module 39). WordPerfect lets you set the limits as to how far spaces can be stretched for justified text and how much they can be squeezed. The default setting for justified text is 400 percent expansion, or up to 4 spaces, and 60 percent compression, or 6/10 of a space. To change this, type a percentage for compression, press Enter, then type a percentage for expansion and press Enter. Press F7 to return to the document.

UNDERLINE SPACES AND TABS   WordPerfect normally underlines spaces between words, but does not underline the space between two tabs. You might want to change this to underline only words and/or to underline tabs. Underlining tabs is particularly helpful when preparing tables. To change the settings, type 7 or U from the Other Format menu. Then type Y or N for each setting as appropriate. Press F7 to return to the document.

APPLICATIONS

The Other Format menu helps you change a variety of settings. Use overstrike when preparing special characters in scientific or mathematical documents; change the language setting in multi-lingual documents; adjust kerning for desktop publishing applications; change word or letter spacing as desired; and underline tabs in tables.

TYPICAL OPERATION

This typical operation illustrates the effect of compressing or expanding justified text.

1. Create a document similar to the following:

```
                                          February 24, 1987


Brian Snyder
607 E. Park
Carbondale, IL 62901

Dear Brian:

I can't tell you what a pleasure it was to speak with you last
week. I am hopeful we can begin a fruitful business relationship.
We expect that with you as our Sales Manager for large
corporations, we can increase our overall sales by 35% to more than
one million dollars per year. And, if you can continue (and we can
get you some help), we think sales could be in excess of five
million dollars by 1992. That would make several of us very rich,
Brian. I am looking forward to working with you.


                              Sincerely,


                              Jack Belew
                              Controller

                              Doc 1 Pg 1 Ln 2.33" Pos 1"
```

2. Move the cursor to the beginning of the paragraph, press **Shift-F8**, type **4** or **O**, then **6** or **P**.

3. Type **4** or **J**. Type **20**, press **Enter**, then type **100** and press **Enter**. Press **F7** to save the changes and return to the document. The printed version of the justified document without compression or expansion alteration looks like this:

```
                                            February 24, 1987


Brian Snyder
607 E. Park
Carbondale, IL 62901

Dear Brian:

I can't tell you what a pleasure it was to speak with you last
week. I am hopeful we can begin a fruitful business relationship.
We expect that with you as our Sales Manager for large
corporations, we can increase our overall sales by 35% to more than
one million dollars per year. And, if you can continue (and we can
get you some help), we think sales could be in excess of five
million dollars by 1992. That would make several of us very rich,
Brian. I am looking forward to working with you.


                              Sincerely,

                              Jack Belew
                              Controller
```

4. Save the document as SNYDER.WPF.

5. Turn to Module 30 to continue the learning sequence.

Module 49
OUTLINE

DESCRIPTION

You do not need an outline generator program if you have WordPerfect. That's because WordPerfect includes an Outline feature (Shift-F5) to let you create your own outlines. Outlines are a good way to organize your thoughts. You can create better, more organized documents if you outline them first. And if you use WordPerfect instead of an outline generator program, you do not have to convert the outlined text to WordPerfect format when you use the outline to create another document.

The Outline feature automatically numbers paragraphs in outline format. Eight levels of numbering — I., A., 1., a., (1), (a), i), a) — among others — are available. (See Changing the Numbering Style for examples.)

NOTE
Paragraph numbering, a related topic, is
discussed in Module 52.

Each time you press Enter in outline mode, you create a new outline number. And each time you press Tab, you change the numbering level. When you edit an outline and add or delete numbers or levels, WordPerfect automatically renumbers the document. To outline text:

NOTE
Do not use the Tab key when outlining text unless
you want to go to the next numbering level. Use
F4, the Indent key (Module 35) to move the cursor
to the next tab stop. Press Spacebar, then Tab
to use the Tab key without changing the
numbering level.

1. Press **Shift-F5**. Then type **4** or **O**. Notice the Status Line.

```
Outline                                              Doc 1 Pg 1 Ln 1" Pos 1"
```

2. Press **Enter**. Notice the roman numeral "I" appears on-screen. Then press **F4**, type your text, for example, **Introduction**, and press **Enter**.

```
  I.   Introduction
 II.
Outline                                         Doc 1 Pg 1 Ln 1.33" Pos 1.3"
```

3. Notice the second outline number has been introduced. Press **Tab** to move to the next level of numbering. Notice the "II." has changed to "A."

4. Press **F4**, type the text for this level, for example, **How the West was won**, and press **Enter**.

```
    I.    Introduction
          A.   How the West was won
    II.
    Outline                              Doc 1 Pg 1 Ln 1.5" Pos 1.3"
```

5. Continue creating the outline in this way until you are finished. Then press **Shift-F5** again and type **4** or **O** to turn the Outline mode off. Notice the "Outline" message on the Status Line disappears.

The Outline key works as a toggle switch. Press Shift-F5, and then type 4 or O to turn it on, and the same sequence to turn it off.

TIP: After you turn Outline mode off, edit the outline by adding blank lines between entries and other editing touches.

CHANGING THE NUMBER LEVELS   WordPerfect lets you change the number level (back to "II" from "A," for example). To do this, press Shift-Tab or move the cursor to the left of the number to change and press Del. Either method automatically moves to the previous number level. The rest of the numbers are automatically updated as you move through the outline.

CHANGING THE NUMBERING STYLE   WordPerfect creates a default numbering style for outlines called, appropriately enough, "outline style." If you wish to change this style, however, you may. Five styles are available:

• Paragraph Style	1.	a.	i.	(1)	(a)	(i)	1)	a)
• Legal Style	I.	A.	1.	a.	(1)	(a)	i)	a)
• Outline Style	1	.1	.1	.1	.1	.1	.1	.1
• Bullet Style	•	o	–	■	*	+	·	×
• User-defined								

Using the fifth style, user-defined, you can create your own style using lowercase and uppercase letters, and Roman numerals, numbers, and legal-style numbers. You can punctuate these with and without periods, and with single or double parentheses.

You can change the numbering style of an outline either before or after you write it. To change the numbering style of the outline:

1. Move the cursor to the beginning of the outline and press **Shift-F5**. Then type **6** or **D**.

```
Paragraph Number Definition

    1 - Starting Paragraph Number        1
        (in legal style)

                                                 Levels
                                 1     2     3     4     5     6     7     8
    2 - Paragraph               1.    a.    i.   (1)   (a)   (i)   1)    a)
    3 - Outline                 I.    A.    1.    a.   (1)   (a)   i)    a)
    4 - Legal (1.1.1)           1     .1    .1    .1    .1    .1    .1    .1
    5 - Bullets                 •     o     -     ■     *     +     ·     ×
    6 - User-defined

    Current Definition          I.    A.    1.    a.   (1)   (a)   i)    a)

        Number Style                    Punctuation
        1 - Digits                      #   - No punctuation
        A - Upper case letters          #.  - Trailing period
        a - Lower case letters          #)  - Trailing parenthesis
        I - Upper case roman            (#) - Enclosing parentheses
        i - Lower case roman            .#  - All levels separated by period
        Other character - Bullet              (e.g.  2.1.3.4)


    Selection: 0
```

In Outline mode, the default is selection 3 or O. That default is listed in the table in the middle of the illustration. To change the numbering method, type 2 or P for paragraph numbering, 4 or L for legal numbering, 5 or B for bullet numbering, and 6 or U for user-defined numbering. The numbers underneath the "Number Style" and "Punctuation" headings at the bottom of the illustration are provided for reference if you are selecting your own method of paragraph numbering.

The Starting Paragraph Number selection (1 or S) lets you change the beginning number of an outline. This is useful when you continue numbering from a previous outline or document.

You can also define numbering to begin at a level other than the first level. If you do this, press Tab to move the number to your chosen level before typing.

APPLICATIONS

Use the Outline feature to organize your thoughts for time management, problem solving, planning, or writing purposes. Also use it when you are writing outlines for use by themselves.

TYPICAL OPERATION

In this example, you develop an outline for a hypothetical banquet.

1. Create a document similar to the following:

```
                        FLG OFFICE SUPPLY
                         ANNUAL BANQUET
                            AGENDA


                                          Doc 1 Pg 1 Ln 1.5" POS 1"
```

2. Press **Shift-F5** and type **4** or **O** to turn Outline mode on. Press **Enter**.

3. Press **F4**, type **Welcoming Speech**, and press **Enter**.

4. Press **Tab**, then **F4**, and type **FLG welcomes employees, associates, customers, and friends of the company.**

```
        I.    Welcoming Speech
              A.    FLG welcomes employees, associates, customers, and
                    friends of the company.

  Outline                                 Doc 1 Pg 1 Ln 2" Pos 4.3"
```

5. Press **Enter**, then **F4** and type **Dinner**.

6. Press **Enter**, then **Tab** and **F4** and type **Entree - Roast Duck**.

7. Press **Enter**, **Tab** twice, and **F4**. Type **Sides - salad, potatoes, carrots, peas**.

8. Press **Enter**, **Tab** twice, and **F4**. Type **Dessert - chocolate mousse**.

9. Press **Enter** and **F4**. Type **Keynote Address - Professor Philip Feinsilver, Southern Illinois University.**

10. Press **Enter**, **Tab**, and **F4**. Type **Topic - The Evolution of the Office**.

11. Press **Shift-F5** and type **4** or **O** to turn Outline mode off.

12. Add blank lines in the outline by pressing **Enter** at the end of the two major dividing lines in the outline (after "company." and "mousse"). The final outline looks like this:

```
                        FLG OFFICE SUPPLY
                         ANNUAL BANQUET
                            AGENDA

        I.    Welcoming Speech
              A.    FLG welcomes employees, associates, customers, and
                    friends of the company.

        II.   Dinner
              A.    Entree - Roast Duck
                    1.    Sides - salad, potatoes, carrots, peas
                    2.    Dessert - chocolate mousse

        III. Keynote Address - Professor Philip Feinsilver, Southern
             Illinois University
              A.    Topic - The Evolution of the Office

                                          Doc 1 Pg 1 Ln 3.66" Pos 1"
```

13. Move the cursor to the top of the document, press **Shift-F5**, and type **6** or **D**.

14. Type **2** or **P** and press **F7**. Then press **Home**, **Home**, **Down Arrow** to move the cursor to the bottom of the document. The outline now looks like this:

```
                        FLG OFFICE SUPPLY
                        ANNUAL BANQUET
                           AGENDA

    1.    Welcoming Speech
          a.    FLG welcomes employees, associates, customers, and
                friends of the company.

    2.    Dinner
          a.    Entree - Roast Duck
                i.    Sides - salad, potatoes, carrots, peas
                ii.   Dessert - chocolate mousse

    3.    Keynote Address - Professor Philip Feinsilver, Southern
          Illinois University
          a.    Topic - The Evolution of the Office


                                    Doc 1 Pg 1 Ln 3.66" Pos 1"
```

15. Save the document as BANQUET.WPF.

16. Turn to Module 52 to continue the learning sequence.

Module 50

PAGE BREAKS

DESCRIPTION

Like typed documents, WordPerfect breaks up its documents into pages. The length of these pages is determined by you. You can keep typing until you fill up the number of lines on a page as determined by the size of paper you use. WordPerfect then automatically creates a new page. This is explained in Module 51. This is called a soft page break. You can also press Ctrl-Enter at any point to create a new page. This is called a hard page break.

No matter how you create a new page, WordPerfect shows you a separation between pages with a dashed line.

```
   text here is on one page
===================================================================================
   text here is on the next
```

The dashed line is considered a character and may be deleted, just like any other character.

To delete a page break, move the cursor to the space before the page break and press Del.

SOFT PAGE BREAK   WordPerfect creates a soft page break when the end of a page has been reached. Lines on a page are determined by the size and type of paper you are using. This is explained in Module 51.

Soft page breaks occur when you run out of space on a page. For example, assume you are on line 54 of a page. If there are not any more text lines available on the page when the word wraps around to the next line, WordPerfect creates a new page.

```
     In reference to the Wilson's account, please tell them that
we can no longer afford to keep supporting them. They have been
-----------------------------------------------------------------
late with
```

Doc 1 Pg 2 Ln 1" Pos 1.9"

In addition to the size and type of paper you are using, the number of text lines available on a page is affected by headers and footers (Module 32), page numbers (Module 51), footnotes (Module 28) and endnotes (Module 23). Widow and orphan protection (Module 39) affects where a page break occurs as well.

HARD PAGE BREAK   You can create a hard page break at any time. Move the cursor where you want the page break to occur and press Ctrl-Enter. A hard page break is useful for separating text or for making sure a table or chart fits on one page. Hard page breaks are distinguished from soft page breaks on-screen by a double dashed line instead of a single one:

===

APPLICATIONS

Use the Page Break feature any time you are creating a document longer than one page. Let WordPerfect create soft page breaks when you are typing text that can be separated. Use a hard page break to separate text at the end of chapters, or to make sure an illustration stays together on one page.

TYPICAL OPERATION

In this operation, you type a letter that includes a table for emphasis. One-half of the table is on one page and one-half is on another. Use a page break to correct the problem.

1.   Create the following document leaving blank lines at the top of the first page so that a second page is required:

```
We need a major client support person. Here is a table that
outlines the problems we have had with clients who we haven't
properly serviced. Note that before we lost Russo, (June of 1985),
sales were much higher to those clients than after:

CUSTOMER              AVG. MONTHLY SALES
                  BEFORE 6/85      AFTER 6/85
Imperial Palace    $1250            $ 975
National            1570            1240
Orbison's           3470            2150
Ortega's             435             395
-----------------------------------------------------------------
Snyder Travel        250             175
Miller Men Shop      625             490
Orbital Link        2350            1895
Total:             $9950           $7320

The difference in just these clients alone more than pays for
Russo's salary. I recommend trying to hire her back. What do you
think?

                              Doc 1 Pg 2 Ln 2.33" Pos 1"
```

2. Move the cursor to the "C" in "CUSTOMER" on the table heading and press **Ctrl-Enter**. This moves the table to the next page.

```
We need a major client support person. Here is a table that
outlines the problems we have had with clients who we haven't
properly serviced. Note that before we lost Russo, (June of 1985),
sales were much higher to those clients than after:


==================================================================================
CUSTOMER              AVG. MONTHLY SALES
                   BEFORE 6/85       AFTER 6/85
Imperial Palace     $1250            $ 975
National             1570             1240
Orbison's            3470             2150
Ortega's              435              395
Snyder Travel         250              175
Miller Men Shop       625              490
Orbital Link         2350             1895
Total:              $9950            $7320

The difference in just these clients alone more than pays for
Russo's salary. I recommend trying to hire her back. What do you
think?
                                          Doc 1 Pg 2 Ln 1" Pos 1"
```

3. Save the document as SUPPORT.WPF.

4. Turn to Module 34 to continue the learning sequence.

Module 51
PAGE FORMAT

DESCRIPTION

There are many decisions that go into editing a document besides typing text. Do you want page numbers? Where do you want them to go? How many lines of text should be on the page? How much blank space should be at the top? Would you like this page centered?

The Page Format command (Shift-F8) gives you the tools to answer those questions and others. Use the Page Format key to number pages; select page numbers; make page numbers odd or even; position page numbers on a page; center pages; determine the paper size; set the top and bottom margins; create headers and footers (described in Module 32); and suppress page formatting for the current page.

NOTE

The default number of text lines per page is 54.
But, because many of these options take up space
on a printed page, they reduce the number of text
lines available to you per page.

Select the Page Format command by pressing Shift-F8 and typing 2 or P.

WordPerfect lists the default settings to the right of the various options on this menu. If you want to change those settings, you do so at this menu.

CENTER PAGE TOP TO BOTTOM   This command centers everything on a page vertically, from top to bottom. It is especially useful for title pages, letters, and other documents that don't occupy all of the space on a page. You cannot tell a page is centered by looking at it on-screen. WordPerfect centers the page when it is printed. To center a page, type 1 or C from the Page Format menu. You see the setting change to "Yes." Press F7 to return to the document.

To turn page centering off, Press Alt-F3, Reveal Codes (Module 59), and delete the [Center Pg] code.

FORCE ODD/EVEN PAGE   This command is useful if you are writing a chapter in a book that must start on an odd-numbered (right-hand) or even-numbered (left-hand) page. To force an odd- or even-numbered page, type 2 or o from the Page Format menu. When the "Odd or Even" prompt appears, type 1 or O to force an odd numbered page, 2 or E to force an even-numbered page. Then press F7 to return to the document.

TOP AND BOTTOM MARGINS   The default setting for WordPerfect top and bottom margins is 1-inch at the top and 1-inch at the bottom. Standard paper is 11-inches and you can fit 6 lines of text on each line. So the largest number of lines you can fit on a page is 6 x 11 or 66. With 1 inch at the top and bottom reserved for a margin, the most lines on a page is 9 x 6 or 54. Headers, footers, and footnotes further reduce this number. You can reset the top and bottom margins to give you more or less room for text. To do this, type 5 or M from the Page Format menu. Type the new top margin, press Down Arrow, then type the new bottom margin. Then press F7 to save the new settings and return to the document.

NEW PAGE NUMBER   This option lets you select the proper page number for your document. If your document is a chapter in a book, for example, and the chapter begins on page 150, this option lets you change the first page of your document to 150. This is also useful for documents that include a title page and table of contents before the beginning of text. The first page after the front matter might be eight pages into the document. This option lets you number that page one.

WordPerfect lets you number pages in Arabic (1,2,3) and lowercase Roman numerals (i,ii,iii). Lowercase Roman numerals are appropriate for prefaces, forewords, and other similar documents. When you change page numbers in the document, the page number on the Status Line also changes. To change the current page number:

1.   Move the cursor to the top of the current page and press **Shift-F8**. Type **2** or **P**, then **6** or **N**.

2.   Type a page number, for example, **256**, and press **F7**.

3.   Press **F7** again to return to the document. Notice the Status Line.

Doc 1 Pg 256 Ln 1" Pos 1"

PAGE NUMBERING   Page numbering is normally off in WordPerfect. However, this option turns page numbering on. It offers you a variety of choices for the location of the page number on the printed page. Page numbers can also be placed in headers and footers, as described in Module 32.

WordPerfect subtracts two lines of text for the page number: one for the page number itself and the other to separate it from the text. These page numbers do not appear on-screen, you see them only when the document is printed out.

Page numbers are pre-set to print at position 10 for the left side, 42 for the center, and 74 for the right. WordPerfect numbers pages on line 7 at the top of a page, and line 59 at the bottom.

To set a page number position:

1.   Move the cursor to the beginning of the page where you want page numbering to begin and press **Shift-F8**. Then type **2** or **P** and **7** or **P**.

```
Format: Page Numbering
```

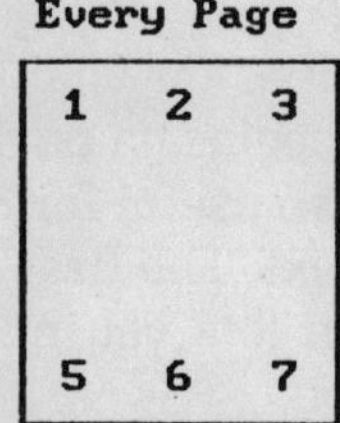
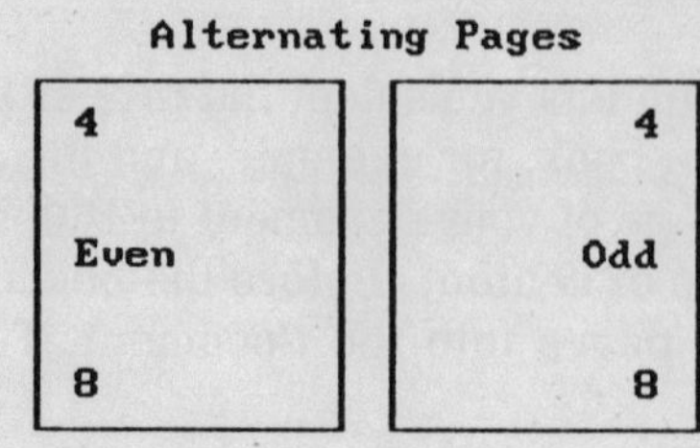

```
      Every Page                Alternating Pages

   ┌───────────┐        ┌───────────┐  ┌───────────┐
   │ 1   2   3 │        │ 4         │  │         4 │
   │           │        │           │  │           │
   │           │        │ Even      │  │      Odd  │
   │           │        │           │  │           │
   │ 5   6   7 │        │ 8         │  │         8 │
   └───────────┘        └───────────┘  └───────────┘

        9 - No Page Numbers

   Selection: 0
```

2. Select the page numbering option of your choice. For example, type **8** if you want page numbers at the bottom of each page, alternating between the left and right side (like this book). Press **Enter**.

```
    7 - Page Numbering                  Bottom Alternating
```

NOTE

You can turn page numbering off at any point
in the document by typing option 9 or N in the
Page Numbering menu.

3. Press **F7** to return to the document.

PAPER SIZE   WordPerfect is pre-set to print on standard letter-size paper (8½" by 11"), but several other options are available. You can also set it to print on standard-size paper sideways (landscape mode); legal-size paper, both standard and sideways; envelopes; half-sheets; government paper; and size A4 engineering documents, both standard and sideways. It also lets you print on a variety of forms, including standard-size paper, bond, letterhead, labels, envelopes, transparencies, and index cards.

To set the paper size:

1. Move the cursor to the top of the page where you want the new settings to begin and press **Shift-F8**. Type **2** or **P**, then **8** or **S**.

```
Format: Paper Size

    1 - Standard               (8.5" x 11")

    2 - Standard Landscape     (11" x 8.5")

    3 - Legal                  (8.5" x 14")

    4 - Legal Landscape        (14" x 8.5")

    5 - Envelope               (9.5" x 4")

    6 - Half Sheet             (5.5" x 8.5")

    7 - US Government          (8" x 11")

    8 - A4                     (210mm x 297mm)

    9 - A4 Landscape           (297mm x 210mm)

    0 - Other
```

2. Type the appropriate option, for example, **2** or **t**.

```
Format: Paper Type

    1 - Standard

    2 - Bond

    3 - Letterhead

    4 - Labels

    5 - Envelope

    6 - Transparency

    7 - Cardstock

    8 - Other
```

3. Type the appropriate type of paper on which WordPerfect will be printing the document. Press **F7**. If your printer is unable to print on the type of paper you've chosen, either because it requires a sheet feeder, or because your printer can't print sideways, the following message appears:

```
    8 - Paper Size             *8.5" x 8.5"
            Type               Standard
                               (*requested form is unavailable)
```

4. Press **F7** again to return to the document.

SUPPRESS PAGE FORMATTING FOR CURRENT PAGE ONLY This command lets you suppress all or some of the page formatting commands for the current page only. This is useful when you are creating a title page somewhere in a document. This command also lets you move page numbering to the bottom center of the current page only.

For example, assume you have a document with two headers, two footers, and page numbering. For one page only, you want to suppress Header A and Footer B and the page number at the bottom center of the page.

1. Move the cursor to the beginning of the desired page and press **Shift-F8**. Type **2** or **P**, then **9** or **u**.

```
Format: Suppress (this page only)

        1 - Suppress All Page Numbering, Headers and Footers

        2 - Suppress Headers and Footers

        3 - Print Page Number at Bottom Center   No

        4 - Suppress Page Numbering              No

        5 - Suppress Header A                     No

        6 - Suppress Header B                     No

        7 - Suppress Footer A                     No

        8 - Suppress Footer B                     No

    Selection: 0
```

2. Type **3** or **B**, **5** or **H**, and **8** or **o**. Notice the message next to those selections change to "Yes."
3. Press **F7** twice to save the selections and return to the document.

APPLICATIONS

Any time you are preparing a document for printing, you should consider changing the page formats from WordPerfect's default settings. You might want page numbering, but you might not like it to begin with page one of the document. If you are typing a short letter, you might want to center the document on a page. There are any number of reasons for formatting the pages in a document before you print it.

TYPICAL OPERATION

In this operation, you create a legal brief to be printed on legal-size paper. You want a centered title page, page numbering beginning on page 3, and the page number appearing at the bottom center of every page.

1. Create a document similar to the following:

```
                            LEGAL BRIEF

                        FLG OFFICE SUPPLIES


    =================================================================

    =================================================================
    This is a legal document pertaining to the operations of FLG Office
    Supply, Carbondale, Illinois. This store has been in business since
    1975 supplying Southern Illinois with a wide variety of supplies
    for office, school, computers, and electronic equipment.


                                            Doc 1 Pg 1 Ln 1" Pos 1"
```

2. With the cursor at the top of the title page, press **Shift-F8**. Type **2** or **P**, then **8** or **S**.
3. Type **3** or **L**, then **1** or **S** to set the document to print on legal-size standard paper.
4. Type **1** or **C** to center the title page. Then press **F7** to leave the Page Format menu.
5. Press **Ctrl-Home**, the Go To key. Type **3** and press **Enter**. The cursor moves to page 3.
6. Press **Shift-F8** and type **2** or **P**. Then type **6** or **N**, then **1**. Press **F7**.
7. Type **7** or **P**. Then type **6** to put page numbers at the bottom center of every page.
8. Press **F7** to return to the document.

```
    =================================================================
    This is a legal document pertaining to the operations of FLG Office
    Supply, Carbondale, Illinois. This store has been in business since
    1975 supplying Southern Illinois with a wide variety of supplies
    for office, school, computers, and electronic equipment.


                                            Doc 1 Pg 3 Ln 1" Pos 1"
```

9. Save the document as LEGALDOC.WPF.
10. Turn to Module 12 to continue the learning sequence.

Module 52

PARAGRAPH NUMBERING

DESCRIPTION

If you are typing a list of procedures, similar to those found in the Typical Operation sections in this book, WordPerfect can help you. No longer do you have to retype half the numbers just because you add a step in the middle. For example, if you add step 12 in a 30-step procedure, WordPerfect automatically renumbers steps 13 through 30 for you.

This is done with the Paragraph Number feature (Shift-F5). Paragraph numbering is similar to the Outline feature (Module 49), but instead of adding numbers every time you press Enter, WordPerfect adds them when you need them. You tell WordPerfect when you want to add a number and it does it. If you add a step in the middle, all the other paragraphs are re-numbered. There are two ways to set paragraph numbers: automatic and fixed.

AUTOMATIC PARAGRAPH NUMBERING   Eight levels of numbering — 1., a., i., (1), (a), (i), 1), a), among others are available. Automatic paragraph numbering works similarly to the Outline feature. Each time you press Tab, WordPerfect changes to the next level. In other words, if you press Tab twice and then press Enter, WordPerfect assumes you are on the third paragraph level. This feature is useful for creating outlines. To set paragraph numbers automatically:

1.   Press **Shift-F5** and type **5** or **P**.

```
Paragraph Level (Press Enter for Automatic):
```

2.   Press **Enter**.

```
I.
```

Doc 1 Pg 1 Ln 1.16" Pos 1"

Notice the roman numeral "I" appears on-screen. This is the first paragraph level. If you had moved the cursor to the "I" and pressed Tab six times and pressed Down Arrow, the screen would look like this:

```
                               i)
```

Doc 1 Pg 1 Ln 1" Pos 1.2"

Type whatever text you like. You do not need to create another paragraph number until you want to. When you want to add another paragraph number, repeat steps 1 and 2.

FIXED PARAGRAPH LEVEL   If you always want to be on the same level, such as when you are typing a set of procedures, use the fixed paragraph level. To set a fixed paragraph level, press Shift-F5 and type 5 or P. Type the paragraph level you want and press Enter. This remains fixed until you change it.

CHANGING THE NUMBER LEVELS   You may not always type the right key. You might want to change the number level back to "II" from "A," for example. To do this, move the cursor to the tab stop before the number and press Del. This lets you move up to another level. The rest of the paragraph numbers are automatically updated as you move through the document. If you want to move down to another level, press Tab, then Down Arrow. To delete a paragraph number at any level, move the cursor to the number you want to delete and press Del. The number disappears.

NOTE

If you accidentally create an extra paragraph
number on a line, delete it using the procedure
in this section, then continue typing.

CHANGING THE NUMBERING STYLE   WordPerfect creates a default numbering style for paragraphs called, appropriately enough, "paragraph style." If you wish to change this style, however, you may. Five styles are available:

• Paragraph Style	1.	a.	i.	(1)	(a)	(i)	1)	a)
• Legal Style	1	.1	.1	.1	.1	.1	.1	.1
• Outline Style	I.	A.	1.	a.	(1)	(a)	i)	a)
• Bullet Style	•	o	–	■	✳	+	·	×
• User-defined								

You can also create your own style using lowercase and uppercase letters, Roman numerals, numbers, and legal-style numbers. You can punctuate these with and without periods, and with single or double parentheses.

You can change the numbering style either before or after you write it. To change the numbering style, move the cursor to the beginning of the outline and press Shift-F5. Then type 6 or D.

```
Paragraph Number Definition

    1 - Starting Paragraph Number          1
          (in legal style)

                                        Levels
                         1     2     3     4     5     6     7     8
                        ___   ___   ___   ___   ___   ___   ___   ___
    2 - Paragraph        1.    a.    i.   (1)   (a)   (i)    1)    a)
    3 - Outline          I.    A.    1.    a.   (1)   (a)    i)    a)
    4 - Legal (1.1.1)     1    .1    .1    .1    .1    .1    .1    .1
    5 - Bullets           •     o     -     ■     *     +     ·     x
    6 - User-defined

    Current Definition    I.    A.    1.    a.   (1)   (a)    i)    a)

       Number Style                  Punctuation
       1 - Digits                    #    - No punctuation
       A - Upper case letters        #.   - Trailing period
       a - Lower case letters        #)   - Trailing parenthesis
       I - Upper case roman          (#)  - Enclosing parentheses
       i - Lower case roman          .#   - All levels separated by period
       Other character - Bullet          (e.g.  2.1.3.4)

    Selection: 0
```

The default is selection 3 or O. That default is listed in the table in the middle of the illustration. To change the numbering method, type 2 or P for paragraph numbering, 4 or L for legal numbering, 5 or B for bullet numbering, and 6 or U for user-defined numbering. The numbers underneath the "Number Style" and "Punctuation" headings at the bottom of the illustration are provided for reference if you are selecting your own method of paragraph numbering.

The Starting Paragraph Number selection (1 or S) lets you change the beginning number of a paragraph. This is useful when you continue numbering paragraphs from a previous document, or when you want to start numbering paragraphs over again.

APPLICATIONS

Use the Paragraph numbering feature to more easily create long procedures. You can also use it to create outlines if you are not comfortable with WordPerfect's Outline feature.

TYPICAL OPERATION

This example illustrates how to automatically number a set of rules.

1. Start WordPerfect and create a document similar to the following:

```
                        FLG OFFICE SUPPLY
                        RULES OF BEHAVIOR


                                           Doc 1 Pg 1 Ln 1.5" Pos 1"
```

2. Press **Shift-F5** and type **5** or **P**.

3. Type **1** to fix the paragraph level at 1 and press **Enter**. Press **F4** and type **Employees are expected to be on time, all the time.** Press **Enter**.

4. Press **Shift-F5**, type **5** or **P**, and press **Enter**. Press **F4** and type **Employees are to be courteous at all times to our customers.** Press **Enter**.

```
                          FLG OFFICE SUPPLY
                          RULES OF BEHAVIOR

    I.    Employees are expected to be on time, all the time.
    II.   Employees are to be courteous at all times to our customers.


                                           Doc 1 Pg 1 Ln 1.83" Pos 1"
```

5. Press **Shift-F5**, type **5** or **P**, and press **Enter**. Press **F4** and type **Employees are to wear clothing appropriate for work. No jeans, cut-offs, or other overly casual attire is allowed on the sales floor.** Press **Enter**.

```
                          FLG OFFICE SUPPLY
                          RULES OF BEHAVIOR

    I.    Employees are expected to be on time, all the time.
    II.   Employees are to be courteous at all times to our customers.
    III.  Employees are to wear clothing appropriate for work. No jeans,
          cut-offs, or other overly casual attire is allowed on the
          sales floor.

                                           Doc 1 Pg 1 Ln 2.33" Pos 1"
```

6. Move the cursor to the top of the document and press **Shift-F5**. Type **6** or **D**.

7. Type **2** or **P** to select paragraph numbering and press **F7** twice. Press **Home, Home, Down Arrow** to move the cursor to the bottom of the document. The document now looks like this:

```
                          FLG OFFICE SUPPLY
                          RULES OF BEHAVIOR

    1.    Employees are expected to be on time, all the time.
    2.    Employees are to be courteous at all times to our customers.
    3.    Employees are to wear clothing appropriate for work. No jeans,
          cut-offs, or other overly casual attire is allowed on the
          sales floor.

                                           Doc 1 Pg 1 Ln 2.33" Pos 1"
```

8. Save the document as RULES.WPF.

9. Turn to Module 48 to continue the learning sequence.

Module 53

PASSWORD PROTECTION

DESCRIPTION

WordPerfect offers you file security with its File Locking feature. File Locking lets you protect a file with a password, meaning no one else can access that file unless they know the password. If you have a file with confidential contents, use the password feature to make sure unauthorized personnel cannot access it. Each time you lock a file, you must type the password twice. Each time you retrieve it, you must type the password once. A document cannot be retrieved, looked at, or printed without the correct password.

CAUTION
When you lock a file, remember the password.
If you do not remember the password, there is
no way to retrieve the file.

LOCK A FILE   You may lock an existing file or a new file. To lock a file:

1.   Create or retrieve a file. Name it "LOCK.WPF." Press **Ctrl-F5**, then type **2** or **P**.

```
Password: 1 Add/Change; 2 Remove: 0
```

2.   Type **1** or **A**.

```
Enter Password:
```

3.   Type any password (up to 24 characters) and press **Enter**. The letters you type will not appear on-screen. You will be prompted to re-enter your password. At this time, retype the same password and press **Enter**. This ensures that you typed the password correctly the first time. If you type a different password the second time, WordPerfect gives you an error message and prompts you to enter the password again.

CAUTION
Remember your password! If you forget it, it is
not possible to retrieve the document.

4.   Press **F7**, type the name of the file you want to save (LOCK.WPF in this example) and press **Enter** to save it.

SAVE A FILE AFTER IT HAS BEEN PROTECTED   To save a file after it has been password protected, you can use either the Save/Exit key (F7) or the Save key (F10).

RETRIEVE A PROTECTED FILE   After a file has been protected, you can open it only with the password. There are two ways to unlock a file: through List Files (F5) or Retrieve a file (Shift-F10). To unlock the example file through List Files:

1. Make sure your screen is blank. Press **F5** to access the List Files menu. Type the directory location of the file and press **Enter**. If the file is on your default directory, just press **Enter**.

2. Move the cursor to the LOCK.WPF and type **1**. Then type the password for the file and press **Enter** to retrieve it.

NOTE
If you get an error message while trying to retrieve the file, you have typed the wrong password. Try again.

3. Edit the document and save the file.

To retrieve the protected example file using the Retrieve key:

1. Make sure your screen is blank. Press **Shift-F10**. Type **LOCK.WPF** and press **Enter**.

2. Type the password and press **Enter** to retrieve the file.

3. Edit the document and save the file.

CHANGING YOUR PASSWORD   The procedure for changing your password is similar to the procedure for locking a document. To change your password:

1. Press **Shift-F10**, type the filename and press **Enter**. Then type the old password and press **Enter** to retrieve the protected file LOCK.WPF.

2. Press **Ctrl-F5**, type **2** or **P**, then **1** or **A**.

3. Type the new password and press **Enter**. Then retype it.

4. Press **F7**, type the name of the file you want to save, and press **Enter** to save it.

REMOVING PASSWORD PROTECTION   The need for security can be fleeting. Some files that may at first appear to need password protection may later not need it. WordPerfect offers a remedy in this situation by letting you remove password protection from a document. To remove password protection:

1. Press **Shift-F10**, type the filename, and press **Enter**. Then type the old password and press **Enter**.

2. Press **Ctrl-F5** and type **2** or **P**.

3. Type **2** or **R**. Password protection is removed.

APPLICATIONS

Use password protection to "lock" files of a confidential nature. These may be files containing trade or government secrets or other security information.

TYPICAL OPERATION

In this example, you protect a file that is of a confidential nature.

1. Create a document similar to the following:

```
MEMO

CONFIDENTIAL

From: FLG
To: JM, MD
Subject: New advertising campaign.

We are about to go full-force after SIU Office Supply. We are
readying a $20,000 ad campaign that will run in the Southern
Illinoisan, the Daily Egyptian, WTAO, Channel 8, and Channel 6.
Enclosed is the ad copy. DON'T LET ANYONE ELSE SEE THIS DOCUMENT!

                                        Doc 1 Pg 1 Ln 1" Pos 1"
```

2. Press **Ctrl-F5**. type **2** or **P**, then **1** or **A**.

3. At the "Enter Password" prompt, type **flgads** and press **Enter**. Type it again at the "Re-enter Password" prompt.

4. Save the document as ATTACK.WPF.

5. Turn to Module 58 to continue the learning sequence.

Module 54

PRINTER ADVANCE

DESCRIPTION

The Printer Advance key (Shift-F8) lets you insert a code that tells your printer to print text a specified distance from the current printing position. Advance up and down contrasts with superscripts and subscripts (Module 59), which let you print text one-third of a line up or down.

The advance left or right or to a specific column features are useful when printing text on pre-printed forms. Advancing left or right moves the cursor a specific distance from the current cursor position. Advancing to a column moves the cursor to a specific position number.

The Printer Advance key also lets you advance the printer to a specific line on the page. Advancing to a specific line lets you create a blank space on the page without inserting blank lines. This is particularly helpful when you are inserting a number of blank lines to make room for information that will be pasted into the text later.

Advance commands are not reflected by blank space on the screen. Rather, they are reflected in the status line. The "Ln" indicator on the Status Line reflects up, down, and line advances. The "Pos" indicator reflects left, right, and specific column advances.

Advance features can be used separately or together. If trying to fill out a form, for example, you can type text at the left margin that needs to be printed 5" from the right margin and 2" from the top and advance text accordingly. This saves you the trouble of trying to line up text on the screen.

NOTE

Not all printers support the advance features. To check, try to print the PRINTER.TST file (Appendix E) and see if it works with your printer.

To use the advance feature:

1. Position the cursor where you want to begin. Press **Shift-F8**, type **4** or **O**, then **1** or **A**.

```
Advance: 1 Up; 2 Down; 3 Line; 4 Left; 5 Right; 6 Position: 0
```

2. Select the appropriate advance feature: type **1** or **U** to advance text up; **2** or **D** to advance text down; **3** or **i** to advance text to a specific line; **4** or **L** to advance text left; **5** or **R** to advance text right; **6** or **C** to advance text to a specific column.

3. Type the distance, line number, or column number you want and press **F7** twice to advance text to that position or that distance. Notice the Status Line change accordingly.

4. Type the text you want to advance. If you want the printer to return to the original position when you have finished, press **Shift-F8** and type **4** or **O**. Select the appropriate advance method (same as the one selected in step 2).

5. Type **0** and press **F7** twice to turn Printer Advance off.

If you have already typed the text you want advanced:

1. Move the cursor to the beginning of the text you want advanced and press **Shift-F8**, type **4** or **O**, then **1** or **A**.

2. Select the appropriate advance feature: type **1** or **U** to advance text up; **2** or **D** to advance text down; **3** or **i** to advance text to a specific line; **4** or **L** to advance text left; **5** or **R** to advance text right; **6** or **C** to advance text to a specific column.

3. Type the distance, line number, or column number you want and press **F7** twice to advance text to that position or that distance. Notice the Status Line change accordingly.

4. Move the cursor to the end of the text you want advanced. Press **Shift-F8** and type **4** or **O**. Select the appropriate advance method (same as the one selected in step 2).

5. Type **0** and press **F7** twice to turn Printer Advance off.

APPLICATIONS

Use the printer advance up or down feature when you are advancing several characters or words up or down. This is useful for equations, lining up text on a page, and a variety of other applications. Use the advance to a line feature when you are inserting a large number of blank lines on a page. This is especially useful if you are going to be adding an illustration to a document later and want to make room for it.

Use the advance left or right feature when printing on forms or other pre-printed documents. This lets you type text anywhere on a page without measuring the distance on the form where text actually needs to be printed. The advance to a column feature works for similar applications. Advance features can be used together for filling out forms and other pre-printed data.

TYPICAL OPERATION

In this example, you create a document that will benefit from some extra white space on a page for a chart.

1. Start WordPerfect and create a document similar to the following:

```
MEMO
FROM: FLG
TO: ALL STAFF
SUBJECT: GOOD NEWS!


As you can tell from the above chart, sales at FLG are going up!
Congratulations. Each one of you will get an extra day off next
week. Keep up the good work.

                                        Doc 1 Pg 1 Ln 1.66" Pos 1"
```

2. Make sure your cursor is on the blank line after "SUBJECT" and press **Shift-F8**. Type **4** or **O**, then type **1** or **A**, and **3** or **i**.

3. The chart takes up 10 lines (2.16") of text, so advance 3" down the page. Type **3** and press **Enter**. Then press **F7** to turn the advance to a line feature on.

```
SUBJECT: GOOD NEWS!
-
As you can tell from the above chart; sales at FLG are going up!
                                          Doc 1 Pg 1 Ln 3" Pos 1"
```

4. Move the cursor to the "a" in "are" on the next line and press **Shift-F8**. Type **4** or **O**, **1** or **A**, then **1** or **U**.

5. Type **.1** and press **F7** twice to turn the advance up feature on.

```
As you can tell from the above chart, sales at FLG are going up!
                                        Doc 1 Pg 1 Ln 3.86" Pos 6.1"
```

6. Move the cursor to the end of the sentence and press **Shift-F8**. Type **4** or **O**, then **1** or **A**.

7. Type **2** or **D**, then **.1**, and press **F7** twice to turn the advance up feature off.

8. The printed document looks like this with space for the chart to be pasted in later.

```
MEMO
FROM: FLG
TO: ALL STAFF
SUBJECT: GOOD NEWS!




As you can tell from the above chart, sales at FLG are going up!
Congratulations. Each one of you will get an extra day off next
week. Keep up the good work.
```

9. Save the document as GOODNEWS.WPF.

10. Turn to Module 57 to continue the learning sequence.

Module 55

PRINTER CONTROL

DESCRIPTION

Module 56 teaches you how to print outside a document. Module 57 teaches you to print inside a document. This module teaches you how to control your printer, both before and during printing. You use the control printer selection on the Print menu as well as the options from that same menu.

Before printing, WordPerfect lets you set the binding width (the amount of room left in the margins for punch holes or bindings), the number of copies to print, which printer to use, (you can select as many as you want), the quality of graphics in the document, and the text quality. You can also display the printers and fonts you have selected.

During printing, you can cancel a print job (Module 56), display print jobs, rush a print job to the head of the print queue (Module 56), or stop printing entirely.

Before you do anything else, however, you have to select printers.

SELECT PRINTERS   Before you make any choices in the print process, it is necessary to tell WordPerfect which printer or printers you are using. You can choose as many printers as you like to work with WordPerfect. After you select the appropriate printer or printers and set them up to work with WordPerfect, you can edit the settings, delete the printer definition, or copy the printer definition to use it with a similarly defined printer.

The printer files are located on four diskettes that come with WordPerfect. If you are using WordPerfect on a hard-disk-based system, you should have copied the printer files to your hard disk in Module 2. If you are using a floppy-based system, remove your data diskette from drive B and replace it with the Printer diskette.

To access the Print menu, press Shift-F7:

```
Print

        1 - Full Document
        2 - Page
        3 - Document on Disk
        4 - Control Printer
        5 - Type Through
        6 - View Document
        7 - Initialize Printer

    Options

        S - Select Printer          Toshiba P1340
        B - Binding                 0"
        N - Number of Copies        1
        G - Graphics Quality        Medium
        T - Text Quality            Draft
```

To select a new printer, type S from the Print menu, then type 2 or A. If necessary, type the location of the printer files and press Enter.

NOTE

On a floppy-based system, it may be necessary to exchange printer diskettes to access the printer files you want to use.

```
Select Printer: Additional Printers

    Alphacom Alphapro 101
    Alps ALQ200/300/P2400C
    Alps P2000/P2100
    AMT Office Printer (Diablo)
    AMT Office Printer (IBM Color)
    Apple ImageWriter / DMP
    Apple ImageWriter II
    Apple Laserwriter Plus
    AST TurboLaser
    AST TurboLaser/PS
    Blaser
    Brother HR-15XL/35
    Brother HR-20
    C.ITOH 8510 Prowriter
    C.ITOH C-310 CP
    C.ITOH C-310 EP/CXP
    C.ITOH C-715F
    C.ITOH C-815
    C.Itoh D10-40
    C.ITOH ProWriter jr. Plus
    C.Itoh Starwriter/Printmaster

  1 Select; 2 Other Disk; 3 Help; 4 List Printer Files; N Name Search: 1
```

This is the beginning of an alphabetical listing of printers available to you in WordPerfect. In all, WordPerfect fully supports more than 100 printers.

To select a printer, move the cursor to that printer using the Down Arrow key. You can also use WordPerfect's Name Search feature (Module 61) to quickly move to the printer of your choice. Press Enter twice and observe the text that tells you helpful hints about the printer. Then press F7 and the Printer Selection menu appears:

```
 Select Printer: Edit

        Filename                         TOSHP134.PRS

     1 - Name                            Toshiba P1340

     2 - Port                            LPT1:

     3 - Sheet Feeder                    None

     4 - Forms

     5 - Cartridges and Fonts

     6 - Initial Font                    10 pitch

     7 - Path for Downloadable
             Fonts and Printer
             Command Files

     Selection: 0
```

This menu lets you tell WordPerfect all of the important information about your printer. You can change the initial font (type style) your printer will print text in (Module 27), indicate the types of forms your printer is using, select whether you are using a sheet feeder or not, etc.

Name   Type 1 or N from the Printer Selection menu. Notice the cursor move to the first character in the printer name. This option lets you change the name of the printer. This is useful if you are using a printer that is compatible with the one selected. Either type a new name for the printer and press Enter, or press F1 to cancel the operation.

Port   Type 2 or P from the Printer Selection menu.

```
 Port: 1 LPT 1; 2 LPT 2; 3 LPT 3; 4 COM 1; 5 COM 2; 6 COM 3; 7 COM 4; 8 Other: 0
```

This option lets you tell WordPerfect which port your printer is connected to. Generally, dot-matrix or daisy-wheel printers are connected to a parallel printer port, signified by the "LPT" designation. A laser printer is generally connected to a serial port, signified by the "COM" designation. Type a number for the desired port and press Enter.

Sheet Feeder   Type 3 or S from the Printer Selection menu.

```
Select Printer: Sheet Feeder

  BDT MF 850 (3 Bin)
  Diablo Single/Dual/Envelope
  HP 2603A 3 Bin
  Kyocera F Series
  Mechanical

1 Select; 2 None; 3 Help; N Name search: 1
```

A sheet feeder is a device that connects to the back of your printer. It makes it easier to feed different forms through your printer, i.e., one bin can hold letterhead, another can hold blank paper, another can hold envelopes, etc. The above illustration lists all the sheet feeders supported by both WordPerfect and the Toshiba P1340. Your printer may support more or less of the WordPerfect-compatible sheet feeders. If you are using a sheet feeder, move the cursor to the sheet feeder connected to your printer and type 1 or S. If you are not using a sheet feeder, type 2 or o. Like printer selection, you can also use the Name Search feature to quickly move to the sheet feeder of your choice.

Forms   Type 4 or F from the Printer Selection menu.

```
Select Printer: Forms
                                         Orient Init            Offset
Form type                 Size           P L    Pres Location   Top     Side

Standard                  8.5" x 11"     Y N     Y   Contin     0"      0"
[ALL OTHERS]              Width ≤ 8.5"           N   Manual     1"      0"

If the requested form is not available, then printing stops and WordPerfect
waits for a form to be inserted in the ALL OTHERS location.  If the requested
form is larger than the ALL OTHERS form, the width is set to the maximum width.

1 Add; 2 Delete; 3 Edit: 3
```

The forms selection screen lets you tell WordPerfect what kinds of forms — paper types — your printer supports. The menu lets you select the form type; size; orientation (portrait, a straight up and down view, or landscape, a sideways view); whether this form type is initially present (the default); where the paper is located, important for a sheet feeder-supported printer; and how much space to leave at both the top and sides of the form.

To add a form type, type 1 or A. To delete a form type, move the cursor to the form type you want to delete and type 2 or D, then Y. To edit a form type, that is, change the settings defined on the menu, type 3 or E and make the appropriate changes.

If you type 1 or A, the following screen appears:

```
Select Printer: Form Type

        1 - Standard

        2 - Bond

        3 - Letterhead

        4 - Labels

        5 - Envelope

        6 - Transparency

        7 - Cardstock

        8 - [ALL OTHERS]

        9 - Other

    Selection: 1
```

Type the appropriate letter (or number) for the form you want to add. For example, if you type
2 or B, you see:

```
Select Printer: Forms

        Filename                    TOSHP134.PRS

        Form Type                   Bond

    1 - Form Size                   8.5" x 11"

    2 - Orientation                 Portrait

    3 - Initially Present           Yes

    4 - Location                    Continuous

    5 - Page Offsets - Top          0"
                       Side         0"

    Selection: 0
```

As described above, change the settings as desired, then press F7 to save them and add the
form. When you are printing a document and are ready to change the form, insert a paper change
code using the paper type option in the Page Format menu (Module 51). You can add as many
forms as you like.

Cartridges and Fonts   Type 5 or C from the Printer Selection menu. Many printers support plug-in modules, print wheels, or downloadable fonts that let you change the font. For example, here are the available fonts and cartridges for the Texas Instruments 855 and 857 printers.

```
Select Printer: Cartridges and Fonts

Font Category                    Resource                    Quantity

Font Slot                        Slot 3                         1
Font Slot                        Slot 2                         1
Font Slot                        Slot 1                         1

1 Select Fonts; 2 Change Quantity; N Name search: 1
```

These are the available font resources for the printer. As you can see, three slots are available on the TI 855/857 for fonts. To actually select fonts, move the cursor to the slot you want to select and type 1 or F.

```
Select Printer: Cartridges and Fonts

                                        Total Quantity:      1
                                    Available Quantity:      1

Font Slot                                           Quantity Used

Courier                                                  1
Courier Italic                                           1
Gothic 96                                                1
Modern (PS)                                              1

Mark Fonts:  * Present when print job begins        Press Exit to save
                                                    Press Cancel to cancel
```

These are the fonts available with this particular cartridge. Move the cursor to the font you want to use with your printer and type * to mark it as present when the print job begins. These fonts are used in the Base Font menu (Module 27) and can be used when you switch fonts in the middle of a document. Press F7 to save the settings.

Initial Font   Type 6 or I from the Printer Selection menu.

```
Select Printer: Initial Font

* 10 pitch
  12 pitch
  17 pitch Condensed
  5 pitch Double Wide
  Proportional

1 Select; N Name search: 1
```

This option lets you set the initial font your printer will be using when you start WordPerfect. Note that this font is identical to the one that appears when you use the Base Font menu in Module 27. Move the cursor to the font of your choice and press Enter to choose it.

Type 7 or d. This option lets you set the path where downloadable fonts and printer command files (Appendix E) are located. Type the location (either drive or directory information or both) and press Enter.

Press F7 twice to save all the settings.

OPTIONS   Options available at the Print menu let you change the current printer; the binding width (the amount of space between the left margin and the edge of the page taking into account whether a page is numbered odd or even); the number of copies to print; the quality of the graphics; and the quality of the text you print. These options are changed for the remainder of the session until you exit WordPerfect. Many of the selections are saved with the document. The options are described as follows.

When you are finished, press F7 to return to your document.

Select Printers   Type S from the Print menu:

```
Print: Select Printer

    Apple Laserwriter Plus
    DOS Text Printer
    Epson FX-80/100
    Epson MX-80 Graftrax
    TI 855/857
 *  Toshiba P1340


  1 Select; 2 Additional Printers; 3 Edit; 4 Copy; 5 Delete; 6 Help: 1
```

Move the cursor to the printer of your choice. Type 1 or S to select it; 2 or A to select a different printer from among the 100 + models supported by WordPerfect; 3 or E to edit a particular printer selection; 4 or C to copy a particular definition; 5 or D to delete a definition; or 6 or H for help. Press F7 to return to the Print menu.

Binding   Type B from the Print menu. WordPerfect normally shifts text to the right on odd-numbered pages and to the left on even-numbered ones. This lets you punch holes in or bind two-sided copies without losing any text. If you are printing one-sided pages, you might want to increase the left margin to compensate for the additional space. To change the binding width, type the new binding width and press Enter.

Number of Copies   Type N from the Print menu. Then type the number of copies you want to print and press Enter.

Graphics Quality   Type G from the Print menu.

```
Graphics Quality: 1 Do Not Print; 2 Draft; 3 Medium; 4 High: 3
```

This lets you set the quality at which your printer prints graphics (Module 30). The higher the quality, the longer they take to print. Type 1 or N if you do not want to print graphics; 2 or D for draft quality; 3 or M for medium quality; 4 or H for high quality.

Text Quality   Type T from the Print menu. This option offers you the same options for text as you were presented with above for graphics. Type 1 or N if you do not want to print text; 2 or D for draft quality; 3 or M for medium quality; 4 or H for high quality.

PRINTER CONTROL   WordPerfect's Printer Control menu lets you manage the way documents flow from WordPerfect to the printer. You can change the order of documents in queue, cancel print jobs, stop them, and more.

When the printer is already printing a document and you select another for printing, WordPerfect assigns that document a print job number and puts it in line, or in a print queue. The Printer Control menu lists both the document being printed and up to two additional documents. To access the Printer Control menu, press Shift-F7 and type 4 or C.

```
Print: Control Printer

Current Job

Job Number: 1                          Page Number:  1
Status:       End of job               Current Copy: 1 of 1
Message:      None
Paper:        Standard 8.5" x 11"
Location:     Continuous feed
Action:       None

Job List

Job  Document              Destination        Print Options
 1   (Screen)              LPT 1
 2   (Screen)              LPT 1

Additional Jobs Not Shown: 0

 1 Cancel Job(s); 2 Rush Job; 3 Display Jobs; 4 Go (start printer); 5 Stop: 0
```

There are two parts to this menu. The first part (Current Job) tells you which document is currently being printed, what page is being printed, which copy, and whether anything is wrong with the printer. The second part (Job List) tells you which documents are in the print queue. Up to three print jobs are displayed on this menu. If you are printing more than three documents at a time, the remaining documents are listed in a job list, which you access by typing 3 or D from this menu. The number of documents not shown on the Printer Control menu is listed at the bottom of the menu as "additional jobs not shown." Each printed document is given a print job number, sent to a certain printer, and "knows" whether the printer can handle continuous form paper or not.

CANCEL PRINT JOBS   Once you have put a document in the print queue, whether it has begun printing or not, it is assigned a print job number (Module 56). You can cancel printing of any document at any time, whether it has begun printing or not. To cancel a print job, assume at least one document is in the print queue. Press Shift-F7 and type 4 or C, then 1 or C.

```
Cancel which job? (*=All Jobs) 1
```

Type the number of the print job you wish to cancel. If you want to cancel all print jobs, type * and Y to confirm this and press Enter. The print job is canceled. To start printing again, you have to send the printer a "go," described later in this module.

RUSH PRINT JOB   If you are printing a number of documents, but want to print one before all the others, you can "rush" that print job to the head of the print queue. To do this:

Assume there are 14 documents in the print queue.

1.   Type **2** or **R** from the Printer Control menu.

```
Rush which job? 14
```

2.   WordPerfect assumes you are trying to rush the last print job to the head of the line. If you are, press **Enter**. If you are not, type the print job you want to rush to the head of the line and press **Enter**.

```
Interupt current job? (Y/N) N
```

3.   If you are really in a hurry and want the document printed fast (especially if the document currently printing is fairly long), you can interrupt the current print job. If you do not want to interrupt the current print job, press **Enter**. The document will print as soon as the current one is finished.

If you want to interrupt, type **Y**. WordPerfect stops what it's printing, resets the printer to the top of the next page and prints the rushed document. After the rushed print job is finished, WordPerfect resumes printing the current document at the top of the page where printing was interrupted.

DISPLAY ALL PRINT JOBS   WordPerfect displays the next three print jobs on the Job List section of the Printer Control menu. If more than three print jobs have been sent to the print queue, WordPerfect tells you the number of additional print jobs at the bottom of the Printer Control menu. If you want, you can see all the print jobs, including the ones on the Printer Control menu, on a separate job list. To display all print jobs:

1.   Type **3** or **D** from the Printer Control menu.

```
Job List

    Job  Document              Destination      Print Options
     3   C:\WP50\ALIGNTXT.WPF  LPT  1           text=draft
     4   C:\WP50\BLOCKTXT.WPF  LPT  1           text=draft
     5   C:\WP50\BREAKTXT.WPF  LPT  1           text=draft
     6   C:\WP50\CANCLTXT.WPF  LPT  1           text=draft

Press any key to continue
```

2.   The job list lists the print job, the document, where the document is to be printed, and the type of form it will be printed on. If a print job has already been printed, it moves out of the queue and is not listed. Press Enter twice to return to the document.

"GO" RESUME PRINTING   If you cancel all print jobs or stop printing for any other reason, WordPerfect temporarily suspends printing. In order to start printing again, you must inform WordPerfect that everything is okay again. Normally, this is because you need to realign or add printer paper, change a ribbon or a print wheel, or perform some other maintenance task on your printer. The Printer Control menu looks like this when you need to send the printer a "go" signal:

```
Print: Control Printer

Current Job

Job Number: 3                        Page Number:  1
Status:      Stopped                 Current Copy: 1 of 1
Message:     None
Paper:       Standard 8.5" x 11"
Location:    Continuous feed
Action:      Adjust paper (press FORM FEED or advance paper to top of page)
             Press "G" to restart, "C" to cancel

Job List

Job  Document              Destination      Print Options
 3   (Screen)              LPT 1
 4   (Screen)              LPT 1

Additional Jobs Not Shown: 1

1 Cancel Job(s); 2 Rush Job; 3 Display Jobs; 4 Go (start printer); 5 Stop: 0
```

To send the printer a "go," type G from the Printer Control menu. If there are any print jobs in the print queue, they begin printing again.

STOP PRINTING   You can stop printing at any time. You might have to answer the telephone and the printer is making too much noise. Or maybe an emergency situation occurs with the printer, like the ribbon runs out of ink. To stop printing, type S from the Printer Control menu. This temporarily stops printing without canceling any print jobs. If you want to start printing again, send the printer a "go." WordPerfect starts printing the current print job where it left off.

APPLICATIONS

There are many applications for printer control. Before printing a document, you must tell WordPerfect something about the printer or printers you are using. You might need to print more than one copy of a document. And there are many instances where you need to control the print queue. If you do not know which documents were selected, display all the print jobs and check. If there is a document you do not want to print, cancel it. If you have a problem with your printer, stop printing and solve the problem. Then send the printer a "go" signal to resume. And if you are printing a fairly large document and want to rush a short document to the head of the line, use the rush print job option.

TYPICAL OPERATION

In this example, you use the Printer Control menu to control the print job queue. The procedures required for printing documents are described in Modules 56 and 57.

1. Start WordPerfect and retrieve any document. Then press **Shift-F7** and type **1** or **F**. Repeat this four times. Then press **Shift-F7** and type **4** or **C**.

```
    Job List

    Job  Document              Destination          Print Options
     2   (Screen)              LPT 1
     3   (Screen)              LPT 1
     4   (Screen)              LPT 1

    Additional Jobs Not Shown: 1


    1 Cancel Job(s); 2 Rush Job; 3 Display Jobs; 4 Go (start printer); 5 Stop: 0
```

2. Type **2** or **R**, then **5**, and press **Enter** to rush the fifth print job to the front of the queue. When prompted to let the current job print to completion, type **N**.

3. Type **5** or **S** to stop printing.

4. Reset the printer to the top of the page by using the top of page command on your printer. Type **4** or **G** to resume printing.

5. Type **1** or **C**, then ***** and **y** to cancel all print jobs.

6. Turn to Module 54 to continue the learning sequence.

Module 56

PRINTING OUTSIDE A DOCUMENT

DESCRIPTION

The Print key (Shift-F7) lets you print a document being edited or a document on disk. This module describes printing a document on disk. Module 57 describes printing a document that is being edited.

NOTE

In order to save space, WordPerfect gives you the option of "Fast Saving" documents in unformatted fashion. You select this through the Setup key (Shift-F1), discussed in Appendix B. If you selected fast save for documents, you must either retrieve documents before you can print them, or format them immediately before saving them by pressing Home, Home, Down Arrow, then Home, Home, Up Arrow.

This module assumes you have not used the Fast Save option for documents, or that you have formatted the documents before saving them. If you used Fast Save and did not format the document immediately before saving it, the following error message appears when you try to print documents that have not been retrieved: "ERROR: Document was Fast Saved — Must be retrieved to print." If you have used the Fast Save option, disregard this module.

You can select as many documents for printing as you like. WordPerfect assigns each document a print job number. These documents are lined up in a "print queue," which prints one document after another.

You can also select which printer to send the document to (if you have more than one), the number of copies you want to print, the binding width of the document, and the graphics and text quality of the document. All of these options are discussed in Module 55, Printer Control.

There are two ways to print a document from disk. You can print either from the List Files (Module 40) menu, or from the Print menu (Module 55).

PRINTING FROM THE LIST FILES MENU   To print a document from List Files:

1. Press **F5**, then **Enter**. Your List Files menu looks similar to this:

```
06/14/88  12:37              Directory C:\WP50\DOCS\*.*
Document size:        0   Free:  4476928   Used:      61459        Files:  44

 . <CURRENT>    <DIR>                    .. <PARENT>    <DIR>
ANNUAL   .WPF    2611  06/13/88 08:43   ATTACK   .WPF     880  06/10/88 15:50
AVERAGE  .WPF    2619  06/08/88 10:28   BANQUET  .WPF    1184  06/13/88 13:11
BIRTHDAY.WPF     566  06/08/88 14:29   CONCERN  .WPF     886  06/09/88 14:41
DRESS    .WPF     582  06/08/88 15:36   FINANCES.WPF    2944  06/13/88 08:11
HOURS    .WPF    1193  06/09/88 13:01    IDEAS   .WPF    1050  06/13/88 08:11
INDEX    .WPF    3338  06/13/88 09:16   JAMES    .WPF    1922  06/09/88 16:37
JOG      .WPF     846  06/10/88 08:31   LEAGUE   .WPF     798  06/08/88 15:57
LEGALDOC.WPF    1102  06/09/88 11:36   LIPSON   .WPF     890  06/09/88 15:07
LIST     .WPF     429  06/13/88 08:04   LISTS    .WPF    1680  06/13/88 09:44
```

2. Move the cursor to the document you want to print and type **4** or **P**.

```
   Page(s): (All)
```

3. Select the range of pages to print (see Page Ranges later in this module) and press **Enter**. If you want to print all the pages, just press **Enter**. The document prints.

PRINTING FROM THE PRINT MENU   To print a document from the Print menu:

1. Press **Shift-F7**. You see the Print menu:

```
Print

     1 - Full Document
     2 - Page
     3 - Document on Disk
     4 - Control Printer
     5 - Type Through
     6 - View Document
     7 - Initialize Printer

Options

     S - Select Printer          Epson FX-80/100
     B - Binding                 0"
     N - Number of Copies        1
     G - Graphics Quality        Medium
     T - Text Quality            High

Selection: 0
```

2. Type **3** or **D**. You see the "Document name" prompt. Type the name of the document you want to print and press **Enter**. Select the range of pages to print and press **Enter**. To print all the pages, just press **Enter**. The document prints.

3. Repeat this procedure as many times as you like.

PRINTING SEVERAL FILES AT A TIME   If you want to print several files at once, you can mark them on the List Files menu. The Mark Text key, Alt-F5, marks every file in a directory. You can then print those files. If you want to mark only certain files for printing:

1. From the List Files menu, move the cursor to the first file to print and type *. Then move the cursor to the next file to mark and type *.

2. Continue marking files in this manner. If you change your mind about marking any file, type * again with the cursor at that file to remove the mark.

3. Type **4** or **P**.

```
Print marked files? (Y/N) No
```

4. Type **Y** and press **Enter**. The files print in alphabetical order.

PAGE RANGES   As illustrated before, WordPerfect lets you select a range of pages before you print a document. There are several options open to you at the "Pages(All)" prompt, as illustrated in the following list:

Keystrokes	Results
Enter	Prints all pages.
1, Enter	Prints page 1.
1, 3 Enter	Prints pages 1 and 3.
1, 4, 6 Enter	Prints pages 1, 4, and 6.
1-4, 6 Enter	Prints pages 1 through 4 and 6.
1-4, 6-10 Enter	Prints pages 1 through 4 and 6 through 10.
10-Enter	Prints from page 10 through the end of the document.
-10 Enter	Prints from the beginning of the document through page 10.

APPLICATIONS

Use the Print menu to print a document or part of a document. Use the List Files menu when you are not sure the name of the file to print. List Files is especially convenient for printing a large number of documents at once because you can simply move the cursor to the documents and type *. You can monitor the printing of any document from the Print menu.

TYPICAL OPERATION

In this example, you use both the Print menu and List Files to print a number of documents.

1. Start WordPerfect and press **F5** from a blank screen. Change the directory to correspond to where you keep documents and press **Enter**.

```
06/14/88  12:41              Directory C:\WP50\DOCS\*.*
Document size:        0   Free:   4433920   Used:      61459        Files:  44

.  <CURRENT>     <DIR>                    ..  <PARENT>     <DIR>
ANNUAL   .WPF      2611  06/13/88 08:43   ATTACK   .WPF       880  06/10/88 15:50
AVERAGE  .WPF      2619  06/08/88 10:28   BANQUET  .WPF      1184  06/13/88 13:11
BIRTHDAY.WPF        566  06/08/88 14:29   CONCERN  .WPF       886  06/09/88 14:41
DRESS    .WPF       582  06/08/88 15:36   FINANCES.WPF      2944  06/13/88 08:11
HOURS    .WPF      1193  06/09/88 13:01   IDEAS    .WPF      1050  06/13/88 08:11
INDEX    .WPF      3338  06/13/88 09:16   JAMES    .WPF      1922  06/09/88 16:37
JOG      .WPF       846  06/10/88 08:31   LEAGUE   .WPF       798  06/08/88 15:57
LEGALDOC.WPF       1102  06/09/88 11:36   LIPSON   .WPF       890  06/09/88 15:07
LIST     .WPF       429  06/13/88 08:04   LISTS    .WPF      1680  06/13/88 09:44
MEMO     .WPF       968  06/09/88 10:08   MEMOS    .WPF      1751  06/07/88 15:54
MILLER   .WPF      1538  06/10/88 13:47   MONTH    .WPF      1373  06/09/88 15:32
PAPERLES.WPF        819  06/10/88 09:33   PERFORM  .WPF      1291  06/09/88 12:14
PRACTICE.WPF        720  06/06/88 08:20   PURPOSE  .WPF       517  06/08/88 08:21
REST     .WPF       667  06/13/88 08:11   RESUME   .WPF      1703  06/08/88 12:48
REVIEW   .WPF       702  06/08/88 09:14   RULES    .WPF       631  06/09/88 14:07
RUSSO    .WPF      1329  06/10/88 07:55   SALE     .WPF       657  06/07/88 13:36
SHOP     .WPF       440  06/08/88 10:47   SNYDER   .WPF      1183  06/13/88 14:18
SORRY    .WPF      1403  06/07/88 13:58 ▼ SORRY2   .WPF      1663  06/07/88 16:28

1 Retrieve; 2 Delete; 3 Move/Rename; 4 Print; 5 Text In;
6 Look; 7 Other Directory; 8 Copy; 9 Word Search; N Name Search: 6
```

2. Move the cursor to a document, ("ANNUAL.WPF," for example) and type **4** or **P**. Press **Enter** to print all the pages in the document and **Enter** again to return to the menu. Press **F7** to return to the document.

3. Press **Shift-F7**. Type **3** or **D**.

4. Type a document name (SALE.WPF, for example) and press **Enter**. Type **3-5** to print pages 3 to 5 in the document and press **Enter**.

5. When the documents are finished printing, turn to Module 13 to continue the learning sequence.

Module 57

PRINTING WITHIN A DOCUMENT

DESCRIPTION

The Print key (Shift-F7) lets you print the document being edited or a document on disk. This module describes printing the document being edited. Module 56 describes printing a document on disk.

While editing a document, you have the following printing options:

- Print the entire document.
- Print a page of the document.
- Print a block of text.
- Use the printer as a typewriter, typing through one character at a time.
- Previewing a document before it is printed.

Anything you print, whether it be a page, a block of text, or an entire document, is printed complete with headers, footers, footnotes, or endnotes.

You can also select which printer to send the document to (if you have more than one), the number of copies you want to print, the binding width of the document, and the graphics and text quality of the document. All of these options are discussed in Module 55, Printer Control.

PRINT A DOCUMENT You can print a document from anywhere inside that document. You can print multiple copies (Module 55) of that document as well. You can leave the document before printing is completed. To print a document:

1. Press **Shift-F7**.

```
Print

        1 - Full Document
        2 - Page
        3 - Document on Disk
        4 - Control Printer
        5 - Type Through
        6 - View Document
        7 - Initialize Printer

    Options

        S - Select Printer          Epson FX-80/100
        B - Binding                 0"
        N - Number of Copies        1
        G - Graphics Quality        Medium
        T - Text Quality            High

    Selection: 0
```

2. As discussed in Module 55, select the printer you wish to use, and set the binding width, number of copies, and graphics and text quality to your specifications.

3. Type **1** or **F**. Notice the "*Please wait*" prompt. The document prints.

PRINT A PAGE   You can also print a page of the document you are editing. The cursor needs to be resting in that page before you print. To print a page, move the cursor anywhere in the page to print and press Shift-F7. After setting the options to your specifications, type 2 or P. The page prints.

PRINT A BLOCK   Besides printing an entire document or a page in that document, you can also print a block (Module 8) of text. That block can be as long or as short as you want. To print a block:

1. Move the cursor to the beginning of the block to print and press **Alt-F4**. Move the cursor to the end of the block to print and press **Shift-F7**.

```
Print block? (Y/N) No
```

2. Type **Y**. The block prints.

TYPE THROUGH   The Type Through command essentially turns your printer into a typewriter. Everything you type while in Type Through mode either goes directly to the printer or goes to the printer when you press Enter.

The advantage of waiting until you press Enter for text to go to the printer is that if you make a mistake you can correct it before it is sent to the printer. The Type Through feature is useful for printing short amounts of text, such as that on envelopes and forms. To use Type Through:

NOTE

Type Through doesn't work on all printers. If your printer doesn't support this feature, WordPerfect gives you the following message: "Feature not available on this printer."

1. Move the cursor anywhere you want and press **Shift-F7**. Type **5** or **Y**.

```
Type Through by: 1 Line; 2 Character: 0
```

2. To send characters to your printer when you press **Enter**, type **1** or **L**. To send characters to your printer as you type, type **2** or **C**.

```
Character Type Through printing

Function Key            Action

Move                    Retrieve the previous line for editing
Format                  Do a printer command
Enter                   Print the line
Exit/Cancel             Exit without printing
```

This menu explains how Type Through printing works. If you want to edit the previous line, press Ctrl-F4, the Move key (Module 47). If you want to send the printer a command, press Shift-F8, the Other Format key (Module 48). If you are in the line Type Through printing mode, press Enter to print a line. And if you don't want to print anything, press F7, the Exit key (Module 60), or F1, the Cancel key (Module 10).

NOTE

Other keys also work in Type Through mode. You can insert and delete text, for example. The cursor control keys control the printer. Up Arrow moves the printer carriage up one line, Down Arrow moves it down one line, Left Arrow moves it left one character, and Right Arrow or Spacebar moves it right one character.

Before you begin typing, position the form or other document on your printer.

Begin typing. If you are in the character Type Through mode, every character you type is printed immediately. If you are in the line Type Through mode, you can type up to 200 characters before you have to press Enter to send the characters to the printer. There is no word-wrapping, however, so type only the number of characters your printer can print on a line.

When you are finished using Type Through, press F7 or F1 to return to the document.

VIEW DOCUMENT   The View Document feature gives you a preview of what a document looks like before it is printed. This is useful for making sure that a document looks like you want it to, that headers and footers are properly placed, that page numbers fall where you want, that text flows evenly, and especially, that graphics look like they should (graphics don't appear on-screen at any other time). To use View Document, press Shift-F7 and type 6 or V.

This is a long-distance look at one page of your document as it will be sent to the printer. If you want to see it more closely, type 1 to see it displayed at 100 percent. If you want to see just a specific part of the page, type 2 to see the page at 200 percent. Typing 4 puts facing pages on the screen, and typing 3 makes the document look as it does when View Document starts. Cursor control keys, like PgUp, PgDn, Screen Up, and Screen Down keys let you scroll through the document.

APPLICATIONS

Use the Print Within a Document feature of WordPerfect to print the document you are currently editing. Select the page option to print only one page of a document. Mark a block to print more than a page, but less than an entire document. Type Through is useful for printing small amounts of text, filling out a form, or addressing an envelope. View Document helps you make sure a document is ready for printing, that page numbers, headers, footers, footnotes, and graphics appear in the places you want them.

TYPICAL OPERATION

This example illustrates various methods of printing within a document.

1. Start WordPerfect and retrieve "FINANCES.WPF" (created in Module 15, Cursor Control):

```
                                        Jack Belew
                                        FLG Office Supplies
                                        124 N. Main
                                        Carbondale, IL 62901
                                        February 24, 1987

William Levin
345 N. Olive
Carterville, IL 62966

Dear Bill:

It was a pleasure speaking with you last week about your new
position with the Bank of Carterville. I hope you can help us with
our financial needs in the future.

Per your request, I am enclosing some recent financial statements.
I think you'll agree that FLG Office Supplies is in fine financial
shape. And with your help, we hope to be even better.

                                Sincerely,

                                Jack Belew
                                Controller
                                        Doc 1 Pg 1 Ln 1" Pos 1"
```

2. Move the cursor to the beginning of the next page.

```
                          INCOME STATEMENT
                        FLG OFFICE SUPPLIES
                  FOR YEAR ENDED DECEMBER 31, 1986

     Sales:                    $625,000




C:\WP50\DOCS\FINANCES.WPF                    Doc 1 Pg 2 Ln 1" Pos 1"
```

3. Press **Alt-F4** and move the cursor to the end of the document. Then press **Shift-F7** and type **Y** to print the block.

4. Press **Shift-F7** and type **5** or **Y**. Type **1** to set up line Type Through printing.

5. Insert an envelope in your printer. Position it in the address area and type **William Levin** and press **Enter** to send this to the printer.

6. Press **Down Arrow** to move the printer to the next line. Type **345 N. Olive** and press **Enter** to send this to the printer.

7. Press **Down Arrow** to move the printer to the next line. Type **Carterville, IL 62966** and press **Enter** to send this to the printer.

8. Press **Down Arrow** to move the printer to the next line and press **F7** to exit Type Through mode.

9. Exit the document.

10. Turn to Module 56 to continue the learning sequence.

Module 58

REDLINE AND STRIKEOUT

DESCRIPTION

Two old terms from pen and paper editing days are *redline* and *strikeout*. Redlined text is text that the editor recommends be added to a document. Text that is marked for strikeout means the editor recommends it be deleted from a document. WordPerfect lets you use both the Redline and the Strikeout feature while editing a document. Redline and strikeout appear most frequently when you are comparing two documents (Module 20).

REDLINED TEXT   Redlined text appears in red on-screen with a color monitor. It appears in reverse video on a monochrome monitor. This can be altered using WordPerfect's Colors/Fonts/Attributes Feature (Appendix C). When it is printed, it can appear any variety of ways, including in red or with a vertical bar in the left or right margins. Your printer might even put dots under all the letters that are redlined.

NOTE

You may change the way redlined text is printed
using the Redline Format command, described
later in this module or with the Printer.exe
command, described in Appendix E.

To redline text:

1.   Move the cursor to the space where you want to add text and press **Ctrl-F8**. Then type **2** or **A**.

```
1 Bold 2 Undrln 3 Dbl Und 4 Italc 5 Outln 6 Shadw 7 Sm Cap 8 Redln 9 Stkout: 0
```

2.   Type **8** or **R**. Notice the Status Line. On a color monitor, the number next to Pos has turned red. In monochrome, the number is in reverse video. This indicates you are in Redline mode. Type the text to be added.

3.   Press **Ctrl-F8** and type **3** or **N**. This turns Redlining off.

USING THE BLOCK KEY TO REDLINE TEXT   If you have already typed text that you want to redline, you can use the Block key (Module 8).

1.   Move the cursor to the beginning of the block to redline and press **Alt-F4**. Then move the cursor to the end of the block to redline and press **Ctrl-F8**.

2.   Type **2** or **A**, then type **8** or **R**. The text is redlined.

STRIKEOUT TEXT   Strikeout text is displayed as green on a color monitor and appears with dashes through it on a monochrome monitor and when printed:

Since you are marking text for deletion, you usually use the Block key to strikeout text. But you can type text marked for strikeout as well. To type strikeout text:

1. Press **Ctrl-F8**, type **2** or **A**, then type **9** or **S**. This turns on the Strikeout mode.

2. Type the text you want to strikeout.

3. Press **Ctrl-F8**, then type **3** or **N** to turn Strikeout off.

To strikeout text using the Block key:

1. Move the cursor to the beginning of the block to strikeout and press **Alt-F4**. Then move the cursor to the end of the block to strikeout and press **Ctrl-F8**.

2. Type **2** or **A**, then type **9** or **S**. The text is marked for strikeout.

The number next to "Pos" on the Status Line turns green to indicate text is marked for strikeout. On a monochrome monitor, the number has a line through it.

REDLINE FORMAT   The Redline Format command lets you choose how redlined text will be displayed when it is printed. You have several choices in formatting redlined text. You can let the printer choose how redlined text will be marked. A color printer, by the way, can print redlined text in red. Or, it can identify redlined text with a bar in the left margin, or with a bar in the left margin on even-numbered pages and the right margin on odd-numbered pages. To choose redline format:

1. Press **Shift-F8**. Type **3** or **D**.

```
Format: Document

     1 - Display Pitch - Automatic        Yes
                          Width            0.1"

     2 - Initial Codes

     3 - Initial Font                      10 CPI

     4 - Redline Method                    Printer Dependent

     5 - Summary

 Selection: 0
```

2. Type **4** or **R**.

```
Redline Method: 1 Printer Dependent; 2 Left; 3 Alternating: 1
```

3. Type **1** or **P** for printer dependent redlining, **2** or **L** for bars in the left margin, or **3** or **A** for alternating bars in the left margin on even pages and the right margin on odd.

REMOVING REDLINE OR STRIKEOUT MARKINGS   When you mark text for redline or strikeout, WordPerfect inserts a code marking the beginning and end of the redlined or strikeout text. Use Reveal Codes, Alt-F3 (Module 59) to delete these codes.

However, if you decide to accept these markings, you may remove all text marked for strikeout while adding all text marked for redline in a document. To do this:

1. Position the cursor anywhere in the document and press **Alt-F5**.

```
1 Auto Ref; 2 Subdoc; 3 Index; 4 ToA Short Form; 5 Define; 6 Generate: 0
```

2. Type **6** or **G**.

```
Mark Text: Generate

    1 - Remove Redline Markings and Strikeout Text from Document

    2 - Compare Screen and Disk Documents and Add Redline and Strikeout

    3 - Expand Master Document

    4 - Condense Master Document

    5 - Generate Tables, Indexes, Automatic References, etc.

Selection: 0
```

3. Type **1** or **R**.

```
Delete redline markings and strikeout text? (Y/N) No
```

4. Type **Y**.

APPLICATIONS

Redline text that you want to add to a document. If you are editing a document for someone else, this gives that person the option of adding your redlines or deleting them. Strikeout text you want to remove from a document. Again, this gives the originator of the document the option of accepting or rejecting your changes. Once all redlines and strikeouts have been made to a document, the Remove command accepts them. Redline and strikeout markings are created automatically by WordPerfect when using the Document Compare feature (Module 19).

TYPICAL OPERATION

Imagine you have received a trip report and have been asked to edit it. In this example, you create redlined text, strikeout other text, and use the Remove command to delete the markings from the redlined text and delete the text marked for strikeout.

1. Create a document similar to the following:

```
Monday, March 16. Traveled to Washington. Met with representatives
of the Office Automation Society. Talked about the state of the
industry.

Tuesday, March 17. Met with Acme Folder Company. Told them of our
requirements for folders. They made us a very attractive offer. We
can get a 60% margin on folders if we buy all of our folders from
them.

Wednesday, March 18. Gave a speech at the meeting. Was well
received. Decided to leave town early, since the meeting with
Computer Forms fell through.

                                        Doc 1 Pg 1 Ln 1" Pos 1"
```

2. Move the cursor to the end of the second paragraph and press **Enter** twice. Then press **Ctrl-F8** and type **2** or **A**. Type **8** or **R** to turn Redline on. Type **Set up meeting with Computer Forms for Thursday morning.**

3. Press **Ctrl-F8** and type **3** or **N** to turn Redline off.

4. Move the cursor to the "W" in "Was" in the next paragraph and press **Alt-F4** to turn Block on. Type . to highlight the sentence as a block. Then press **Ctrl-F8**, type **2** or **A** and type **9** or **S**. This is what the document looks like when it is printed:

```
Monday, March 16. Traveled to Washington. Met with representatives
of the Office Automation Society. Talked about the state of the
industry.

Tuesday, March 17. Met with Acme Folder Company. Told them of our
requirements for folders. They made us a very attractive offer. We
can get a 60% margin on folders if we buy all of our folders from
them.

Set up meeting with Computer Forms for Thursday morning.

Wednesday, March 18. Gave a speech at the meeting. Was well
received. Decided to leave town early, since the meeting with
Computer Forms fell through.
```

5. Press **Alt-F5**. Type **6** or **D**, then **1** or **R**.

6. Type **Y** to add all redlines and remove all strikeouts from the document.

7. Move the cursor to the spaces after the period in "meeting" and press **Del** to delete one of them. This is what the final document looks like:

```
Monday, March 16. Traveled to Washington. Met with representatives
of the Office Automation Society. Talked about the state of the
industry.

Tuesday, March 17. Met with Acme Folder Company. Told them of our
requirements for folders. They made us a very attractive offer. We
can get a 60% margin on folders if we buy all of our folders from
them.

Set up meeting with Computer Forms for Thursday morning.

Wednesday, March 18. Gave a speech at the meeting. Decided to
leave town early, since the meeting with Computer Forms fell
through.
```

8. Save the document as WASHTRIP.WPF.

9. Turn to Module 44 to continue the learning sequence.

Module 59
REVEAL CODES

DESCRIPTION

You use many special features in the course of creating and editing a document. You change spacing, set tabs, create new pages, and more. Whenever you use any special feature, WordPerfect inserts a code into the text for the printer. Because it would be distracting to see symbols for those functions on-screen all the time, WordPerfect hides them. If you want to see where a tab is or when you changed spacing from single to double, use the Reveal Codes key (Alt-F3). The preceding text looks like this when you press Alt-F3:

```
    screen all the time, WordPerfect hides them. If you want to see
    where a tab is, or when you changed spacing from single to double,
    use the Reveal Codes key (Alt-F3). The preceding text looks like
    this when you press Alt-F3:

                                              Doc 1 Pg 1 Ln 1" Pos 1"
[   ▲    ▲    ▲    ▲    ▲    ▲    ▲    ▲    ▲    ▲    ▲   }    ▲    ▲
Screen all the time, WordPerfect hides them. If you want to see[SRt]
where a tab is, or when you changed spacing from single to double,[SRt]
use the Reveal Codes key ([BOLD]Alt[-]F3[bold]). The preceding text looks like[S
Rt]
this when you press [BOLD]Alt[-]F3[bold]:[HRt]

Press Reveal Codes to restore screen
```

WordPerfect divides the screen in half and shows several lines above and below the cursor on each half, plus the current line. On the top half, it displays text as it would normally be seen on the screen. On the bottom, it displays text with all codes included. A complete list of codes is included in Appendix L. The above illustration includes the following codes:

- Boldface on ([Bold])
- Boldface off ([bold])
- Soft return ([SRt])
- Hard return ([HRt])

The cursor is always highlighted and does not blink.

WordPerfect lets you perform complete editing tasks while in Reveal Codes. You can add text, edit, move the cursor around, even use the Search and Replace feature to search and replace codes.

The main use for Reveal Codes is to delete unwanted functions. Use the Del or Backspace key to delete any function, space, or character. Reveal Codes also give you a status report, displaying codes at a glance.

The only way to leave the Reveal Codes screen is by pressing Alt-F3, the Reveal Codes key.

DELETING CODES   You delete a code because you no longer need that function in place. For example, you might center a word and then decide later you do not want that word centered. One way to delete the center is to use the Reveal Codes key. Pressing Alt-F3 reveals the location of the center code ([Cntr]).

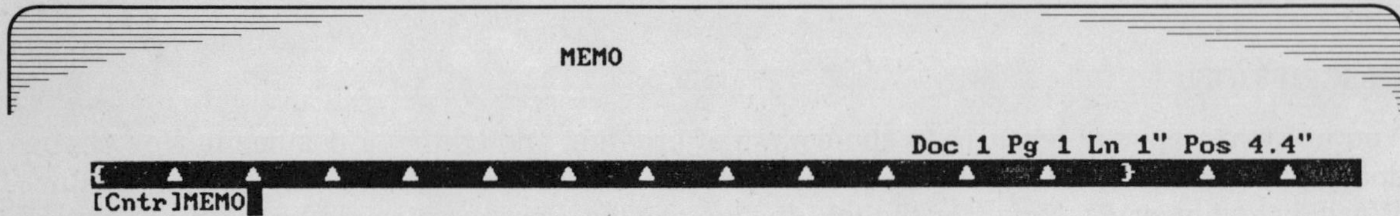

To delete the center command, move the cursor to the right of the center code and press Backspace, or move the cursor to the left of the code and press Del.

SEARCHING FOR CODES   There are times, especially in long documents, when you want to search for a code, for example, the next underline code. To search forward for an underline code, you can either have the Reveal Codes screen active or not. If you press F2, then F8 you see:

Press F2 and the cursor moves to the next underline code. You can delete the code to remove the underline, or perform any other editing functions you want. If there are no more underline codes, a "*not found*" message appears on the screen.

You can also search backward, or use the search command to search and replace. (The Search functions are described in Module 61.)

APPLICATIONS

Use Reveal Codes to delete unwanted codes from text and to make sure the right codes have been used. Reveal Codes is particularly helpful for printing, because it informs you of the location of each code. Reveal Codes is very helpful in troubleshooting a document that will not print or otherwise behaves erratically. If you are having problems with any WordPerfect document, there is a good chance there is a code in the wrong place. The only way to find this out is through Reveal Codes.

TYPICAL OPERATION

Imagine you decide to delete all boldfaced text from a document. In order to do this, you use the Search key and perform search and replace functions. This operation can be accomplished without using Reveal Codes, but we use it here to add clarity to the example.

1. Create a document similar to the following:

```
MEMO
To: ALL FLG PERSONNEL
From: FLG
Subject: DRESS CODE

Until further notice, there is no dress code at FLG. Dress as you'd
like. But you had better look professional at all times! So while
there is no dress code, there are limits!

Thanks,

FLG


                                        Doc 1 Pg 1 Ln 1" Pos 1"
```

2. Press **Alt-F3**. Notice all the bold codes in the text. These codes identify where boldface starts and ends.

```
MEMO
To: ALL FLG PERSONNEL
From: FLG
Subject: DRESS CODE

Until further notice, there is no dress code at FLG. Dress as you'd
like. But you had better look professional at all times! So while
there is no dress code, there are limits!

Thanks,
                                        Doc 1 Pg 1 Ln 1" Pos 1"

MEMO[HRt]
To: [BOLD]ALL FLG PERSONNEL[bold][HRt]
From: [BOLD]FLG[bold][HRt]
Subject: [BOLD]DRESS CODE[bold][HRt]
```

3. Press **Alt-F2**, the Search and Replace key (Module 61). Type **N** in response to the prompt "w/Confirm? (Y/N)." The command works much faster this way.

4. Type **F6**, the Bold key (explained in Module 5).

NOTE
You cannot type [Bold] when performing a search
and replace. The command does not work with
codes in that manner, only with the appropriate
function key.

```
-> Srch: [BOLD]
```

5. Press **F2**, then press **Del** and **F2** again. This indicates you want to delete the boldface items. Then press **Alt-F3** to leave Reveal Codes.

```
MEMO
To: ALL FLG PERSONNEL
From: FLG
Subject: DRESS CODE

Until further notice, there is no dress code at FLG. Dress as you
want. But you had better look professional at all times! So while
there is no dress code, there are limits!

Thanks,

FLG
                                        Doc 1 Pg 1 Ln 2.83" Pos 1.3"
```

6. Press **Alt-F3**. Notice that all the boldface codes have been removed. Press **Alt-F3** to exit Reveal Codes.

7. Save the document as DRESCODE.WPF.

8. Turn to Module 31 to continue the learning sequence.

Module 60
SAVE TEXT/EXIT

DESCRIPTION

Before you turn off your computer, you must exit WordPerfect. More importantly, before you exit WordPerfect, you should save the text you created during the session. If you don't save your text, you lose everything you created during the session.

WordPerfect lets you save text in one of two ways: by using the Exit key (F7) or by using the Save key (F10). Use the Exit key to save a document you are finished editing. Also use the Exit key to leave WordPerfect. (When you use the Exit key, you don't have to save the document you are editing in a separate step). If you use the Save key, you are telling WordPerfect you want to save the document and then continue editing it.

You can save text either unformatted (Fast Save) or formatted with WordPerfect commands. If you save text unformatted, you cannot print documents without retrieving them. However, it takes less time to save documents to disk in unformatted fashion and you can print documents after they have been retrieved. Fast Save is explained in Appendix B.

You can print documents from disk even with Fast Save enabled. Simply press Home, Home, Down Arrow, then Home, Home, Up Arrow immediately before saving and exiting the file. This bypasses Fast Save and saves the file in formatted fashion on disk.

USING THE SAVE KEY WordPerfect lets you save data through the use of the Save key (F10). If you have not saved the document before, the following prompt appears when you press F10:

```
Document to be saved:
```

To save a new document, type the name you want to use and press Enter. If you already saved the document you are working with — let's call it "MEMOS.WPF" and say it is in the \WP\DOCS subdirectory on drive C: — the following prompt appears when you press F10:

```
Document to be saved: C:\WP50\DOCS\MEMOS.WPF
```

If you press Enter, you see:

```
Replace C:\WP50\DOCS\MEMOS.WPF? (Y/N) No
```

NOTE
To save a document under a different filename,
thereby keeping the original, type N at this point,
type the new filename, and press Enter.

Typing Y saves the document. WordPerfect returns you to the document when it is finished saving it.

USING THE EXIT KEY Press the Exit key to end the current session. When you press F7, the following prompt appears:

```
    Save document? (Y/N) Yes
```

If text has not been modified since the last time you saved the document, the following message appears:

```
    Save document? (Y/N) Yes                          (Text was not modified)
```

If text has been modified since the last time you saved it, no message appears on the right-hand side of the screen.

If you save a document by pressing F10, you are not notified whether text was modified or not. When the "Save Document?" prompt appears, you have the following options:

Keystrokes	Result
y (filename) Enter n	Saves a new document and clears the screen.
y Enter y n	Saves a previously saved document and clears the screen.
y (filename) Enter y	Saves a new document and exits WordPerfect.
y Enter yy	Saves a previously saved document and exits WordPerfect.
y (filename) Enter F1	Saves a new document and returns to it.
y Enter y F1	Saves a previously saved document and returns to it.
n n	Clears the screen (doesn't save the document).
n y	Exits WordPerfect (doesn't save the document).

APPLICATIONS

Saving and editing a document are two of the most important features of WordPerfect. If you do not save a document, you lose it. After you are finished using WordPerfect, exit the program either to use other applications or to get ready to turn off your computer.

If you are working with a document for a long period of time, remember to save it periodically (every fifteen minutes is a good idea). This is true especially if you are not using WordPerfect's automatic backup feature (Appendix B). If something catastrophic happens, like a power failure or a lightning strike, this ensures you do not lose a great deal of data.

TYPICAL OPERATION

In this example, you save a document that has never been saved before and exit from WordPerfect.

1. Start WordPerfect and create a document similar to the following:

```
This is a test.
```

2. Press **F7**, then **Enter**.
3. Type **C:\WP50\DOCS\TEST.WPF** and press **Enter**.

```
Exit WP? (Y/N) No                                    (Cancel to return to document)
```

4. Type **Y** to exit WordPerfect.
5. Turn to Module 65 to continue the learning sequence.

Module 61

SEARCH AND REPLACE

DESCRIPTION

One of the nice things about word processing is being able to search through a document to find a word. If you have a twenty page document, for example, and are not sure where you mentioned Dr. Jones, WordPerfect's Search feature finds the good doctor for you in a flash. If you are on the last page in that document, use the Backward Search (Shift-F2) feature to search back to page 1. If you are on page 1, use the Forward Search (F2) feature.

WordPerfect also includes a Word Search feature that lets you search through a number of documents for a specific word. This is useful if you are trying to find a document that mentions aspirin, for example, but are not sure which of the fifty documents on your hard disk is the right one.

A related feature to Search is Replace. The Replace feature (Alt-F2) lets you move through a document and change every occurrence of a word or words to something else — PC to Personal Computer, for example. WordPerfect even includes a Confirm option that gives you a chance to verify each Replace before it happens.

NOTE
The Replace feature works forward only, while the Search feature works both forward and backward. Replace also does not work in conjunction with Word Search.

WordPerfect searches for characters, strings of characters, or codes in a document or a block of text. If you type letters all lowercase, WordPerfect finds all instances of the word, both uppercase and lowercase. If you type uppercase letters, WordPerfect only looks for occurrences of the word with uppercase letters:

- If you type "test" WordPerfect finds all occurrences of the word — test, Test, TEST.
- If you type "Test" WordPerfect only finds Test.
- If you type "TEST" WordPerfect only finds TEST.

There are two exceptions to this: WordPerfect always capitalizes the first letter of every sentence and it always capitalizes the proper I in words like I and I'm.

To search or replace in a block, define a block, as described in Module 8.

If WordPerfect does not find the string of characters you typed, it displays a "*Not found*" message.

TIP: When searching for whole words, put a space both before and after the word. That way, if you are looking for the word "the," WordPerfect will not stop each time it sees "the" in a word (then, other, etc.).

FORWARD SEARCH WordPerfect can search forward from the cursor position for any character, phrase, or code. To search forward:

1. Press **F2**. The arrow in the prompt tells you that you are searching forward.

2. Type the word, phrase, or code you are looking for. (The cursor, Backspace, Delete, and Insert keys all work normally.)
3. Press **F2**. The cursor moves to the first occurrence of the text you were searching for. To search for that same string again, press **F2** twice.

BACKWARD SEARCH WordPerfect can search backward from the cursor position for any character, phrase, or code. To search backward:

1. Press **Shift-F2**. Notice the difference between this prompt and the one for Forward Search.

2. Type the string of characters you are looking for and press **Shift-F2**. WordPerfect moves to the first previous occurrence of the word. To search for that same string again, press **Shift-F2** twice.

WORD SEARCH WordPerfect has a feature that lets you search through all the documents on your disk for a certain word or group of words. This can be very helpful when you are not sure which document or documents mention a specific subject. Word Search is located in the List Files directory. To use Word Search:

1. Press **F5**. Select the directory you want to search and press **Enter**.

```
06/09/88  16:05            Directory C:\WP50\DOCS\*.*
Document size:       305    Free:  7073792   Used:      28663           Files:  25

.  <CURRENT>    <DIR>                    .. <PARENT>    <DIR>
AVERAGE  .WPF      2619  06/08/88 10:28   BIRTHDAY.WPF       566  06/08/88 14:29
CONCERN  .WPF       886  06/09/88 14:41   DRESS    .WPF       582  06/08/88 15:36
FINANCES.WPF       3172  06/07/88 15:06   HOURS    .WPF      1193  06/09/88 13:01
IDEAS    .WPF      1418  06/08/88 08:54   LEAGUE   .WPF       798  06/08/88 15:57
LEGALDOC.WPF       1102  06/09/88 11:36   LIPSON   .WPF       890  06/09/88 15:07
MEMO     .WPF       968  06/09/88 10:08   MEMOS    .WPF      1751  06/07/88 15:54
MONTH    .WPF      1373  06/09/88 15:32   PERFORM  .WPF      1291  06/09/88 12:14
PRACTICE.WPF        720  06/06/88 08:20   PURPOSE  .WPF       517  06/08/88 08:21
REST     .WPF       895  06/06/88 16:15   RESUME   .WPF      1703  06/08/88 12:48

  1 Retrieve; 2 Delete; 3 Move/Rename; 4 Print; 5 Text In;
  6 Look; 7 Other Directory; 8 Copy; 9 Word Search; N Name Search: 6
```

2. Type **9** or **W**.

```
Search: 1 Doc Summary; 2 First Page; 3 Entire Doc; 4 Conditions: 0
```

3. Type **1** or **D** to search the Document Summary (Module 21) only; **2** or **F** to search the first page of every document; **3** or **E** to search each document entirely. See Conditional Word Search if you want to type **4** or **C** and set conditions for the search.

```
Word pattern:
```

4. Type the word pattern to search for. It can be anything up to 20 characters. The word pattern can be in a variety of formats:

   - One word — type one word by itself.
   - Two or more words — enclose the phrase in quotes.
   - A wildcard — use an asterisk or question mark to find words that match a certain pattern. Typing T* for example, finds all words that begin with T. Typing to?n finds all the words that match that pattern like torn, town, etc.
   - One word and another word — use a semi-colon or space between words to identify files that include both words. Typing paper;pencils looks for files where both words are found.
   - One word or another word — use a comma between words to identify files that include either word. Typing paper,pencils looks for files where either word is found.

5. Press **Enter**. The Word Search begins. When the search is complete, WordPerfect puts an asterisk next to the files that include the designated word pattern.

CONDITIONAL WORD SEARCH WordPerfect lets you set a number of conditions when conducting a search. You can search only those documents created between one date and another; you can select the files to search; you can search parts of the document summary; and more. You can also change search conditions and undo the effects of the last search. To perform a Conditional Word Search, type 9 or W, then 4 or C from the List Files menu.

```
    Word Search

        1 - Perform Search on              All 25 File(s)

        2 - Undo Last Search

        3 - Reset Search Conditions

        4 - File Date                       No
              From (MM/DD/YY):              (All)
              To   (MM/DD/YY):              (All)

                      Word Pattern(s)

        5 - First Page
        6 - Entire Doc
        7 - Document Summary
              Creation Date (e.g. Nov)
              Descriptive Name
              Subject/Account
              Author
              Typist
              Comments

        Selection: 1
```

Perform Search On   This option lists the number of files involved in the search. The number changes after each search has been executed to reflect the number of files that meet the search conditions. Typing 1 or P from the Word Search menu executes the search.

Undo Last Search   Type 2 or U from the Word Search menu. This option resets the search back to its condition before the last search. If a search resulted in 20 files being selected and a second search resulted in 40 files being selected, typing 2 or U resets the conditions so only 20 files are selected.

Reset Search Conditions   Type 3 or R from the Word Search menu to clear the search conditions and start completely over. The Perform Search On selection then lists all the files in the current directory.

File Date   Type 4 or D from the Word Search menu. This option lets you select only files modified within a certain time period. For example, if you want to search only files created between March and December 15 of 1989, type 3//88 and press Enter. Then type 12/15/89 and press Enter. Type 4 or D to turn the File Date feature off, thus selecting files from all time periods.

First Page   This option lets you search through the first page (or first 4,000 characters, which ever comes first) of selected documents for specific word patterns. To do this, type 5 or F from the Word Search menu. Type the word pattern and press Enter.

Entire Doc   This option lets you search through a series of selected documents for specific word patterns. To do this, type 6 or E from the Word Search menu. Type a word pattern and press Enter.

Document Summary   This option lets you search specific parts of document summary for desired word patterns. To do this, type 7 or S from the Word Search menu, move the cursor to the desired section to search, type the word pattern, and press Enter.

EXTENDED SEARCH   Extended Search searches beyond text through headers, footers, endnotes, and footnotes. Access Extended Search by pressing the Home key with the Forward (F2) or Backward (Shift-F2) Search keys or the Replace key (Alt-F2). For example, pressing Home-F2 brings up the following screen:

```
-> Extended srch:
```

NAME SEARCH   While most of WordPerfect's Search options deal with individual documents, Name Search helps you navigate through menus and lists. Several WordPerfect features — List Files (Module 40), Printer Selection (Module 55), Fonts (Module 27), and others — make use of the Name Search feature. This feature quickly searches through a listing as you type the name of a font, printer, file, or other entity. For example, if you were looking for the Toshiba P1340 printer while selecting printers, you would type 1 or N to enter the Name Search mode. Then, typing "t" takes you to the first printer beginning with "t," typing "o" takes you to Toshiba.

SEARCH AND REPLACE   This is one of the most useful features in WordPerfect. It lets you search through a document and replace the characters you do not want with those you do. And it works very quickly. You can search through a fairly lengthy document and replace occurrences in just a few seconds. To use Search and Replace:

1.   Press **Alt-F2**. The message "w/Confirm? (Y/N) N" appears.

2.   If you type **Y**, the cursor stops at each occurrence of the specified character string and asks you if you really want to replace it in this location. If you type **N**, it replaces all occurrences. The Confirm option is useful for documents where you might want to replace a phrase or code only in certain locations. After you type Y or N, the "Srch" prompt appears.

If you had previously searched for a phrase or code, it would also be displayed in the above message. The " – > Srch" prompt is displayed.

3.   Type the phrase or code to find and replace. Lowercase characters match both lowercase and uppercase. Uppercase characters match only uppercase.

NOTE

WordPerfect includes a special feature that lets
you include a "wildcard" character, by pressing
Ctrl-V first, then Ctrl-X. If you want to replace all
words that start with "I," for example, you can
type I, and then press Ctrl-X (^ X).

4. Press **F2**. The message "Replace with:" appears.

5. Type the phrase or code you want to replace the searched for phrase or code with. To delete the searched for phrase or code, leave this space blank. Then press **F2** to begin replacing.

SEARCHING AND REPLACING CODES   Besides searching for words or other characters, WordPerfect also lets you add bold, underlines, or other codes to words in a document. Take the following text for example:

```
This is a sample text string.
```

If you want to boldface the word "text," in a document follow this example:

1. Press **Alt-F2** and type **N**.
2. Type **text**, then press **F2**.
3. Press **F6**, type **text**, and press **F6** again.

```
Replace with: [BOLD]text[bold]
```

Notice that the first time you pressed F6, WordPerfect gave you the code to turn bolding on. The second time, it gave you the code to turn it off. This is the way WordPerfect works. Pressing a function once gives you the beginning code. Pressing it again gives you the ending code. Notice also that text in the string is unbolded, while codes are bolded. This search and replace operation, then, should bold the word "text" every time it occurs in the example.

4. Press **F2**.

```
This is a sample text string.
```

APPLICATIONS

The Search feature helps you quickly locate phrases in a document or block. Name Search lets you find items in a list quickly. Word Search lets you identify all documents containing certain words or phrases. Extended Search lets you search through headers, footers, endnotes, and footnotes in addition to the document itself. Search and Replace quickly updates changes or revisions in a document. It is useful for form letters, business documents, reports, and other text.

TYPICAL OPERATION

Assume you have written a form letter to a person and find that the person you are sending the letter to is not the right person after all. Search and replace can help you make these last minute changes very quickly, as follows:

1. Create a document similar to the following:

```
                                        Michael David
                                        FLG Office Supplies
                                        124 N. Main
                                        Carbondale, IL 62901
                                        March 17, 1990


Laura Caron
Quality Leasing
1208 S. Wall St.
Carbondale, IL 62901

Dear Laura:

How many times have you found yourself without office supplies?
Then you had to break up a busy day to run down to the store and
pay high, low-volume prices for that supply. Didn't you promise
yourself you'd never let it happen again?

Well, now you can do that with FLG's special business
discount/volume buying plan. All you have to do is guarantee that
you will buy a specified quantity of office supplies this year
(minimum: $200), and we will set up a volume buying plan for you
based on that number. And Laura, as a member of the plan, if you
run out of office supplies in the middle of the day, WE'LL DELIVER
REPLACEMENTS (maximum of two deliveries per year)!

We can only put a limited number of companies into this plan, so
hurry. Please feel free to call me at the office about this plan.
Of course, Laura, if you don't call us, we'll call you!

                                        Have a nice day,

                                        Michael David

                                Doc 1 Pg 1 Ln 6.5" Pos 1"
```

2. Move the cursor to the top of the document and press **Alt-F2**. Type **N** to conduct an unconfirmed search and replace.

3. Type **Laura** and press **F2**. Then type **James** and press **F2**. WordPerfect makes the specified changes.

4. Press **Ctrl-Home** twice to move the cursor back to where it was before the Search and Replace operation. Then press **Alt-F2** and type **N**.

5. Type **WE'LL DELIVER REPLACEMENTS** and press **F2**. Then type **we'll deliver replacements** and press **F2** again. WordPerfect makes the changes.

```
                                    Michael David
                                    FLG Office Supplies
                                    124 N. Main
                                    Carbondale, IL 62901
                                    March 17, 1990


James Caron
Quality Leasing
1208 S. Wall St.
Carbondale, IL 62901

Dear James:

How many times have you found yourself without office supplies?
Then you had to break up a busy day to run down to the store and
pay high, low-volume prices for that supply. Didn't you promise
yourself you'd never let it happen again?

Well, now you can do that with FLG's special business
discount/volume buying plan. All you have to do is guarantee that
you will buy a specified quantity of office supplies this year
(minimum: $200), and we will set up a volume buying plan for you
based on that number. And James, as a member of the plan, if you
run out of office supplies in the middle of the day, we'll deliver
replacements (maximum of two deliveries per year)!

We can only put a limited number of companies into this plan, so
hurry. Please feel free to call me at the office about this plan.
Of course, James, if you don't call us, we'll call you!

                                    Have a nice day,

                                    Michael David

                                    Doc 1 Pg 1 Ln 4.83" Pos 6.4"
```

6. Save the document as JAMESCAR.WPF.

7. Turn to Module 50 to continue the learning sequence.

Module 62
SORT

DESCRIPTION

The Sort command (Ctrl-F9) lets you sort a secondary merge file (Module 46), a block of text, or a regular non-merge file. You can sort by lines or paragraphs, alphabetically or numerically, in ascending or descending order. This is useful for documents where information needs to be alphabetically or numerically sorted. Employee and vendor lists, glossaries, and address lists are some examples.

WordPerfect's Sort feature is as powerful as any low-end database management software program. It lets you sort by field (Module 46), select key words in the field, and prioritize up to nine key words in a sort. You can also select specific items or records to sort using if-then logic. For example, you can sort all the vendors from California with which you do more than $50,000 in annual business.

WordPerfect sorts *records*. A record is a collection of *fields*. Each line in a line sort is a record. Lines are separated by hard or soft returns. Each paragraph in a paragraph sort is a record. Paragraphs are separated by two consecutive hard returns. Each record in a merge sort (Module 46) is a record. Records in secondary files are separated by a code (^ E).

Fields are the components of records. On a line or paragraph sort, fields are separated by tabs or indents. On a merge sort, fields are separated by ^ R codes. Fields should be consistent. Field one should always mean the same thing (e.g. last name), as should every other field in a record. You can have as many fields as you want in a record. If one record has more fields than another, identify unused fields with a "?" as described in Module 46.

Records are sorted by *key words*. You select what word in what field should be the key word. If you have more than one key word, you can prioritize. Up to nine key words can be chosen for any sort, but they must be ranked.

An alphanumeric sort lets you sort either words or numbers. If the numbers to be sorted are all of the same length (telephone numbers, zip codes, etc.), use this option. A numeric sort lets you sort numbers that are not of the same length (a list from 1 to 20, columns of numbers, etc.).

DEFINING A SORT   There are three steps to a sort:

1. Decide what you want to sort. You can sort entire files, merge files, and blocks of text. Always save your document before sorting it.
2. Decide how you want to sort it by defining the sort criteria.
3. Sort.

DECIDING WHAT TO SORT   To identify what to sort:

1. Press **Ctrl-F9**.

```
1 Merge; 2 Sort; 3 Sort Order: 0
```

NOTE
Option 1, merge, is described in Module 46.

2. Type **2**.

```
Input file to sort: (Screen)
```

3. You can sort either the file that is on-screen, or a file on disk. Either type the filename of another file and press **Enter**, or, if you are sorting the file that is on-screen, press **Enter**.

```
Output file for sort: (Screen)
```

4. Tell WordPerfect where you want the sorted file to appear. Press **Enter** if you want it to replace the on-screen file. Type a filename if you want the sorted file somewhere else. The following screen appears:

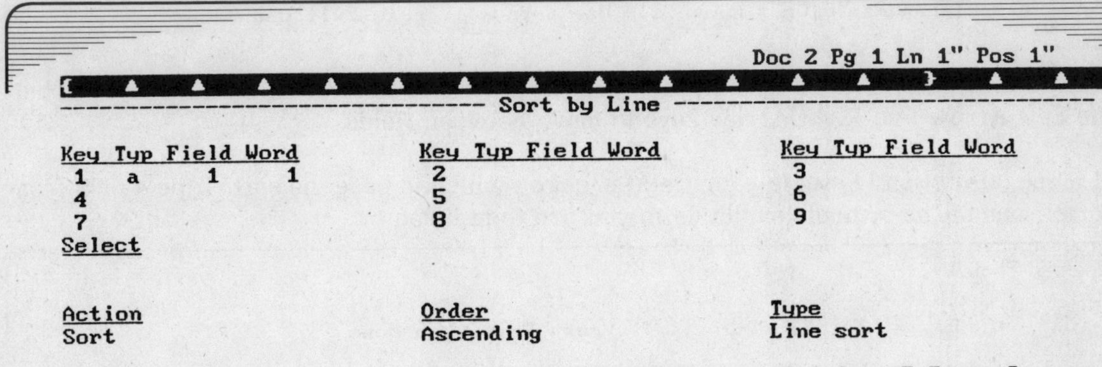

This is the Sorter menu. Use it to define sorting criteria.

DEFINING SORT CRITERIA   Default sort values are: an alphanumeric line sort in ascending order with one key word (the first word in the first field). To sort your data based on these criteria, type 1 or P to begin the sort. After a few moments, WordPerfect completes the sort. The sorting criteria remain the same for the next time you sort the file. To change the sorting criteria, refer to the following paragraphs.

View   While the Sorter menu takes up half the screen, the document takes up the other half. If you want to see more of the document, type 2 or V to let you move your cursor through the document. You can use the cursor control keys or the Search key (F2) to move through the document. When you are finished, press F7 to return to the Sorter menu.

Keys   Use this option to move the cursor through the Sorter menu. This lets you select the key fields, the key words in the fields, and whether a sort is alphanumeric or numeric. For example, if you have a list of names to sort by last name, and the first name is listed first, then you need to change the criteria to sort by the second word in the first field. If there is a difficulty in defining words from left to right, you may define them from right to left. For example, assume you want to sort a list by last name. If the list contains some names with first and last names and some names with first, middle, and last names, the last name is sometimes the second word and sometimes the third. But from right to left, it is always the first word. In this case, use negative numbers to locate the word. Since it is always the first word on the right, use − 1 as its location.

You can have up to nine keys in a sort. For example, in that same listing, if you are sorting by last name, what happens if two or more people have the same last name? You need a "tie-breaker." A good choice would be the first name. So, the last name would be the first keyword and the first name would be the second. You can also use keywords for a multi-level sort. This is illustrated in the Typical Operation section of this module.

To use keys, type 3 or K from the Sorter menu. The following screen appears:

```
Type: a = Alphanumeric; n = Numeric;  Use arrows;  Press Exit when done
```

If you have previously defined keys in this session, press Del to clear those definitions. Then use the Left Arrow and Right Arrow keys to move between fields.

Select   Use this option to create a logic statement on which to base the sort. Type 4 or S from the Sorter menu. The symbols available to you are then listed:

```
+(OR), *(AND), =, <>, >, <, >=, <=;  Press Exit when done
```

A typical selection might read: keyg = CA + TX. The "g" after key is a global select option that tells WordPerfect to select all people who are in California or Texas.

Select statements are ordered from left to right unless parentheses are used. For example, key1 = Henderson * (key5 = 30510 + key5 = 75240) finds all people with the last name of Henderson in Zip Codes 30510 and 75240. If parentheses were not used, the selection would list all people named Henderson in Zip Code 30510 and everyone in Zip Code 75240.

These symbols are described in the following table:

Select Symbol	Meaning
+	Or. This selects records that meet conditions set forth by either key. For example, key1 = Henderson + key5 = 30510 selects all people with the last name of Henderson and all people who live in Zip Code 30510.
*	And. This selects records that meet the conditions set forth by both keys. For example, key1 = Henderson * key3 = 30510 only selects people with the last name of Henderson if they live in Zip Code 30510.
=	Equals. This selects records that meet the condition set forth by the key. For example, key1 = Henderson will find all people with the last name of Henderson.
< >	Not equal to. This selects records that do not match the conditions set forth by either key. For example, key1 = Henderson < > key3 = 30510, selects all people without the last name of Henderson who do not live in Zip Code 30510.
>	Greater than. This selects records alphabetically or numerically greater than the conditions set forth by the key. For example, key1 > Henderson will find all people with a last name alphabetically greater than Henderson.
> =	Greater than or equal to. This selects records alphabetically or numerically greater than or equal to the conditions set forth by the key. For example, key1 > = Henderson will find all people with a last name alphabetically greater than or equal to Henderson.
<	Less than. This selects records alphabetically or numerically less than the conditions set forth by the key. For example, key1 < Henderson will find all people with a last name alphabetically less than Henderson.
< =	Less than or equal to. This selects records alphabetically or numerically less than or equal to the conditions set forth by the key. For example, key1 < = Henderson will find all people with a last name alphabetically less than or equal to Henderson.

Action   This option works only when you have used the select option. If you have not used the select option, the action is always to sort just the text. If you have used the select option, the action on the Sorter menu changes automatically to select and sort. To change that to select the records but not sort them, use this option. Type 5 or A from the Sorter menu, if you have already used the select option, the following menu appears:

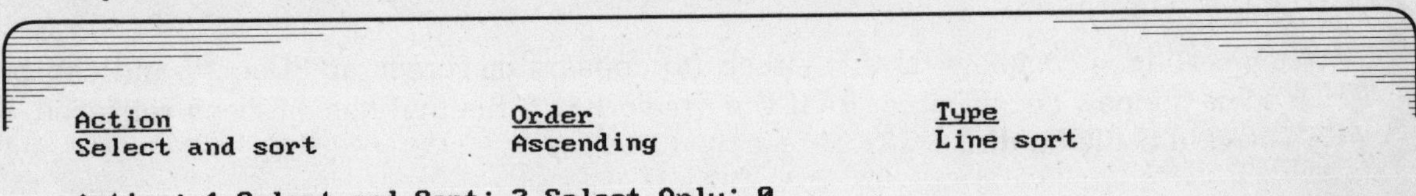

Type 1 or S to select and sort, 2 or O to select the records without sorting them.

Order   This option lets you change a sort from ascending (A-Z) to descending (Z-A) order. To change the order, type 6 or O from the Sorter menu.

```
   Order: 1 Ascending; 2 Descending: 0
```

Type 1 or A to put the sort in ascending order; 2 or D to put the sort in descending order.

Type   This option lets you change the type of sort. The default is a line sort, which sorts a document line-by-line. This means that each line is a record. Each line must be separated by a hard return. A paragraph sort is used to sort a document by paragraph. WordPerfect identifies a paragraph by two consecutive hard returns. A merge sort is used to sort a secondary file of a merge document. To change the type of sort, type 7 or T from the Sorter menu.

```
   Type: 1 Merge; 2 Line; 3 Paragraph: 0
```

Type 1 or M for a merge sort, 2 or L for a line sort, and 3 or P for a paragraph sort.

PERFORMING A SORT   Once you've defined the sort criteria, you're ready to sort. WordPerfect usually sorts based on English and European characters. You can also sort based on Scandinavian Characters.

1. Press **Ctrl-F9**. Type **3** or **O**.

```
   Sort Order: 1 US/European; 2 Scandinavian: 0
```

2. Type **1** for US/European characters; **2** for Scandinavian.

Performing A Line Sort   Use a line sort to sort each line of a non-merge file. To perform a line sort:

1. Press **Ctrl-F9**, then type **2** or **S**.
2. Select the input and output files, define the sorting criteria, and type **1** or **P** to start the sorting process.
3. When sorting is complete the file either: (a) appears on-screen as "Doc 3" and can be saved as the new document, or (b) if you are sorting a file that has not been retrieved, it is saved in a file on disk.

Performing A Paragraph Sort   Select a paragraph sort to sort each paragraph of a document. To perform a paragraph sort:

1. Press **Ctrl-F9**, then type **2** or **S**.

2. Select the input and output files and type **7** or **T** from the Sorter menu.

3. Type **3** or **P** to select paragraph sort, define the sorting criteria, and type **1** or **P** to start the sorting process.

Sorting A Secondary File Of A Merge Document   Select merge sort to sort a secondary file of a merge document. To sort a secondary file:

1. Press **Ctrl-F9**, then type **2** or **S**.

2. Select the input and output files and type **7** or **T** from the Sorter menu.

3. Type **1** or **M** to select merge sort, define the sorting criteria, and type **1** or **P** to start the sorting process.

Sorting A Block   You do not have to sort an entire document. If you have created a chart that is part of a larger document, for example, you may want to sort it and leave the rest of the document alone. WordPerfect can sort a block only from the screen to the screen. To sort a block of text:

1. Move the cursor to the beginning of the block and press **Alt-F4**. Move the cursor to the end of the block and press **Ctrl-F9** to move directly to the Sorter menu.

2. Define the sorting criteria and type **1** or **P** to start the sorting process.

APPLICATIONS

Use the Sort feature to alphabetize charts, lists, glossaries, secondary merge files, and other documents. You can also put lists and financial information in numerical order. If you sort the same files often, you can use macros to automatically change the sort criteria and sort the files.

TYPICAL OPERATION

In this example, sort a vendor list according to several criteria.

1. Start WordPerfect. Press **Shift-F8**, type **1** or **L**, then **7** or **M**. Change the margins (Module 43) to 0" for the left and 0" for the right.

2. Press **Shift-F8**, type **1** or **L**, then **8** or **T**. Press **Ctrl-End** to delete all tabs (Module 70). Set tabs at 2", 3.5", and 6" and press **F7** twice to save the tabs and return to the document.

3. Create a vendor list similar to the following:

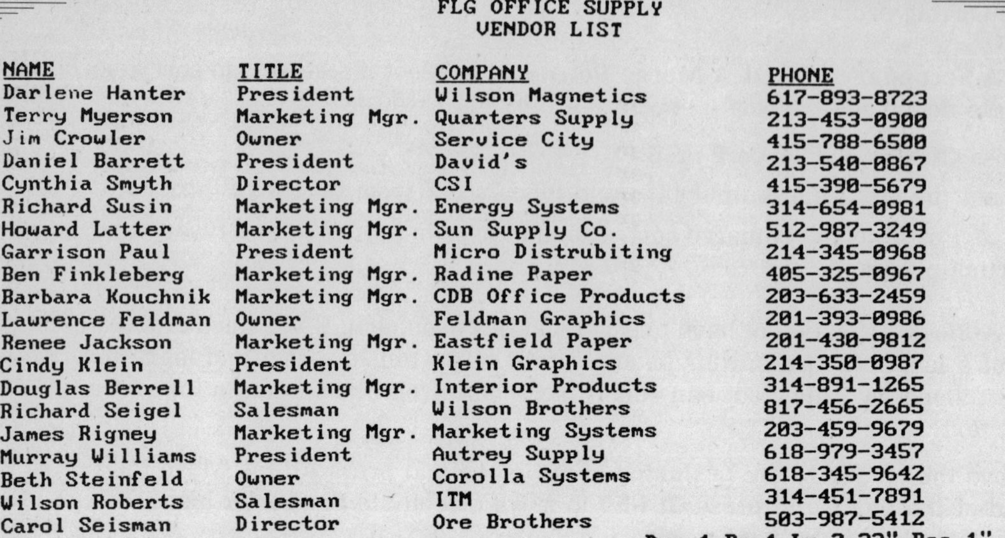

```
                              FLG OFFICE SUPPLY
                                VENDOR LIST

NAME                TITLE          COMPANY               PHONE
Darlene Hanter      President      Wilson Magnetics      617-893-8723
Terry Myerson       Marketing Mgr. Quarters Supply       213-453-0900
Jim Crowler         Owner          Service City          415-788-6500
Daniel Barrett      President      David's               213-540-0867
Cynthia Smyth       Director       CSI                   415-390-5679
Richard Susin       Marketing Mgr. Energy Systems        314-654-0981
Howard Latter       Marketing Mgr. Sun Supply Co.        512-987-3249
Garrison Paul       President      Micro Distrubiting    214-345-0968
Ben Finkleberg      Marketing Mgr. Radine Paper          405-325-0967
Barbara Kouchnik    Marketing Mgr. CDB Office Products    203-633-2459
Lawrence Feldman    Owner          Feldman Graphics      201-393-0986
Renee Jackson       Marketing Mgr. Eastfield Paper       201-430-9812
Cindy Klein         President      Klein Graphics        214-350-0987
Douglas Berrell     Marketing Mgr. Interior Products     314-891-1265
Richard Seigel      Salesman       Wilson Brothers       817-456-2665
James Rigney        Marketing Mgr. Marketing Systems     203-459-9679
Murray Williams     President      Autrey Supply         618-979-3457
Beth Steinfeld      Owner          Corolla Systems       618-345-9642
Wilson Roberts      Salesman       ITM                   314-451-7891
Carol Seisman       Director       Ore Brothers          503-987-5412
                                          Doc 1 Pg 1 Ln 2.33" Pos 1"
```

4. Move the cursor to the "D" in "Darlene Hanter" and press **Alt-F4**. Then move the cursor to the end of the list and press **Ctrl-F9**. Type **3** or **K**. To sort first by title, then by company, then by last name, then by phone number, set the following characteristics in the table:

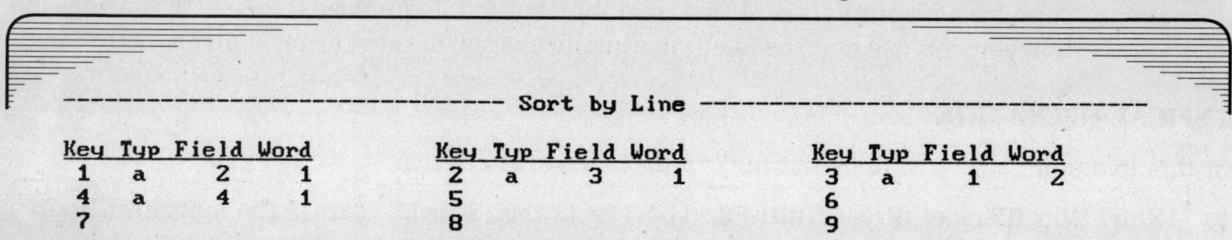

```
------------------------------------ Sort by Line ------------------------------------

Key Typ Field Word      Key Typ Field Word      Key Typ Field Word
 1   a    2    1          2   a    3    1          3   a    1    2
 4   a    4    1          5                        6
 7                        8                        9
```

5. Press **F7** and type **1** or **P** to start executing the sort.

```
                        FLG OFFICE SUPPLY
                          VENDOR LIST

NAME                 TITLE            COMPANY                PHONE
Cynthia Smyth        Director         CSI                    415-390-5679
Carol Seisman        Director         Ore Brothers           503-987-5412
Barbara Kouchnik     Marketing Mgr.   CDB Office Products     203-633-2459
Renee Jackson        Marketing Mgr.   Eastfield Paper        201-430-9812
Richard Susin        Marketing Mgr.   Energy Systems         314-654-0981
Douglas Berrell      Marketing Mgr.   Interior Products      314-891-1265
James Rigney         Marketing Mgr.   Marketing Systems      203-459-9679
Terry Myerson        Marketing Mgr.   Quarters Supply        213-453-0900
Ben Finkleberg       Marketing Mgr.   Radine Paper           405-325-0967
Howard Latter        Marketing Mgr.   Sun Supply Co.         512-987-3249
Beth Steinfeld       Owner            Corolla Systems        618-345-9642
Lawrence Feldman     Owner            Feldman Graphics       201-393-0986
Jim Crowler          Owner            Service City           415-788-6500
Murray Williams      President        Autrey Supply          618-979-3457
Daniel Barrett       President        David's                213-540-0867
Cindy Klein          President        Klein Graphics         214-350-0987
Garrison Paul        President        Micro Distrubiting     214-345-0968
Darlene Hanter       President        Wilson Magnetics       617-893-8723
Wilson Roberts       Salesman         ITM                    314-451-7891
Richard Seigel       Salesman         Wilson Brothers        817-456-2665
                                      Doc 1 Pg 1 Ln 1.66" Pos 0.23"
```

NOTE

If the sort does not execute properly, check the
number of tabs or indents in each line. Make
sure there is one tab or one indent between
each field. If there are too many, delete the
extras. If there are not enough, add some.

6. Define the same block of text again and press **Ctrl-F9**. Type **3** or **K**. To sort by phone
    number, set the following criteria:

```
---------------------------------- Sort by Line -----------------------------------

Key Typ Field Word          Key Typ Field Word          Key Typ Field Word
 1   a    4    1              2                           3
 4                            5                           6
 7                            8                           9
```

7. Press **F7** and type **1** or **P** to start the sorting process. The table looks as follows:

```
                            FLG OFFICE SUPPLY
                              VENDOR LIST

     NAME                TITLE            COMPANY              PHONE
     Lawrence Feldman    Owner            Feldman Graphics     201-393-0986
     Renee Jackson       Marketing Mgr.   Eastfield Paper      201-430-9812
     Barbara Kouchnik    Marketing Mgr.   CDB Office Products  203-633-2459
     James Rigney        Marketing Mgr.   Marketing Systems    203-459-9679
     Daniel Barrett      President        David's              213-540-0867
     Terry Myerson       Marketing Mgr.   Quarters Supply      213-453-0900
     Garrison Paul       President        Micro Distrubiting   214-345-0968
     Cindy Klein         President        Klein Graphics       214-350-0987
     Richard Susin       Marketing Mgr.   Energy Systems       314-654-0981
     Douglas Berrell     Marketing Mgr.   Interior Products    314-891-1265
     Wilson Roberts      Salesman         ITM                  314-451-7891
     Ben Finkleberg      Marketing Mgr.   Radine Paper         405-325-0967
     Jim Crowler         Owner            Service City         415-788-6500
     Cynthia Smyth       Director         CSI                  415-390-5679
     Carol Seisman       Director         Ore Brothers         503-987-5412
     Howard Latter       Marketing Mgr.   Sun Supply Co.       512-987-3249
     Darlene Hanter      President        Wilson Magnetics     617-893-8723
     Beth Steinfeld      Owner            Corolla Systems      618-345-9642
     Murray Williams     President        Autrey Supply        618-979-3457
     Richard Seigel      Salesman         Wilson Brothers      817-456-2665
                                          Doc 1 Pg 1 Ln 1.66" Pos 0.23"
```

8. Save the document as VENDORS.WPF.

9. Turn to Module 45 to continue the learning sequence.

Module 63
SPACING AND LEADING

DESCRIPTION

As with a typewriter, spacing is the number of lines in between text. Single spacing means lines are spaced with no lines separating them, so each line of text takes up one line on a page. Double spacing means lines are spaced with one line separating each, so each line of text takes up two lines. WordPerfect initially sets spacing at single spacing. However, you can change spacing to any number you want as many times as you want. For example, 2 for double spacing, 1.5 for one-and-a-half line spacing, even .5 for equations. WordPerfect sets spacing on-screen to the nearest whole number. For example, 2.5 line spacing looks like triple spacing on-screen. Check the Status Line to determine the correct line you are on in these instances.

Text can be single spaced in one part of a document, double spaced in another.

The amount of space in between each line is also determined by leading (pronounced ''ledding''), or line height.

SETTING SPACING   Spacing is changed using the Line Format key (Shift-F8). To set spacing:

1.   Press **Shift-F8** and type **1** or **L**.

```
Format: Line

    1 - Hyphenation                        Off

    2 - Hyphenation Zone - Left            10%
                          Right            4%

    3 - Justification                      Yes

    4 - Line Height                        Auto

    5 - Line Numbering                     No

    6 - Line Spacing                       1

    7 - Margins - Left                     1"
                  Right                    1"

    8 - Tab Set                            0", every 0.5"

    9 - Widow/Orphan Protection            No

Selection: 0
```

2. Type **6** or **S**. Then type whatever you want spacing to be set to and press **Enter**. Then press **F7**. Spacing is now changed from this point in the document until the end or until you change spacing again.

LEADING   Leading is the amount of space that each line is assigned. This includes the height of the characters and the space between each line. WordPerfect provides automatic leading that is dependent on the font and/or attribute that you are using. If you want even line spacing throughout a document no matter what font you are using, you can change leading from automatic to fixed. It is recommended, however, that you leave leading at automatic for most applications.

NOTE
Fixed leading does not work with printers that
can only print six lines per inch, which includes
most older dot-matrix printers.

To change the leading:

1. Press **Shift-F8**. Type **1** or **L**, then **4** or **H**.

```
    1 Auto; 2 Fixed: 0
```

2. Type **1** or **A** for automatic leading; **2** or **F** for fixed. If you type **1** or **A**, press **Enter**, then **F7** to return to the document.

3. If you type **2** or **F**, the reading by line height changes from Auto to 0.16", the typical line height in WordPerfect. You can change this to any number you like. WordPerfect automatically converts it to inches. Press **Enter**, then **F7** to return to the document. Leading is now changed from this point in the document until either the end or until you change it again.

APPLICATIONS

Change spacing whenever you feel a document would read better if text were spaced differently. If you are sending a report that needs editing to someone, for example, it is advisable to double or triple space the text. The more spaces in between the lines, the easier it is to edit text. Leading changes are appropriate for newsletters and other documents that require a professional look when printed.

TYPICAL OPERATION

In this example, you change spacing from single spacing to one and one-half line spacing and observe the difference.

1. Create a document similar to the following:

```
MEMO

From: FLG
To:   JYM
Subject: Performance Review

John:

It is time for your ninety-day review. I've scheduled it for next
Monday, the 27th, at 3:00 p.m. in my office. Per company policy,
you are not due a raise in pay at this time. We will discuss your
performance and if I believe it is exceptional, I may make an
exception.

If I were you, John, I'd be optimistic!

FLG
```

Doc 1 Pg 1 Ln 3.66" Pos 1.3"

2. Move the cursor to the "M" in "MEMO" and press **Shift-F8**. Type **1** or **L**, then type **6** or **S**.

3. Type **1.5** and press **Enter**. Then press **F7**.

```
MEMO



From: FLG

To:   JYM

Subject: Performance Review



John:



It is time for your ninety-day review. I've scheduled it for next

Monday, the 27th, at 3:00 p.m. in my office. Per company policy,

you are not due a raise in pay at this time. We will discuss your

performance and if I believe it is exceptional, I may make an
```

Doc 1 Pg 1 Ln 1" Pos 1"

4. Move the cursor to the "M" in "Monday." Notice the Status Line.

Even though text looks like it is double-spaced, there are only one and one-half lines in between each line of text.

5. Save the document as REVIEW.WPF.

6. Turn to Module 70 to continue the learning sequence.

Module 64
SPELLER

DESCRIPTION

Nobody likes to have misspelled words in their documents. It's embarrassing to send someone a letter, only to find out later that words in the letter were misspelled. WordPerfect's Speller command (Ctrl-F2) gives you the opportunity to correct misspelled words before you submit a document to someone else.

The Speller checks the spelling of words in your document by comparing each word to WordPerfect's 115,000-word dictionary. The Speller lets you check words, pages, blocks, or entire documents. The Speller checks words included both on-screen and in headers, footers (Module 32), footnotes (Module 28), and endnotes (Module 23).

Misspelled words are highlighted in context, and WordPerfect offers possible replacement words for the misspelled word. WordPerfect also lets you check words phonetically (by sound) and in word patterns (a*t, for example, lists all the words in the dictionary that begin with a and end with t). It identifies double occurrences of the same word, and gives you the number of words in a particular block, page, or document.

The dictionary is revisable. You may add words to it and delete words from it. In the interest of speed, when WordPerfect looks up a word, it first looks at a common word list. If the word is not in that word list, it looks at a larger main word list, and if that word is not in either of those lists, WordPerfect looks at a supplemental word list, which is created by you. While you can revise the dictionary while spell-checking, you can also add words at any time by retrieving the dictionary as a WordPerfect file and adding words to it or by typing a list of words and saving it as an auxiliary file, also described in Appendix B.

You can also change dictionaries using the Speller Utility, which is described in Appendix G.

SPELL CHECK If you have a hard disk, you loaded the Speller on it when you installed WordPerfect (described in Module 2). If you do not, you must keep the Speller diskette in drive B at all times while performing spell-checking procedures.

To use the Speller, first make sure the document you wish to spell-check is on-screen. Then move the cursor to the word or page to check. If you are checking a document, the cursor need only be in that document.

If you have a floppy-based system, remove the diskette from drive B and replace it with the Speller diskette. If you have a hard disk system, you should already have installed the Speller on the hard disk.

CAUTION
Always save a document before beginning spell-checking.

1. Press **Ctrl-F2**.

```
Check: 1 Word; 2 Page; 3 Document; 4 New Sup. Dictionary; 5 Look Up; 6 Count: 0
```

2. Type **1** or **W** to check a word, **2** or **P** to check a page, or **3** or **D** to check a document. For example, assume you are spell-checking a document and have misspelled the word "computer," by spelling it "compter." WordPerfect gives you the following message:

```
===============================================================================
        A. compeer              B. compte              C. computer
        D. copter

Not Found: 1 Skip Once; 2 Skip; 3 Add Word; 4 Edit; 5 Look Up:  0
```

3. Notice that WordPerfect highlights the misspelled word and offers alternative spellings. You have the choice of:

   - Selecting one of the alternative choices to replace the word.
   - Skipping this occurrence of the word and going on to the next misspelled word.
   - Skipping all occurrences of this word.
   - Adding the word to the dictionary.
   - Rejecting the choices offered, and editing the word yourself. To do this, edit the word and press **Enter** to correct it and return to spell-checking.
   - Looking up words that match a pattern. For example, typing **com*r** at this selection would list all the words that begin with "com" and end with "r." Typing **com?r** lists all five-letter words beginning with "com" and ending with "r."
   - Looking up words that match this word phonetically. This option gives you all the words that sound like the chosen word. In this case, WordPerfect lists the same words it chose for alternative spellings. But if you misspell a word like diskette, spelling it "diskete," WordPerfect lists only "diskette" as an alternative spelling, but lists discoid, and disquiet in addition to diskette as phonetic spellings.

4. Type **c** to correct the spelling of the word computer. WordPerfect continues to identify words not found in any part of its dictionary. When it is finished, the following message appears on-screen:

```
Word Count:  102          Press any key to continue
```

NOTE

WordPerfect always gives you a count of the words it has spell-checked. If you are spell-checking a document and stop the spell-checking prematurely by pressing F1, the Cancel key (Module 10), it gives you a count of only those words that were spell-checked, not the number of words in the document.

5. Press any key, then **Enter** to leave the Speller. If you have a floppy-based system, remove the Speller diskette from drive B and replace it with the diskette that was formerly in drive B.

SPELL-CHECK A BLOCK OF TEXT   WordPerfect also lets you spell-check a block (Module 8) of text. To spell-check a block of text:

1. If you have a floppy-based system, remove the diskette from drive B and replace it with the Speller diskette. If you have a hard disk system, proceed to step two.

2. Position the cursor where you want spell-checking to begin and press **Alt-F4**. Then move the cursor where you want spell-checking to end and press **Ctrl-F2**. WordPerfect automatically spell-checks the block of text, identifying words not found in any part of its dictionary. When it is finished, it gives you a count of the words in the block and tells you to press any key to continue. Do this and then press **Enter** to leave the Speller.

3. If you have a floppy-based system, remove the Speller diskette from drive B and replace it with the diskette that was formerly in drive B.

DOUBLE OCCURRENCE OF A WORD   If WordPerfect finds that a word appears twice in a row, the following message appears on-screen:

```
Double Word: 1 2 Skip; 3 Delete 2nd; 4 Edit; 5 Disable Double Word Checking
```

Typing 1 or 2 skips the word for the remainder of the spell-checking session. Typing 3 deletes the second occurrence of the word, 4 lets you edit the word and 5 disables double word checking for this spell-checking session.

NEW SUPPLEMENTAL DICTIONARY   You do not have to use WordPerfect's dictionary when spell-checking a document. You have the option of using a different dictionary through the Speller Utility (Appendix G). This includes third-party dictionaries such as Turbo Lightning from Borland International, Scotts Valley, California.

You can also change supplemental dictionaries after you have saved them as auxiliary files, as described in Appendix B. To change supplemental dictionaries, press Ctrl-F2 and type 4 or N. Notice the "Supplemental dictionary name:" prompt. Type the name of the supplemental dictionary to use and press Enter. Begin spell-checking.

LOOK UP   Like the Look Up option during a spell-check, this option gives you all the words in the dictionary that sound like the one you selected, or all the words that match a certain word pattern. The advantage of this is that you can select the word or word pattern without doing a spell-check first. To use the Look Up feature:

1.   If you have a floppy-based system, make sure the Speller diskette is in drive B.

2.   Press **Ctrl-F2** and type **5** or **L**. After the "Word or word pattern" prompt, type a word to get a list of all the words that sound like it, or a word pattern to get a list of all the words that match that pattern. For example, type **age**.

3.   Press **Enter**.

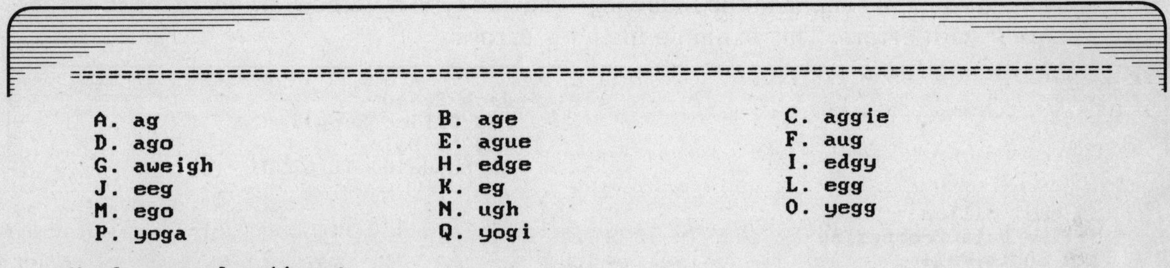

These are all the words that sound like "age." You now have the option of typing another word or word pattern, or returning to the document. To return to the document, proceed to step 4.

4.   Type **ag?** and press **Enter** to find all the three-letter words that begin with "ag."

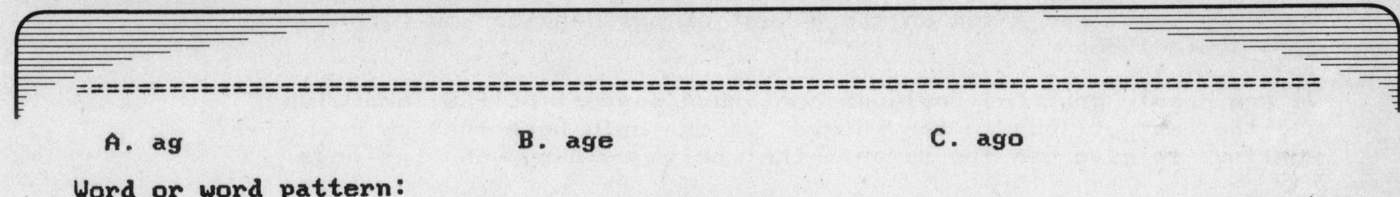

5.   Press **Enter** twice to return to your document.

WORD COUNT   Anyone writing a report or an article likes to know how many words are in the document. WordPerfect automatically gives you a word count whenever you spell-check a block, page, or document. That word count corresponds to either the block, page, or document. You can also count words alone without spell-checking. To perform a word count:

1.   Make sure the document is on-screen. If you have a floppy-based system, make sure the Speller diskette is in drive B. Press **Ctrl-F2** and type **6** or **C**. After a few seconds, the following display appears:

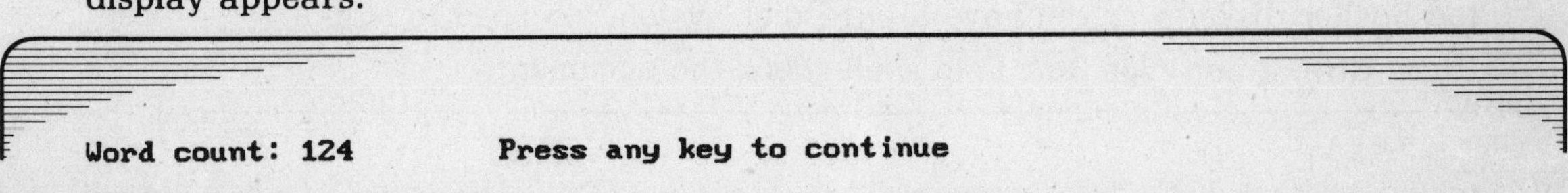

2.   Press any key, then press **Enter** to return to the document.

APPLICATIONS

Spell-checking is useful for reports, letters, memos, articles, term papers, theses, or any other document that someone else will read. It's always good practice to spell check a document.

Use the Look Up feature if you are unsure of the word you want to use. Use the Word Count feature to count words in reports and articles.

TYPICAL OPERATION

This example teaches you to spell-check a document.

1. Create a document similar to the following: You can type it without trying to make errors, or type it with errors. This example includes errors.

```
                                        Jack Belew
                                        FLG Office Supplies
                                        124 N. Main
                                        Carbondale, IL 62901


Michael Miller
Miller Data Processing
123 South Wall
Carbondale, IL 62901

Dear Mike:

Please accept the inclosed gift as an expression of our gratitude
for being chosen as our number one customor. Your company was
chosen based on two facters: The result of a poll of our employees
and suppliers, and based on the amount of merchandise you purchased
from us in 1986.

We are deeply grateful for your continued support of FLG, and wish
you the best of luck in the future. We can only hope that we can
continue to give you the support that helps us eary your business.

                                        Sinerey,

                                        Jack Belew
                                        Controller

                                Doc 1 Pg 1 Ln 5.33" Pos 1"
```

CAUTION
Do not remove the Speller diskette from drive B
while performing spell-checking procedures.

2. If you have a floppy-based system, remove the diskette from drive B and replace it with the Speller diskette. If you have a hard disk system, proceed to step 3.

3. Press **Ctrl-F2** and type **3** or **D** to spell-check the document.

```
                                    Jack Belew
=====================================================================================
    A. bedew              B. below              C. blew
    D. bellow             E. billow             F. bylaw
  Not Found: 1 Skip Once; 2 Skip; 3 Add Word; 4 Edit; 5 Look Up:   0
```

4. Since Belew is one of the officers of FLG, type **3** to add his last name to the dictionary.

5. Type **3** to add FLG to the dictionary.

```
Please accept the inclosed gift as an expression of our gratitude
for being chosen as our number one customor. Your company was

===============================================================================

    A. customer              B. costumer              C. costumier

Not Found: 1 Skip Once; 2 Skip; 3 Add Word; 4 Edit; 5 Look Up:  0
```

6. Type **A** to select customer.

```
Dear Mike:

Please accept the inclosed gift as an expression of our gratitude
for being chosen as our number one customer. Your company was
chosen based on two facters: The result of a poll of our employees
and suppliers, and based on the amount of merchandise you purchased
from us in 1986.

We are deeply grateful for your continued support of FLG, and wish
you the best of luck in the future. We can only hope that we can

===============================================================================

    A. factors               B. falters               C. factories

Not Found: 1 Skip Once; 2 Skip; 3 Add Word; 4 Edit; 5 Look Up:  0
```

7. Type **A** to select factors.

8. Type **D** to select earn.

9. Notice WordPerfect cannot find the correct spelling for "Sinerey." Type **5** to look up the word according to a word pattern. Then type **sin∗y** and press **Enter**.

```
                                            Sinerey,

===============================================================================

    A. sincerely         B. sincerity         C. sinewy
    D. sinfully          E. singlehandedly    F. singly
    G. singularity       H. singularly        I. sinisterly
    J. sinistrality      K. sinistrally       L. sinistrocularity
    M. sinistrorsally    N. sinistrorsely     O. sinlessly
    P. sinuosity         Q. sinuously         R. sinusoidally
    S. sinusotomy

Select Word: 0
```

10. Type **A**.

<pre>
Word count: 117   Press any key to continue
</pre>

11. Press any key then **Enter** to return to the document.
12. Save the document as THANKYOU.WPF.
13. Turn to Module 71 to continue the learning sequence.

Module 65

STATUS LINE

DESCRIPTION

When you first enter WordPerfect, the Status Line is the only thing on the screen. The Status Line is always displayed at the bottom of the screen. It tells you where your cursor currently is and whether you are editing document 1 or document 2. (WordPerfect lets you edit two documents at once; see Module 22 for details.) Your cursor position is defined as the page of the document, the line, and the position on that line.

WordPerfect also uses the Status Line to tell you if the Caps Lock or Num Lock keys have been activated; whether text is being boldfaced, underlined, italicized, or otherwise highlighted (Module 5); whether text is being redlined or struck out (Module 58); whether you are in Math (Module 45) or Column (Module 13) mode; and what file you are currently editing. The Status Line also displays messages from the system.

Here is what the Status Line typically looks like upon entering a WordPerfect document:

```
                                                  Doc 1 Pg 1 Ln 1" Pos 1"
```

NOTE

WordPerfect automatically sets the left and right margins at 1 inch. Therefore when you enter a WordPerfect document, the cursor is in position 1". See Module 43 to learn how to change margins.

NOTE

This Status Line is set up to display inches. Using WordPerfect's Setup feature (Appendix B), you can alternatively set it up to display WordPerfect 4.2 units, centimeters, or points. For example, if you set it up for WordPerfect 4.2 units, the Status Line will display Ln 1 Pos 1 when you first start WordPerfect.

As you can see, the Status Line tells you that you are editing document 1 and are on page 1, 1" from the top margin and 1" from the left margin. The position changes with each letter you type, and the line changes every time your cursor moves to the next line. The page changes as you move from page to page, and the document changes as you move between documents.

If you are editing a document that has previously been saved, the Status Line looks like this:

```
  C:\WP50\DOCS\SAMPLE.WPF                          Doc 1 Pg 1 Ln 1" Pos 1"
```

By observing the filename at the bottom of the screen, you always know what document you're editing. Also, you know if you've saved and named a document yet. If you haven't, this feature serves as a gentle reminder to you to save it.

USING THE STATUS LINE IN CAPS LOCK MODE   When you press the Caps Lock key, the Status Line looks like this:

```
                                                 Doc 1 Pg 1 Ln 1" POS 1.3"
```

When "Pos" is all uppercase, you are in Caps Lock mode and all the text you type will be capitalized. Press Caps Lock again to turn the capitalization mode off. When "Pos" is normal, Caps Lock mode is off.

USING THE STATUS LINE IN NUM LOCK MODE   When you press the Num Lock key, the "Pos" indicator on the Status Line flashes on and off. This informs you that the numbers on your numeric keypad are activated and the cursor control keys won't work. To turn Num Lock off, press it again. "Pos" stops flashing.

USING THE STATUS LINE FOR MESSAGES   Nearly every time you press a key, the Status Line changes, even when you press function keys. Press F7. Notice the following display:

```
  Save document? (Y/N) Yes
```

When some function key commands are pressed, cursor position disappears on the Status Line and a message line appears. This occurs whether or not the length of the message would have interfered with the cursor information. When a message removes cursor position from view, it means that message is more important at present than your cursor position and that you should pay attention to it. The above message, for example, asks if you want to save the document (see Module 60). Other messages that appear on-screen include those for print formatting, macros, spell-checking, search and replace, and many others.

APPLICATIONS

The Status Line gives you important information about the document being edited and can help you work more efficiently. It is the place for messages, cursor position, document number, filename, appearance, and more. Refer to it often.

TYPICAL OPERATION

In this illustration, observe how the Status Line keeps you informed.

1. Start WordPerfect and type the following document:

```
                SALE IN PROGRESS AT FLG OFFICE SUPPLIES

        FLG Office Supplies, 124 N. Main, in Carbondale, is having a whale
        of a sale. Now 'til Tuesday, FLG is selling school supplies,
        computer supplies, and office furniture at low, low prices. For
        example, a box of no-perf computer paper, regularly $39.95, is now
        just $19.95._


                                            Doc 1 Pg 1 Ln 2" Pos 2.2"
```

2. Press **Ctrl-Enter** to create a new page.

```
        _


                                            Doc 1 Pg 2 Ln 1" Pos 1"
```

3. Press **PgUp**.

```
        _       SALE IN PROGRESS AT FLG OFFICE SUPPLIES

        FLG Office Supplies, 124 N. Main, in Carbondale, is having a whale
        of a sale. Now 'til Tuesday, FLG is selling school supplies,
        computer supplies, and office furniture at low, low prices. For
        example, a box of no-perf computer paper, regularly $39.95, is now
        just $19.95.


                                            Doc 1 Pg 1 Ln 1" Pos 1"
```

4. Press **Right Arrow** three times. Note that "Pos" is now at 1.3".
5. Press **Caps Lock** and observe that "POS" is uppercase.
6. Press **Caps Lock** again. Notice "POS" change back to "Pos." Then press **F6**, the Boldface key (Module 5).

```



                                            Doc 1 Pg 1 Ln 1" Pos 1.3"
```

7. Press **F6** again to turn the number next to ''Pos'' back to normal. Then press **F8**, the Underline key (Module 5).

```
                                                    Doc 1 Pg 1 Ln 1" Pos 1.3"
```

8. Press **F7**, the Save Text key (Module 60).

```
    Save document? (Y/N) Yes
```

9. Press **Enter**. Then type **SALE.WPF** and press **Enter** to save the document.
10. Exit Wordperfect by typing **Y**.
11. Turn to Module 33 to continue the learning sequence.

Module 66
STYLES

DESCRIPTION

WordPerfect's Styles feature lets you set up pre-defined "templates" for business letters, reports, or other documents that require consistent formatting. Styles let you present a consistent appearance. For example, letters, book chapters, or reports can have the same margins, tabs, fonts, and indent style. While each document can have several style settings, a style library (Appendix B) can be created using the Setup key (Shift-F1).

Two types of styles are available in WordPerfect — paired and open. A paired style, which is the default in WordPerfect, has a beginning and an end. Use it when a style is really just a code, like italics or underlined text. This lets you set a style by defining it as a block, or by turning it on, then turning it off when you are finished. When using a paired style, you can redefine the function of the Enter key to turn the style off, then on again.

Open styles only have a beginning. These are useful for formatting changes like margins and tabs. Open styles cannot be turned off.

When creating styles, you can name them, offer a description as long as 54 characters, and change the function of the Enter key.

To create styles:

1. Press **Alt-F8**.

```
  Styles

    Name          Type  Description

    1 On; 2 Off; 3 Create; 4 Edit; 5 Delete; 6 Save; 7 Retrieve; 8 Update: 1
```

2. Type **3** or **C**.

```
  Styles: Edit

        1 - Name

        2 - Type           Paired

        3 - Description

        4 - Codes

        5 - Enter          HRt
  Selection: 0
```

3. Type **1** or **N**, type a name for the style, and press **Enter**.

4. Type **2** or **T**, then **1** or **P** for paired styles, **2** or **O** for open.

5. Type **3** or **D**, type a description of the file, and press **Enter**.

6. Type **4** or **C**. If you are using paired styles, the following screen appears. If you are using open styles, the same screen appears, minus the comment (Module 19):

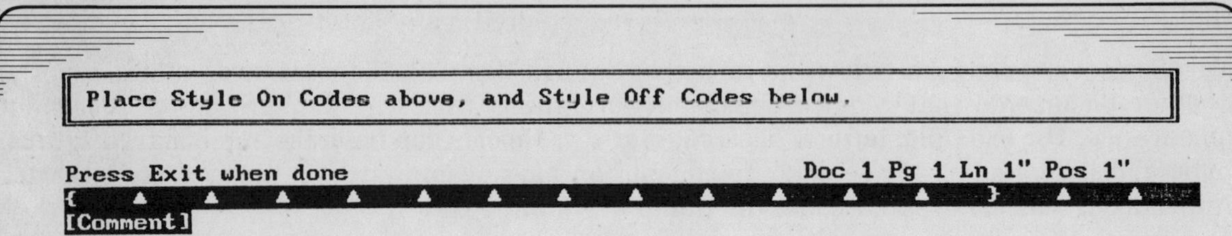

7. The comment comes up whenever you retrieve a style. It reminds you to turn style on and off before and after styles. Insert the codes and text you want to include in the style. Type the text you want, then press **F7** to return to the Style menu.

8. If you are using open styles, press **F7** to return to the Style menu. If you are using paired styles, type **5** or **E**.

9. This lets you define the function of the **Enter** key. To let it work as it normally does, type **1** or **H**. To have it turn off a style only, type **2** or **F**. To have it turn styles off and on (only when in styles that have already been defined), type **3** or **O**. Press **F7** to return to the Style menu.

10. Note that the Style menu now includes the name of the style, a description, and its type. Press **F7** to return to the document.

TIP: You can create a paired style by defining a block of text, pressing Alt-F8, and typing 3 or C.

USING STYLES   When a style has been created, you can use it anywhere in a document. To use styles:

1. Move the cursor where you want the style inserted and press **Alt-F8**. Move the cursor to the style you want to use and type **1** or **O**.

2. Type text normally. Everything that you do will be treated according to the style you defined.

3. If you are using a paired style, when you are finished, press **Alt-F8** and type **2** or **f**. Or, if you defined the **Enter** key to turn a style off, press **Enter**.

STYLE MENU OPTIONS   Several options are available for altering styles on the Style menu. You can edit styles, changing them according to your needs; delete them; save them as a separate document that can then be used with other documents; retrieve styles from other documents; or update the style library (Appendix B).

APPLICATIONS

There are many applications for styles. One of the best reasons for styles, however, is uniformity. Defining certain items as styles insures that all of your like documents will have the same "look and feel." These include form letters, memos, annual reports, and other documents.

Other styles can be used for convenience, much the same way as macros (Module 42), since a style essentially repeats a task that previously required many keystrokes.

TYPICAL OPERATION

The following example illustrates the creation of a set format for the front of a business letter:

1. Start WordPerfect, press **Alt-F8**, and type **3** or **C**.

2. Type **1** or **N** and type **memotop**. Press **Enter**.

3. Leave the style type as "paired." Type **3** or **C**, then **standard top of business letter**. Press **Enter**.

4. Type **4** or **C**.

5. Move the cursor to the right of the comment. Press **Shift-F8**, type **1** or **L**, then **7** or **M** to set the margins. Type **.5** and press **Enter**, and type **.5** and press **Enter** again.

6. Type **8** or **T**. Press **Ctrl-End** to delete all the tabs. Then type **5.5** and press **Enter**. Then press **F7** twice.

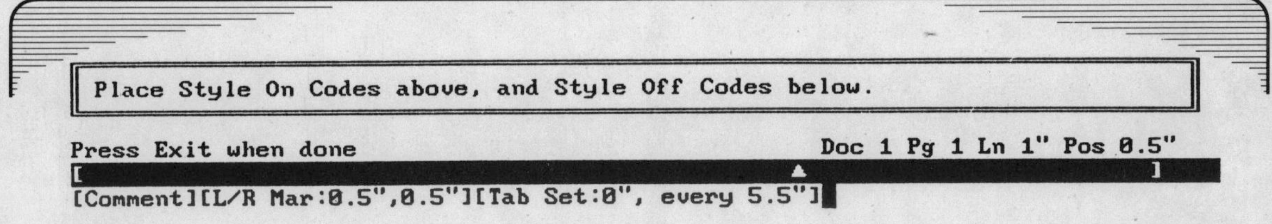

7. Press **Tab**, then press **F6**. Type **FLG Office Supply** and press **Enter**. Press **F6** to turn boldface off.

8. Press **Tab**, then type **124 N. Main** and press **Enter**. Press **Tab**, then type **Carbondale, IL 62901** and press **Enter**.

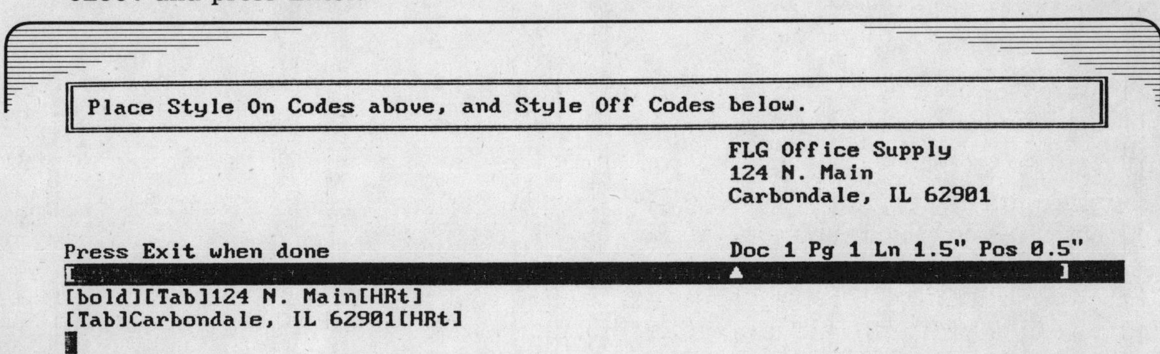

9. Press **F7** to save the style.

10. Press **Alt-F8** and type **1** or **O**. Notice the text is retrieved into the document. Then press **Alt-F8** and type **2** or **f**. Margins and tab settings are different in the style than they are in the rest of the document.

11. Press **Alt-F8** and type **6** or **S**. Type **MEMOTOP.WPF** and press **Enter** to save the style in a file that can be used by other WordPerfect documents. If you have a style library, type **8** or **U** to update it.

12. Clear the screen.

13. Turn to Module 46 to continue the learning sequence.

Module 67
SUBSCRIPTS AND SUPERSCRIPTS

DESCRIPTION

Superscripts place text ⅓ line above the text, while subscripts place it ⅓ line below the text. Superscripts look like this when they are printed:

IBM^r

Subscripts look like this when they are printed:

$$X_1 + X_4 = X_5$$

NOTE

WordPerfect offers other ways to print text up or down from a line. The Advance key (Shift-F8) is explained in Module 54, Footnotes (Ctrl-F7) are explained in Module 28 and Endnotes (Ctrl-F7) are explained in Module 23.

To use superscripts:

1. Press **Ctrl-F8**. Then type **1** or **S**.

```
1 Suprscpt; 2 Subscpt; 3 Fine; 4 Small; 5 Large; 6 Vry Large; 7 Ext Large: 0
```

2. Type **1** or **p**. Notice the Status Line change next to "Pos." On a color monitor, this resembles a light blue background with white characters. This tells you that superscript is activated. Whenever it is on, every character you type until you turn it off is superscripted and will look like the colors on the Status Line. Type the character(s) you want superscripted.

3. When you are done typing superscripted characters, press **Ctrl-F8** and type **3** or **N** to turn superscript off. Press Reveal Codes, **Alt-F3** (Module 59) to see the superscript symbol on-screen.

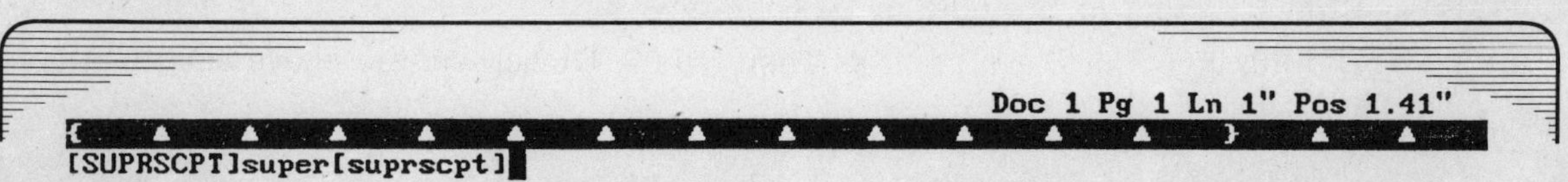

To use subscripts:

1. Press **Ctrl-F8**. Type **1** or **S**. Then type **2** or **b**.

2. Notice the Status Line change next to "Pos." On a color monitor, this resembles a light blue background with light red text inside. This tells you that subscript is activated. Whenever it is on, every character you type until you turn it off is subscripted and will look just like the colors on the Status Line. Type the character(s) you want subscripted.

3. When you are done typing subscripted characters, press **Ctrl-F8** and type **3** or **N** to turn subscript off. Press Reveal Codes, **Alt-F3** (Module 59) to see the subscript symbol on screen.

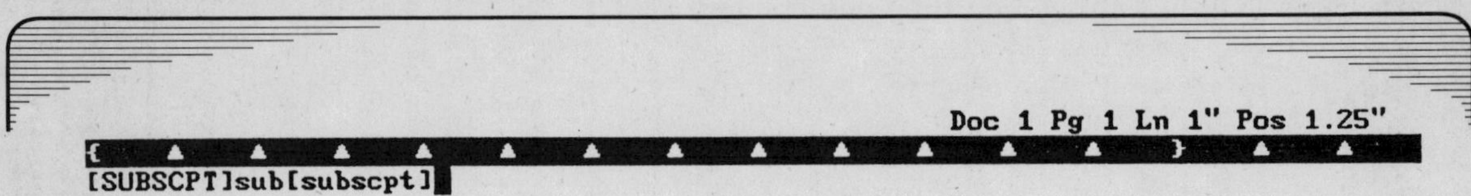

NOTE

To delete a superscript or subscript, use the Reveal Codes key (Alt-F3) and follow the procedures in Module 59 for deleting codes.

APPLICATIONS

Subscripts are most commonly used in mathematical equations. Superscripts are used for trademarks, patent marks, and also in mathematical equations.

TYPICAL OPERATION

This operation shows you how to subscript and superscript text in a document. Assume you are creating an equation.

1. Start WordPerfect. Type **x**. Press **Ctrl-F8**, type **1** or **S**, and **2** or **b**. Then type **1**.

2. Press **Ctrl-F8**, type **1** or **S**, and **1** or **p**. Then type **2**.

3. Then press **Ctrl-F8** and type **3** or **N**.

4. Press the **Spacebar** and type **+**. Then press the **Spacebar** and type **x**.

5. Press **Ctrl-F8**, type **1** or **S**, and **2** or **b**. Then type **2**.

6. Press **Ctrl-F8**, type **1** or **S**, and **1** or **p**. Then type **3**.

7. Press **Ctrl-F8** and type **3** or **N**.

8. Press the **Spacebar** and type **=**. Then press the **Spacebar** and type **x**.

9. Press **Ctrl-F8**, type **1** or **S**, and **2** or **b**. Then type **3**.

10. Press **Ctrl-F8**, type **1** or **S**, and **1** or **p**. Then type **5**. On-screen, the above equation looks like this:

`x12 + x23 = x35`

When it is printed, the above equation looks like this:

$$x_1^{\,2} + x_2^{\,3} = x_3^{\,5}$$

11. Save the document as EQUASION.WPF.
12. Turn to Module 28 to continue the learning sequence.

Module 68
TABLE OF AUTHORITIES

DESCRIPTION

Lawyers and others in the legal profession use a table of authorities to cite cases, statutes, regulations, etc. WordPerfect lets you mark text to generate such a table. Up to sixteen sections can be defined, such as one for cases, one for statutes, one for references to the Constitution. Use the Mark Text key (Alt-F5) to define the table of authorities.

Creating a table of authorities is really not much different than creating a table of contents (Module 69) or generating an index (Module 36). Just as in list, index, or table of contents creation, there are three steps to generating a table of authorities:

1. Mark the text
2. Define the table of authorities
3. Generate the table of authorities

If you use WordPerfect's Master Document feature, a table of authorities can be generated for a series of linked documents. Master Documents are explained in Module 44.

MARKING TEXT FOR A TABLE OF AUTHORITIES   The best way to mark text for a table of authorities is as you create the document. Whenever you type a word or phrase that you feel should be marked for the table of authorities, do so. The text you mark for your table of authorities is given a code that cannot be seen without using Alt-F3, the Reveal Codes key (Module 59). If you make a mistake while marking text, use the Reveal Codes key to delete the code and then re-mark the text. To mark text for a table of authorities:

1. Move the cursor to the beginning of the text to mark and press **Alt-F4**, the Block key (Module 8). Then move the cursor to define the block of text to mark and press **Alt-F5**.

```
    Mark for: 1 ToC; 2 List; 3 Index; 4 ToA: 0
```

2. Type **4** or **A**.

```
    ToA Section Number (Press Enter for Short Form only):
```

3. Type the section number where you want this entry to be listed and press **Enter**. An editing screen appears with your block of text in it. Edit the text as you want it to appear in the table of authorities. You can put up to 30 lines of text in this screen. You can also use the Appearance key (Module 5) to make changes like underline and boldface. Then press **F7**.

```
Short Form:
```

4. The short form is the nickname for this legal heading. It lets you quickly mark other occurrences of this authority in a document. Type a short form and press **Enter**.

CAUTION
Be sure to enter a unique short form name. If you
enter a short form that has already been defined
for another authority, the table of authorities will
not be properly generated.

MARKING SHORT FORM TEXT   Short form text lets you quickly mark other occurrences of the authority. Each authority is assigned one unique short form that must be entered correctly. To mark text for an authority using the short form, first move the cursor to a word you want in the table and press Alt-F5. Type 4 or A. Then type the short form for the authority and press Enter.

DEFINE THE STYLE OF THE TABLE OF AUTHORITIES   Before you can generate the table of authorities, you must define a style for it. Would you like page numbers? Where would you like them? How would you like them to look? WordPerfect gives you several choices to help you answer these questions. To define the style:

1. Move the cursor to the place you want the table to begin. Then type a heading for the table and press **Alt-F5**. Type **5** or **D**.

```
Mark Text: Define

     1 - Define Table of Contents

     2 - Define List

     3 - Define Index

     4 - Define Table of Authorities

     5 - Edit Table of Authorities Full Form



Selection: 0
```

2. Type **4** or **A**. Then type the section number you want to define and press **Enter**.

```
Definition for Table of Authorities 1

     1 - Dot Leaders                         Yes

     2 - Underlining Allowed                 No

     3 - Blank Line Between Authorities      Yes



Selection: 0
```

3. This is the Definition menu for the table of authorities. In it, you can select whether you want dot leaders between the citation and the page number, whether you want underlining in the table, and whether you want a blank line between authorities. Make changes accordingly and press **F7** to save them.

4. Repeat the definition procedure for each section in the table.

5. Press **F7** to save the changes.

GENERATE A TABLE   Once you have marked the text and defined the style for the table, you are ready to generate it. To generate a table of authorities:

1. With the cursor anywhere in your document, press **Alt-F5**. Then type **6** or **G**.

```
Mark Text: Generate

     1 - Remove Redline Markings and Strikeout Text from Document

     2 - Compare Screen and Disk Documents and Add Redline and Strikeout

     3 - Expand Master Document

     4 - Condense Master Document

     5 - Generate Tables, Indexes, Automatic References, etc.



Selection: 0
```

2. Type **5** or **G**.

3. WordPerfect automatically deletes old tables. If you have previously created a table of authorities in this document, either delete it before continuing or WordPerfect deletes it for you. Use the Block Delete command to delete it (Module 17). If you have deleted the table of authorities, type **Y**.

4. WordPerfect now generates the table of authorities. While it is being generated, a "counter" at the bottom left of the screen counts from one to ten to inform you of its progress. When it is completed, the table of authorities appears on-screen.

NOTE

If you are generating a particularly large table of authorities, you might need to create a separate document. WordPerfect prompts you in this case to switch documents by pressing Shift-F3 (Module 22) and will generate the table of authorities there.

EDITING A TABLE OF AUTHORITIES   Editing capabilities are provided to help you change a table of authorities. To do this:

1. Using Reveal Codes (Module 59), move the cursor to the immediate right of the ToA code and press **Alt-F5**. Then type **5** or **D**.

2. Type **5** or **E**. The editing screen comes up. Make your changes and press **F7**.

3. Type the section number and press **Enter**.

4. Regenerate the table of authorities as defined before.

APPLICATIONS

The most popular use for a table of authorities is in legal briefs and other legal documents. This feature can be used to generate nearly any kind of table, however.

TYPICAL OPERATION

The following typical operation illustrates the creation of a table of authorities.

1. Create a document similar to the following:

```
The 211 years since the Declaration of Independence was signed in
1776 has been a struggle for this country. Many wars have been
fought, many battles have been won, many lives have been lost in
a struggle for freedom.

The War of 1812 was our first test as a country. This tested our
mettle and determination as the British actually burned down the
White House.

The Civil War literally tore our country apart. The sting from the
Civil War is something that we haven't completely recovered from.

World Wars I and II represented a very difficult time in our
history. We struggled against oppression, fought, and won.

The assassinations of our leaders, like John Kennedy and Abraham
Lincoln, also brought trying times to America.

Through all of this hardship, the country has managed to stay
together. In fact, in times of crisis, in every instance but the
Civil War, the country has united, disregarding minor differences
and fighting together. After all, everyone is an American first.
And that attitude has kept our contry strong. The signers of the
Declaration of Independence might not be completely happy with our
country as it is today, but they would be proud of our ability to
come together in a crisis.


                                        Doc 1 Pg 1 Ln 5.33" Pos 1"
```

2. Move the cursor to the "t" in "the" in the middle of the first sentence, press **Alt-F4** and define "the Declaration of Independence" as a block of text. Press **Alt-F5**. Type **4** or **A**.

3. Type **1** (the section number in which you want the blocked text to appear) and press **Enter**. Change the "t" in "the" to "T" and press **F7** to exit the block in the table of authorities.

4. Type **Declaration** as the short form for this authority and press **Enter**.

5. Press **End** to move the cursor to the end of the line. Then press **Home-F2**, the Extended Search key (Module 61). Type **Declaration** and press **F2**.

<u>Declaration</u> of Independence might not be completely happy with our

6. Press **Alt-F5** and type **4** or **A**. Then press **Enter**.

7. Move the cursor to the "W" in "World Wars I and II" at the beginning of the fourth paragraph and define "World Wars I" as a block of text. Press **Alt-F5**. Type **4** or **A**.

8. Type **2** (the section number in which you want the blocked text to appear) and press **Enter**. Type **World War I** to change the wording for the table of authorities and press **F7**.

9. Type **World War I** as the short form for this authority and press **Enter**.

10. With the cursor still on the "W" in "World Wars I and II" at the beginning of the fourth paragraph, re-define "World Wars I and II" as a block of text. Press **Alt-F5**. Type **4** or **A**.

11. Type **2** (the section number in which you want the blocked text to appear) and press **Enter**. Type **World War II** to change the wording for the table of authorities and press **F7**.

12. Type **World War II** as the short form for this authority and press **Enter**.

13. Continue this procedure, marking The War of 1812 and the Civil War in section 2, and the assassinations of Lincoln and Kennedy in section 3. Using steps 7 through 12 above, create separate entries for the Kennedy and Lincoln assassinations.

14. After all the text is marked, move the cursor to the top of the document, press **Ctrl-Enter** to create a new page, and move the cursor back to the top of the document. Press **Shift-F6** and type **United States History Table of Authorities**. Press **Enter** twice. Then type **Major Events**, press **Alt-F6**, type **Page:** and press **Enter** twice.

15. Press **Alt-F5**, type **5** or **D**, and type **4**.

16. Type **1** to define section 1 and press **Enter** twice.

17. Type **Wars**, press **Enter** twice, then repeat steps 15 and 16, substituting **2** for the section number.

18. Type **Tragedies**, press **Enter** twice, then repeat steps 15 and 16, substituting **3** for the section number.

19. Press **Alt-F5**, type **6** or **G**, then type **5** or **G**, and press **Enter**. Momentarily, WordPerfect creates the new table of authorities. If it appears, ignore the warning message "Warning: New page num not found between ToA def and first mark (press any key)," which basically tells you that all ToA marks are on the same page. Press **Enter** twice:

United States History Table of Authorities

Major Events	Page:
The Declaration of Independence.	.2

Wars

The Civil War.	.2
The War of 1812.	.2
World War I.	.2
World War II	.2

Tragedies

Abraham Lincoln Assassination.	.2
John Kennedy Assassination	.2

==

Doc 1 Pg 1 Ln 4.66" Pos 1"

20. Save the document as HISTORY.WPF.

21. Turn to Module 49 to continue the learning sequence.

Module 69
TABLE OF CONTENTS

DESCRIPTION

Many reports, term papers, and books include a table of contents. Creating a table of contents is no easy task, unless you use WordPerfect, which creates it for you. WordPerfect also helps you generate up to nine lists (Module 41), an index (Module 36), and a table of authorities for legal documents (Module 68). The table of contents can have up to five levels for things like parts of a book, sections in that part, and chapters in that section. Text for the table of contents comes from the document, usually chapter titles, part numbers, and the like. Use the Mark Text key (Alt-F5) to define the table of contents.

There are three steps to creating a table of contents:

1. Mark the text
2. Define the style of the table of contents
3. Generate the table of contents

MARKING TEXT FOR A TABLE OF CONTENTS The best way to mark text for a table of contents is as you create the document. Whenever you type a chapter or section title that you feel should be in a table of contents, mark it. The text you mark for the table of contents is given a code that cannot be seen without using Alt-F3, the Reveal Codes key (Module 59). If you make a mistake while marking text, use the Reveal Codes key to delete the code and then re-mark the text. You can also delete codes later to remove entries from the table. And, you can change the text for marked entries by replacing the text between the [mark] and [endmark] codes. To mark text for a table of contents:

1. Move the cursor to the beginning of the text to mark and press **Alt-F4**, the Block key (Module 8). Then move the cursor to define the block of text to mark and press **Alt-F5**. Then type **1** or **C**.

```
ToC Level:
```

2. Type the level of the table of contents for which you want the text marked.

DEFINE THE STYLE OF THE TABLE OF CONTENTS Before you can generate a table of contents, you must define a style for it. Would you like page numbers? Where would you like them? How would you like them to look? WordPerfect gives you several choices to help you answer these questions. To define the style:

1. Position the cursor where you want the table of contents to begin. It's recommended that you put the table of contents at the very beginning of a document. If you do not, the table might not be properly generated. Press **Ctrl-Enter** to create a new page. Then type a heading for the table of contents and press **Enter** a few times to separate the heading from the rest of the table.

2. Press **Alt-F5** and type **5** or **D**.

```
Mark Text: Define

        1 - Define Table of Contents

        2 - Define List

        3 - Define Index

        4 - Define Table of Authorities

        5 - Edit Table of Authorities Full Form

   Selection: 0
```

3. Type **1**.

```
Table of Contents Definition

        1 - Number of Levels                    1

        2 - Display Last Level in               No
              Wrapped Format

        3 - Page Numbering - Level 1            Flush right with leader
                             Level 2
                             Level 3
                             Level 4
                             Level 5

   Selection: 0
```

This is the Table of Contents Definition menu. You can generate it anywhere you want in a document. You must define page number position for each level in the table of contents.

4. Type **1** and then type the number of levels in the table of contents. Levels are things like parts, chapters, sections, paragraphs, etc. You can have up to five levels.

5. Type **2** to select the last level in wrapped format.

Wrapped format is useful when you have many levels because the text introducing items on that level might be too long to fit on a line. In that case, WordPerfect wraps it to the next line. This provides a neater looking table of contents. (Wrapped and unwrapped tables of contents are compared in the Typical Operation section of this module.)

However, you will not usually need wrapped format. Type N if you do not want page numbers in wrapped format, Y if you do.

NOTE

If you use wrapped format, the last level cannot
use flush right or flush right with leader for page
numbering.

6.   Type **3**.

```
1 None; 2 Pg # Follows; 3 (Pg #) Follows; 4 Flush Rt; 5 Flush Rt with Leader
```

This option lets you tell WordPerfect how you want page numbers displayed. For every level you define, WordPerfect automatically creates a default page number position of flush right with the dot leader. A leader is a dotted line connecting the entry and the page number. If you want to change this, move the cursor to the level(s) you want to change and type 1 or N if you want list headings with no page numbers, 2 or P if you want page numbers following list entries, 3 or (if you want page numbers in parentheses following list entries, 4 or F if you want flush right (Module 23) page numbers, or 5 or L if you want the page numbers flush right with the dot leaders. Then type F7 to save the settings.

GENERATE A TABLE OF CONTENTS   Once you have marked the text and defined the page numbering style for your table of contents, you are ready to generate it. To generate a table of contents:

1.   Leave the cursor in the same location where you defined the style and press **Alt-F5**. Then type **6**.

```
Mark Text: Generate

     1 - Remove Redline Markings and Strikeout Text from Document

     2 - Compare Screen and Disk Documents and Add Redline and Strikeout

     3 - Expand Master Document

     4 - Condense Master Document

     5 - Generate Tables, Indexes, Automatic References, etc.

Selection: 0
```

2.   Type **5**.

```
Existing tables, lists, and indexes will be replaced.  Continue? (Y/N) Yes
```

3. Type **Y**. WordPerfect automatically deletes your old table of contents while generating a new one. WordPerfect now generates the table of contents. While the table of contents is being generated, a message at the left-hand side of the Status Line informs you of its progress. When it is completed, the table of contents appears on-screen.

NOTE

If you are generating a particularly large table of contents, you might need to create a separate document. WordPerfect prompts you in this case to switch documents by pressing Shift-F3 (Module 22) and generates the table of contents there.

APPLICATIONS

A table of contents is useful for reports, books, chapters, theses, and a variety of other documents. The Table of Contents feature helps create a table of contents quickly, efficiently, and with a minimal amount of effort.

TYPICAL OPERATION

In this example, you generate a three-level table of contents in a fictional document.

1. Create a document that looks similar to the following. The broken lines signify new pages.

```
                    The Myth of the Paperless Office

                         by John Mathews
                         FLG Office Supply
                         Carbondale, IL


   ========================================================================
   Part I. History
   ========================================================================
   Chapter 1. The Beginning
   ========================================================================
   Figure 1. Use of paper in American offices 1940-present
   ========================================================================
   Chapter 2. Computers begin to bloom
   ========================================================================
   Part II. Office Workers
   ========================================================================
   Chapter 1. Secretaries
   ========================================================================
   Chapter 2. Executives
   ========================================================================
   Figure 1. Executives' use of paper - 1940 to present


                                          Doc 1 Pg 9 Ln 1" Pos 6.2"
```

2. Move the cursor to the "P" in "Part I," which is located on page 2 and press **Alt-F4**. Then press **End** to highlight the entire title and press **Alt-F5**. Type **1** and then **1** again to set the ToC level at 1.

3. Move the cursor to the "C" in "Chapter 1," which is located on page 3 and press **Alt-F4**. Press **End** to highlight the entire title and press **Alt-F5**. Then type **1** and then **2** to set the ToC level at 2.

4. Move the cursor to the "F" in "Figure 1," which is located on page 4 and press **Alt-F4**. Press **End** to highlight the entire title and press **Alt-F5**. Then type **1** and then **3** to set the ToC level at 3.

5. Move the cursor to the "C" in "Chapter 2," which is located on page 5 and press **Alt-F4**. Press **End** to highlight the entire title and press **Alt-F5**. Type **1** and then **2** to set the ToC level at 2.

6. Repeat these procedures for the rest of the "Part," "Chapter," and "Figure" numbers, setting ToC levels of 1 for the parts, 2 for the chapters, and 3 for the figures.

7. Move the cursor to the top of the document and press **Ctrl-Enter** to create a new page (Module 50).

NOTE

The page locations of the parts, chapters, and figures change now that you have created a new page. You could use the New Page Number function (Module 51) to change the numbers of the pages after the table of contents.

8. Move the cursor up to the new page and press **Shift-F6**, the Center key (Module 10). Then press **F6**, the Boldface key (Module 5) and type **TABLE OF CONTENTS**. Then press **F6** again.

9. Press **Enter** twice. Then press **Alt-F5** and type **5**. Type **1** to define the table of contents.

10. Type **1** then **3** to define the table of contents for three levels and leave the last level in unwrapped format. Leave flush right dot leader page number positioning for all levels. Press **F7** to save the settings.

11. Leave the cursor in the same location where you defined the style and press **Alt-F5**. Type **6**, **5**, and then **Y** in response to the prompt. WordPerfect generates the table of contents.

The completed table of contents looks like this:

```
                    TABLE OF CONTENTS


    Part I. History. . . . . . . . . . . . . . . . . .    3
        Chapter 1. The Beginning. . . . . . . . . . . .    4
            Figure 1. Use of paper in American offices 1940-
                present . . . . . . . . . . . . . . . . .    5
        Chapter 2. Computers begin to bloom . . . . . . . .    6


    Part II. Office Workers. . . . . . . . . . . . . .    7
        Chapter 1. Secretaries. . . . . . . . . . . . . .    8
        Chapter 2. Executives . . . . . . . . . . . . . .    9
            Figure 1. Executives' use of paper - 1940 to
                present . . . . . . . . . . . . . . . . .   10
```

The same table of contents with the last level wrapped looks like this:

```
                          TABLE OF CONTENTS

       Part I. History. . . . . . . . . . . . . . . . . . . . .  3
          Chapter 1. The Beginning. . . . . . . . . . . . . .  4
             Figure 1. Use of paper in American offices 1940-
             present (5)
          Chapter 2. Computers begin to bloom . . . . . . . . .  6

       Part II. Office Workers. . . . . . . . . . . . . . . . .  7
          Chapter 1. Secretaries. . . . . . . . . . . . . . . .  8
          Chapter 2. Executives . . . . . . . . . . . . . . . .  9
             Figure 1. Executives' use of paper - 1940 to present
             (10)
```

12. Save the document as CONTENT.WPF.

13. Turn to Module 68 to continue the learning sequence.

Module 70
TABS

DESCRIPTION

Typists set tabs on their typewriters to set levels of indentation, starting points for addresses, starting points for columns within tables, and for a variety of other reasons. When tabs are set, pressing the Tab key moves the carriage or the carrier to the next tab, where the typist continues.

WordPerfect's tab settings work in a similar fashion. Instead of a carriage or a carrier, the cursor moves to the next Tab setting when the Tab key is pressed. Pressing Shift-Tab moves the cursor back to the previous tab setting.

WordPerfect initially sets tabs 0.5 inches apart from the left margin to the right margin. (5 spaces at the default setting of 10 characters per inch.) You can reset these in any manner you like.

WordPerfect offers four kinds of tabs: left-justified, right-justified, centered, or decimal.

- Left-justified tabs, the default setting, are the way normal tabs are set. Text appears at the left-most portion of the tab.
- Right-justified tabs result in right-justified text. Text moves to the left as you type, with the tab setting serving as the right margin. This is similar to the flush right feature.
- Decimal tabs are decimal aligned. Text moves to the right until you type a decimal point. These are helpful for columns of numbers.
- Centered tabs result in centered text. The tab setting serves as the center of the text.

You can set tabs as many times in a document as you like. Realize, however, that the only text affected by a tab setting is text that occurs after that tab setting and before the next one.

SETTING TABS   Tabs are set using the Line Format key (Shift-F8). To set tabs:

1. Press **Shift-F8** and type **1** or **L**. Notice the initial tab setting. It means that there is one tab stop every half-inch from the left margin to the right margin.

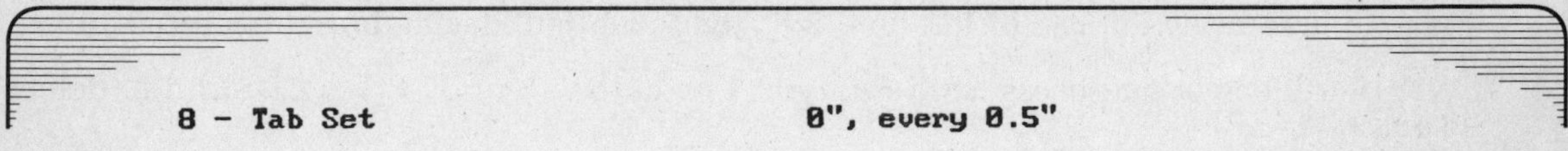

2. Type **8** or **T**.

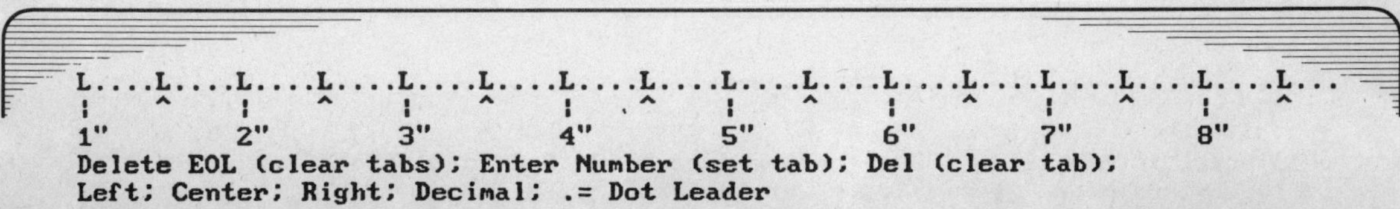

These are tab settings. Each time you press the Tab key, you get to the next space where a tab has been set. Each "L" signifies a left-justified tab has been placed on that space. Notice tabs are set 0.5" (five spaces apart) from 0 to 80.

Typing a period (.) before L, R, or D gives you a dot leader before the text. "C" tabs do not have a dot leader. These tabs can be combined in the same entry. Any tab that is set with a dot leader appears in reverse video.

While setting tabs, control the cursor through either the Left Arrow or Right Arrow key, or by typing the inch setting you want. Keystrokes used in changing tabs are:

NOTE
If you are using left-justified tabs, you do not
need to enter a tab style letter. Also, before
typing the tab style letter, add the step of typing
a period if you want dot leaders.

Keystrokes	Results
Ctrl-End, F7	Clears all tabs.
Tab-style letter, any number, Enter, F7	Moves cursor to that number, sets tab.
Tab-style letter, any number, Enter, Delete, F7	Moves cursor to that number, deletes tab.
Tab-style letter, any number, comma, any number, Enter, F7	Sets evenly spaced tabs. The first number is the beginning column number, the second number is the number of spaces between tabs. For example, to place tabs 2 inches apart beginning 2.5-inches from the left margin, at column 25, type 2.5,2, Enter, F7.

APPLICATIONS

Among other applications, tabs are helpful in setting indent levels for paragraphs, and for setting columns in tables and charts. Right-justified tabs are good for tables, as are centered tabs. Decimal tabs are useful in columns of numbers. Adding dot leaders is helpful in figures, tables, lists, and other documents.

TYPICAL OPERATION

This example illustrates the use of left-justified, right-justified, decimal, and centered tabs.

1. Start WordPerfect and press **Shift-F8**, type **1** or **L**, then **8** or **T**. Press **Ctrl-End** to delete all the tabs.

2. Type **3** and press **Enter**, then **4** and press **Enter**, then **5** and press **Enter**, then **6.5** and press **Enter**.

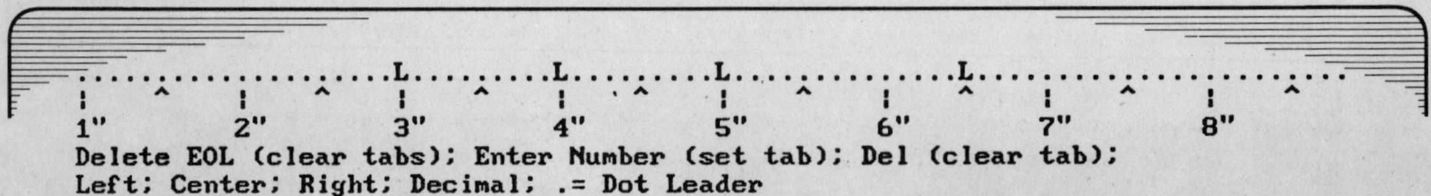

3. Press **F7** twice to return to your document.

4. Using those tabs, create the following document:

```
                    FLG ROGUES TEAM BATTING AVERAGE
                    AB        H         AVG          DEPT.
        David
        Belew
        Mathews
        Wilson
```

5. With the cursor on the "D" in David, press **Shift-F8** and type **1** or **L**. Type **8** or **T**.

6. Type **3** and press **Enter**. Type **.R**. This sets a right-justified tab with a dot leader preceding it.

7. Type **4** and press **Enter**. Type **R**.

8. Type **6.5** and press **Enter**. Type **C**. Press **F7** twice to return to the document.

9. Using the tab keys, fill in the table so it looks like this:

```
              FLG ROGUES TEAM BATTING AVERAGE
              AB        H         AVG          DEPT.
  David. . . . . . 250      61        .244      Accounting
  Belew. . . . . . .50      15        .300        Sales
  Mathews. . . . . 500     129        .258     Administration
  Wilson . . . . . 100      38        .380      Sanitation
```

Notice that tabs under AB and H are right-justified, the tab under .AVG is left-justified, and the tab under DEPT. is centered.

10. Save the document as AVGS.WPF.

11. Turn to Module 39 to continue the learning sequence.

Module 71

THESAURUS

DESCRIPTION

The Speller (Module 64) makes sure all the words in your document are spelled right. The Thesaurus (Alt-F1) makes sure all the words in your document have just the right meaning. The Thesaurus works just like a book version, but with the convenience of being electronic. WordPerfect does the searching for you; you don't have to thumb through a book.

The Thesaurus lets you select many of the words in your document. Words that can be selected are called headwords. WordPerfect includes synonym and antonym references for more than 10,000 such headwords. If a word can't be selected, WordPerfect gives you a "Word not found" message.

The synonyms and antonyms WordPerfect retrieves are called references and are listed on the Reference menu. References are organized into subgroups. Subgroups are groups of references with the same connotation. The Thesaurus also separates references into nouns (n), verbs (v), adjectives (a), and antonyms (ant). There may be more than one subgroup in any of these classifications.

You can search among references that are headwords (identified by a bullet) to find even more references. Or you can find references for unrelated headwords. In this way, you can put up to three headwords and their references on-screen at any time.

All references are listed in columns. There is room for three columns of words. You can select words from only one column at a time. Words in a non-selected column do not have letters next to them. Use the cursor control (Module 15) keys to move between columns. You can also use Ctrl-Home or the Go To key (Module 29) to move between subgroups.

To use the Thesaurus:

1. Move the cursor to the word you want to find synonyms for. You can also type the word once you have started the Thesaurus. In this case, assume you are looking for synonyms for the word "better."

2. If you have a floppy-based system, put the Thesaurus diskette in drive B. If you have a hard disk-based system, you should have already copied the Thesaurus onto your hard disk (Module 2). If the Thesaurus is not in the same directory as the WordPerfect file, you are asked to provide the directory that the Thesaurus is in, for example, \ WP50 \ THESARUS.

CAUTION

Do not remove the Thesaurus diskette from drive
B until you are through using it.

3. Press **Alt-F1**.

```
  I'm looking for a word that's [better] than this.

 ┌better-(a)─────────────────────┬──────────────────────────┐
 │ 1 A  finer          better-(ant)─────────                │
 │   B  improved       5    ·inferior                        │
 │   C  preferable          ·failing                         │
 │   D  ·superior                                            │
 │                     6    ·worsen                          │
 │ 2 E  convalescing                                         │
 │   F  improving                                            │
 │   G  recovering                                           │
 │                                                           │
 │better-(v)─────────────                                    │
 │ 3 H  ·ameliorate                                          │
 │   I  ·improve                                             │
 │   J  ·refine                                              │
 │   K  ·revamp                                              │
 │                                                           │
 │ 4 L  ·exceed                                              │
 │   M  ·surpass                                             │
 │   N  ·top                                                 │
 1 Replace Word; 2 View Doc; 3 Look Up Word; 4 Clear Column: 0
```

Notice there are six subgroups for "better," two adjective subgroups, two verb subgroups, and two antonym subgroups. Notice also that there is no letter next to the word "inferior" in the second column. That's because you can select only words in column one. But you can move inferior over to column one by using the Down Arrow key. That is described later in the module.

Notice that all of the verb and antonym references have bullets next to them, making them headwords, while only one of the adjective references is a headword.

There are four options at the bottom of the screen — Replace Word, View Doc, Look Up Word, and Clear Column.

4. To replace the word in the text, type **1**.

```
  Press letter for word
```

5. Assume you want to replace "better" with "finer." Type **A**, the letter next to finer in column one.

```
  I'm looking for a word that's finer than this.
```

6. When you are finished using the Thesaurus, press **F1**, **F7**, or the **Spacebar** to return to normal editing.

VIEW DOC This option lets you move around your document while still using the Thesaurus. It is useful for seeing more of the text around a word. You can also use View Doc to look up other words in the document. To use the View Doc option:

1. With the cursor on the word "finer," press **Alt-F1**. Notice the references are for the word "fine," a form of finer.

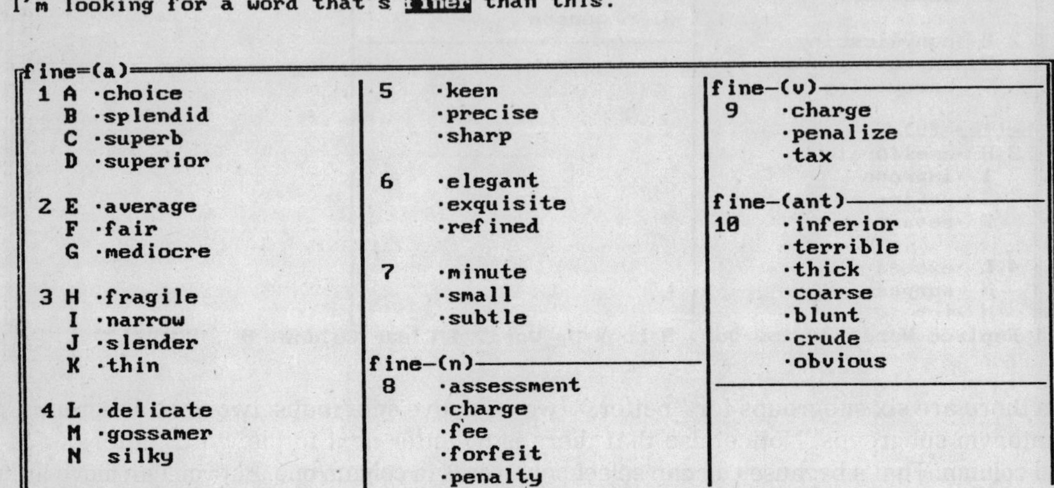

2. Type **2**.

You can now move the cursor anywhere in the document you are editing.

3. Move the cursor to the word "looking" in the same sentence and press **Alt-F1**. Notice entries for "look" appear on the screen. Press **F7** to return to the document.

LOOK UP WORD Any time you are in the Thesaurus, you can look up words. It does not matter what word you have previously looked up.

1. Move the cursor to the word "finer" from the previous example and press **Alt-F1**.
2. Type **3**. Then type **choice** and press **Enter**.

```
 fine=(a)                  choice=(n)                        ·select
   1    ·choice            1 A ·alternative                  ·superior
        ·splendid            B ·decision
        ·superb              C ·option              choice-(ant)
        ·superior                                   5    ·mediocre
                           2 D ·pick
   2    ·average            E ·preference
        ·fair               F ·selection
        ·mediocre
                           3 G ·array
   3    ·fragile            H ·assortment
        ·narrow             I ·stock
        ·slender            J ·supply
        ·thin               K ·variety

   4    ·delicate         choice-(a)
        ·gossamer          4 L ·elite
         silky               M ·exceptional
                             N ·fine
 1 Replace Word; 2 View Doc; 3 Look Up Word; 4 Clear Column: 0
```

3. Type **H**.

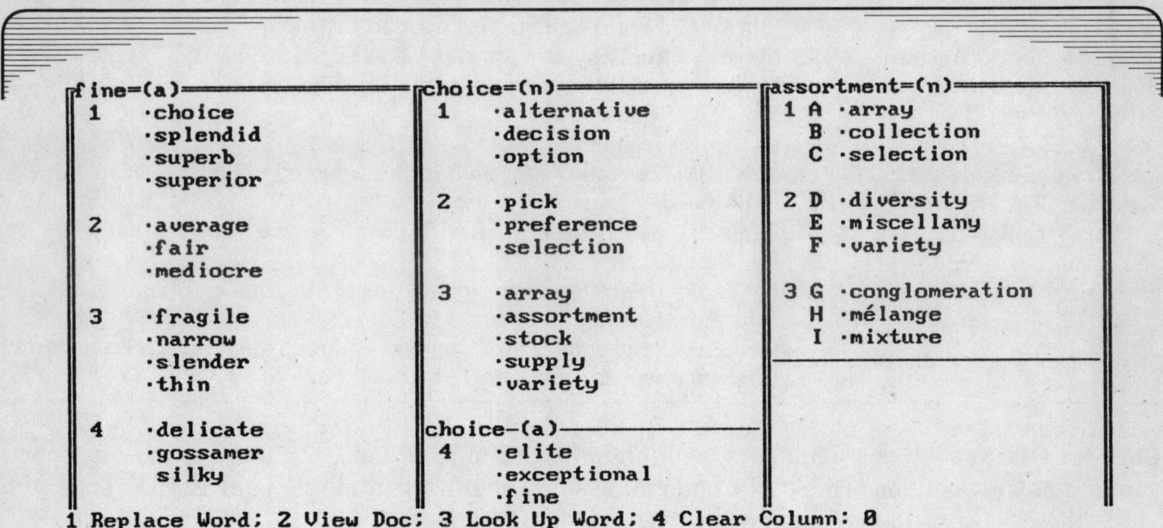

```
 fine=(a)                  choice=(n)              assortment=(n)
   1    ·choice            1   ·alternative        1 A ·array
        ·splendid               ·decision            B ·collection
        ·superb                 ·option              C ·selection
        ·superior
                           2   ·pick               2 D ·diversity
   2    ·average              ·preference           E ·miscellany
        ·fair                 ·selection            F ·variety
        ·mediocre
                           3   ·array              3 G ·conglomeration
   3    ·fragile              ·assortment           H ·mélange
        ·narrow               ·stock                I ·mixture
        ·slender              ·supply
        ·thin                 ·variety

   4    ·delicate         choice-(a)
        ·gossamer          4   ·elite
         silky                ·exceptional
                              ·fine
 1 Replace Word; 2 View Doc; 3 Look Up Word; 4 Clear Column: 0
```

Notice there are two ways to look up words. Either type 3, type the word and press Enter, or if the word has a letter next to it, simply type the letter.

CURSOR CONTROL INSIDE THE THESAURUS   Notice the letters have moved over to column three, where assortment begins. Notice also that several subgroups for "fine" and "choice" have disappeared. They have not disappeared for good, however.

1. Press **Left Arrow**. Notice the letters have moved over to column two, under "choice."

2. Press **Down Arrow**. Notice the reference words that were in column three before and seemed to have disappeared when we selected references for "assortment." Notice that those words now have letters next to them.

3. Press **Left Arrow**. Notice the letters move back to column one.

4. Press **PgDn**. Notice the words for fine are still there, they were just out of view. PgDn or Screen Down (+ on the numeric keypad) both accomplish the same thing. The following table describes the functions of the cursor control keys in the Thesaurus.

Thesaurus Cursor Control

Key	Function
Left Arrow	Moves the letters to a previous column.
Right Arrow	Moves the letters to a later column.
Down Arrow	Moves down in a column to let you view any subgroups that did not fit on the screen before. When only one or two headwords have been selected, this key also moves subgroups over and assigns them letters.
Up Arrow	Moves up in a column to let you see any subgroups that did not fit on the screen before. When only one or two headwords have been selected, this key "pushes" subgroups over to the next column.
Home, Home, Up Arrow	Moves to the first subgroup in the selected column.
Home, Home, Down Arrow	Moves to the last subgroup in the selected column.
PgUp or Screen Up	Moves the column up.
PgDn or Screen Down	Moves the column down.
Ctrl-Home, Subgroup #	Moves to a specific subgroup in the selected column.
Spacebar, F1, or F7	Exits the Thesaurus.
1, Specific letter	Replaces the selected word with the reference word at that letter on the menu.
Specific letter	Looks up reference word, changes current menu to references for reference word.
3	Looks up reference word, changes current menu to references for reference word.

CLEAR COLUMN   If you want to select another word to reference, but there is not any room, you can clear a column. To clear a column, assume you are continuing your earlier example. Move the cursor to the column you want to clear and type 4.

APPLICATIONS

A Thesaurus helps improve the quality of your writing. Use it whenever you want a better word than the one you have chosen. WordPerfect lets you choose synonyms, in the form of nouns, verbs, and adjectives, and antonyms (words that are the opposite of the selected word).

TYPICAL OPERATION

Use the Thesaurus in this example to improve the writing quality in a memo.

1. Create a document similar to the following:

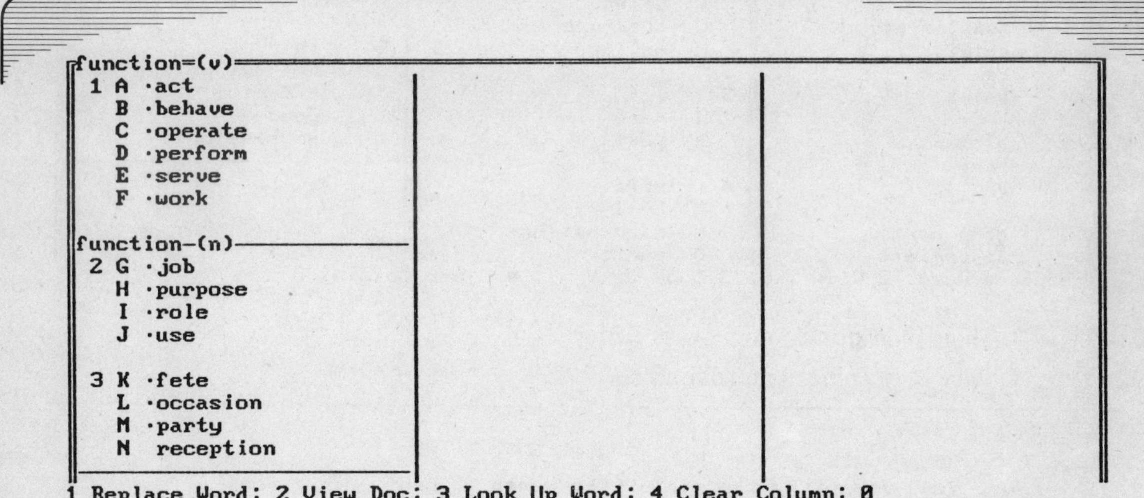

```
From: FLG
To:   RAW

While the main function of the average office is work, many office
personnel rely on their place of work as a hub of social activity.
Therefore, it might be pertinent if we start to sell merchandise
that is not related to the office, like magazines.

I want to investigate this matter. I'm going to put you in charge
of this program, Roger. Go to the library and do some market
research. Also do some studies. Find out what types of items people
hope to find in office supply stores. Find out what we're missing.

I'd like a full report by the end of the month. I want your report
to list all of the items we aren't carrying that we should be
carrying. I'd also like an estimated sales volume for those items.

FLG
```

Doc 1 Pg 1 Ln 1" Pos 1"

2. Move the cursor to the word "function" on line four and press **Alt-F1**.

```
function=(v)
  1 A ·act
    B ·behave
    C ·operate
    D ·perform
    E ·serve
    F ·work

function-(n)
  2 G ·job
    H ·purpose
    I ·role
    J ·use

  3 K ·fete
    L ·occasion
    M ·party
    N  reception

1 Replace Word; 2 View Doc; 3 Look Up Word; 4 Clear Column: 0
```

3. Type **1**, then **H** to select the word "purpose."

```
While the main purpose of the average office is work, many office
```

Doc 1 Pg 1 Ln 1.5" Pos 3.2"

4. Move the cursor to the word "work" on the next line and press **Alt-F1**. Notice the references for work appear on-screen.

5. Press **Right Arrow** to move the menu over to the next column and type **1**. Then type **D** to replace "work" with "employment."

personnel rely on their place of employment as a hub of social activity.

                                        Doc 1 Pg 1 Ln 1.66" Pos 5.3"

6. Move the cursor to the word "items" on the second line of the third paragraph and press **Alt-F1**. Notice the references for item appear on-screen.

7. Type **B** to look up references for "thing."

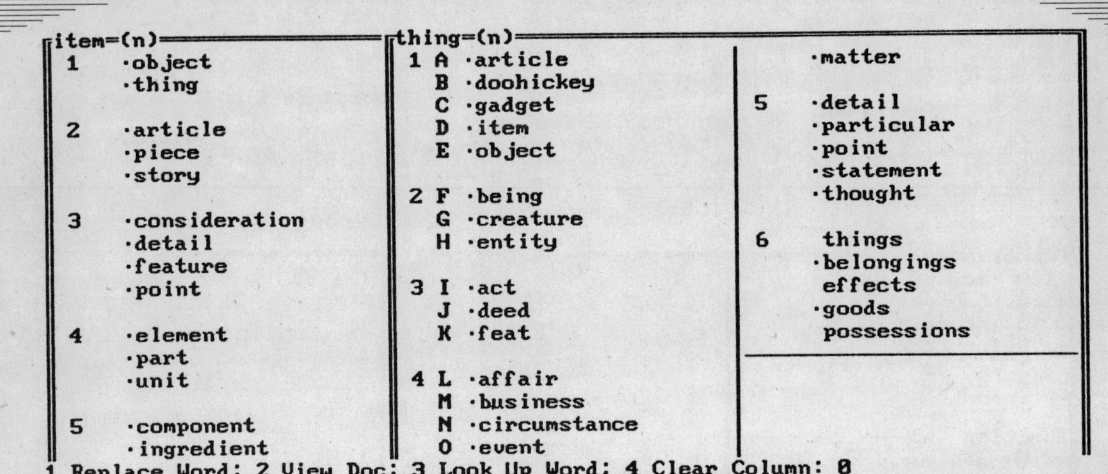

8. Type **3**. Then type **goods** and press **Enter**.

9. Type **1**, then **B** to select "merchandise."

I'd like a full report by the end of the month. I want your report to list all of the merchandise we aren't carrying that we should be carrying. I'd also like an estimated sales volume for those items.

FLG

                                        Doc 1 Pg 1 Ln 3.5" Pos 8.1"

10. Save the document as MAGAZINE.WPF.

11. Turn to Module 53 to continue the learning sequence.

Module 72
WORKING WITH DOS

DESCRIPTION

You save most documents in WordPerfect format when using WordPerfect. But if you are exchanging documents with others who use either other versions of WordPerfect or other word processing software, the Text In/Out key (Ctrl-F5) offers you several useful options. You can save and retrieve DOS text files (ASCII files), which is helpful for transferring information to other computers via a modem. You can save documents in generic format, which makes them easier to use with other word processors. Or you can save documents in WordPerfect 4.2 format for use with WordPerfect 4.2, WordPerfect for the Macintosh, or other WordPerfect software. You can also print files to disk to save text files.

SAVING AND RETRIEVING DOS TEXT OR GENERIC FILES   Save files as DOS files if you send files over telephone lines. DOS text files are immediately ready to send to another computer or use as ASCII files, because they include a hard carriage return at the end of every line.

On the other hand, save files as generic files if you are going to be using them with other word processing software. Generic files include a hard return at the end of each paragraph instead of the end of every line. This is much more convenient when using other software.

Both DOS text files and generic files convert feature codes, like paragraph numbers, dates, and other automatically entered information to ASCII text. Space generated in tabs, indents, centers, margins, etc. is converted to individual spaces.

Both types of files lose boldface, underline, italics and other text appearance changes. They also do not convert text from footnotes and endnotes.

There is no need to use the WordPerfect's Convert utility (Appendix D) when either saving or retrieving DOS text or generic files. The Convert utility saves and retrieves documents to formats used by other applications software. WordPerfect automatically converts DOS text or generic files to WordPerfect format when it retrieves them.

To save files as DOS text or generic files:

1.   Press **Ctrl-F5**.

```
1 DOS Text; 2 Password; 3 Save Generic; 4 Save WP 4.2; 5 Comment: 0
```

2.   Type **1** or **T** to save the files as DOS text files, **3** or **G** to save them as generic files.

3. Type **1** or **S** to save the file as a DOS text file. If the file has never been saved before, type the filename and press **Enter**. If the file has been saved before, you are asked if you want to replace the file. Type **Y** if you do. The file is then saved as a DOS text file.

   To save the file as a generic file, type the filename if the file has never been saved before and press **Enter**. If the file has been saved before, press **Enter** to save the document as the same filename and type **Y** to confirm. You are then returned to the document.

NOTE

You do not have to save this file as a DOS or generic file. If you want to keep a copy of it in WordPerfect format, give it another name and press Enter. The new file is saved as a DOS or generic file.

NOTE

If you did not change the filename or location, make sure you do not save the file again, or WordPerfect will save it in its own format and replace the DOS text file.

4. Press **F7**, then type **N** to exit WordPerfect.

To retrieve a DOS or generic file:

1. Press **Ctrl-F5**. Type **1** or **T** for DOS text files or **3** or **G** for generic text files. Then type **2** or **R** to retrieve the file with hard carriage returns at the end of every line (DOS text), or **3** or **e** to retrieve the file with soft carriage returns at the end of most lines, and hard carriage returns at the end of every paragraph (generic files). You can use either option for generic and DOS text files, but it is usually better to use option 3 when retrieving documents.

2. Type the filename and location of the document to be retrieved and press **Enter**.

To retreive a DOS text or generic file using List Files (Module 40):

1. Press **F5**, type the directory location of the DOS text file, and press **Enter**.

2. Move the cursor to the DOS text file and type **5** or **T**, then **Y** to retrieve it.

SAVING FILES IN WORDPERFECT 4.2 FORMAT   If you intend to share a file with someone who is using WordPerfect 4.2 or Macintosh WordPerfect, you need to save it in WordPerfect 4.2 format. To do this:

1. Press **Shift-F7**. Type **S** and move the cursor to the printer you normally use.

```
   1 Select; 2 Additional Printers; 3 Edit; 4 Copy; 5 Delete; 6 Help: 1
```

2. Type **3** or **E**.

```
Select Printer: Edit

        Filename                      EPFX80.PRS

     1 - Name                         Epson FX-80/100

     2 - Port                         LPT1:

     3 - Sheet Feeder                 None

     4 - Forms

     5 - Cartridges and Fonts

     6 - Initial Font                 10 CPI

     7 - Path for Downloadable
           Fonts and Printer
           Command Files

  Selection: 0
```

3. Type **2** or **P**.

```
  Port: 1 LPT 1; 2 LPT 2; 3 LPT 3; 4 COM 1; 5 COM 2; 6 COM 3; 7 COM 4; 8 Other: 0
```

4. Type **8**.

```
  Device or Filename:
```

5. Type the directory location and filename you want the file printed to. If you type only a filename, the document prints on the current directory.

6. Press **F7** twice to return to the Print menu. Then type **1** or **F** to print the document you are currently editing. You can also type **3** or **D** and print a document on disk, as long as that document has not been Fast Saved (Module 60).

7. Repeat this procedure for as many files as you want to print to disk. You must change the filename each time you print a document to disk, however, repeating steps 1 through 6. When you are finished, change printing back to the regular port for your printer.

APPLICATIONS

When saving files for use with other word processing software, save them as generic files. If sending files via modem to other users, save them as DOS text files. If you do not want to lose headers, footers, boldface, and other information, print the file to disk as a DOS file.

TYPICAL OPERATION

In this example, you save a regular WordPerfect file as a DOS file.

1. Retrieve the income statement created in Module 15, "FINANCES.WPF."

2. Press **PgDn** to display the income statement.

```
                        INCOME STATEMENT
                       FLG OFFICE SUPPLIES
                 FOR YEAR ENDED DECEMBER 31, 1986

   Sales:                   $625,000
   Less: Cost of Goods:      375,000
   Gross Margin:                                $250,000

   Operating Expenses:

   Rent:                    $ 36,000
   Utilities:                  8,000
   Salaries:                  95,000
   Misc. Expenses:            46,525
   Total Operating Expenses:                     185,525
   Gross Profit:                                $64,475
   Taxes:                                       $19,343

   Net Profit:                                  $45,132
```

3. Press **Ctrl-F5**, type **1** or **T**, then **1** or **S**.

```
   Document to be saved (Dos Text): C:\WP50\DOCS\FINANCES.WPF
```

4. Type **FINANCES.WPF** and press **Enter**. The file is saved as a DOS text file, while keeping FINANCES.WPF as a regular WordPerfect file.

5. Press **F7** and type **N**.

6. Turn to Module 38 to complete the learning sequence.

Appendix A
TERMS AND DEFINITIONS

Term	Definition
Alignment Character	A certain character along which columns of numbers or text are aligned vertically. The typical alignment character is a period.
Alphanumeric	Including both letters and number characters.
Application	Use. Sometimes an application program is shortened to "application."
ASCII	Acronym for *American Standard Code for Information Interchange*. It is the character set used in data communications. Files saved as DOS text files.
Append	To add a block of text at the end of a selected file.
Auto Rewrite	Command that automatically rewrites (rewraps lines of text) to account for editing changes.
Automatic Reference	A WordPerfect feature that automatically enters the correct page number for a referenced item when a document is complete.
Backup	An additional copy of a diskette or program that acts as insurance in case something happens to the original. The process of creating a backup copy is called "backing up" a diskette or file.
Backspace Key	A key that deletes characters and codes to the left of the cursor. (The delete key deletes characters and codes to the right of the cursor.)
Binding Width	The width used to determine the available space for binding text or putting punch holes in a document.
Bit	A single binary digit used in combination with others to form characters that are usable by computers. In general, eight bits make a byte.
Block	A selected segment of a document. Blocks can be manipulated — copied, deleted, underlined, etc.
Boilerplate	In publishing and word processing jargon this refers to standard passages of text, such as report paragraphs, tables, or formatting commands, that serve as patterns to help create new documents.
Boldface	A means of darkening or highlighting text so that it stands out from the rest of a document.
Boot	To load the disk operating system (DOS) into a computer.
Buffer	A temporary area of data storage. Blocks of text and documents waiting to be printed are kept in buffers by the computer.

Term	Definition
Byte	A single computer character made up of eight binary digits called bits.
Cancel	WordPerfect's "oops" key that lets you undo or nullify a particular action.
Case Conversion	A feature that changes a block of text to either all uppercase or all lowercase letters. In the case of all lowercase letters, the first word of each sentence retains initial capitalization, as do words like I and I'm.
Center	An editing function that positions the designated text so that approximately the same number of characters appears to the right of center as to the left.
Character	A single letter, number, space, punctuation mark, or other symbol placed on the monitor by the computer keyboard.
Character String	A continuous sequence of characters that can include letters, numbers, blank spaces, and symbols.
Codes	Symbols that tell your printer and computer where to insert a tab, change spacing or margins, and many other functions. WordPerfect hides these codes so you only see them when you use Reveal Codes.
Colors	Feature that lets you change the on-screen color of a variety of text.
Column Definition	The process of defining a group of columns. Columns may be parallel, where independent information is kept separately, or newspaper style, where information flows continuously.
Computer	A machine that helps you manipulate information like words and numbers.
Copy	An editing function that duplicates a designated body of text. It lets you position the copied text in another part of the document and leaves the original section intact.
Cursor	A screen indicator that shows you where the next character you type will appear.
Cursor Control	Term referring to the activity of using keystrokes to manipulate the position of the cursor on the screen.
Data	Information. Data can be in many forms including words, figures, and commands. Data is also the information that you use to create documents and the documents themselves.
Date	A command that inserts today's date in various formats at the current cursor position.
Default	The value that the program automatically designates. The default remains in effect until you change it. You can set the default repeat value to 16, for example. It remains 16 until you change it. You can also change the default directory or drive, so WordPerfect accesses a different directory on your command.
Delete	The word processing function whereby text is erased from a document.

Term	Definition
DIF	Acronym for Data Interchange Format. Spreadsheets are often converted to this file format in order to send files over a modem or to send information between different application packages.
Directory	A location on a disk (hard or floppy) designated to keep certain groups of files. A directory can be compared to a drawer in a filing cabinet.
Disk	See diskette or hard disk.
Diskette	A magnetic object that stores programs and data. Also called a disk.
Diskette Jacket	The covering or casing that protects the magnetic surface of the diskette.
Diskette Envelope	The sleeves or folders that house the diskette for storage when the diskette is not being used in the disk drive.
Display	The name given to the picture on the monitor or a simulation of it in a document.
Document	The name given to a word processing file.
Document Comments	A WordPerfect feature that adds comments to a document that can be seen on-screen but are not printed in the printed version.
Document Compare	A WordPerfect feature that analyzes and compares two documents and displays the differences between them on-screen.
DOS	Acronym for Disk Operating System. DOS lays the ground rules for computer operation. It gives the computer instructions to tell it how to read and write data from the diskettes, how to display it on the screen, etc.
Drive	A device that houses diskettes or a hard disk. It serves as the mechanism to record and retrieve data on the diskettes or hard disk.
Dual Document Editing	A feature that lets you edit two documents at once.
Edit	A word processing function that permits creation of new files and modification of existing ones.
Endnote	Information, at the end of a document, that provides further details about a subject in the text.
Escape	A command that uses a repeat value to let you perform the same activity (like deleting or typing a specific character) a set number of times.
Execute	To carry out a command or instruction. Both the computer and the operator can execute a command.
File	A computer-generated document or program.
Filename	The name given to a file. It is usually up to eight characters and identifies the contents of the file.

Term	Definition
Flush Right	Term that describes text flush against the right margin.
Font	A specific typeface, point size, and weight, such as 10 point pica italic.
Footer	A portion of text that is placed at the end of a page and repeated throughout the document.
Footnote	Information, at the end of a page, that provides further details about a specific point in the text.
Format	The physical arrangement of a document, including margins and character and line spacing, that contributes to determining the appearance of a printed page. Also, the process of preparing your diskettes so they can store data.
Go To	A word processing function used to send the cursor to a specific place in a document or a specific page.
Hard Copy	The printed version of a file.
Hard Disk	A rigid disk that is more rugged and stores more data than a floppy diskette. It can be inside the computer or in a separate drive.
Hard Space	A space positioned between two characters that prevents them from separating during editing or pagination.
Header	One or more standard lines of text, such as a chapter title, located at the top of a page within a document.
Help	A WordPerfect function that summarizes the functions and keys to help you choose what action to take. It can be used while you are in your document and serves as a first step before using the manual or this book.
Hyphenation	An option that separates a long word at the end of a line so that lines of text are more equal. This improves the appearance of the printed version of the document.
Import	The process of bringing information from another source (a file, for example) into the current document.
Indent	To align text along a tab stop. Pressing the Indent key moves the cursor to a tab stop. This temporarily changes the left margin so that all text you type until you press Enter lines up along the tab stop.
Index	A WordPerfect function that lets you automatically generate an index. The index can include the location of special terms used in a document.
Insert	An editing function that allows the introduction of characters, words, entire passages of text, figures, or other information at a designated point in an existing document.
Italics	A text treatment that slants letters to the right. It is a means of making text stand out from the rest of the document.

Term	Definition
Justification	The creation of an even right margin by printing the last character on each line in the same right column. It is achieved by printing a document with extra space between words (and sometimes characters, depending on the printer used). Document justification is a printing, not an editing, function.
Kerning	Spacing between letters. WordPerfect sets letter spacing automatically to eliminate excessive white space.
Leading	Pronounced "ledding." The spacing between lines. WordPerfect measures leading in terms of line height, which is the distance from the top of one line to the top of the next.
Learning Diskette	The WordPerfect diskette that contains lessons on how to use WordPerfect.
Line Drawing	A WordPerfect function that makes it easier to draw lines on the screen. It is used to draw borders around text, create graphics images, etc.
Line Format	A WordPerfect function that sets the format for each line of text in a document. It sets tabs, margins, hyphenation, spacing, widow/orphan protection, line height, and line numbering.
Lines Per Inch	The number of lines printed in a vertical inch. The standard line spacing is six lines per inch.
List	A WordPerfect function that lets you create up to nine lists per document. The lists can be lists of tables or illustrations in a document, or used for any other purpose.
List Files	A WordPerfect function that lists all the files in a particular directory. It includes options for copying, deleting, renaming, retrieving, printing, searching for, and looking at a file. Options are also available for changing the default directory and retrieving DOS files.
Macro	A feature that lets you "record" a series of keystrokes into a file for "playback" at a later time.
Mark Text	A WordPerfect function that marks text for use in index, list, and table of contents generation. This key also marks text for redlining and strikeout of text.
Master Document	A document that lets you create indexes, lists, tables of authorities, and tables of contents, and formatting changes for an unlimited number of subdocuments.
Math	A command that turns WordPerfect into a calculator at its simplest and a spreadsheet at its most complex.
Menu	A list of options from which to select an activity.

Term	Definition
Merge	The process of combining two documents to form a third. Printed merge documents are created from a "primary file," which contains boilerplate material, and a "secondary file," which lists the variable items, such as names and addresses.
Mode	Term to describe a function taking place. Some modes of operation include block, math, and column.
Monitor	A device that attaches to a computer to display what is entered on the keyboard.
Move	An editing function used to identify an area of text (from a single character, up to entire pages) and position it at another point in a document.
Outline	A WordPerfect mode that acts as a "thought organizer." Each time Enter is pressed, the next level of the outline is reached. Levels can be changed (i.e., from II to A) by pressing Tab.
Page	A designated number of lines that constitute a single page within a document. Pages are divided automatically by WordPerfect based on the selected number of lines on a page.
Page Break	The boundary between two pages. Soft page breaks are created automatically by WordPerfect. Hard page breaks are created by the user.
Paragraph Numbering	A WordPerfect feature that automatically keeps track of paragraph numbers. This is useful for procedural steps, where adding a step in the middle of a long procedure used to result in having to renumber the paragraphs by hand. WordPerfect automatically renumbers the paragraphs or steps.
Print	The process of sending a document or part of a document to an attached printer so a hard copy of the document can be printed or distributed. WordPerfect lets you print a document, a page, or a block of text.
Printer Advance	A WordPerfect command that automatically advances the printer a specific distance up or down.
Printer Control	A menu at which the printer is controlled. Documents being sent to the printer can be manipulated, and the printer can be stopped and started. A listing on the menu tells which documents are in the print cycle.
Proportional Spacing	An option that divides spaces between characters so text appears more uniform. It is similar to typesetting on more complex equipment.
Protect	A WordPerfect function that keeps all of a designated block of text together on the same page.

Term	Definition
RAM	Acronym for Random Access Memory. It is temporary memory devoted to currently used computer information. RAM is erased when the power is turned off.
ROM	Acronym for Read Only Memory. It is permanent memory used by the computer to run. ROM is not erased when the power is turned off.
Rectangle	A block of text that is defined as the space between the upper lefthand corner and the lower righthand corner of the block. This lets you move or copy portions of lines rather than whole lines of text. Rectangular blocks are useful for moving or copying addresses, columns of tables, and other uses.
Redline	A mark that identifies text an editor recommends be added to a document.
Replace	A WordPerfect function that lets you substitute a character string in a document.
Screen	The group of lines in a document that are visible on the monitor at any one time.
Search	A WordPerfect function that lets you locate a character string in a document. You can search forward or backward in a document at any time.
Search and Replace	A function similar to search, except once a character string is located, it is replaced. A confirm option gives you the option of not replacing this occurrence of the character string.
Sort	A function that sorts secondary merge files, paragraphs, or lines of text in alphabetical or numerical order based on a variety of criteria.
Spell-check	To use the WordPerfect Speller utility to check the spelling of each word in a document.
Split Screen	A WordPerfect option that lets you see two documents on screen at the same time, for editing or other purposes.
Status Line	The last line on the screen. It shows you the document number, page, line, and position number. It also shows the mode of operation and screen messages.
Strikeout	A mark that identifies text an editor recommends be deleted from a document.
Styles	A method by which you can create pre-defined "templates" for documents that require consistent formatting.
Tab	A WordPerfect feature that places tabs and indents in specific locations in a document.

Term	Definition
Tab Ruler	Divides the screen during split screen editing. Symbols in the tab ruler point to the document being edited. Symbols are divided by tab stops.
Table of Authorities	A WordPerfect feature that automatically generates a table of authorities based on information provided in a document.
Table of Contents	A WordPerfect feature that automatically generates a table of contents based on information provided in a document.
Text In/Out	A WordPerfect feature that makes, retrieves, and saves DOS (ASCII), Generic, and WordPerfect 4.2 files.
Thesaurus	A WordPerfect feature that offers synonyms and antonyms for selected words in a document.
Troubleshooting	The practice or technique of narrowing possibilities to discover how to correct a malfunction or problem.
Typeover	Opposite of insert. Types over text, deleting old letters and inserting new simultaneously.
Type-through	An option that temporarily turns your printer into a typewriter. Each character typed is sent to the printer either as it is typed or when Enter is pressed.
Underline	The effect of putting a line underneath text to make it stand out from the rest.
Widow/Orphan	A widow is the first line of a paragraph appearing by itself on the last line of a page. An orphan is the last line of a paragraph appearing by itself as the first line of a page.
Word Count	The number of words in a document. The Speller utility provides a word count.
Word Processing	The activity or computer program that lets you manipulate (edit) words in a document.
Word Wrap	A feature that automatically moves text that does not fit on one line down to the next.

Appendix B
WORDPERFECT SETUP

Following are procedures for using WordPerfect's Setup menu. The Setup menu sets system defaults, which affect initial settings of tabs, page length, pitch, and so on in all documents. Locate the Setup menu by pressing Shift-F1 after starting WordPerfect.

```
Setup

    1 - Backup

    2 - Cursor Speed              30 cps

    3 - Display

    4 - Fast Save (unformatted)   No

    5 - Initial Settings

    6 - Keyboard Layout

    7 - Location of Auxiliary Files

    8 - Units of Measure

Selection: 0
```

BACKUP OPTIONS Normally, WordPerfect does not backup your files. But, you can instruct WordPerfect to backup your files automatically every few minutes. You can also have WordPerfect automatically backup the original version of a revised document, giving it a ".BK!" extension. This lets you make changes to a document and later use the Document Compare feature (Module 20) to see what changes were made. WordPerfect stores backup files in a location you determine through the auxiliary files option, described later in this appendix. To set backup options:

1. Type **1** or **B** from the Setup menu.

```
Setup: Backup

        Timed backup files are deleted when you exit WP normally.  If you
        have a power or machine failure, you will find the backup file in the
        backup directory indicated in Setup: Location of Auxiliary Files.

            Backup Directory

        1 - Timed Document Backup                 No
            Minutes Between Backups               30


        Original backup will save the original document with a .BK! extension
        whenever you replace it during a Save or Exit.

        2 - Original Document Backup              No


    Selection: 0
```

2. Type **1** or **T** and type **Y** to select timed document backups. Then set the number of minutes between backups and press **Enter**.

3. If you want to backup the original of a document, type **2** or **O** and type **Y**.

4. Press **F7** to return to the document.

CURSOR SPEED   WordPerfect keeps up with most of us. Its default setting of 30 characters per second (cps) repeats characters and moves the cursor down a page or across the screen fast enough for most of our tastes. However, you can make the cursor repeat characters or move faster or slower than that by adjusting the cursor speed. To do this:

1. Type **2** or **C** from the Setup menu.

```
Setup

        1 - Backup

        2 - Cursor Speed                 30 cps

        3 - Display

        4 - Fast Save (unformatted)      No

        5 - Initial Settings

        6 - Keyboard Layout

        7 - Location of Auxiliary Files

        8 - Units of Measure


    Characters Per Second: 1 15; 2 20; 3 30; 4 40; 5 50; 6 Normal: 0
```

2. Type **1** to set cursor speed to 15 cps, **2** for 20, **3** for 30, **4** for 40, **5** for 50, or **6** or **N** to set it back to normal (30).

3. Press **F7** to return to the document.

DISPLAY SETTINGS Your main communications link with WordPerfect is the screen. WordPerfect lets you set the screen to your preferences. You can set Automatic Rewrite (Module 6) on or off; select screen colors and fonts (Appendix C); decide whether to display document comments (Module 19) on-screen or not; put the filename on the Status Line (Module 65); select the proper screen type for your computer (WordPerfect normally senses this information for you); display hard returns on screen; select the appearance (Module 5) of mnemonic menu letters; and set columns (Module 13) to display either side-by-side or on separate pages. To do this:

1. Type **3** or **D** from the Setup menu.

```
Setup: Display

        1 - Automatically Format and Rewrite    Yes

        2 - Colors/Fonts/Attributes

        3 - Display Document Comments            Yes

        4 - Filename on the Status Line          Yes

        5 - Graphics Screen Type                 Hercules 720x348 mono

        6 - Hard Return Display Character

        7 - Menu Letter Display                  BOLD

        8 - Side-by-side Columns Display         Yes


    Selection: 0
```

These are the default settings for the display.

2. Type the appropriate option number or letter and change the setting as desired. Then press **F7** to return to the document.

FAST SAVE The Fast Save option lets you save documents (Module 60) in an unformatted fashion. As its name implies, this saves documents much faster. The only drawback to this option is it does not let you print documents directly from disk (Module 56). As a default, Fast Save is on. To change this, type 4 or F from the Setup menu and type y or n to change the setting. Then press F7 to return to the document.

INITIAL SETTINGS This option lets you change the initial defaults for a variety of options. It lets you change the initial settings for tabs, hyphenation, margins, and many other commands.

This setting changes the default for all documents you create from now on. For example, you could change tabs from 1 every ½ inch to 1 every inch. To change initial settings type 5 or I from the Setup menu.

```
Setup: Initial Settings

    1 - Beep Options

    2 - Date Format                    3 1, 4

    3 - Document Summary

    4 - Initial Codes

    5 - Repeat Value                   8

    6 - Table of Authorities



Selection: 0
```

Typing 1 or B lets you set whether WordPerfect beeps on errors, hyphenations, or search failures. Typing 2 or D lets you change the default date setting (Module 16). Typing 3 or S lets you decide whether WordPerfect prompts you to create a document summary (Module 21) when you exit WordPerfect. It also lets you select the character or characters immediately preceding the subject of a document ("RE:" is the default). Typing 4 or I lets you change the initial formatting codes. This option differs from the initial codes setting in Module 48 only in that this setting is for all documents, while the option in Module 48 is for only the current document. Typing 5 or R lets you change the repeat value (Module 24). Typing 6 or A lets you set the defaults for the creation of a table of authorities (Module 68).

KEYBOARD LAYOUT   WordPerfect lets you set up your keyboard to fit a variety of definitions. WordPerfect includes three such keyboard definitions. The alternate keyboard definition moves Help to F1 (from F3) and Cancel to the Escape key. This eliminates the repeat value function described in Module 24 and moves WordPerfect operation to a manner more consistent with many other software programs. The enhanced keyboard definition takes advantage of the F11 and F12 keys included on some computer keyboards. It also changes some cursor control definitions. The macros definition includes a variety of macros (Module 42) to make using the program easier. WordPerfect also lets you change the commands to fit your own custom made definition. To use the keyboard layout feature:

1.   Type **6** or **K** from the Setup menu.

```
Setup: Keyboard Layout

    ALTRNAT
    ENHANCED
    MACROS




    1 Select; 2 Delete; 3 Rename; 4 Create; 5 Edit; 6 Original; N Name search: 1
```

2. Move the cursor to the keyboard definition of your choice. Type **1** or **S** to select it as the new definition; **2** or **D** to delete it; **3** or **R** to rename it; **5** or **E** to edit it. Use Name Search (Module 61) to search quickly through the available definitions. Type **6** or **O** to return to the original definition.

3. Press **F7** to return to the document.

To create a new definition:

1. Type **6** or **K** from the Setup menu, then type **4** or **C**.

2. Type a keyboard filename and press **Enter**.

```
Keyboard: Edit

  Name: TEST

  Key                     Description                          Macro




  Key: 1 Edit; 2 Delete; 3 Move; 4 Create;  Macro: 5 Save; 6 Retrieve: 1
```

3. Type **4** or **C** to create a new keyboard definition. Then press the key you want to change. For example, assume you want to change the definition of F1 from cancel (Module 10) to help (Module 33). Press **F1**.

```
 ┌─────────────────────────────────────────────────────────────────┐
 │                                                                   │
 │   Key: Edit                                                       │
 │                                                                   │
 │       Key                 F1                                      │
 │                                                                   │
 │     1 - Description                                               │
 │                                                                   │
 │     2 - Action                                                    │
 │                                                                   │
 │            ┌──────────────────────────────────────────────────┐  │
 │            │ {Cancel}                                          │  │
 │            │                                                  │  │
 │            │                                                  │  │
 │            │                                                  │  │
 │            │                                                  │  │
 │            │                                                  │  │
 │            └──────────────────────────────────────────────────┘  │
 │                                                                   │
 │     Selection: 0                                                  │
 │                                                                   │
 └───────────────────────────────────────────────────────────────────┘
```

4. Type **1** or **D**, then type **Help** to describe the key's function. Press **Enter**.

5. Type **2** or **A**, then press **F3** to change the key's function to help. Press **Enter**.

6. Continue in this manner, defining all the keys you want to change. The others will remain the same as they were before. Press **F7** to return to the document.

AUXILIARY FILES   Auxiliary files include a variety of information about hyphenation (Module 34), spelling (Module 64), styles (Module 66), the Thesaurus (Module 71), and other files. In order for WordPerfect to use them no matter what directory or subdirectory you are in, you need to tell WordPerfect where these files are located. To do this:

1. Type **7** or **L** from the Setup menu.

```
 ┌─────────────────────────────────────────────────────────────────┐
 │                                                                   │
 │   Setup: Location of Auxiliary Files                              │
 │                                                                   │
 │         1 - Backup Directory                                      │
 │                                                                   │
 │         2 - Hyphenation Module(s)                                 │
 │                                                                   │
 │         3 - Keyboard/Macro Files                                  │
 │                                                                   │
 │         4 - Main Dictionary(s)                                    │
 │                                                                   │
 │         5 - Printer Files              C:\WP50                    │
 │                                                                   │
 │         6 - Style Library Filename                                │
 │                                                                   │
 │         7 - Supplementary Dictionary(s)                           │
 │                                                                   │
 │         8 - Thesaurus                                             │
 │                                                                   │
 │      Selection: 0                                                 │
 │                                                                   │
 └───────────────────────────────────────────────────────────────────┘
```

2. Type the appropriate number or letter key of the desired auxiliary files, then type the full pathname of the particular directory, and press **Enter**.

UNITS OF MEASURE   WordPerfect lets you decide how you want line and position numbers on the Status Line (Module 65) and measurements in margins (Module 43), tabs (Module 70), and other features displayed. You have a choice of inches, centimeters, points (approximately 1/72 of an inch), or WordPerfect 4.2 units (line and column numbers). To set units of measure:

1. Type **8** or **U** from the Setup menu.

```
Setup: Units of Measure

        1 - Display and Entry of Numbers          "
              for Margins, Tabs, etc.

        2 - Status Line Display                    "


    Legend:

        " = inches
        i = inches
        c = centimeters
        p = points
        u = WordPerfect 4.2 Units (Lines/Columns)




    Selection: 0
```

2. Type **1** or **D**, then choose the display of your choice for margins and tabs.

3. Type **2** or **S** and choose the method of your choice for the Status Line.

4. Press **F7** to return to the document.

Appendix C
COLORS/FONTS/ATTRIBUTES

The Colors/Fonts/Attributes feature lets you change the way text is displayed on-screen. If you are using a color monitor, this lets you change the background, foreground, italics, underline, boldface, and a variety of other colors. If you are using a monochrome monitor, you have fewer options. Since WordPerfect gives you the ability to edit two documents at once (Module 22), you must change colors for both "Doc 1" and "Doc 2." Once you change colors, they are changed permanently until you change them again. Default colors are listed below:

Type	Color
Background	Blue
Foreground	White
Underline	Black
Boldface	Light Blue
Boldface and Underline	Light Green
Strikeout	Green
Double Underline	Pink
Redline	Red
Italics	White
Subscript	Light Green on White
Superscript	Red on White

WordPerfect automatically senses the type of monitor and graphics card you are using and sets colors and/or attributes accordingly. WordPerfect supports four main display types. Monochrome lets you change attributes to display as bold, underlined, blocked, blinking, or normal. CGA (Color Graphics Adapter) lets you assign foreground and background colors for a variety of attributes. EGA/VGA (Enhanced Graphics Adapter/Video Graphics Array) lets you select from eight to sixteen foreground colors and decide which font you want to use as the primary foreground attribute. Hercules RamFont or InColor cards let you select reverse video, boldface, underline, and strikeout display options. The following example illustrates the setup procedure for EGA/VGA monitors:

1. To access the Colors command, press **Shift-F1**, then type **3** or **D**.

```
Setup: Display

     1 - Automatically Format and Rewrite     No

     2 - Colors/Fonts/Attributes

     3 - Display Document Comments            Yes

     4 - Filename on the Status Line          Yes

     5 - Graphics Screen Type                 IBM EGA 640x350 16 color

     6 - Hard Return Display Character

     7 - Menu Letter Display                  BOLD

     8 - Side-by-side Columns Display         Yes


Selection: 0
```

2. Type **2** or **C**.

```
Setup: Colors/Fonts

     1 - Screen Colors

     2 - Italics Font, 8 Foreground Colors

    *3 - Underline Font, 8 Foreground Colors

     4 - Small Caps Font, 8 Foreground Colors

     5 - 512 Characters, 8 Foreground Colors

     6 - Normal Font Only, 16 Foreground Colors


Selection: 0
```

3. Type **1** or **S**. If you are using an EGA or VGA color monitor, the following screen appears:

```
Setup: Colors/Fonts

   Attribute              Font   Foreground   Background   Sample
   Normal                  N         H            B        Sample
   Blocked                 N         B            H        Sample
   Underline               Y         H            B
   Strikeout               N         C            B        Sample
   Bold                    N         G            B        Sample
   Double Underline        N         F            B        Sample
   Redline                 N         E            B        Sample
   Shadow                  N         A            D        Sample
   Italics                 N         B            D        Sample
   Small Caps              N         E            D        Sample
   Outline                 N         F            D        Sample
   Subscript               N         G            D
   Superscript             N         H            D
   Fine Print              N         B            A        Sample
   Small Print             N         C            A        Sample
   Large Print             N         D            A        Sample
   Very Large Print        N         E            A        Sample
   Extra Large Print       N         F            A        Sample
   Bold & Underline        N         A            C        Sample
   Other Combinations      N         A            G        Sample

   Switch to switch; Move to copy settings        Doc 1
```

4. Note that the default font for all attributes is normal. By adjusting the foreground and/or background colors, the sample text at the right of the screen changes. After moving the cursor to select a particular attribute to change, adjust the foreground and background colors to meet your needs. The corresponding foreground and background colors appear at the top of the screen as you move between the foreground and background settings. The letters listed in the preceding illustration correspond to particular colors.

5. If you want to set the characteristics for "Doc 2" at this time, press **Shift-F3** and set them. If you want to retain the document 1 settings for document 2, press **Ctrl-F4** and type **y**.

6. Press **F7** to save your results and return to the document you are editing.

FOREGROUND ATTRIBUTE   The EGA and VGA adapters have the ability to utilize one font in foreground appearance. You can select italics, underline, or small caps as this font, or you can decide to display 512 characters instead of 256 in the current font. All fonts except normal result in 8 foreground colors available. Normal fonts result in 16 foreground colors.

CHANGING DISPLAY TYPES   WordPerfect automatically senses the type of monitor you are using. However, under certain conditions, it may be necessary to change display types. To do this:

1. Press **Shift-F1**, type **3** or **D**, then **5** or **G**.

```
Setup: Graphics Screen Type

    Text (no graphics)
    Hercules 720x348 mono
    Hercules InColor 720x348 16 color
    IBM CGA 640x200 mono
    IBM EGA 640x350 mono
    IBM EGA 640x200 16 color
    IBM EGA 640x350 4 color
  * IBM EGA 640x350 16 color
    IBM VGA 640x480 mono
    IBM VGA 640x480 16 color
    IBM VGA 320x200 256 color
    AT&T 6300 640x400 mono
    Compaq Prtble plasma 640x400 mono
    IBM 8514/A 1024x768 256 color
    MDS Genius2 1280x1024 mono dual
    Multisync 800x560 16 color
    MDS Genius   736x1008 mono portrt
    WYSE Wy-700 1280X800 mono




  1 Select: 1
```

The asterisk (*) marks the current screen type.

2. Move the cursor to the desired display type and type **1** or **S**.

3. Press **F7** to return to the document.

Appendix D

FILE CONVERSION

WordPerfect's Convert utility lets you convert files to and from many different formats:

NOTE
If you want to convert or import an ASCII file,
use the Text In/Out key (Ctrl-F5). This is
described in Module 72.

- Revisable-Form Text, Final-Form Text, or Document Content Architecture. This is the format of IBM Mainframe DISOSS and the IBM Displaywriter. Common extension: .RF

- Navy DIF Standard. This is the format specified by the Navy for DIF (document interchange format) files. Common extension: .DIF

- WordStar 3.3. This is the format of documents generated in MicroPro International's Wordstar. Common extension: .WS.

- MultiMate 3.22. This is the format of documents generated in Ashton-Tate's MultiMate. Common extension: .DOC.

- Seven-bit transfer format. Use this format when transferring WordPerfect files over telephone lines if you cannot send the file in WordPerfect format. When the receiver gets the file, it can be transferred back to WordPerfect format and no codes are lost. You can also use ASCII text format, available here and through the Text In/Out key (Module 72).

- Mail merge. Use this when transferring dBase files (Ashton-Tate), WordStar mail merge files, or any other mail merge files. WordPerfect adds a ^R code to the end of each field and ^E codes to the end of each record. Merge files are explained in Module 46. Common extension: varies.

- WordPerfect Secondary Merge. Use this when converting secondary files to DIF format for use with spreadsheets like Lotus 1-2-3 from Lotus Development Corp. Records become rows and fields become cells. Common extension: varies.

- WordPerfect 4.2. WordPerfect 5.0 normally automatically converts WordPerfect 4.2 files to 5.0 format. If you find that conversion doesn't work automatically, use this option.

- Spreadsheet DIF. This is the opposite of WordPerfect Secondary Merge. It converts DIF format spreadsheet files to WordPerfect. Rows become records and cells become fields. Common extension: .DIF.

To use the Convert utility:

1. Start from the "C>" (or "A>") prompt. If you are not using a hard disk, insert the Learning diskette in drive A. Type **convert** and press **Enter**. Momentarily, the following prompt appears:

```
Name of Input File?
```

2. Type the directory location and name of the input file and press **Enter**.

```
Name of Input File? charactr.doc
Name of Output File?
```

3. Type the directory location and name of the output file and press **Enter**.

```
Name of Input File? charactr.doc
Name of Output File? charactr.dic

1 WordPerfect to another format
2 Revisable-Form-Text (IBM DCA Format) to WordPerfect
3 Navy DIF Standard to WordPerfect
4 WordStar 3.3 to WordPerfect
5 MultiMate 3.22 to WordPerfect
6 Seven-Bit Transfer Format to WordPerfect
7 WordPerfect 4.2 to WordPerfect 5.0
8 Mail Merge to WordPerfect Secondary Merge
9 WordPerfect Secondary Merge to Spreadsheet DIF
A Spreadsheet DIF to WordPerfect Secondary Merge

Enter number of Conversion desired
```

4. If you type any number other than 1, WordPerfect automatically converts the input file to WordPerfect format. Spreadsheet DIF files are converted to WordPerfect Secondary Merge files and vice-versa.

5. If you type **1**, the following menu appears:

```
1 Revisable-Form-Text (IBM DCA Format)
2 Final-Form-Text (IBM DCA Format)
3 Navy DIF Standard
4 WordStar 3.3
5 MultiMate 3.22
6 Seven-Bit Transfer Format
7 ASCII text file

Enter number of output file format desired
```

6. Type the number of the output file type and press **Enter**. WordPerfect converts the file.

Appendix E
PRINTER INFORMATION

WordPerfect includes a printer definition program to help you customize your printer to best work with WordPerfect. You can change characters, such has how your printer underlines text; add, delete or rename printers; and change or add definitions for sheet feeders. Because WordPerfect supports more than 100 printers, there is little likelihood that you will ever need to use this utility. For additional help, use the help screens included with the program.

NOTE
If you are not familiar with printer definition codes,
it is not recommended that you use this utility.

Printer definition codes for ASCII characters, commands, sheet feeder operations, and printer operations, are listed in the form of decimal codes. If you are creating a definition for a printer or sheet feeder or changing a character table, refer to your printer or sheet feeder manual for assistance.

To use the printer definition program:

1. On a floppy-based system, put the WordPerfect diskette into drive A and insert the PTR Program diskette in drive B. Then change the prompt to B>. On a hard disk system, change to the C:\WP50 directory.

2. Type **ptr** and press **Enter**. After a few moments, the following screen appears:

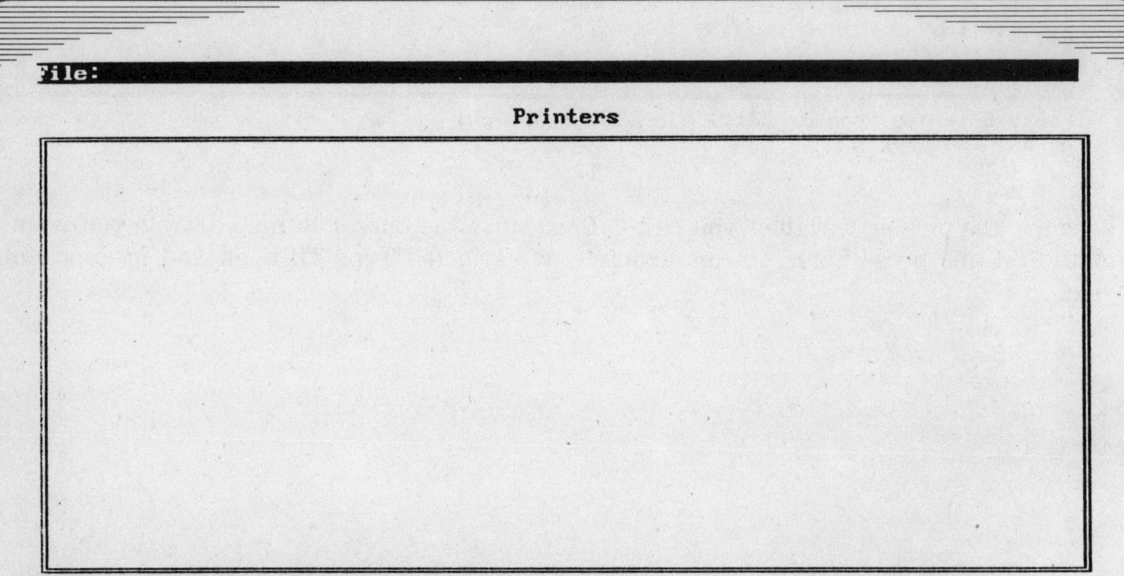

This is the printer definition program. A great deal of on-line help information is included to help you navigate through this program. To access help, press F3. If you are going to use this program, read the help information. Type 1 to add, 2 to delete, 3 to rename, or 4 to copy the printer definitions.

TIP: If you are editing a printer definition, copy it first.

Move the cursor to the desired printer definition file, then press Enter to edit or look at it. For example, if your printer does not make text bold enough, you can change it.

To add a printer definition, type 1, then the filename for the printer you want to add and press Enter. Type 1 if it is a standard printer, 2 if it is a Postscript printer. Press Enter.

```
File:

                    Printer: toshiba

    Initialize and Reset
    Horizontal Motion
    Vertical Motion
    Margins and # Fonts/Page
    Type Through
    Miscellaneous Printer Commands
    Miscellaneous Information
    Fonts
    Groups
    Resources
    Forms
    Graphics Resolutions
    Bitmap Graphics
    Rules and Shaded Boxes
    Bold
    Underline
    Double Underline
  ▼ Italics

Press Enter to Look or Edit; A - Z Name Search;
Do all that apply
```

These are the printer variables you can define. Move the cursor to the variable you want to define first and press Enter. In this example, we selected Type Through and pressed Enter twice:

```
                          Printer: toshiba
                            Type Through
                      Type Through Expressions

    ┌─────────────────────────────┬──────────────────────────────────┐
    │ Function                     │ Expression                       │
    ├─────────────────────────────┼──────────────────────────────────┤
    │ Initialize Type Through      │                                  │
    │ Flush Printer's Buffer       │                                  │
    │ Reset Type Through           │                                  │
    │ Perform Backspace            │                                  │
    │ Perform Carriage Return      │                                  │
    │ Perform Line Feed            │                                  │
    │                              └──────────────────────────────────┤
    │                                                                 │
    │                                                                 │
    │                                                                 │
    └─────────────────────────────────────────────────────────────────┘

    A - Z Name Search;
    Press Enter to Edit
```

Select the proper printer expression for each of the functions and press Enter.

Continue this procedure for all remaining printer variables. When you are finished, press F7 to save the file. WordPerfect then verifies the file and informs you if any errors may be present. You can edit printers in much the same way.

PRINTER TEST FILE The printer test file is included on your Learning diskette. This helps you determine the compatibility of your printer with various WordPerfect features. It checks the ability of your printer to support right justification, boldface, underline, italics, shadow, large and small fonts, overstrike, super- and subscript, pitch, and a number of other printer functions.

Appendix F
TROUBLESHOOTING TIPS

You may run into some snags when using WordPerfect from time to time. Many of the troubles you may encounter when using WordPerfect are discussed in the module pertaining to the particular subject. A few other troubles are described here, along with tips to correct the problem.

SCREEN

1. There is no picture.

    a. Check the controls and connectors for proper adjustment and fit.

2. The cursor "locks" (meaning it freezes and will not move).

    a. Press the various cursor controls.
    b. Press Ctrl-Alt-Del. This "resets" the system. You can lose everything you have not saved, so it is recommended that you save your data often and use the backup feature in the Setup menu (Appendix B).

3. Text suddenly "jumps" to the extreme right.

    a. Move the cursor to the right to try and move the text back over.
    b. Delete the most recent characters you added.

4. A document previously used with WordPerfect 4.2 does not format properly.

    a. Save the document in WordPerfect 4.2 format using the Text In/Out key (Ctrl-F5), then retrieve it into WordPerfect 5.0.

5. Text does not remain centered.

    a. Delete the center code and re-center text.

PRINTER

1. If the printer does not operate, check to see that:

    a. All cables are connected properly.
    b. The printer is "on-line."
    c. The printer queue is empty.
    d. The printer has paper.
    e. The printer type is listed and selected on the Print Options menu.
    f. The printer ribbon is installed correctly.
    g. The printer is not waiting for a "Go."

2. You may also:

    a. Turn the printer off and on again, then resubmit the file for printing.
    b. Turn the system off and on again, then resubmit the file for printing.
    c. Press Shift-PrtSc to print whatever is on the screen.

    • If the printer does not print the screen, call your printer dealer.
    • If the printer does screen print, consult your printer manual or your dealer.

Appendix G

SPELLER UTILITY

Operation of WordPerfect's Speller, which checks the spelling of words, is described in Module 64. The Speller utility lets you add or delete words in the Speller dictionary, display the common word list, create new dictionaries, check the location of a word (which dictionary it is in), and look up words. To use the Speller utility:

1. On a floppy-based system, make sure the "A>" prompt is on the screen. Put the Speller diskette in drive A. Type **spell** and press **Enter**.

2. On a hard disk system, change the directory to \ **wp50**, type **spell** and press **Enter**.

```
 Spell -- WordPerfect Speller Utility                    wp{wp}en.lex

 0 - Exit
 1 - Change/Create dictionary
 2 - Add words to dictionary
 3 - Delete words from dictionary
 4 - Optimize dictionary
 5 - Display common word list
 6 - Check location of a word
 7 - Look up
 8 - Phonetic look up
 9 - Convert 4.2 Dictionary to 5.0

 Selection:
```

This is WordPerfect's Speller utility. A description of each option follows.

CHANGE/CREATE DICTIONARY   This option lets you use dictionaries other than the ones supplied with WordPerfect. You can use either dictionaries from other word processors (like the dictionary with MultiMate from Ashton-Tate), or a stand-alone dictionary (like Turbo Lightning from Borland International). You can also create dictionaries from scratch.

To change or create a dictionary, type 1 from the Speller utility, then type the name and location of the dictionary you want to use and press Enter.

ADD WORDS TO DICTIONARY   WordPerfect includes two word lists. In the interest of speed, the dictionary includes both a common word list and a main word list, sometimes called the main dictionary. When spell-checking, WordPerfect first checks the common word list.

The common word list is a smaller list than the main dictionary, but it includes words that are used more often, so spell-checking is faster. If the word is not found, WordPerfect checks the main dictionary.

This option lets you add words to the first dictionary in either the common word list or main dictionary. And you can enter the words either from the keyboard or from a file.

To add words to the dictionary:

NOTE

No matter how many or how few words you add to the dictionary, it takes about 20 minutes for WordPerfect to add them. So add everything you want to add before selecting exit.

1. Type **2** from the Speller utility menu.

```
 Spell -- Add Words                                         wp{wp}en.lex

    0 - Cancel - do not add words
    1 - Add to common word list (from keyboard)
    2 - Add to common word list (from a file)
    3 - Add to main word list (from keyboard)
    4 - Add to main word list (from a file)
    5 - Exit

 Selection:
```

2. If you are using the keyboard to add words to the common word list, type **1**. If you are using the keyboard to add words to the main word list, type **3**. Then type the words and press **Enter** when finished.

3. If you are adding a file to the common word list, type **2**. If you are adding a file to the main word list, type **4**. Then type the filename or filenames and press **Enter** when finished.

4. Type **5** to exit the option when finished. Words, files, or both are added at this time.

DELETE WORDS FROM DICTIONARY   This option lets you delete words from either the common word list or main word list. You can erase individual words or complete files. To delete words from the dictionary:

NOTE

No matter how many words you delete from the dictionary, it takes about 20 minutes to delete them. So enter everything you want to delete before selecting exit.

1. Type **3** from the Speller utility menu.

```
 Spell -- Delete Words                                        wp{wp}en.lex

 0 - Cancel - do not delete words
 1 - Delete from common word list (from keyboard)
 2 - Delete from common word list (from a file)
 3 - Delete from main word list (from keyboard)
 4 - Delete from main word list (from a file)
 5 - Exit

 Selection:
```

2. If you are using the keyboard to delete words from the common word list, type **1**. If you are using the keyboard to delete words from the main word list, type **3**. Type the words to delete. Press **Enter** when finished.

3. If you are deleting a file from the common word list, type **2**. If you are deleting a file from the main word list, type **4**. Then type the filename or filenames to delete and press **Enter** when finished.

4. Type **5** to exit the option when finished. Words, files, or both are deleted at this time.

OPTIMIZE DICTIONARY   Use this option to create a common and main word list in an optional dictionary. This will make your optional dictionary as fast as WordPerfect's.

DISPLAY COMMON WORD LIST   This option displays all words in the common word list. Words are displayed one screen at a time. If you wish to leave the list at any time, press F1.

CHECK LOCATION OF A WORD   This option lets you find out if a word is in the common word list or main dictionary. For example, to find out if the word "signature" is in the common word list or main dictionary:

1. Type **6** from the Speller utility menu and press **Enter**.

```
 Spell -- Check Spelling                                      wp{wp}en.lex

 Word to check:
```

2. Type **signature** and press **Enter**.

```
 Spell -- Check Spelling                                      wp{wp}en.lex

 Word to check: signature
 Found in main dictionary
```

3. Either check another word, or press **Enter** to return to the Speller utility menu.

LOOK UP This option lets you look up words that match a pattern. For example, typing re*l at this selection would list all the words that begin with "re" and end with "l." Typing re?l lists all four-letter words beginning with "re" and ending with "l."

To use the look up feature:

1. Type **7** from the Speller utility menu.

2. Type **re*l** and press **Enter**. A partial listing is:

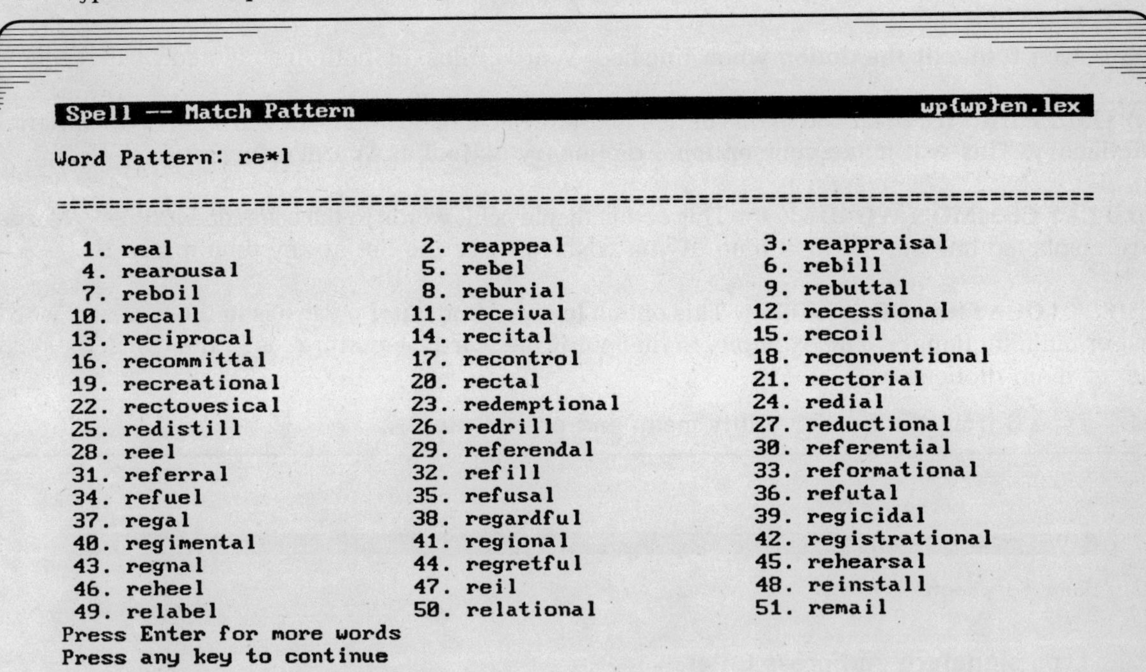

This is the first of three screens full of words that match the pattern. There are 109 words in all.

3. Press **Enter** three times to return to the Main menu, or press **Enter** twice and select another word pattern.

PHONETIC LOOK UP   The look up feature lets you select words that match a word pattern. This feature lets you match words that sound like certain words. For example, see what words sound like the word "real."

1.   Type **8** from the Speller utility menu. Then type **real** and press **Enter**.

```
 Spell -- Match Phonetic Pattern                              wp{wp}en.lex

Word: real


==============================================================================

      1. rail              2. real              3. reel
      4. reil              5. rial              6. riel
      7. rile              8. rill              9. riyal
     10. roil             11. role             12. roll
     13. royal            14. rule
```

2.   Press **Enter** to leave this option.

CONVERT 4.2 DICTIONARY TO 5.0   If you have used earlier versions of WordPerfect, odds are you have added a lot of words to the dictionary. WordPerfect lets you convert your WordPerfect 4.2 dictionary to 5.0 so you do not have to add these words again. To do this, type 9 from the Speller utility menu. Then type the directory location and name of the WordPerfect 4.2 dictionary and press Enter.

Appendix H
COMPOSE

WordPerfect's Compose feature lets you create digraphs and diacriticals on the keyboard. It also lets you access the 12 built-in and one user-defined character sets available in WordPerfect.

DIGRAPHS AND DIACRITICALS A digraph is a group of two consecutive letters. WordPerfect lets you put those letters closer together than usual (æ) for special character creation. A diacritical, on the other hand, is a letter with a special symbol above it, such as the tilde in Spanish (ñ).

To create a digraph or diacritical, press Ctrl-2 or Ctrl-v, type the first character, then type the second character. WordPerfect creates a digraph or diacritical depending upon which letters you type. After you type two characters, you automatically resume normal typing. Not all characters work as digraphs or diacriticals, so you will have to experiment some to find the ones you are looking for.

Digraph examples include typing -L to result in £, ss to result in β, and AE to result in Æ. Diacritical examples include typing shift dash and any letter to result in a letter with a line above it (ā), and quotation mark and any letter to result in the letter with two dots above it (ë). Remember to press the Compose key (Ctrl-2 or Ctrl-v) before typing the digraph or diacritical.

SPECIAL CHARACTER SETS WordPerfect supports twelve special character sets including Hebrew and Japanese. Many digraphs and diacritcals are included in character set 1. All character sets are illustrated in the WordPerfect manual. You can also define one additional character set using the Printer Definition program (Appendix E). Not all character sets are necessarily available, however. It depends whether your printer supports them. To access a character set, press Ctrl-2 or Ctrl-V, then type the character set number, comma, and the particular character.

Appendix I

WORDPERFECT START COMMANDS

The most common command to start up WordPerfect each day is typing wp and pressing Enter. While this gets you into the program, it does not begin to take advantage of the many program start options available to you. Some of these options are listed here. Realize that you can even combine these options to create a new startup procedure.

The DOS SET command and batch files can be used to make your desired startup command the default startup procedure. See your DOS manual for more details about these procedures.

Typing WP/B- and any number tells WordPerfect to start and also sets the Backup feature to a certain number of minutes (Appendix B). Example: WP/B-10 sets automatic backup to every ten minutes.

Generally, your program files are in a different directory than your data files. To start the program and automatically change the current drive and/or directory, type WP/D-drive/directory. Example: WP/D-C:\WP50\DOCS changes the current directory to WP50\DOCS.

Rather than starting WordPerfect and getting a blank screen, you can immediately start into a file by typing WP filename. Example: WP WP50\DOCS\FINANCES.WPF automatically retrieves that file as soon as WordPerfect is started.

You can also invoke a macro (Module 42) as soon as WordPerfect starts by typing WP/M-macroname. Example: WP/M-flg invokes a macro that types the name and address of FLG Office Supply.

If you do not want to use expanded memory, type WP/NE. If you want to load certain files into expanded memory, type WP/R. If you decide you want to restore the setup files (Appendix B) to their default values, type WP/X.

Appendix J
SCREEN CAPTURE UTILITY

WordPerfect's Screen Capture utility helps retrieve files that are not retrievable with the Graphics feature (Module 30). The Screen Capture utility is a RAM-resident program that makes a copy of the graphics on the screen and stores them in a file called "GRAB.WPG." This image can then be retrieved by WordPerfect. The second captured file is stored in a file called "GRAB1.WPG." Each consecutive file is stored in a new file up to "GRAB9999.WPG." These files are stored in the directory where the utility is located.

To change the filename of captured files, for example, to picture, type GRAB/F = PICTURE. This changes successive files from GRAB.WPG to PICTURE.WPG. These files are still numbered consecutively. To change the directory where these files are located, for example to \WP50\PIX, type GRAB/D = \WP50\PIX.

Before using the Screen Capture utility, you must install it in memory. In order to use it, it must be installed before you start any other program.

TIP: If you find you use it often, include the Screen Capture utility in your AUTOEXEC.BAT file to install it each time you start your system. AUTOEXEC.BAT is described in your DOS user's manual.

To install the Screen Capture utility:

1. Start your computer. If you have a floppy-based system, put the Fonts/Graphics diskette in drive A. If you have a hard disk, change to the directory where the screen capture utility is located. For example, if you installed WordPerfect using the procedures described in Module 2, this is the \WP50 directory. In this case, type **CD\WP50** and press **Enter**.

2. Type **GRAB** and press **Enter**.

```
C:\WP50\DOCS>cd\wp50

C:\WP50>grab

┌─────────────────────────────────────────────────────────────────┐
│ Screen Capture Utility                    Release 1.0  October 1, 1987 │
│                                                                   │
│ Copyright (c) WordPerfect Inc., 1987, All rights reserved         │
└─────────────────────────────────────────────────────────────────┘
Screen capture utility successfully installed
Activation (hot key) sequence is "<ALT><SHIFT><F9>"
Output goes to active directory at time of capture
Output file name is "GRAB.WPG"
For help, type "grab /h"

C:\WP50>
```

This installs the Screen Capture utility. Help is available by typing GRAB /H. To remove the Screen Capture utility at any time, type GRAB/R.

To use the Screen Capture utility:

1. Get an image that you want to capture on-screen and press **Alt-Shift-F9**. If a low-pitched buzz sounds, you are not in graphics mode or your monitor does not support the utility. A two-tone chime tells you the utility is ready to capture the image.

2. A box appears on-screen. Use the cursor control keys to position the box around the picture you want to capture. Use the Shift key in conjunction with the cursor control keys to re-size the box. Use the Ins key to switch between large and small increments in the re-sizing process. When you are ready to capture the contents of the box, press **Enter**. A two-tone chime indicates screen capture was successful.

3. To import the captured image into WordPerfect, use the Graphics feature as described in Module 30.

Appendix K
WORDPERFECT COMMAND LIST

Function	Keystrokes
Add Password	Ctrl-F5, 2 or P, 1 or A
Additional Printers	Shift-F7, S, 2 or A
Advance	Shift-F8, 4 or O, 1 or A
Advance Down	Shift-F8, 4 or O, 1 or A, 2 or D
Advance to Line	Shift-F8, 4 or O, 1 or A, 3 or i
Advance Up	Shift-F8, 4 or O, 1 or A, 2 or U
Advanced Macros	Ctrl-PgUp
Alignment Character set	Shift-F8, 4 or O, 3 or D
Appearance	Ctrl-F8, 2 or A
Append Block (Block on)	Ctrl-F4, 1 or B, 4 or A
Automatic Backup	Shift-F1, 1 or B
Automatic Format and Rewrite	Shift-F1, 3 or D, 1 or A
Automatic Reference	Alt-F5, 1 or A
Auxiliary Files	Shift-F1, 7 or L
Backspace	←
Backward Search	Shift-F2
Base Font	Ctrl-F8, 4 or F
Beep Options	Shift-F1, 5 or I, 1 or B
Beginning of Text	Home, Home, Up Arrow
Beginning of Line (Text)	Home, Home, Left Arrow
Beginning of Line (Codes)	Home, Home, Home, Left Arrow
Binding Width	Shift-F7, B
Block	Alt-F4
Block, Append (Block On)	Ctrl-F4, 1 or B, 4 or A
Block, Center (Block On)	Shift-F6
Block Copy (Block on)	Ctrl-F4, 1 or B, 2 or C
Block, Delete (Block On)	Del
Block Move (Block on)	Ctrl-F4, 1 or B, 1 or B
Block, Print (Block On)	Shift-F7
Block Protect (Block on)	Shift-F8
Block, Rehighlight	Alt-F4, Ctrl-Home
Bold	F6 or Ctrl-F8, 2 or A, 1 or B
Border Style	Alt-F9; 1, 2, 3, or 4; 4 or O; 1 or B
Calculate (Math On)	Alt-F7, 2 or a
Cancel	F1
Cancel Hyphenation	F1
Cancel Print Job	Shift-F7, 4 or C, 1 or C
Capitalization lock	Caps Lock

Function	Keystrokes
Caption Number Style	Alt-F9; 1, 2, 3 or 4; 4 or 0; 6 or C
Caption Position	Alt-F9; 1, 2, 3 or 4; 4 or 0; 7 or P
Cartridges and Fonts	Shift-F7, S, 3 or E, 5 or C
Case Conversion, Lowercase (Block on)	Shift-F3, 2 or L
Case Conversion, Uppercase (Block on)	Shift-F3, 1 or U
Center	Shift-F6
Center Page Top to Bottom	Shift-F8, 2 or P, 1 or C
Center Tabs	Shift-F8, 1 or L, 8 or T, C
Change Directory	F5, =, new directory, Enter
Change Password	Ctrl-F5, 2 or P, 1 or A
Change Print Options	Shift-F7
Codes	Alt-F3
Colors	Shift-F1, 3 or D, 2 or C
Columns On/Off	Alt-F7, 3 or C
Column Definition	Alt-F7, 4 or D
Concordance	Alt-F5, 5 or D, 3 or I
Condense Master Document	Alt-F5, 6 or G, 4 or o
Conditional End of Page	Shift-F8, 4 or O, 2 or C
Convert Comment to Text	Ctrl-F5, 5 or C, 3 or T
Convert Text to Comment (Block on)	Ctrl-F5, Y
Compose	Ctrl-V
Copy (List Files)	F5, Enter, 8 or C
Copy Block (Block on)	Ctrl-F4, 1 or B, 2 or C
Copy Rectangle (Block on)	Ctrl-F4, 3 or R, 2 or C
Copy Tabular Column (Block on)	Ctrl-F4, 2 or C, 2 or C
Count	Ctrl-F2, 6 or C
Create Directory	F5, Enter, 7 or O
Current Document Size	F5, Enter
Cursor Movement	Home, arrow keys
Cursor Movement, Specialized	Go To, Esc, Page/Screen Up & Down
Cursor Speed	Shift-F1, 2 or C
Date/Time	Shift-F5
Date Code	Shift-F5, 2 or C
Date Format	Shift-F5, 3 or F
Date Text	Shift-F5, 1 or T
Decimal Character	Shift-F8, 4 or O, 3 or D
Define Index	Alt-F5, 5 or D, 3 or I
Define List	Alt-F5, 5 or D, 2 or L
Define Outline Numbering Style	Shift-F5, 6 or D
Define Macro	Ctrl-F10
Define Table of Authorities	Alt-F5, 5 or D, 4 or A
Define Table of Contents	Alt-F5, 5 or D, 1 or C
Delete	Del
Delete Block (Block on)	Ctrl-F4, 1 or B, 3 or D
Delete Directory	F5, Enter, 2 or D

Function	Keystrokes
Delete to End of Line	Ctrl-End
Delete to End of Page	Ctrl-PgDn
Delete File	F5, Enter, 2 or D
Delete Left	←(Backspace)
Delete Rectangle (Block on)	Ctrl-F4, 3 or R, 3 or D
Delete Right	Del
Delete Tabular Column (Block on)	Ctrl-F4, 2 or C, 3 or D
Delete to Word Boundary	Home-Backspace or Home-Del
Delete Word	Ctrl-Backspace
Digraphs and Diacriticals	Ctrl-V
Display Disk Space	F5, Enter
Display Document Comments	Shift-F1, 3 or D, 3 or D
Display Filename on Status Line	Shift-F1, 3 or D, 4 or F
Display Hard Return	Shift-F1, 3 or D, 6 or H
Display Pitch	Shift-F8, 3 or D, 1 or D
Display Print Jobs	Shift-F7, 4 or C
Display Printers and Fonts	Shift-F7, S
Display Setup	Shift-F1, 3 or D
Document Backup	Shift-F1, 1 or B, 2 or O
Document Comments Creation	Ctrl-F5, 5 or C, 1 or C
Document Comments Editing	Ctrl-F5, 5 or C, 2 or E
Document Compare	Alt-F5, 6 or G, 2 or C
Document Summary Creation	Shift-F8, 3 or D, 5 or S
Document Summary Editing	Shift-F8, 3 or D, 5 or S
Document Summary Setup	Shift-F1, 5 or I, 3 or S
DOS Text	Ctrl-F5, 1 or T
Downloadable Fonts	Shift-F7, S, 3 or E, 7 or D
Double Underline	Ctrl-F8, 2 or A, 3 or D
Dual Document Editing	Shift-F3
Edit Table of Authorities	Alt-F5, 5 or D, 5 or E
End of Field	F9
End of Line	End or Home, Home, Right Arrow
End of Record	Shift-F9, E
End of Text	Home, Home, Down Arrow
Endnote	Ctrl-F7, 2 or E
Enhanced Keyboard Definition	Shift-F1, 6 or K
Enter	←
Erase to End of Line	Ctrl-End
Erase to End of Page	Ctrl-PgDn
Escape	Esc
Executive macro	Alt-F10
Execute merge	Ctrl-F9, 1 or M
Exit/Restart	F7
Expand Master Document	Alt-F5, 6 or G, 3 or E
Extended Backward Search	Home, Shift-F2
Extended Forward Search	Home, F2

Function	Keystrokes
Extended Search and Replace	Home, Ctrl-F2
Extra Large Type	Ctrl-F8, 1 or S, 7 or E
Fast Save Setup	Shift-F1, 4 or F
Figure Box Creation	Alt-F9, 1 or F, 1 or C
Figure Box Editing	Alt-F9, 1 or F, 2 or E
File Management	F5, Enter
File Size	F5, Enter
Fine Type	Ctrl-F8, 1 or S, 3 or F
Fixed Paragraph Numbering	Shift-F5, 5 or P
Flush Right	Alt-F6
Font	Ctrl-F8
Footers	Shift-F8, 2 or P, 4 or F
Footnotes	Ctrl-F7, 1 or F
Force Odd/Even Page	Shift-F8, 2 or P, 2 or o
Forms	Shift-F7, S, 3 or E, 4 or F
Forward Search	F2
Full Text Print	Shift-F7, 1 or F
Generate Index	Alt-F5, 6 or G, 5 or G
Generate List	Alt-F5, 6 or G, 5 or G
Generate Table of Authorities	Alt-F5, 6 or G, 5 or G
Generate Table of Contents	Alt-F5, 6 or G, 5 or G
Generic Format	Ctrl-F5, 3 or G
Go (Resume Printing)	Shift-F7, 4 or C, 4 or G
Go To	Ctrl-Home
Go to DOS	Ctrl-F1, 1 or G
Graphics	Alt-F9
Graphics Quality Print Select	Shift-F7, G
Graphics Screen Type	Shift-F1, 3 or D, 5 or G
Gray Shading (% of black)	Alt-F9; 1, 2, 3, or 4; 4 or O; 9 or G
Hard Hyphen	-
Hard Page	Ctrl-Return
Hard Return	Return
Hard Return Display Character	Shift-F1, 3 or D, 6 or H
Hard Space	Home-Space
Headers	Shift-F8, 2 or P, 3 or H
Help	F3
Home	Home
Horizontal Line	Alt-F9, 5 or L, 1 or H
Hyphen, Hard	-
Hyphen, Soft	Ctrl--
Hyphenation On/Off	Shift-F8, 1 or L, 1 or Y
Hyphenation Auxiliary File Location	Shift-F1, 7 or L, 2 or H
Hyphenation Zone	Shift-F8, 1 or L, 2 or Z
Indent	F4
Indent, Left and Right	Shift-F4
Index Generation	Alt-F5, 6 or G, 5 or G

Function	Keystrokes
Initial Codes	Shift-F8, 3 or D, 2 or C
Initial Font, Document	Shift-F8, 3 or D, 3 or F
Initial Font, Printer	Shift-F7, S, 3 or E, 6 or I
Initial Settings, Default	Shift-F1, 5 or I
Initial Settings, Document	Shift-F8, 3 or D, 2 or C
Initialize Printer	Shift-F7, 7 or I
Initially Present Cartridges and Fonts	Shift-F7, S, 3 or E, 5 or C
Initially Present Forms	Shift-F7, S, 3 or E, 4 or F
Insert Date/Time	Shift-F5, 1 or T
Insert Date Code	Shift-F5, 2 or C
Insert Printer Command	Shift-F8, 4 or O, 6 or P, 2 or C
Insert/Replace	Ins
Invisible Soft Return	Home-Enter
Invoke Macro	Shift-F10
Italics	Ctrl-F8, 2 or A, 4 or I
Justification On/Off	Shift-F8, 1 or L, 3 or J
Kerning	Shift-F8, 4 or O, 6 or P, 1 or K
Keyboard Layout	Shift-F1, 6 or K
Landscape Orientation, Fonts	Shift-F7, S, 3 or E, 4 or F, 3 or E
Landscape Orientation, Forms	Shift-F7, S, 3 or E, 4 or F, 3 or E
Landscape Orientation, Paper	Shift-F8; 2 or P; 8 or S; 2 or t or 4 or g
Language	Shift-F8, 4 or O, 4 or L
Large Type	Ctrl-F8, 1 or S, 5 or L
Leading	Shift-F8, 1 or L, 4 or H
Left Margin Release	Shift-Tab
Left and Right Margins	Shift-F8, 1 or L, 7 or M
Letter/Word Spacing	Shift-F8, 4 or O, 6 or P, 1 or K
Line Draw	Ctrl-F3, 2 or L
Line Format	Shift-F8, 1 or L
Line, Graphics	Alt-F9, 5 or L
Line Height	Shift-F8, 1 or L, 4 or H
Line Numbering	Shift-F8, 1 or L, 5 or N
Line Spacing	Shift-F8, 1 or L, 6 or S
List Files	F5, Enter
Lists (Block on)	Alt-F5, 2 or L
Location of Auxiliary Files	Shift-F1, 7 or L
Location of Forms	Shift-F7, S, 3 or E, 4 or F
Lock Document	Ctrl-F5, 2 or P
Look at a File	F5, Enter, 6 or L
Look Up	Ctrl-F2, 5 or L
Lowercase Conversion (Block on)	Shift-F3, 2 or L
Macro Commands	Ctrl-PgUp
Macro Definition	Ctrl-F10
Macro Execution	Alt-F10
Main Dictionary Location	Shift-F1, 7 or L, 4 or M
Manual Hyphenation	Shift-F8, 1 or L, 1 or y

Function	Keystrokes
Margin Release	Shift-Tab
Margins Left/Right	Shift-F8, 1 or L, 7 or M
Margins Top/Bottom	Shift-F8, 2 or P, 5 or M
Mark Reference	Alt-F5, 1 or R, 1 or R
Mark Reference and Target	Alt-F5, 1 or R, 3 or B
Mark Target	Alt-F5, 1 or R, 2 or T
Mark Text	Alt-F5
Master Document Compression	Alt-F5, 6 or G, 4 or o
Master Document Expansion	Alt-F5, 6 or G, 3 or E
Math Definition (Math Off)	Alt-F7, 2 or e
Math On/Off	Alt-F7, 1 or M
Menu Letter Display Settings	Shift-F1, 3 or D, 7 or M
Merge	Ctrl-F9, 1 or M
Merge Codes	Shift-F9
Merge End of Record	Shift-F9, E
Merge Return	F9
Minimum Offset From Paragraph	Alt-F9; 1, 2, 3 or 4; 4 or O; 8 or M
Minus Sign	Home- –
Move	Ctrl-F4
Move Block (Block on)	Ctrl-F4, 1 or B, 1 or M
Move a File	F5, Enter, 3 or M
Move Page	Ctrl-F4, 3 or A
Move Paragraph	Ctrl-F4, 2 or A
Move Rectangle (Block on)	Ctrl-F4, 3 or R, 1 or M
Move Sentence	Ctrl-F4, 1 or S
Move Tabular Column (Block on)	Ctrl-F4, 2 or C, 1 or M
New Footnote Number	Ctrl-F7, 3 or N
New Page	Ctrl-Enter
New Page Number	Shift-F8, 2 or P, 6 or N
New Supplemental Dictionary	Ctrl-F2, 4 or N
Newspaper Columns	Alt-F7, 4 or D, 1 or T
Normal Font	Ctrl-F8, 3 or N
Number of Copies	Shift-F7, N
Offsets, Page	Shift-F7, S, 3 or E, 4 or F, 3 or E
On-screen Attributes	Shift-F1, 3 or D, 2 or C
Orientation, Forms	Shift, F7, S, 3 or E, 4 or F, 3 or E
Original Document Backup	Shift-F1, 1 or B
Other Directory	F5, Enter, 7 or O
Other Format	Shift-F8, 4 or O
Outline	Shift-F5, 4 or O
Outline Style Text	Ctrl-F8, 2 or A, 5 or O
Outside Border Space	Alt-F9; 1, 2, 3, or 4; 4 or O; 2 or O
Overstrike	Shift-F8, 4 or O, 5 or O
Page Down	PgDn
Page Format	Shift-F8, 2 or P
Page Format, Suppress	Shift-F8, 2 or P, 9 or u

Function	Keystrokes
Page Length	Shift-F8, 2 or P, 8 or S
Page Number in Text	Ctrl-B
Page Numbering	Shift-F8, 2 or P, 7 or P
Page Offsets	Shift-F7, S, 3 or E, 4 or F, 3 or E
Page Print	Shift-F7, 2 or P
Page Up	PgUp
Paragraph Numbering	Shift-F5, 5 or P
Paragraph Number Definition	Shift-F5, 6 or D
Paper Location, Printer	Shift-F7, S, 3 or E, 2 or P
Paper Size/Type	Shift-F8, 2 or P, 8 or S
Password Protection	Ctrl-F5, 2 or P
Path for Downloadable Fonts	Shift-F7, S, 3 or E, 7 or D
Path for Printer Command Files	Shift-F7, S, 3 or E, 7 or D
Position of Caption	Alt-F9; 1, 2, 3 or 4; 4 or 0; 7 or P
Primary File, Merge	Ctrl-F9, 1 or M
Print	Shift-F7
Print (List Files)	F5, Enter, 4 or P
Print a Block (Block on)	Shift-F7
Print a Document	Shift-F7, 3 or D
Print a Page	Shift-F7, 2 or P
Print Color	Ctrl-F8, 5 or C
Print a Document on Disk	F5, Enter, 4 or P. Or, Shift-F7, 3 or D
Print Graphics Quality	Shift-F7, G
Print Text Quality	Shift-F7, T
Printer Command Files Path	Shift-F7, S, 3 or E, 7 or D
Printer Control	Shift-F7, 4 or C
Printer Files Location	Shift-F1, 7 or L, 5 or P
Printer Functions	Shift-F8, 4 or O, 6 or P
Printer Port	Shift-F7, S, 3 or E, 2 or P
Printer Selection	Shift-F7, S
Printer Status	Shift-F7, 4 or C
Protect Block (Block on)	Shift-F8
Rectangle, Move/Copy (Block on)	Ctrl-F4, 3 or R
Redline Method	Shift-F8, 3 or D, 4 or R
Redline Text	Ctrl-F8, 2 or A, 8 or R
Reference	Alt-F5, 1 or R, 1 or R
Remove Redline and Strikeout	Alt-F5, 6 or G, 1 or R
Rename File	F5, Enter, 3 or M
Repeat Value (n)	Esc
Repeat Value, Initial Settings	Shift-F1, 5 or I, 5 or R
Replace	Alt-F2
Restore	F1, 1 or R
Required Hyphen	Alt–
Retrieve Block	Ctrl-F4, 4 or R, 1 or B
Retrieve DOS Text File	Ctrl-F5; 1 or T; 2 or R, or 3 or e
Retrieve DOS Text File (List Files)	F5, Enter, 5 or T

Function	Keystrokes
Retrieve File	Shift-F10
Retrieve File (List Files)	F5, Enter, 1 or R
Retrieve Rectangle	Ctrl-F4, 4 or R, 3 or R
Retrieve Tabular Column	Ctrl-F4, 4 or R, 2 or C
Reveal Codes	Alt-F3
Reverse Search	Shift-F2
Rewrite Screen	Ctrl-F3, 0 or R
Rush Print Job	Shift-F7, 4 or C, 2 or R
Save Document	F10
Save/Exit	F7
Screen Down	+ (Numeric Keypad)
Screen Type	Shift-F1, 3 or D, 5 or G
Screen Up	← (Numeric Keypad)
Search Forward	F2
Search Backward	Shift-F2
Search & Replace	Alt-F2
Secondary File, Merge	Ctrl-F9, 1 or M
Select Printers	Shift-F7, S
Set Pitch	Shift-F8, 3 or D, 1 or D
Set Printer Attributes	Shift-F7, S
Shadow Text	Ctrl-F8, 2 or A, 6 or a
Sheet Feeder Selection	Shift-F7, S, 3 or E, 3 or S
Short Form Table of Authorities	Alt-F5, 4 or A
Side-by-Side Column Display	Shift-F1, 3 or D, 8 or S
Small Caps Text	Ctrl-F8, 2 or A, 7 or C
Small Text	Ctrl-F8, 1 or S, 4 or S
Soft Hyphen	Ctrl--
Sort	Ctrl-F9, 2 or S
Sort Order	Ctrl-F9, 3 or O
Spacing	Shift-F8, 1 or L, 6 or S
Spell Check Document	Ctrl-F2, 3 or D
Spell Check Page	Ctrl-F2, 2 or P
Spell Check Word	Ctrl-F2, 1 or W
Split Screen	Ctrl-F3, 1 or W
Status Line Display	Shift-F1, 3 or D, 4 or F
Stop Printing	Shift-F7, 4 or C, 5 or S
Strikeout Text	Ctrl-F8, 2 or A, 9 or S
Strikeout Text (Block On)	Ctrl-F8, 2 or A, 9 or S
Style	Alt-F8
Style Library Filename	Shift-F1, 7 or L, 6 or L
Subdocument	Alt-F5, 2 or S
Subscript	Ctrl-F8, 1 or S, 2 or b
Summary	Shift-F8, 3 or F, 5 or S
Superscript	Ctrl-F8, 1 or S, 1 or p
Suppress Page Format	Shift-F8, 2 or P, 9 or u
Switch Documents	Shift-F3

Function	Keystrokes
Tab	Tab
Tab Align	Ctrl-F6
Table	Alt-F9, 2 or T
Table of Authorities (Block on)	Alt-F5, 4 or A
Table of Contents (Block on)	Alt-F5, 1 or C
Tab Settings	Shift-F8, 1 or L, 8 or T
Tabular Column Copy (Block on)	Ctrl-F4, 2 or C, 2 or C
Tabular Column Move (Block on)	Ctrl-F4, 2 or C, 1 or M
Target, Mark	Alt-F5, 2 or T
Text Box	Alt-F9, 3 or B
Text In (List Files)	F5, 5 or T
Text In/Out	Ctrl-F5
Text Quality	Shift-F7, T
Thesaurus	Alt-F1
Thousand's Separator	Shift-F8, 4 or O, 3 or D
Time	Shift-F5
Timed Document Backup	Shift-F1, 1 or B, 1 or T
Top/Bottom Margin	Shift-F8, 2 or P, 5 or M
Typeover Mode	Ins
Type Through to Printer	Shift-F7, 5 or y
Undelete	F1
Underline	F8; or Ctrl-F8, 2 or A, 2 or U
Underline Spaces and Tabs	Shift-F8, 4 or O, 7 or U
Units of Measure	Shift-F1, 8 or U
Unlock a Document	Ctrl-F5, 2 or P
Uppercase a Block (Block on)	Shift-F3, 1 or U
User-defined Box	Alt-F9, 4 or U
Vertical Line	Alt-F9, 5 or L, 2 or V
View Document	Shift-F7, 6 or V
Very Large Type	Ctrl-F8, 1 or S, 6 or V
Widows and Orphans	Shift-F8, 1 or L, 9 or W
Window	Ctrl-F3
Word Count	Ctrl-F2, 6 or C
Word Left	Ctrl-Left Arrow
Word/Letter Spacing	Shift-F8, 4 or O, 6 or P, 3 or W
Word Right	Ctrl-Right Arrow
Word Search	F5, Enter, 9 or W
Word Spacing Justification Limits	Shift-F8, 4 or O, 6 or P, 4 or J
WP 4.2 Format, Save File	Ctrl-F5, 4 or W
WordPerfect Character Set	Ctrl-V

Appendix L

REVEAL CODES ABBREVIATIONS

Abbreviation	Function
[ ]	Hard Space
[-]	Hyphen
-	Soft hyphen
/	Cancel Hyphenation
[Adv]	Advance
[Align]	Tab Align (beginning)
[Block]	Block
[BlockPro:Off]	Block Protect Off
[BlockPro:On]	Block Protect On
[BOLD]	Boldface (beginning)
[bold]	Boldface (end)
[Box Num]	Caption in Graphics Box
[C/A/Fl Rt]	End of Centering, Tab Align, or Flush Right
[Cntr]	Centering
[Center Pg]	Center Current Page (top to bottom)
[Cndl EOP n:]	Conditional end of page (n equals number of lines)
[Col Def]	Column Definition
[Col Off]	End of Text Columns
[Col On]	Beginning of Text Columns
[Comment]	Document Comment
[Date:n]	Date/Time function (n equals format)
[Decml/Algn Char:]	Decimal Character/Thousands Separator
[Def Mark:Index,n]	Index Definition (n equals format)
[Def Mark:List,n]	List Definition (n equals List Number)
[Def Mark:ToA,n]	Table of Authorities Definition (n equals section number)
[Def Mark:ToC,n]	Table of Contents Definition (n equals Table of Contents Level)
[DSrt]	Detectible Soft Return
[EndDef]	End of Index, List, Table of Authorities, or Table of Contents
[End Mark:Index,n]	End marked text (n equals Index format)
[End Mark:List,n]	End marked text (n equals List Number)
[End Mark:ToA,n]	End marked text (n equals section number)
[End Mark:ToC,n]	End marked text (n equals Table of Contents Level)
[End Opt]	Endnote Options
[Endnote]	Endnote
[Endnote Placement]	Endnote Placement
[Ext Large]	Extra Large Print
[Figure]	Figure Box
[Fig Opt]	Figure Box Options
[Fine]	Fine Print

Abbreviation	Function
[Flsh Rt]	Flush Right
[Font]	Base Font
[Footnote]	Footnote
[Footer]	Footer
[Force]	Force Odd/Even Page
[Ftn Opt]	Footnote Options
[Full Form]	Table of Authorities, Full Form
[HLine]	Horizontal Line
[Header]	Header
[HPg]	Hard Page
[HRt]	Hard Return
[Hyph On]	Hyphenation On
[Hyph Off]	Hyphenation Off
[HZone Set;n,n]	Reset size of hyphenation zone (n equals left, right)
[→Indent]	Indent
[→Indent←]	Left/Right Indent
[Index]	Index Entry
[ISRt]	Invisible Soft Return
[Italc]	Italics
[Just]	Right Justification
[Just Lim]	Word/Letter Spacing Justification Limits
[Kern]	Kerning
[L/R Mar]	Left/Right Margins
[Lang]	Language
[Large]	Large Print
[Line Height]	Line Height
[Ln Num]	Line Numbering
[<-Mar Rel]	Left Margin Release
[Mark:List]	List Entry (n equals list number)
[Mark:ToC]	Table of Contents Entry (n equals ToC level)
[Math Def]	Definition of Math Columns
[Math Off]	End of Math
[Math On]	Beginning of Math
!	Formula Calculation
t	Subtotal Entry
+	Calculate Subtotal
T	Total Entry
=	Calculate Total
*	Calculate Grand Total
[Note Num]	Footnote/Endnote Reference
[Outln]	Outline Text
[Ovrstk]	Overstrike
[Paper Sz/Typ]	Paper Size and Type
[Par Num]	Paragraph Numbering
[Par Num:Auto]	Automatic Paragraph Numbering
[Par Num Def]	Paragraph Numbering Definition

Abbreviation	Function
[Pg Num:n]	New Page Number (n equals new page number)
[Pg Numbering]	Page Number Position
[Ptr Cmnd:]	Printer Command
[RedLn]	Redline
[Ref]	Reference (Automatic Reference)
[Set End Num]	Set New Endnote Number
[Set Fig Num]	Set New Figure Box Number
[Set Ftn Num]	Set New Footnote Number
[Set Tab Num]	Set New Table Box Number
[Set Txt Num]	Set New Text Box Number
[Set Usr Num]	Set New User-Defined Box Number
[Shadw]	Shadow Print
[Sm Cap]	Small Caps
[Small]	Small Print
[SPg]	Soft New Page
[SRt]	Soft Return
[StkOut]	Strikeout
[Style]	Styles
[Subdoc]	Subdocument
[SubScrpt]	Subscript
[SuprScrpt]	Superscript
[Suppress:n]	Suppress Page Format Options (n equals formats to suppress)
[T/B Mar]	Top and Bottom Margins
[Tab]	Move to Next Tab Stop
[Tab Set]	Tab Set
[Table]	Table Box
[Target]	Target (Automatic Reference)
[Tbl Opt]	Table Box Options
[Text Box]	Text Box
[Txt Opt]	Text Box Options
[UND]	Underlining (beginning)
[und]	Underlining (end)
[Undrln]	Underline Spaces/Tabs
[Usr Box]	User-Defined Box
[UsrOpt]	User-Defined Box Options
[VLine]	Vertical Line
[Vry Large]	Very Large Text
[W/O Off]	Widow/Orphan Protection Off
[W/O On]	Widow/Orphan Protection On
[Wrd/Ltr Spacing]	Word and Letter Spacing

Appendix M
WORDPERFECT EXERCISES

1. ABOUT THIS BOOK
    a. What is word processing software and what do you think it will do for you?
    b. What is each module in this book centered around? Why do you think this structure was selected?
    c. What is the logic behind the order of the modules presented in the Table of Contents? Who is the audience?

2. WORDPERFECT SYSTEM OVERVIEW
    a. Why do you need to make working copies of diskettes? Backup copies?
    b. The WordPerfect program collection is made up of what individual diskettes?
    c. Can you identify the steps in loading the WordPerfect program into your computer?
    d. How does creating a new WordPerfect document differ from editing an existing document?

3. A SAMPLE SESSION WITH WORDPERFECT 5.0
    a. How are key sequences indicated in this book?
    b. What are function keys? How do they differ from standard typing keys in what they do for you?
    c. Describe the function of the following special keys:
        Enter
        Esc
        Delete (Del)
        Insert (Ins)
        End
        PgDn

4. ALIGNING TEXT
    a. Describe the alignment character. What does it do?
    b. Why is it useful?
    c. What are the best applications for it?

5. APPEARANCE
    a. What is the difference between boldface and underlined text?
    b. When should you change the appearance of text?

6. AUTO REWRITE
    a. When is it necessary to rewrite the screen?
    b. Why would you want to turn Auto Rewrite off?

7. AUTOMATIC REFERENCE
   a. What are some of the situations where Automatic Reference is handy?
   b. What is the difference between a reference and a target?
   c. What can be referenced?

8. BLOCK
   a. What are some of the applications where the Block key is useful?
   b. What is the difference between a rectangular and a regular block of text?

9. BLOCK PROTECT
   a. What is the chief purpose of the Block Protect feature?
   b. Why would you want to protect a block of text?
   c. What is the difference between the Protect feature and the Conditional End of Page feature?

10. CANCEL
    a. What are the two main functions of the Cancel key?
    b. Name five functions you can leave without performing the operation.

11. CASE CONVERSION
    a. What happens when you convert a block to all lowercase text?
    b. Name some applications where case conversion is useful.

12. CENTER
    a. How does the Center function compare with centering text on a typewriter?
    b. Name three uses for the Center command.

13. COLUMN DEFINITION
    a. What is the difference between newspaper style and parallel style columns? What are some applications for each style?
    b. How many columns can you fit on a page?
    c. Name three applications for columnar text.

14. COPY
    a. What is the purpose of the Copy command?
    b. Name two ways to copy text.
    c. How do you copy columns of text defined with the column definition key?

15. CURSOR CONTROL
    a. How do you send the cursor to the top of a document? page?
    b. How do you send the cursor to the beginning of the current line?
    c. What overall benefit does cursor control give you?

16. DATE
    a. Name three applications for the Date function.
    b. What will the date read if you do not have a clock/calendar card and you did not enter the date when you turned your computer on?

17. **DELETE**
    a. Name three ways you can delete text.
    b. What is the chief purpose of deleting text?
    c. How does the Backspace key delete text? The Del key?

18. **DIRECTORY**
    a. Explain the concept of a default directory.
    b. How do you temporarily change directories?

19. **DOCUMENT COMMENTS**
    a. What are comments similar to in the "paper and pencil" world?
    b. How do you change comments to text? Text to comments?

20. **DOCUMENT COMPARE**
    a. When is the Compare feature useful?
    b. How does it work?

21. **DOCUMENT FORMAT**
    a. What is the purpose of the Document Format menu?
    b. What results in more characters on-screen, a display pitch of .1" or .5"?
    c. What is the difference between initial codes in the Setup menu and initial codes in this menu?
    d. What is the purpose of a document summary?

22. **DUAL DOCUMENT EDITING**
    a. Name three instances where dual document editing would be appropriate.
    b. What does the tab ruler do?

23. **ENDNOTES**
    a. Where are endnotes used most often?
    b. Explain the difference between a footnote and an endnote.

24. **ESCAPE**
    a. What is the default repeat value?
    b. How do you change the default value temporarily? permanently?
    c. Name five uses for the repeat value.

25. **FILE MANAGEMENT**
    a. Contrast a computerized file and one kept in a filing cabinet.
    b. What are the two ways to retrieve files?
    c. How do you copy or delete more than one file at a time?

26. **FLUSH RIGHT**
    a. Name three uses for the Flush Right key.
    b. Name two ways to create text that is flush right.

27. **FONT**
    a. Is 10-point New Century Schoolbook Bold a different font than 10-point New Century Schoolbook Italic? Why or why not?
    b. What is the purpose of the Font feature? When is it useful to change fonts?

28. **FOOTNOTES**
    a. What is the difference between footnotes and endnotes?
    b. How do you look at footnotes?
    c. How do you delete footnotes?

29. **GO TO**
    a. How is the Go To command used in regular text? columns? blocks of text?
    b. What is the difference between using the Go To command in regular text and using it in columns?
    c. When would you use the Go To command to restore a block of text?

30. **GRAPHICS**
    a. What is the purpose of the Graphics function?
    b. Under what conditions can you view graphics on-screen?
    c. Name the four types of graphics boxes. How do they differ?

31. **HARD SPACE**
    a. What is the chief purpose of the Hard Space feature?
    b. Name four applications for it.

32. **HEADERS AND FOOTERS**
    a. What is the purpose of a header? footer?
    b. What kinds of information does a header or footer contain?
    c. How many headers and footers can you have at any time in a document?

33. **HELP**
    a. How do you get help when editing a document?
    b. Why is the Help function called "on-line" help?
    c. What are the two ways to get help for a particular command?

34. **HYPHENATION**
    a. Describe hyphenation.
    b. What is the advantage of using it?
    c. What is the H-Zone?

35. **INDENT**
    a. What is the difference between Tab and Indent?
    b. How do you turn Indent off?

36. INDEX
    a. When is the index function used?
    b. What is the difference and use of headings and subheadings?
    c. What are the three steps to creating an index?

37. INSERT
    a. What is the chief purpose of the Insert mode?
    b. How do you turn on the Insert mode? Typeover mode?

38. LINE DRAWING
    a. What is the chief purpose of the Line Drawing function?
    b. How many characters are available to you in Line Draw mode?
    c. Describe the procedure of drawing lines with the Esc key.

39. LINE FORMAT
    a. When can you tell that text is right-justified?
    b. What is the difference between a widow and an orphan?
    c. When is line numbering useful?

40. LIST FILES
    a. What is the chief purpose of the List Files menu?
    b. Describe the major functions available to you from the List Files menu.
    c. How do you list only selected files?

41. LISTS
    a. How many lists can you create with WordPerfect?
    b. What are the three steps to creating a list?
    c. Name three applications where lists would be useful.

42. MACROS
    a. What are macros?
    b. How are macros used?
    c. What is macro chaining?

43. MARGINS
    a. What is the default margin setting?
    b. What should margins be set to when using 12-pitch type?
    c. What are the limits for the left and right margins?

44. MASTER DOCUMENTS
    a. What is the difference between a master document and a subdocument?
    b. What features can be incorporated into subdocuments from a master document?
    c. When is the Master Document feature useful?

45. **MATH**
    a. Name three applications for the Math mode.
    b. Name the steps required to use the Math mode.
    c. Why is the alignment character used in the Math mode?

46. **MERGE DOCUMENTS**
    a. Describe the difference between merge documents and data files.
    b. Describe the difference between primary and secondary merge files.
    c. Describe the difference between a field and a record.

47. **MOVE**
    a. What is the purpose of the Move command?
    b. Name two ways to move text.
    c. What is the value of cut-and-paste?

48. **OTHER FORMAT**
    a. How many languages is WordPerfect available in?
    b. What is the purpose of overstrike?

49. **OUTLINE**
    a. What is the purpose of the Outline mode?
    b. How do you change the way outline numbers appear?
    c. How do you turn the Outline mode off?

50. **PAGE BREAKS**
    a. What is the difference between a soft and a hard page break?
    b. When would you use a soft page break? A hard page break?

51. **PAGE FORMATTING**
    a. Name two situations where you would want to change the number of text lines per page.
    b. Why would you want to center a page?
    c. What is the difference between a widow and an orphan? Why are these undesirable?

52. **PARAGRAPH NUMBERING**
    a. What is the difference between the Paragraph Numbering feature and the Outline feature described in Module 49?
    b. How many levels of paragraph numbering are available?
    c. Name three applications for paragraph numbering.

53. **PASSWORD PROTECTION**
    a. Why would you want to lock a file?
    b. What happens if you cannot remember your password?

54. PRINTER ADVANCE
    a. What is the chief purpose of the Printer Advance feature?
    b. What is the advantage of using Printer Advance over superscripts or subscripts (Module 67)?

55. PRINTER CONTROL
    a. What is a print job?
    b. Describe the Rush Print Job feature.
    c. If you cancel or temporarily stop printing, what must you do before your printer will work again?

56. PRINTING OUTSIDE A DOCUMENT
    a. Name two ways to print a document from disk.
    b. How can you tell what document is currently printing?
    c. What is a print queue?

57. PRINTING WITHIN A DOCUMENT
    a. What is the advantage of the Type-Through mode?
    b. If you want to print more than one page of a document, but less than the whole document, what do you do?
    c. What are the four options you have for printing while editing a document?

58. REDLINE AND STRIKEOUT
    a. What is the difference between redline and strikeout?
    b. How do you remove the redline and strikeout markings from text?

59. REVEAL CODES
    a. Describe the Reveal Codes feature.
    b. How do you delete codes?
    c. What keys can you use while in Reveal Codes?

60. SAVING TEXT/EXITING
    a. Why would you want to save text without exiting?
    b. What happens when you exit WordPerfect?

61. SEARCH AND REPLACE
    a. What is the value of searching through text?
    b. How can you replace some instances of a word with a substitute but not others?

62. SORT
    a. What is the purpose of the Sort command?
    b. Name the three types of information that can be sorted.
    c. What is a multi-level sort? What is the advantage of a multi-level versus a single-level sort?

63. **SPACING**
    a. Why would you want to change the spacing of a document?
    b. How does WordPerfect display text that is one and one-half lines spaced? How do you know that text is one and one-half lines apart?

64. **SPELLER**
    a. Name the three types of spell options available.
    b. What is the look up feature?
    c. What is the value of a word count?

65. **STATUS LINE**
    a. What are the four main things that the Status Line tells you?
    b. What is the left side of the Status Line used for?

66. **STYLES**
    a. What are styles?
    b. When are they useful?
    c. What is the difference between paired styles and open styles? When should each be used?

67. **SUBSCRIPTS AND SUPERSCRIPTS**
    a. What is the difference between a subscript and a superscript?
    b. How can you tell if on-screen text is superscripted? subscripted?

68. **TABLE OF AUTHORITIES**
    a. What is a table of authorities? When is it useful?
    b. What is short form text?

69. **TABLE OF CONTENTS**
    a. What is the difference between level one in a table of contents and level two?
    b. What are leaders?

70. **TABS**
    a. How do you delete all tab settings?
    b. What is the main purpose of tab settings?

71. **THESAURUS**
    a. What is a headword?
    b. What is the value of an on-line thesaurus?

72. **WORKING WITH DOS**
    a. Why would you want to save documents as DOS text files?
    b. What is the difference between text and generic files?

Index

Computer users around the world depend on the ILLUSTRATED Book Series

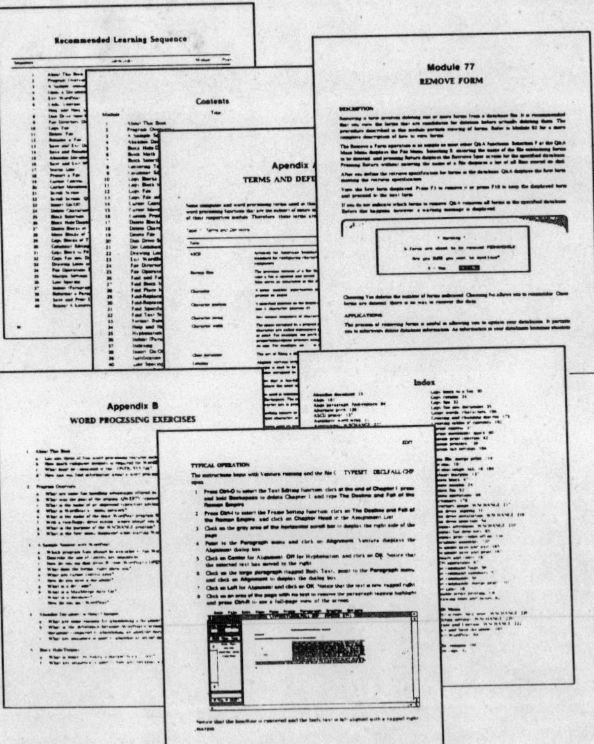

Because . . .
All *ILLUSTRATED* Books feature:

Alphabetized commands provide easy reference.

A simple to complex learning sequence.

Helpful exercises for classroom instruction.

Hands-on learning activities provide practical experience.

Technical audits assure quality and accuracy of material.

Readable style enhances comprehension.

Clarifying descriptions and working examples.

Applications information serve as models.

Glossaries and appendices expand value as a reference tool.

Alphabetical indexes provide quick access to information.

Consistent design and proven format ensures success.

Screen illustrations reinforce user confidence.

Wordware for your software

WORDWARE
Publishing, Inc.
Plano, Texas